Play & Culture Studies
Volume 1
Diversions and Divergences in Fields of Play

PLAY & CULTURE STUDIES

Stuart Reifel, series editor

Volume 1: *Diversions and Divergences in Fields of Play*
edited by Margaret Carlisle Duncan, Garry Chick and Alan Aycock, 1998

Play & Culture Studies
Volume 1
Diversions and Divergences in Fields of Play

series editor
Stuart Reifel
University of Texas–Austin

volume editors
Margaret Carlisle Duncan
University of Wisconsin–Milwaukee

Garry Chick
University of Illinois at Urbana-Champaign

Alan Aycock
Cardinal Stritch College

Ablex Publishing Corporation
Greenwich, Connecticut
London, England

Printed in the United States of America

ISSN: 1096-8911
ISBN: 1-56750-370-5 (cloth)
      1-56750-371-3 (paper)

Ablex Publishing Corporation
55 Old Post Road #2
P.O. Box 5297
Greenwich, CT 06831

Published in the U.K. and Europe by:
JAI Press Ltd.
38 Tavistock Street
Covent Garden
London WC2E 7PB
England

To our children who have taught us a thing or two about play:
John, Katie, Matt, Elizabeth, Katharine, and Melissa

Contents

Part V. Resistant Play

Part VI. Intertextual Play

Series Introduction

This first volume of *Play & Culture Studies* reestablishes the publication efforts of The Association for the Study of Play (TASP). TASP is an organization of scholars dedicated to promoting, stimulating, and encouraging the interdisciplinary study of play. As stated in earlier TASP publication editorial policies, our concern is "furthering our understanding of the phenomenon of play in humans and animals, and across various cultural, social, and activity settings" (*Play & Culture,* 1992). "We view play as a significant subject in its own right, quite apart from the various biological, sociological, and cultural functions it may serve" (*Journal of Play Theory & Research,* 1993), so we investigate play as a legitimate and necessary lens for understanding evolution and behavior.

TASP has sponsored or co-sponsored annual meetings since 1975. In addition to these annual meetings, TASP has also produced a number of publications in which any number of annual meeting and other contributions regarding play have been preserved. That tradition began with Lancy and Tindall's *The Anthropological Study of Play: Problems and Prospects* (1976), and continued through a total of ten annual volumes and two journals, *Play and Culture* (1988–1992) and *Journal of Play Theory & Research* (1993). *Play & Culture Studies,* in which we build on the name of one of our earlier journals, will continue TASP's efforts to publish blind-reviewed materials, many of which may originate at its annual meetings.

Play & Culture Studies: Diversions and Divergences in Fields of Play reflects the critical efforts of its three volume editors: Margaret Carlisle Duncan, Garry Chick, and Alan Aycock. They have organized recent, quality play scholarship into six thematic sections, including Theorizing Play, Traditional Play, Children's Play, Playful Primates, Resistant Play, and Intertextual Play. In terms of the tradition of TASP publications, it is interesting that four of these themes reflect the themes (or sub-themes) of Lancy and Tindall's 1976 volume, including Theoretical Approaches in the Study of Play, Expressive Aspects of Play, and Observational Study of Play in Primates and Young Children. A number of older themes, focusing on disciplinary (ethnographic, linguistic, psychological) approaches, have been replaced by contemporary concerns, such as Resistance and Intertextual Play; some play topics can now be considered Traditional. Theory and Children's Play have proved to be abiding themes for play scholars (see, for examples, Cheska, 1981; Loy, 1982; Mergen, 1986; Sutton-Smith & Kelly-Byrne, 1984), while other themes recur more sporadically. Clearly, play inquiry is evolving.

In the tradition of *Play & Culture, Journal of Play Theory & Research*, and the earlier annual volumes published under the auspices of TASP, the *Play & Culture Studies* series will further scholarship regarding play. Play will remain our organizing focus and the central construct for contributions that appear in the series. We are grateful to Ablex for making these efforts possible, and I am grateful to Margaret Carlisle Duncan, Garry Chick, and Alan Aycock for preparing this first volume.

—Stuart Reifel, Series Editor
University of Texas at Austin

REFERENCES

Cheska, A.T. (Ed.). (1981). *Play as context*. West Point, NY: Leisure Press.
Editorial policy. (1992). *Play & Culture, 5.*
Editorial preface. (1993). *Journal of Play Theory & Research, 1.*
Lancy, D.F., & Tindall, B.A. (Eds.). (1976). *The anthropological study of play: Problems and prospects.* Cornwall, NY: Leisure Press.
Loy, J. (Ed.). (1982). *The paradoxes of play.* West Point, NY: Leisure Press.
Mergen, B. (Ed.). (1996). *Cultural dimensions of play, games, and sport.* Champaign, IL: Human Kinetics Press.
Sutton-Smith, B., & Kelly-Byrne, D. (Eds.). (1984). *The mask of play.* New York: Leisure Press.

part I
Theorizing Play

Part I

Introduction

Margaret Carlisle Duncan

In theorizing play anew, the three chapters comprising Part I each offer an uncommon perspective. Garry Chick and Robert Hood focus on the relationship between work and play. These authors point out that the current body of literature on this topic is confusing, contradictory, and wholly intractable. Most theories lack empirical support, and many employ non-equivalent units of analysis.

In their research on machinists' preferences for outdoor recreation, Chick and Hood endeavor to avoid these pitfalls. The linchpin of this research is the question, do machinists play with machines? In other words, are individuals who work with machines more likely to use machines (such as powerboats, snowmobiles, etc.) in their leisure than their non-machinist counterparts? The authors' concept of "patterned socialization" suggests a more complex relationship than earlier theories of work and nonwork have asserted. Chick and Hood's findings result in a careful delineation of a new model tracing possible connections between work and play.

Mechthild Nagel's theorizing is motivated by a "postmodernism of resistance" and involves a critique of Huizinga's *Homo Ludens*. Nagel uses Heidegger's hermeneutic phenomenology as a vehicle to challenge Huizinga's ideological assumptions about the inauthenticity of play in modern society. Nagel discusses how phenomenology implies a privileged access to the truth. By adopting a phenomenological approach that focuses on the origins and primordality of play, Huizinga need not explain, but only describe play's qualities. Furthermore, like Heidegger, Huizinga succumbs to "Mandarin ideology," in his insistence upon the corruption of play due to technology and the spread of democratic values.

Nagel shows that far from being an historical examination of play, *Homo Ludens*

3

is ahistorical, elitist, and Eurocentric. Huizinga's romanticized version of "authentic" play excludes women, the poor, the working classes, and other subalterns.

David Myers theorizes play as a representational process, evolving from increased complexities in the human organism. Employing a natural-historical perspective, he examines play's tendency toward egocentric behavior. For example, in computer game play, players frequently endow their computer opponents with *human* qualities; hence, the discourse of a "smart" or "dumb" computer. What is the significance of assigning qualities of the self to inanimate objects? Myers argues that such egocentrism creates and extends mental (symbolic) transformations that form the basis of new human cognitions. Thus, play offers us various ways to model and experiment with personhood, different contexts in which we may be selves.

Do Machinists Play with Machines? Work and Outdoor Recreation Among Employees in the Western Pennsylvania Machine-Tool Industry[1]

Garry Chick
Robert D. Hood

> This was no time for play
> This was no time for fun
> This was no time for games
> There was work to be done.
> —Dr. Seuss

In western society, play and leisure[2] have traditionally been regarded as the antonyms of work (Blanchard, 1986). Moreover, work has been seen as the fountainhead of progress while play and leisure are, at best, diversions and, at worst, potential settings for the handiwork of the devil. Work and leisure, thus, have traditionally been viewed as spheres of life that are at the polar ends of a spectrum. The spectrum itself is variously defined but often includes notions of the degree of obligation or constraint (e.g., Dumazedier, 1967) and/or time, as required for subsistence or maintenance as opposed to discretionary use (e.g., Brightbill, 1960). Parker (1983) suggested a combination of activity (constrained or unconstrained) and time (work or non-work)

5

dimensions. Various other sociological or psychological models, such as those of Kelly (1972) and Neulinger (1974), distinguish work and leisure in terms of degree of constraint and "work relation" (Kelly) or degree of intrinsic versus extrinsic motivation (Neulinger).

The relationship between work and play in some non-Western societies or in technologically simple cultures, on the other hand, often has been thought of as quite different from its counterpart in the West. Some leisure scholars (e.g., Nash, 1963; Parker, 1983) have concluded, usually without compelling evidence, that work, play, and leisure meld into a rather uniform "daily cycle" in such societies. Godbey (1985), for example, states that:

> It is hard for us to understand life in primitive societies, where work and leisure were inextricably related. Hunter-gatherer and agrarian societies involved a continuous fusion of work and leisure—the notion of being "at work" would be lost on a Bushman. (p. 83)

We are unaware of any evidence that anyone has ever asked a Bushman whether he or she knows the difference between work and play or leisure. It may be that the fusion of work and leisure is a perception of the analyst rather than that of the Bushmen. Nevertheless, whether work and leisure in Western culture are thought to represent the ends of a continuum or, in non-Western cultures, phenomena that are continuously fused, it is clear that the two are typically considered as being somehow in concert.

It is also possible to regard work and play or leisure to be distinct. In a cultural materialist framework, such as that of Marvin Harris (1979), work is infrastructural—directly involved in the processes of production and reproduction—while expressive forms, including play and leisure, are superstructural. While we may cognitively associate work and leisure, they are, from a materialist perspective, very different. Harris (1979) claims that components of the infrastructure "probabilistically determine" those of the structure and the superstructure, suggesting that work can, thus, influence the nature of leisure. Further, he allows for the possibility of feedback from the superstructure to the structure and from both to the infrastructure, so work and leisure are at least potentially mutually interactive.

If we assume that work and leisure are not at the ends of a continuum, but qualitatively distinct, as a cultural materialist perspective would suggest, it is possible that any given activity may be viewed as being in some measure work-like and, similarly, to some degree leisure-like. Though the two will almost always vary inversely, there is no intrinsic need for them to do so. This may assist understanding of the annoying situation where a professional athlete, for example, truly enjoys playing his or her sport, even though doing so is very hard work (and where they may earn gobs of money playing). The idea that work and leisure are neither mutually exclusive, nor opposite ends of a continuum, is not especially new and several previous writers have expressed similar views (e.g., Dubin, 1956; Bowman, 1987).

The research tradition devoted to determining if and how work and leisure (or play) are related (see, e.g., Wilensky, 1960; Rousseau, 1978; Champoux, 1979) is, in fact, quite substantial. Nevertheless, only equivocal support has been found over the years for any of the theoretical positions that purport to explain the work-leisure relationship. A vexing problem in the comparison of work and leisure is that of units of analysis; that is, exactly what about work and leisure can reasonably be compared? This problem is likely to blame for many of the ambiguous and sometimes contradictory results that have plagued research on work and leisure. Additionally, the three work-leisure theories delineated by Wilensky (1960), and basically adhered to by researchers since, are fundamentally synchronic and unidirectional; that is, it is assumed that work influences leisure in a slice-in-time sense, either to be like work (spillover) or to be different from work (compensation). Even the segmentation perspective—that work and leisure are unrelated—is based on viewing each at a point in time. Given current knowledge of the processes of enculturation and of the constraints placed both on work and leisure by the local ecology, these assumptions seem to be overly simplistic.

In this chapter we look at outdoor recreation activities of a sample of workers in the machine-tool industry of western Pennsylvania in order to examine whether machines play a part in the play of individuals who work with them constantly and to evaluate this relationship in terms of extant and new theory. To some extent, the units-of-analysis problem is solved by using a measure of machine involvement in both work and play. Machinists, of course, interact with large, complex machines on a daily basis at work (see, e.g., Chick & Roberts, 1987; Roberts & Chick, 1987). Though the principles of many common machine-tools (e.g., the lathe, mill, boring machine) were known as long as a thousand years ago, it has been only in the last dozen or so years that the computer has been added to the mix, making the machines conceptually more complex than ever. The question is whether working with machines is related in any way to what one does in their leisure. The spillover perspective on work and play would suggest that machinists should play with machines while a compensation perspective would hold otherwise. Segmentation would imply no relationship. We do not believe that spillover, compensation, or segmentation adequately describes the work-play situation, however. Below we provide some discussion of these perspectives and offer a fourth alternative that, we feel, better describes the relationship between work and play.

WORK AND LEISURE

Over the years the relationship between work and play or leisure has been described primarily from three theoretical points of view: (a) spillover (or generalization) theory suggests that one tends to do similar things in play or leisure as in work; (b) compensation theory indicates that play or leisure compensates for unsatisfactory aspects of work; and (c) segmentation theory holds that work and leisure are essentially unrelated spheres of life (Wilensky, 1960). Champoux (1979) has criticized much of the research on the work-nonwork relationship for focusing on work as a singular determinant of leisure, for assuming that work and nonwork are distinct institutions, and for adhering to the spillover, compensation, or segmentation models of work and nonwork. This would suggest that research should focus either on multiple determinants of leisure or on a dynamic theory of work and leisure that would encompass the multiple interactions of both. We will attempt to delineate a model of the latter sort.

Although a satisfactory dynamic theory of work and nonwork has yet to emerge, Roberts and Cosper (1987) found that blue collar workers in three occupations have related levels of strategic involvement in their workplaces and in the games that they play. This suggests a dynamic formulation of work and nonwork wherein both depend, in part, on antecedent socialization rather than on a relatively static and unidirectional relationship, as mandated by the spillover and compensation models. Further, their data suggests that work and nonwork are not distinct, but complementary. Recent research by Judge and Watanabe (1993) indicates that work satisfaction and life satisfaction are interactively related; that is, each contributes to the other, instead of there being a one-way causal relationship, as suggested by the spillover and compensation theories. There is good reason, therefore, to believe that work and leisure have an interactive relationship. Substantial cross-cultural evidence indicates that children often emulate the work of their parents in their own play so, developmentally, children commonly play before they work, rather than vice versa. So, if work and play are seen in a process sense, then it might be argued that play is antecedent to work. Of course, one might assert that the work of adults is then spilling over to the play of children, again indicating the primacy of work. Nevertheless, the evidence that work determines leisure, or that play determines work, is hardly convincing.

We feel that a "Patterned Socialization" model offers the best opportunity to understand the relationship between work and leisure. Its premise is simple: the fundamental requirement of any living organism is to survive and reproduce. What one does at work and at play (and in virtually every other aspect of life) is the result, first and foremost, of the need to maintain life. Here, we are in agreement with Marvin Harris's cultural materialist principle of infrastructural determinism. Harris (1979) posits that all socio-cultural systems involve four universal components: "...the etic behavioral infrastructure, structure, and superstructure, and the mental and emic superstructure" (p. 54). Key to his theory of cultural materialism is the principal of infrastructural determinism. This states that: "The etic behavioral modes of production and reproduction probabilistically determine the etic behavioral domestic and political economy, which in turn probabilistically determine the behavioral and mental emic superstructures" (Harris 1979, pp. 55–56). In Harris's system, play and leisure are aspects of the superstructure and, as such, are probabilistically determined by elements of the structure, such as family organization, education, and enculturation, which are, in turn, probabilistically determined by infrastructural components, including subsistence technology, ecosystems, and work patterns.

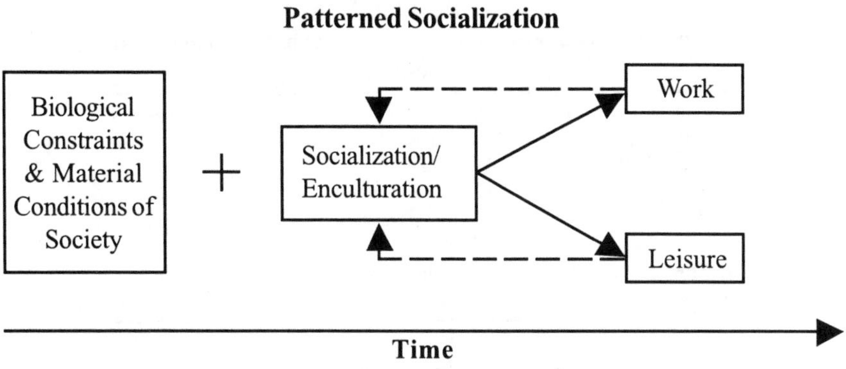

Patterned Socialization

FIGURE 1. The patterned socialization model of the work–play relationship.

Harris's cultural materialist model is not unidirectional, and feedback is presumed to occur from the superstructure to the structure and infrastructure and structure to infrastructure. Hence, infrastructural factors influence socialization and enculturation and lead to what individuals do in play, which may affect, through feedback, what happens in work. We base our model of work and leisure, which we term "Patterned Socialization," on Harris's model of cultural systems. It is depicted in Figure 1.

As a final feature, this model posits agency on part of individuals (effective through feedback) though individual agency may not necessarily be conscious since choices are made on the basis of information assimilated in the past. On the other hand, the spillover and compensation models suggest that the play and leisure activities are externally dictated or constrained and, thus, lack agency.

THE RESEARCH

The data for this study was collected as part of a larger investigation of the styles and quality of life of individuals (and their families) who work in the machine-tool industry of western Pennsylvania. The sample in this study included 316 machinists and 474 non-machinists. The latter group constituted a normative or contrast group and it was designed to mirror the sample of machinists in terms of age and location of residence, but not gender or employment status (employed or unemployed). Hence, for this research, only employed males (all of the machinists are males) were selected from the normative sample as a comparison group for the machinists. When cases with missing data were excluded the final sample included 301 machinists and 231 non-machinists.

All individuals in the sample responded to a survey wherein they were asked to indicate if they participated in any of 24 typical outdoor recreation activities. Specifically, they were asked to "Circle only those activities you do regularly within

TABLE 1.
The original 24 outdoor recreational activities presented to machinists and non-machinists.

1. Fishing	9. Camping	17. Team sports
2. Hunting	10. Canoeing	18. River rafting
3. Four-wheel driving	11. Skiing	19. Bicycling
4. Hiking	12. Snowmobiling	20. Archery
5. Power boating	13. Motorcycling	21. Swimming
6. Bird watching	14. Tennis	22. Golf
7. Cross-country skiing	15. Sightseeing	23. Sailing
8. Horseback riding	16. Shooting	24. Hang gliding

season." The activities were presented in the following format, shown in Table 1.

Informants circled the number in front of activities in which they felt that they participated regularly. This provided a 0–1 matrix where row entries were the informants and columns were the activities. Frequencies of the 24 activities were computed and those in which less than 10 percent of the sample participated were eliminated. Those activities eliminated from further consideration included bird watching, cross-country skiing, horseback riding, skiing, tennis, river rafting, sailing, and hang gliding, leaving the 16 activities analyzed below.

DATA ANALYSIS

A correlation matrix of the 16 outdoor activities was computed in order to investigate patterning of the activities. In particular, we were interested in whether individuals who recreated with any one of the machines (four-wheel driving, power boating, snowmobiling, and motorcycling) tended to also recreate with one or more of the others. Since the data are dichotomous, the correlation matrix was calculated using Jaccard's coefficient. This coefficient is used to relate variables "whose values may represent the presence or absence of an attribute" (Wilkinson, 1989, pp. 53–54). Its formula is $S = a/a+b+c$ where a is the present, present cell of a two by two table while b is present, absent and c is absent, present. Since d, the absent, absent cell, does not clearly convey any information, it is excluded from the formula.

The correlation matrix was then subjected to principal components analysis in order to determine if the "machine-based recreations" grouped together. Component loadings were varimax rotated and the minimum eigenvalue for actor extraction was 1.0 while variables that loaded at .5 or greater and did not cross load were included in factors and interpretations. Results of the factor analysis are given in Tables 2 and 3 below.

The four machine-based recreations comprise the second factor in the three factor solution.[3] Factor 1 may be interpreted as consumptive outdoor activities and factor 3 as non-consumptive outdoor activities. Three activities, team sports, golf, and canoeing, failed to load at the requisite level on any of the factors and were eliminated from

Table 2.

Eigenvalues and Percent of Variance Explained
by Three Factors of the Outdoor Recreation
Activity Correlation Matrix.

Factor	Eigenvalue	Percent of Variance
Factor 1	2.718	16.990
Factor 2	1.849	11.557
Factor 3	2.159	13.495

Table 3.
Varimax Rotated Factor Loadings for 16 Outdoor Recreation Activities.

Activity	Factor 1	Factor 2	Factor 3
Hunting	**0.786**	0.084	0.240
Shooting	**0.736**	0.199	0.177
Fishing	**0.728**	0.072	0.246
Archery	**0.554**	0.299	0.022
Camping	**0.548**	0.180	0.352
Snowmobiling	0.020	**0.665**	−0.011
4-Wheel driving	0.230	**0.553**	0.017
Power boating	0.111	**0.525**	0.181
Motorcycling	0.232	**0.496**	0.183
Sightseeing	0.235	−0.100	**0.605**
Hiking	0.258	−0.012	**0.605**
Biking	−0.074	0.270	**0.591**
Swimming	0.236	0.172	**0.528**
Team sports	0.060	0.422	0.422
Golf	0.222	0.150	0.372
Canoeing	0.254	0.305	0.332

further analyses. Remember that these data are based on what informants indicated that they actually did, rather than on attitudinal information. Hence, these results indicate, quite reasonably, that those who hunt also fish, shoot, camp, and engage in archery. Those who participate in one form of machine-based recreation are likely to participate in others and those who enjoy non-consumptive activities group together.[4]

Next, we were interested in whether the machinists participate more than the contrast group in the machine-based recreations. In order to evaluate this question, the proportion of individuals in each of the two samples who participated or did not participate in each of the 13 activities was calculated. These results are shown in Table 4.

It can be seen that substantially higher percentages of machinists than non-machinists participate in 4-wheel driving, power boating, snowmobiling, and motorcycling. The next question is whether this is due to the fact that machinists enjoy the company of machines or whether some other factor is involved. Other available variables that might have influenced participation in the 13 activities include age (AGE), annual income (INCOME), education level (EDLEVEL), current residence (rural,

Table 4.
Numbers and Percentages of Machinists and Non-machinists
Participating in 13 Outdoor Recreations.

	Machinists (N = 301)		Non-Machinists (N = 231)	
	No	Yes	No	Yes
Fishing	110	191	141	90
	36.54	63.46	61.04	38.96
Hunting	94	207	118	113
	31.23	68.77	51.08	48.92
Four-wheel Driving	241	60	206	25
	80.07	19.93	89.18	10.82
Hiking	205	96	163	68
	68.11	31.89	70.56	29.44
Power Boating	234	67	206	25
	77.74	22.26	89.18	10.82
Camping	150	151	161	70
	49.83	50.17	69.70	30.30
Snowmobiling	259	42	220	11
	86.05	13.95	95.24	4.76
Motorcycling	207	94	208	23
	68.77	31.23	90.04	9.96
Sightseeing	183	118	138	93
	60.80	39.20	59.74	40.26
Shooting	150	151	167	64
	49.83	50.17	72.29	27.71
Bicycling	237	64	196	35
	78.74	21.26	84.85	15.15
Archery	210	91	203	28
	69.77	30.23	87.88	12.12
Swimming	181	120	157	74
	60.13	39.87	67.97	32.03

small town, small city, urban) (LIVENOW), and area where informants grew up (between the ages of five and 18; rural, small town, small city, urban) (GROWUP). The machinist/non-machinist variable is referred to as MACHTOOL in the analyses that follow below.

Summated scores on each of the factors were computed for every individual in the sample. For Factor 1, individuals could participate in none, one, two, three, four, or all five of the activities that comprise the factor, giving a summated score of 0 through 5. Similarly, scores of 0 through 4 were possible on Factors 2 and 3. Each of these summated scores was designated as a dependent variable in a regression analysis, with age, annual income, education level, current residence and area where informants grew up composing the independent variables.[5] The results of these three analysis are shown in Tables 5, 6, and 7.

The results for the first two analyses are statistically significant while that for

TABLE 5.
Regression Analysis of Age, Income, Machine-Tool Employee, Current Residence, Area Where Grew Up, and Education Level on Outdoor Activities Factor 1
(Consumptive Recreation)

Dependent Variable: Consumptive Recreation (Factor 1)

N: 518   Multiple R: 0.437   Squared Multiple R: 0.191
Adjusted Squared Multiple R: 0.181   Standard Error of Estimate: 1.476

Variable	Coefficient	Std Error	Std Coef	Tolerance	t	p (2 tail)
CONSTANT	4.303	0.393	0.000		10.943	0.000
AGE	−0.031	0.006	−0.234	0.773	−5.169	0.000
INCOME	−0.058	0.070	−0.037	0.807	−0.830	0.407
MACHTOOL	0.613	0.149	0.187	0.773	4.123	0.000
LIVENOW	−0.134	0.070	−0.095	0.648	−1.915	0.056
GROWUP	−0.053	0.069	−0.038	0.660	−0.775	0.439
EDLEVEL	−0.223	0.069	−0.135	0.897	−3.222	0.001

Analysis of Variance

Source	Sum of Squares	df	Mean Square	F-Ratio	p
REGRESSION	262.430	6	43.738	20.068	0.000
RESIDUAL	1113.711	511	2.179		

TABLE 6.
Regression Analysis of Age, Income, Machine-Tool Employee, Current Residence, Area Where Grew Up, and Education Level on Outdoor Activities Factor 2
(Machine-Based Recreation)

Dependent Variable: Consumptive Recreation (Factor 1)

N: 518   Multiple R: 0.379   Squared Multiple R: 0.144
Adjusted Squared Multiple R: 0.134   Standard Error of Estimate: 0.862

Variable	Coefficient	Std Error	Std Coef	Tolerance	t	p (2 tail)
CONSTANT	1.447	0.230	0.000		6.300	0.000
AGE	−0.022	0.003	−0.289	0.773	−6.198	0.000
INCOME	−0.002	0.041	−0.002	0.807	−0.048	0.961
MACHTOOL	0.274	0.087	0.147	0.773	3.148	0.002
LIVENOW	−0.010	0.041	−0.012	0.648	−0.233	0.816
GROWUP	−0.021	0.040	−0.027	0.660	−0.532	0.595
EDLEVEL	−0.008	0.041	−0.008	0.897	−0.189	0.850

Analysis of Variance

Source	Sum of Squares	df	Mean Square	F-Ratio	p
REGRESSION	63.814	6	10.636	14.304	0.000
RESIDUAL	379.955	511	0.744		

TABLE 7.
Regression Analysis of Age, Income, Machine-Tool Employee, Current Residence, Area Where Grew Up, and Education Level on Outdoor Activities Factor 3 (Non-Consumptive Recreation)

Dependent Variable: Consumptive Recreation (Factor 1)

N: 518   Multiple R: 0.104   Squared Multiple R: 0.011
Adjusted Squared Multiple R: 0.000   Standard Error of Estimate: 1.069

Variable	Coefficient	Std Error	Std Coef	Tolerance	t	p (2 tail)
CONSTANT	0.974	0.285	0.000		3.422	0.001
AGE	−0.001	0.004	−0.014	0.773	−0.279	0.781
INCOME	−0.017	0.051	−0.017	0.807	−0.345	0.730
MACHTOOL	0.146	0.108	0.068	0.773	1.357	0.175
LIVENOW	−0.006	0.051	−0.007	0.648	−0.127	0.899
GROWUP	−0.050	0.050	0.055	0.660	1.011	0.312
EDLEVEL	−0.062	0.050	0.057	0.897	1.227	0.221

Analysis of Variance

Source	Sum of Squares	df	Mean Square	F-Ratio	p
REGRESSION	6.424	6	1.071	0.938	0.467
RESIDUAL	583.439	511	1.142		

Factor 3 is not. For both Factors 1 and 2, age and whether or not the informant is a machine-tool worker has a significant effect on the dependent variables. For Factor 1 (Consumptive Outdoor Recreation), education level is also (negatively) related to participation while where the informant currently lives also has a small negative effect (that is, living in urban areas is negatively related to consumptive outdoor recreation). Being a machine-tool worker is positively related to participating in consumptive outdoor recreation (Factor 1) and machine-based outdoor recreation (Factor 2) while age is negatively related in both cases. The amount of the variance accounted for was relatively small for both factors: 18.1 percent for Factor 1 and 13.4 percent for Factor 2.

DISCUSSION

The Patterned Socialization model predicts that machinists should participate more frequently than non-machinists in machine-based play and recreation. The above analyses indicate, first, that machine-based outdoor recreational activities tend to go together and, second, that being a machine-tool worker is significantly and positively associated with these activities. It is true that machine-tool workers participate more than others in the consumptive outdoor recreation activities, as well. While this fact might be regarded as negative evidence for any sort of pattern between one's work and play, we choose to interpret it as support for the idea that individuals are socialized into both work and play. Individuals who became machinists appear to exhibit a somewhat greater preference for outdoor recreation in general than is the case with the sample of non-machinists (though not with respect to non-consumptive activities). Given the data, we cannot explain that preference for consumptive outdoor recreation, although ethnographic experience with machinists suggests that activities like hunting, fishing, camping, and so on, are favorites for them.

Age is also important in both consumptive and machine-based outdoor recreation, even more than occupation. Not surprisingly, the effect of age is the same in both cases: the older one gets, the less likely he is to participate in either of the two types of outdoor activity. A factor that should be considered when evaluating these results is that the machinist sample is a relatively homogenous blue-collar group. The contrast sample, on the other hand, is not at all homogenous but contains both blue-collar and white-collar workers, ranging from garbage collectors and insurance agents through school teachers to medical doctors and college professors. Involvement in outdoor activities may be more characteristic of machinists or of blue-collar workers generally than that of the heterogeneous group represented by the contrast sample. More detailed analysis of the contrast sample may offer additional insight on this question.

This study does not directly test the Patterned Socialization model in that it lacks diachronic data. Though information on where informants grew up represents one sort of information about their pasts, it did not contribute significantly in any of the analyses. One could even claim that the results support the spillover model of work and play/leisure just as well as the Patterned Socialization model. However, interviews with a subset of the sample of machinists indicate clearly that their interest in machines preceded their employment, rendering it difficult to believe that their current interest in machine-based recreation is caused by their work. Based on both the survey results reported here and the interviews, we feel that the most parsimonious explanation is that the informants were socialized into machine interest and awareness beginning long before they were employed.

It must also be admitted that the measures of participation in the outdoor recreation activities were crude. We asked informants only to indicate which of the activities they participated in, not how often they did so. This, however, solves another problem—the unreliability of memory. It is more difficult to reliably indicate participation frequency, especially when one does participate quite often, than to reliably indicate whether or not one participates at all (see Bernard, Killworth, Kronefeld, & Sailer, 1984, for a review of informant accuracy). Still, our data consist of self reports of behavior, not actual observations of behavior. It is also clear, given the relatively low amounts of variance accounted for in the regressions, that other variables may be involved or that the appropriate variables were, indeed, identified but simply are not strongly related (remember, both Harris's cultural materialist model and the Patterned Socialization model presented here are probabilistic, not deterministic).

Finally, with respect to machinists and machine-based recreation, we do solve the "units-of-analysis problem" that plagues research that purports to compare qualitatively different activities (see Chick & Barnett, 1994, for a discussion of this problem). That is, how can work and play or work and leisure be meaningfully compared at all? We use the commonalty of the machine in both but this solution is not one that can be used universally. So, do machinists play with machines? The answer is "Yes, to a greater degree than is true of non machinists." Does work determine leisure? The answer to that question is a simple, "No."

NOTES

[1] This research was supported by a National Science Foundation grant (DIR 89-20630) to the first author.

[2] We should make clear that we are not conceptually distinguishing play, recreation, and leisure in this chapter. Play is a word more typically used to describe the activities of children while leisure is characteristic of adults. But even this is not a hard-and-fast rule as adults "play" tennis or "play" bridge, although "leisure" is not commonly used in reference to children. Recreation seems to be an intermediate term that connotes activity in the context of leisure. We feel that play and leisure (and recreation) may be age graded but are difficult to distinguish in terms of content. Hence, we will generally use the word "leisure" in this chapter, as we are concerned with the activities of adults, and we will assume that it encompasses the meanings of play and recreation as well.

[3] The factors here are numbered 1 through 3 based on descending order of the eigenvalues of the unrotated solution.

[4] Multidimensional scaling and cluster analyses of the data provided essentially identical solutions. In each, the four machine-based activities were closely associated.

[5] The 6- and 5-valued dependent variables technically violate assumptions of the regression model which calls for interval level data from − to + infinity. Hence, analyses identical to the regressions reported here were conducted using logit, an appropriate analog of regression appropriate for polytomous dependent variables. As typically happens, interpretations of the results were essentially identical. The regression model is reported here inasmuch as it is more widely understood and the various regression coefficients have more intuitive meaning than those associated with logit.

REFERENCES

Bernard, H. R., Killworth, P., Kronefeld, D, & Sailer, L. (1984). The problem of informant accuracy: The validity of retrospective data. *Annual Review of Anthropology, 13,* 495–517.

Blanchard, K. (1986). Play as adaptation: The work-play dichotomy revisited. In B. Mergen (Ed.), *Cultural dimensions of play, games, and sport* (pp. 79–87). Champaign, IL: Human Kinetics Publishers.

Bowman, J. R. (1987). Making work play. In G. A. Fine (Ed.), *Meaningful play, playful meaning* (pp. 61–71). Champaign, IL: Human Kinetics Publishers.

Brightbill, C. (1960). *The challenge of leisure.* Englewood Cliffs, NJ: Prentice-Hall.

Champoux, J. E. (1979). Work and nonwork: A review of theory and empirical research. Unpublished manuscript.

Chick, G. E., & Barnett, L. A. (1995). Children's play and adult leisure. In A. D. Pellegrini (Ed.), *Play as multi-disciplinary inquiry: Essays in honor of Brian Sutton-Smith*. New York: Cambridge University Press, (pp. 45–69).

Chick, G. E., & Roberts, J. M. (1987). Lathe craft: A study in "part" appreciation. *Human Organization, 46*, 305–317.

Dubin, R. (1956). Industrial workers' worlds: A study in the 'central life interests' of industrial workers. *Social Problems, 3*, 131–142.

Dumazedier, J. (1967). *Toward a society of leisure*. New York: Free Press.

Godbey, G. (1985). *Leisure in your life: An exploration*. State College, PA: Venture Publishing.

Harris, M. (1979). *Cultural materialism: The struggle for a science of culture*. New York: Random House.

Judge, T. A., & Watanabe, S. (1993). Another look at the job satisfaction–life satisfaction relationship. *Journal of Applied Psychology, 78*, 939–948.

Kelly, J. R. (1972). Work and leisure: A simplified paradigm. *Journal of Leisure Research, 4*, 50–62.

Nash, J. B. (1960). *Philosophy of recreation and leisure*. Dubuque, IA: Wm C. Brown.

Neulinger, J. (1974). *The psychology of leisure*. Springfield, IL: Chas. C Thomas.

Parker, S. (1983). *Work and leisure*. London: George Allen & Unwin, Ltd.

Roberts, J. M., & Cosper, R. L. (1987). Variation in strategic involvement in games for three blue collar occupations. *Journal of Leisure Research, 19*, 131–148.

Roberts, J. M., & Chick, G. E. (1987). Human Views of Machines: Expression and Machine Shop Syncretism. In H. R. Bernard & P. J. Pelto, (Eds.), *Technology and Social Change*, (2nd Ed., pp. 301–327, 377–393). Prospect Heights, IL: Waveland Press.

Rousseau, D. M. (1978). Relationship of work and nonwork. *Journal of Applied Psychology, 63*, 513–517.

Wilensky, H. L. (1960). Work, careers and social integration. *International Social Science Journal, 12*, 543–560.

Wilkinson, L. (1989). *SYSTAT: The System for Statistics*. Evanston, IL: SYSTAT, Inc.

2

Play in Culture and the Jargon of Primordiality: A Critique of *Homo Ludens*[1]

Mechthild Nagel

INTRODUCTION

A number of western play theoreticians have paid tribute to the Dutch historian who introduced their subject into the human and social sciences. It was Huizinga who put forth the original thesis that the activity of playing games is not just part of any civilization but makes culture and civilization possible in the first place. In this chapter I will analyze Johan Huizinga's *Homo Ludens* in light of Martin Heidegger's *Being and Time* and later essays on thinking and technology. I will claim that Huizinga's method resembles in a striking fashion the phenomenological method of Heidegger; furthermore, I will show what serious political consequences Huizinga's description of play has. Huizinga, like Heidegger, succumbs to what Fritz Ringer has coined "Mandarin ideology" (Ringer, 1969).

To study the ideological underpinnings of *Homo Ludens* is nothing new: Margaret Carlisle Duncan (1988) has called for a radical critique of this work and of the growing body of play theoreticians who still relish Huizinga's emphatic exclamation that "[t]rue play knows no propaganda; its aim is in itself, and its familiar spirit is happy inspiration" (1950, p. 211). To dispel this naive myth which still dominates in play discourse, Duncan employs a semiological method which examines oppositional concepts. Unlike other critics, such as Caillois,[2] Ehrmann, Geyl, Gombrich, and Gruneau;

Duncan does not stress Huizinga's original work over his romanticization of the past. María Lugones makes a similar case in point; she critiques Huizinga's emphasis on agonistic play and exposes its inherently imperialistic character (Lugones, 1987). In my chapter I will make use of some of the insights of Duncan, Lugones, Ehrmann, and Sutton-Smith (1982, 1984). By employing the tactics of a postmodern discourse of resistance (Foster, 1987), I will try to display the ideological character of Huizinga's methodology, which resembles Heidegger's phenomenological enterprise.

A SUMMARY OF HUIZINGA'S THESES ON PLAY IN
HOMO LUDENS

Phenomenologists share a predilection for an origin (*Ursprung!*), that is, they emphasize that which is original, early or primordial. The following overview of *Homo Ludens* will review those theses where Huizinga most emphatically employs these concepts.

In the first chapter, we encounter the first incidence of that. Play, Huizinga proclaims, is the origin of culture; it is foundational since it is "older than culture" (1950, p. 1). However, this insight needs to be 'uncovered' by the critical gaze of the self-styled phenomenologist. As for play proper, he determines its characteristics as voluntary, outside the ordinary life-boundaries, secluded and limited in time and space, creating order, rule-governed, and surrounding itself with secrecy (pp. 7-13). With these formal elements of play he sets out to show the formation of culture (law, philosophy, poetry, war, art) through the social and agonistic manifestations of play, that is, its "higher forms" (p. 7). In chapter three, Huizinga reveals that through the progressive development of culture the play-element almost vanishes except for its continuous display in the sacred sphere (p. 46). He concludes that "[t]he *original* play-element is then almost completely *hidden behind* cultural phenomena" (p. 46, my emphasis).

The task of uncovering the authentic, original, culture-creating play-feature is a difficult one for the "phenomenologist," since, after all, much of this authenticity has been lost in modernity: "The ever-present play-element, *originally* a real factor in the shaping of [the archaic noble] culture, has now become a mere show and parade" (p. 65, my emphasis). In accord with Heidegger's suspicion of the advances of the technological age and its emphasis on work and production, Huizinga remarks pessimistically that "we have lost touch with play" insofar as civilization "has grown more serious; it assigns only a secondary place to playing. The heroic period is over, and the agonistic phase, too, seems a thing of the past" (p. 75).

Amidst this gray, over-serious sphere of inauthentic dwelling of modern humans, poetry is our last straw to a return to authentic possibilities of playful self-realization. Only poetry constitutes "the stronghold of living and noble play" (p. 134). It is special and authentic due to its "primordial nature" and its relation to "pure play" (p. 119). It exists prior to prose in culture and naturally, "all poetry is born of play"

(p. 129). The art of poetry is unique in its maintaining and preserving a playful quality even when "civilization grows more complicated" (p. 129). Other forms of art are not that lucky. Of the waning of the (archaic) ritual Huizinga says: "All *true* ritual is sung, danced and played. We moderns have lost the sense for ritual and sacred play. Our civilization is worn with age and too sophisticated" (p. 158, my emphasis).

In the last chapter, "The Play-Element in Contemporary Civilization," it should not come as a surprise that we have completely lost the "pure play-quality" (p. 197) of the Hellenic aristocrats and instead are merely inauthentically absorbed into the "systematization and regimentation of sport" (p. 197). Puerilism and a world-wide "bastardization of culture" (p. 205) lead us to the problem of "false play" which lacks spontaneity and carelessness—two important phenomena of genuine play.

Huizinga emphatically calls, therefore, for a return to the origin, to the roots of our culture, where play is simple and pure: "It must not consist in the darkening or debasing of standards set up by reason, faith or humanity. It must not be a false seeming, a masking of political purposes behind the illusion of genuine play-forms. True play knows no propaganda; its aim is in itself, and its familiar spirit is happy inspiration" (p. 211).

TRACING THE PHENOMENOLOGICAL METHOD: THE PROJECT OF *HOMO LUDENS*

I will now proceed to analyze some of the claims of *Homo Ludens* which—I aver—do fit into the project of *Being and Time*.

The Quest for a Pure Aesthetics

The purpose of treating play as a cultural phenomenon is to restrict the study to the aesthetic quality of play. Huizinga wants to focus on the aspects of fun, pleasure, passion and frenzy in games (p. 2). Naturally, this occurs at the explicit exclusion of the biological function argument, which play theoreticians, such as Buytendijk and Zondervan seem to advocate (p. 2). Even though Huizinga acknowledges these theories as "partial solutions to the problems" instead of summarily rejecting them, he is still quite confident that his project is to look at play "as a totality that we must try to understand and evaluate" (p. 3).

Similarly, in *Being and Time*, we are told by Heidegger that in order to understand *Dasein's* primary function as its venture to tackle the question of Being, we need to suspend anthropological, psychological or even ethical interpretations of *Dasein*. (That is one reason why Heidegger prefers the usage of *Dasein* to "person" or "human being.") This de-anthropologizing, as Rainer Marten puts it (1989, p. 101), leads to a de-humanized, ontocentric philosophy. One could draw similar conclusions about Huizinga's own cleansing effort regarding the ludic aspect in culture. After all, Huizinga engages in a malediction of playful activities which are not entirely "pure," such as gambling, or are not strictly limited to the service of poetry and philosophy. Hence, only when one plays aesthetic or metaphysical games for their own sake, one is, to put it into Heideggerian jargon, concernfully engaged with play itself and always already uncovering *aletheia*.

What follows from this totalizing and purification process is a malediction of modern technology that could "spoil" the noble game. Heidegger delineates the method of phenomenology as anti-scientific and anti-technocratic, as a philosophical endeavor that goes "back to the things themselves!" (1979, p. 27). Empirical science has no place in a phenomenology that proclaims that phenomena can only be uncovered through the apophantic gaze of a philosopher who has privileged access to truth. Evidence for the accuracy of such observations need not be provided. The following quote from Heidegger's later work should elucidate the implications of his tendency to despise science. In the *Letter on Humanism* he states, "[One has to] retain the essential help of the phenomenological way of seeing and dispense with the inappropriate concern with 'science' and 'research'" (1976, p. 235).[3]

This suspicion of scientific-technological approaches is mirrored in Huizinga's own misgiving of the "quantitative methods of experimental science" (p. 2). Huizinga emphasizes in the Foreword that his study of play is historical rather than scientific. However, I want to show that his analysis is rather ahistorical and Eurocentric despite his cross-cultural and historically situated posturing. Take for instance, his enthusiasm for the Hellenic society which "was so profoundly imbued with the play-spirit" (p. 141). Apparently, the historian (and expert in Medieval history) seems to have forgotten what small segment of the Greek society in the classical age was able to participate in activities that were fun. In fourth-century Athens, for example, only the property-holding patriarchs were able to participate freely and playfully in the social-political events (as politicians, as jury drawn by a lot, as actors in a tragedy, as gymnasts). Sure enough, those events can be described as playful and agonistic, but Huizinga's uncritical embrace of Hellenic "civilization" is a bit bewildering.

Even more troubling are Huizinga's remarks regarding the behavior of "uncivilized" peoples. Take, for example, his account of the practice of the potlatch ritual: it embodies an adolescent spirit, par excellence. The primitive man [sic], who engages in such practices, has not only access to a mythical, sacred world, where the "spirit of pure play [is] truly understood" (p. 5) but is also still enveloped in "trivial and childish amusements" (p. 141). The potlatch's dominant principle is "the agonistic 'instinct' pure and simple" (61). Its violent spirit is "akin to the thoughts and feelings of the adolescent" (p. 60).

Judgments like this one perhaps justified the Canadian government's decision around the turn of the century to forbid the Native American nations to continue the potlatch practice. (It also justified the confiscation of their totems, goods, etc.) This is not to say that the potlatch does not have any religious significance and does not display agonistic traits. But at issue is why Huizinga adamantly refuses to see the political and economic significance of the potlatch (cf. Franz Boas's important research on this). I claim that Huizinga's insistence on the cultural/mythical/playful value of the potlatch—paradoxically—may have contributed to the legitimation of the cultural genocide of the Native Americans.

Authenticity and Primordiality: "Uncovering" the Jargon of Emphasis in *Homo Ludens*

Phenomenologists always look for something "foundational" which simply cannot be unearthed by the workings of "real science."[4] So if one sets out to look for the origin of culture, of any human culture (!), one always, only and inevitably finds play. This is made quite clear in the opening sentence of the first chapter of *Homo Ludens*: "Play is older than culture, for culture, however inadequately defined, always presupposes human society,..." (p. 1). This claim is repeated in the following exalted way in the Foreword: "[C]ivilization arises and unfolds in and as play." Again, in Chapter Three, we are reminded that "play is primary" in the "twin union of play and culture" (p. 46). The human condition in archaic society (does he mean African culture?) is different insofar as the "primitive peoples" engage in activities, like hunting, which have nothing but a playful character! (p. 46) This is to say, that at the "beginning" of civilization other life-forms, such as hard work, are simply unthinkable. As civilization "progresses" (i.e., classical Greek culture) the historian finds that play "recedes" to the sacred sphere which includes religion, philosophy, poetry and the judiciary. When we come to this stage, real phenomenological work needs to happen because "[t]he original play-element is then almost completely hidden behind cultural phenomena" (pp. 46–47).

From Heidegger, we already know that this is no easy task. Interpretative understanding (of a text) has to occur within the horizon of the "hermeneutic circle." The circular structure of hermeneutics is the key for all philosophical understanding and interpretation (1979, p. 152). The circular structure occurs when understanding moves from the whole to the part and back to the whole (Gadamer, 1986b, p. 57). However, not everybody has this access to understanding and truth: The dictum, "What is decisive is not to get out of the circle but to come into it in the right way," (1979, p. 153) is most telling here. For Heidegger, the "right way" is to disclose and describe things phenomenologically as they originally show themselves, that is, in their *apophantic logos*, and to elucidate them by engaging in the fore-structure of understanding.

Heidegger wants to demarcate this hermeneutic-interpretative understanding from the derivative modes of understanding. Merely understanding the "ontic" phenomena and employing scientific knowledge and analysis is clearly a wrong strategy (1979, p. 143). True understanding only occurs when Dasein really grasps its existence as Being-able-to-be ("Seinkönnen") in the sense of projecting its possibilities and directing those essentially towards Being-towards-death.

This brings us to the issue of authenticity and inauthenticity. These are key terms in *Being and Time* but are also frequently employed in Heidegger's later work. In the *Letter on Humanism*, he reminds us that authenticity has no anthropological meaning; instead it lays out the ecstatic relationship of Dasein towards the truth of Being

(1976, pp. 332–333). Realizing this relationship however only occurs when Dasein comprehends the totality of Being, which is Dasein's "fulfilled existentiality" or Being-towards-death. Thus, authenticity is a rare feature in Dasein's everydayness where it exists indifferently and never realizes its authentic choices. It always falls short of truly and originally "living." After all, the possibility of Being-no-longer-there (*Nichtmehrdasein*) assumes higher ontological status than the mere reality of simply existing.

Huizinga assumes a similarly foundationalist approach in his "historical" study. However, his ploy is to describe play as being irrational (p. 4) so that he can with ease evade the criticism that he owes us an explanation of what exactly makes play or fun primordial. He can safely maintain that this collection of features simply "resists all analysis, all logical interpretation" (p. 3). On the other hand, he has to do hard (logical!) work to show that the play-element has been foundational to the legal system, to poetry, to philosophy and other cultural institutions. All these, he writes, "are rooted in the primaeval soil of play" (p. 5).

Huizinga's view of poetry exemplifies his depth-hermeneutic analysis: to show that poetry *precedes* prose he argues that "the preference for verse form may have been due in part to utilitarian considerations: a bookless society finds it easier to memorize its texts in this way" (p. 127). This is a perfectly sound speculation over the search for beginnings, I think. But Huizinga, the romantic and idealist, immediately disregards these materialistic considerations and goes further: "But there is a deeper reason, namely, that life in archaic society is itself metrical and strophical in structure, as it were. Poetry is still the more natural mode of expression for the 'higher' things." All this of course implies that poetry is the more authentic mode, whereas prose merely rests in inauthentic everydayness, engaged, not with higher things, but as crude chatting (see Heidegger's *Gerede*) with common people.

Emphatic declarations, such as the above mentioned, brush aside questions that deal with the logic of play, for example, why is partaking playfully in culture a separate/exclusive activity which has nothing to do with so-called ordinary life? Or is Huizinga alluding to the concept of culture that German Mandarins would associate only with *Bildung*, which is pure play, not work and alienation? Incidentally, the concept of work is not fully developed here. Huizinga simply focuses on the opposites of play and seriousness which of course, do not constitute a real dichotomy, since play can be serious (p. 7). The only term that comes close to the issue of work is Huizinga's use of "ordinary" life, clearly full of negative connotations (see Duncan's analysis). So-called derivative modes of play are laughter and comic (why not fun?). Without further explanation these "subsidiary" forms of play are brushed aside as "scarcely" defining "genuine play" (p. 6). Similarly, in a good Aristotelian tradition of malediction, he insists that the "primitive play" of infants and young animals should be disregarded (p. 7). Also, we see adult "savages" being excluded from the noble play activity, since their play spheres seem to be similar to those of children (p. 141). Left in the inner circle of good, authentic play are those civilized adult (males) who are able to engage in a meaningful way in the "higher forms" of aesthetic experience, which are the social manifestations of play (p. 141). It seems that his ideal player, namely the Hellenic noble, has to be hermetically sealed off from this threatening lifestyle of "everydayness" to devote himself fully to ludic endeavors that are beautiful and sublime.

Yet oddly, Huizinga is at his best, when he criticizes the differentiation in the Greek language between higher play forms, such as *agon, diagoge*, and *scholazein*, and the lower form, such as *paidia* (= infantile play). He finds that the Greek mind fails to conceptualize a unifying, positive term that is common in other European languages, e.g., *ludus, jeu* or *Spiel* (1950, p. 160).

But the question still remains, who is allowed to play and in which culture? The "savage" priest, the Hellenic noble warriors, the innocent child, poets and thinkers? Who falls outside this imaginary grid? Perhaps, women, the poor, the working class, subaltern subjects, and "barbarians"!

I also take issue with the invocation of an "origin," of "primordial nature of play," authenticity and so forth. All this is a bad romantization of a universal notion of play, which, incidentally, displays cultural imperialistic attitudes. Naturally, access to "origins" is limited to the "usual suspects." The subaltern, who may spoil his monolithic cultural game, cannot be invited to jump into the sacred hermeneutic circle.

Ehrmann (1968) aptly points out the contradictions that evolve out of this exclusionary thought system. On the one hand, Huizinga evokes the image of the "noble savage" who intuitively grasps "true" play, and on the other hand, he characterizes the "savage" as illogical (like children!) and not yet civilized (1968, pp. 49-50). Ehrmann is also troubled by Huizinga's obsession with deriding inauthentic modes of games, especially where money is involved because it only corrupts and taints the game (1968, p. 47). Professional athletes perform dirty work *not* noble play and thus contribute to the degeneration to that idée fixe "culture."

IMPLICATIONS OF A DE-ANTHROPOLOGIZED PLAY THEORY

It is not entirely farfetched to speculate, whether—despite the title of the book—we really need Man [sic] the Player. Given Huizinga's emphasis on the characteristics of play and cultural artifacts[5] it is entirely reasonable and within the scope of the book to suggest that Huizinga essentially sets up a game which could function very well without a player and *Mitspieler*. Huizinga lays out what play is, not what makes players playful and how they interact in a game. (He notes *in passim* the function of the cheat and spoilsport.) All important is his thesis that western civilization arises from play. He concentrates on an analysis of institutions, such as art, religion and law, and concludes that all of these institutions are driven by an agonistic element. But what constitutes a player's attitude, her playfulness, is *not* discussed (cf. Lugones, 1987). This lack of an anthropologizing analysis is mirrored in the studies of his followers and fellow play theoreticians and ontologists. We may recall Fink's postulate of the play (i.e. the world-play) without playing humans (or gods and demons for that matter) (1960, p. 241). This is what I call a ludic independence-drive.

Similarly, Gadamer, although he doesn't agree with Fink's overall conception of play, uses play as the guiding principle (*Leitfaden*) for the art of understanding, that is, hermeneutics, in *Truth and Method*. Play and the art work, for Gadamer, exercise a normative grip on players and spectators alike. When we undergo this aesthetic experience it becomes clear to us that the "actual subject of the game [...] is not the player but the game itself" (1975, p. 95; cf., p. 446). Gadamer acknowledges that the modern anthropological research, in particular that spearheaded by Huizinga, has looked at play in a new light. It has rejected the subjectivist approach of Kant and Schiller vis-à-vis their analysis of the aesthetic consciousness. The concept of play is important since it can be used as a guideline for the ontological explanation of the art-work. Gadamer adds that his analysis of play is conducted in the horizon of phenom-enology, since play then will not be reduced to a mere subjectivist attitude.[6]

Also, interestingly, Gadamer picks up the notion of the sacred sphere that Huizinga much emphasizes, where "play has its own essential relation to the serious." This notion becomes crucial for Gadamer's own development of the Heideggerian hermeneutic circle. And, if one is subjected to the spell of play—then, subjectivity is nothing but a blurred or distorted mirror image: "Play is also there, in fact *authentically*, where no being-for-itself of subjectivity does limit the thematic horizon, and where there are no subjects, who relate playfully to each other."[7]

Gadamer approvingly cites the following passage from *Homo Ludens* to show the general uncertainty about the consciousness of the player in the act, "The savage [sic] knows of no conceptual differentiation between Being and playing, nor of any iden-tity, of image or symbol. That's why it remains questionable whether we shouldn't better approach the spiritual state of the savage when he commits his sacred act, by stating that he simply plays. In our concept of play, we dissolve the differentiation between belief and imitation (make-belief)" (Gadamer, 1986a, p. 110). It follows that play itself takes primacy over the consciousness of the player (p. 110).

Most radically, this departure from humans or "the philosophy of the subject" is manifest in Heidegger's writings. Heidegger speaks about humans as merely "being present" (*anwesend*) in a temporal sense in order to avoid the metaphysical meaning of *essentia*; he thus implies that humans are simply utilized by Being (cf. Marten, 1989, p. 111). So, again, humans succumb to the absolute sovereignty of Being. At best, as we encounter in *The Letter on Humanism*, human beings are mystically described as "the shepherds of Being" (1976, p. 331). Humanism, a term clearly despised by Heidegger, has to yield to ontocentrism. Where Heidegger actually talks about play this attitude is also displayed: In the lecture *Das Ding* we are told not that humans play but that the "world" is consummated by play (see "das Spiegel-Spiel der Welt," 1985, p. 173). Only a human being who is dying or, in the language of *Being and Time*, "is towards death" really inhabits (playfully?) the world as world (1979, p. 175).

CONCLUSION

In my critique of Huizinga's conception of play I have tried to point out the similarities between his philosophical premises and those of Heideggerian ontocentrism and how those premises lead to a bad ideological mapping of play and should be exposed as such. The similarities of their bourgeois attitudes suggest their affinity to the generation of Mandarins. As for Huizinga, he actually confesses an admiration of the patrician way of life in his autobiographical essay "My Path to History" (1968, p. 246).

I do not wish to suggest that Huizinga's *Homo Ludens per se* has fascist tendencies; nor do I think that Heidegger's racist philosophy of *Being and Time* necessarily endorses Nazism. Rather, it is important to point out personal confrontations of those two thinkers with the Nazis: Heidegger, on the one hand, was an enthusiastic and early follower and self-styled leader of that ideology, which, in 1954, he still called apologetically the "movement"; Huizinga, on the other hand, was captured by the Nazis in 1940 and was imprisoned, along with other prominent Dutch intellectuals, and died in February, 1945.[8] But both scholars do subscribe, I think, to the theory of cultural decadence which was developed by ultra-conservative German "Mandarins" after World War I (cf. Ringer, 1969, pp. 269–294); they cherish a nostalgic retreat into the past while decrying the decline and decay of the present. Huizinga states that from the ninteenth century on "culture ceased to be 'played'" (1950, p. 192). Crude utilitarianism starts to dominate. "Work and production became the ideal, and then the idol, of the age" (p. 192). Huizinga attributes "the menaces of Communism and Nazism" to the cultural crisis of Europe which is caused by modern technology and scientific progress (cf. Geyl, 1963, pp. 222–223).

Concluding this chapter, I want to stress that Huizinga indeed made an enormous contribution to play research, but more importantly, he omitted to tell us that play "knows"—and puts itself in the service of—propaganda. In so doing, he cast the die and determined the outcome of *his* game. His crusade for play advocates "happy inspiration"—and nothing else! This naive exclamation has to be critically examined—to put it in Hal Foster's terms—as "the idea that aesthetic experience exists apart, without 'purpose,' all but beyond history, or that art can now effect a world at once (inter)subjective, concrete and universal—a symbolic totality" (1987, p. xv). In our (postmodern) play discourse, this purposeless, disinterested modernist idealism has to be eradicated: Its "end of innocence" (Flax, 1992) has come!

NOTES

[1] Previous versions of this chapter were presented at various talks, including those given at the Eastern and Pacific Divisions of the American Society for Aesthetics and at The Association of the Study of Play, St. Paul, MN. I want to thank Gareth Matthews, Carol White, David Fisher, Marcella T. Goldsmith, Joseph Yeh, and Bernhard Rohrbacher for their critical com-

ments on previous versions of this chapter.

[2] Caillois in his influential book *Man, Play and Games*, sets out to critique Huizinga for viewing play as "denuded of all material interest," only to retract it a few pages later by defining play as "unproductive; creating neither goods, nor wealth."

[3] Heidegger's anti-modern "Mandarin" conviction and his deep distrust of scientific progress and technology explains in part his enthusiasm for the "Blut und Boden" ideology of the Nazis. In the lecture *Introduction to Metaphysics*, held in 1935, Heidegger condemns America and Russia for their "unrootedness" and for engaging in a perverted technological race, but curiously, he seems to think that the National Socialists had no part in that. Heidegger writes "what is passed around as National Socialist philosophy has nothing to do with the inner truth and greatness of National Socialism." In 1953, in the new edition of *Einführung in die Metaphysik*, Heidegger slightly changes the meaning of that sentence by replacing "National Socialism" with "the movement" and adds in parenthesis: "in its encounter with global technology and modern man" (1956, p. 199, cited in Rainer Marten, "Ein rassistisches Konzept von Humanität," *Badische Zeitung*, Freiburg, December 19, 1987, written in response to the philosophical and political upheaval caused by Victor Farias's book *Heidegger et le nazisme* (1987)).

[4] Huizinga's defensiveness vis-à-vis "science" seems to stem from his complex of lacking understanding and knowledge of the natural sciences and from his failure to be a "full-blooded historical research worker" (1968, p. 271).

[5] In his essay "The Aesthetic Element in Historical Thought," Huizinga avers emphatically that the artwork can reveal the "true (!) image of the era" which is "indelibly fixed in your imagination" (1968, p. 240).

[6] "Spiel geht nicht im Bewusstsein des Spielenden auf und ist insofern mehr als ein subjektives Verhalten" (Preface to the 2nd ed., 1986b, p. 446).

[7] "Spiel ist auch dort, *ja eigentlich dort*, wo kein Fürsichsein der Subjektivität den thematischen Horizont begrenzt und wo es keine Subjekte gibt, die sich spielend verhalten" (1986a, p. 108, my emphasis).

[8] See Weintraub for a brief biographical note (1966, p. 208).

REFERENCES

Caillois, R. (1979). *Man, play and games.* New York: Schocken Books.
Colie, R. (1964). Johan Huizinga and the task of cultural history. *American Historical Review, LXIX*(iii), 607–630.
Duncan, M. C. (1988). Play discourse and the rhetorical turn: A semiological analysis of *Homo ludens. Play & Culture, 1*, 28–42.
Ehrmann, J. (1968). *Homo ludens* revisited. *Yale French Studies, 41*, 31–57.
Fink, E. (1960). *Spiel als Weltsymbol.* Stuttgart: Kohlhammer.
Flax, J. (1992). The end of innocence. In J. Butler & J. Scott (Eds.), *Feminists theorize the political* (pp. 445–463). New York: Routledge.
Foster, H. (Ed.). (1987). Postmodernism. A preface. In *The anti-aesthetic. Essays on postmodern culture* (2nd ed., pp. ix–xvi). Seattle: Bay Press.
Gadamer, H. G. (1986a). *Wahrheit und Methode* (5th ed.), Vol. I of *Gesammelte Werke.* Tübingen: Mohr.
Gadamer, H. G. (1986b). *Wahrheit und Methode*, Vol. II. Tübingen: Mohr.

Gadamer, H. G. (1975). *Truth and method.* New York: Seabury Press.

Geyl, P. (1963). Huizinga as an accusor of his age. *History & Theory, II*(3), 231–262.

Gombrich, E. H. (1973). Huizinga's *Homo ludens.* In *Proceedings of J. Huizinga Conference at Groningen 1972* (pp. 133–154). The Hague: Nijhoff.

Gruneau, R. (1983). *Class, sports, and social development.* Amherst: University of Massachusetts Press.

Heidegger, M. (1979). *Sein und Zeit* (15th ed.). Tübingen: Niemeyer Verlag.

Heidegger, M. (1985). *Vorträge und Aufsätze* (5th ed.). Pfullingen: Neske.

Heidegger, M. (1976). Brief über den Humanismus. In *Wegmarken,* Vol. 9 of Gesamtausgabe (pp. 313–364). Frankfurt: Klostermann.

Huizinga, J. (1950). *Homo ludens: A study of the play element in culture.* Boston: Beacon.

Huizinga, J. (1968). My path to history. In P. Geyl & F. Hugenholtz (Eds.), *Dutch civilisation in the seventeenth century and other essays* (pp. 244–276). London: Collins.

Lugones, M. (1987). Playfulness, 'world'-travelling, and loving perception. *Hypatia, 2*(2), 3–19.

Martens, R. (1989). *Denkkunst. Kritik der Ontologie.* Paderborn: Schöningh.

Plessner, H. (1967). Der Mensch im Spiel. In W. Marx (Ed.), *Das Spiel. Wirklichkeit und Methode,* Vol. 13 of *Freiburger Dies Universitatis* (pp. 7–11). Freiburg.

Ringer, F. (1969). *The decline of the German mandarins. The German academic community, (1890-1933).* Cambridge, MA: Harvard University Press.

Sutton-Smith, B. (1982). The play-theory of the rich and poor. In P. K. Smith (Ed.), *Play in animals and humans* (pp. 305–322). London: Blackwell.

Sutton-Smith, B. (1984). The idealization of play: The relationship between play and sport. In Rees & Miracle (Eds.), *Sport and Social Theory* (pp. 85–102). Champaign, IL: Human Kinetics.

Weintraub, K. J. (1966). *Visions of culture.* Chicago: University of Chicago Press.

3

Playing Against the Self: Representation and Evolution

David Myers

I would like to discuss how important it is that we play "against" something when we play. Now, playing "against" something seems to be more obviously the case when we play games of various sorts than when we engage in, for instance, free play or daydreaming or the like. But I would like to develop the argument that it's not, and that, in fact, playing "against" something is what happens all the time, whenever we play.

Admittedly, this requires defining play somewhat apart from all behavioral manifestations of the play phenomenon. Herein, I will conceptualize play as a transformational process operating most fundamentally on mental representations.[1] Thus, physical mimicry—and the like—would be considered play only to the extent that physical mimicry would be associated with mental (symbol) transformations. I will adopt this conceptualization fully realizing that playful behavior seems to exist prior to our species' representational competencies and should have, for that reason, physical as well as mental consequences among a variety of organisms. Nevertheless, I will consider the mental consequences of play of a different sort and, ultimately, of more significance than its physical consequences.

In any case, what I would like to make clear from the beginning is that I do not by this argument mean to imply that play is of two sorts: the "against" sort and the other sort. I would wish to maintain that it's all the same sort, regardless of what consequences are involved. It's all "against."

And, if so, then against what?

A Model of Representational Evolution

The accumulation of characteristic variations leading to speciation is, within Darwinian evolution, a delimited game. The fittest survive and the winners win — within some bounded ecological niche—only to the extent that the non-fit lose and the losers die.

The great distinction of play—perhaps its most significant distinction—is that the losers of play do not die; they run away (or, more normally, simply submit) to play another day. This speculation—that a more playful evolution might well transform Darwinian notions—is the basis of this essay.[2] It leads us to consider how a representational species might evolve beyond the context of its natural-historical environment. Here is the question I then pursue: does the evolution of representational characteristics and skills (wherein I would define play—see Myers, 1991) differ from the evolution of non-representational characteristics and skills in any fundamental way?[3]

For instance, it seems as though the evolution of representational characteristics and their associated skills has occurred much more rapidly than the evolution of non-representational characteristics and skills. Though information about these matters is imprecise, the development of homo sapiens from homo habilis over a period of (approximately) two million years involves a series of quite radical changes.

> The origin of man was a unique evolutionary event in both its rapidity and its extent of development. The only obvious novel factor to account for the evolution of the hominid line at this particular time was man himself. (Campbell, 1985, p. 151)

But, unfortunately, not only is the exact nature of these changes uncertain, the uniqueness of their rapidity is also controversial. There are several related controversies within evolutionary theory (see Mayer, 1991, for a list); the most pertinent here is that between "continuity" and "discontinuity" models of evolution. Either species characteristics evolve through a series of random and rather abrupt leaps (from australopithecus to habilis to erectus to sapiens, for instance), or species characteristics evolve more gradually through much smaller and more continuous variations.

The latter of these two possibilities is the continuity model, and, all in all, the more conservative and traditional of the two. If, indeed, evolution is fundamentally continuous, then hominid evolution, which appears very choppy and discontinuous, is unique and conspicuous in that choppiness and those discontinuities—which we then might well attribute to the unique and conspicuous representational skills of the human species. If, however, evolution is fundamentally discontinuous (as championed by Gould, 1977, among others) then the rapid evolution of hominids is less unique than it would at first appear—and could not so easily be attributed to representationalism alone.

Each of these two models of evolution—continuity and discontinuity—has its own set of beliefs and assumptions. And each of the models has its unsolved problems. The discontinuity version, for instance, must explain—particularly as regards the seemingly over-rapid proliferation of the representational skills of the habilis line—how such random, lucky, and improbable changes ever occurred, in succession, in such a limited time frame. One explanation is teleological—it happened or we wouldn't be here to talk about it—and, for that reason, less than satisfying. Another explanation is that rapid change is the result of the interaction between wide variations in species characteristics and a rapidly changing environment. However, it is unclear how such wide variations in species characteristics could be tolerated: would not species characteristics gravitate toward some mean value offering the relatively greatest survival potential for members of that species?

Pondering this last question leads down some interesting paths and requires extended discussion. At least the kernel of an answer to this question is in the quote below, if I can, for the moment, equate "structural change" with species' characteristics and "behavioral change" with species' skills:

> An adaptation may precede or follow a behavioral change. For instance, if a species begins to become aquatic, foraging more and more in shallow coastal waters, any variation or mutation that enables it to go for longer periods without breathing, or that streamlines its shape, or that adds fatty tissue that will help maintain its temperature level, will be favored and will tend to increase over time. More rarely, perhaps, a structural change will precede a behavioral one, as when certain Hawaiian treecreepers with beaks shorter and more blunt than those of related species began to dig into the bark of trees instead of merely probing their cracks, and were thus able to exploit a rich and hitherto untapped source of food. (Bickerton, 1990, pp. 146–147)

This passage seems a tad misconceived in implication and, as such, indicative of a common misconception that misdirects thinking concerning cognitive evolutionary change, wherein some amount of structural change must *always* precede behavioral change.

If, for instance, in the first example in the quote above, the non-aquatic species were unable to forage in shallow coastal waters to begin with, it would either continue to live on land or die and become extinct. That is, there must be some "latent" characteristic(s) of that—or any—species that allows it to survive within an environment prior to its "adapting" to that environment. This is a subtle point, but an important one, because it means that the second example above is more the rule than the exception. Species adaptation—and thus, over the long term, survival—most often results from the proliferation of characteristics that are *imperfectly* adapted to the species' currently surrounding environment.[4]

Such characteristics would retain the species' capability to exist in alternative environments; most predictably, of course, these alternative environments would be those that had been amenable to that species prior to some previous sequence of differentiation—due to the maintenance of vestigial forms. But these alternative environments could, in fact, co-exist with the species' current environment without being either superseded or masked by that environment.

The treecreepers above, for instance, discovered a new environment (of breakable tree barks) as a result of their imperfect adaptation (variations in beak size) to their old environment (of cracked, but impervious, tree barks)— despite being under little or no ecological pressure (I would assume) to do so. In fact, the lack of ecological pressure (of which the prime example is competition) in this case would make "adaptation" more likely to occur (since the larger the population of treecreepers, the more likely a wide range in treecreeper beak sizes).[5]

However, a large variance of species characteristics would only be of benefit in inverse relationship to the disadvantages of the abnormalities produced. In the case of the treecreepers, for instance, an under-extended beak is most often simply a malformation, gaining its owner no significant advantage in bug-seeking and, in fact, very likely putting its owner at a disadvantage when competing for food with its sharper beaked brethren. And, in any short-lived competition between two treecreeper species identical in all respects but one—the range and frequency of beak abnormalities—the treecreeper species with the broader range of abnormalities would no doubt lose.

Yet, despite disadvantages incurred, it is constant variation in species characteristics of this kind—random and common and seemingly apart from gross mutation— that is the only reasonable explanation for the rapid evolution of organisms under sudden and severe ecological pressures.

> The evolution of cadmium resistance [in aquatic relatives of the earthworm] could have taken no more than 30 years. In fact, [measurements] indicated that the degree of metal tolerance observed could have evolved in just two to four generations—or a couple of years....
>
> The rapid evolution of tolerance for high concentrations of toxins seems to be common. Whenever a new pesticide is brought into use, a resistant strain of pest evolves, usually within a few years. The same thing happens to bacteria when new antibiotics are introduced. Luckily for humans, antibiotic resistance seems to be costly for bacteria to maintain, and susceptible strains usually return to dominance when the use of a drug is discontinued temporarily. (Levinton, 1992, pp. 87–88)

Either the genetic code of the "pests" above continually produces toxin-resistance variations (though few in number and with a low survival potential in non-toxin environments) or these various pest species must depend on very random, very lucky, and very improbable mutations each time a toxin is introduced into their environment. It is much more efficacious to assume the former than the latter.

Now, in the case of treecreepers and flatworms the relationship between characteristic and skill is rather straightforward: for example, the characteristic of toxin-resistance entails the skill of surviving toxin-infested environments. But such relationships are much less clear regarding the cognitive characters and skills of homo sapiens.

Based on medical and neurophysiological evidence (Gazzaniga, 1992), it clearly seems that the sensory apparati of homo sapiens is wired for representationalism just as it is wired for sight, sound, and smell. But, in many quarters and regarding a great many cognitive issues, huge uncertainties remain concerning the location and precise nature of the imbedded representationalism characteristics of homo sapiens—resulting in the inability to correlate these characteristics of representationalism with associated behavioral skills.

For instance, although we know the range of electromagnetic waves that the human eye is capable of perceiving, and we know the range of decibels that the human ear is capable of hearing, we do not know with any comparable degree of accuracy the range of representations the human mind is capable of representing. This is not from lack of trying. Attempts to determine this range have resulted in a great number of scales (Stanford-Binet and the like) that clearly establish ranges and variations of human cognitive skills. However, these sorts of measurements have tended to measure much more of skills and much less of characteristics than do similar scales of visual or aural acuity (resulting in, among other things, arguments over just what the characteristics of the "intelligence" skill actually are (see Gardner, 1983, and Sternberg, 1988).

Further complicating our inability to precisely locate the neurophysiological mechanism(s) of representationalism is the realization that representational characteristics are not associated with skills—as sight and hearing are—that directly interact with our natural-historical environment. Therefore, the only immediate and direct measurement device that we have to indicate the degree of our representational "acuity" is representationalism itself. And, as post-structuralism makes clear (if anything), it is a major problem to measure anything with itself. This is a problem for evolution as well.

The single measurement of classical Darwinian evolution is a test of fitness, of survival. And this test is inevitably a test of competition, or comparison, between two or more skills within the same natural-historical environment. Whereas these natural-historical tests of fitness might apply as equally to non-representational characteristics as non-representational skills—that is, toxin-resistance and toxin-survival—these same tests are not as equally applicable to representational characteristics and representational skills. For instance, when comparing representational and non-representational characteristics and skills, one is immediately struck by the relatively vast over-complexity of representational skills. We can represent, it seems, an infinite number of totally false things. And, furthermore, the great majority of these false representations are wholly beyond any conceivable natural-historical test of fitness. They are, in effect, entirely meaningless to species survival.

Given this enormous amount of representational gobbledy-gook, it is fortunate indeed that representational skills have physical and thus natural-historical, evolutionary consequences only to the extent that these skills actually result in physical manifestations (e.g., a behavioral change). Representational environments ("worlds of the mind") can then substitute for natural-historical environments as measurers/testers of species survival skills solely to the extent that these representational environments are enforced and maintained beyond some isolated and individual set of interior beliefs and conceptualizations (i.e., representationalism itself).

But, here, then, is the rub: the complexity and variety of representational skills is made possible by the isolation of representational skills from direct interaction with the natural-historical environment—leading to greater species adaptability. Yet simultaneously and for the very same reasons, our species' natural-historical environment cannot serve as a test of fitness for the vast majority of representational "skills."

Thus, in separating the world of the mind from the world of the senses, a species such as our own might well gain the ability to retain a great degree of variance in characteristics and skills, but to what end? If these variations are not directly exposed to environmental hardships—ongoing tests of fitness—then there is no species-independent mechanism available to choose among them. And, to the extent there is no species-independent mechanism to choose among them, they will propagate equally and randomly throughout the species. Furthermore, to the extent that these capabilities *are* directly exposed to environmental hardships (this being the final and culminate part of the rub), they are ultimately indistinguishable from non-representational characteristics offering equivalent survival skills.[6]

Given the lack of an environment to serve as proper context for the variation and natural selection of representational skills, it is unlikely that such skills could have evolved. Yet they have evolved. I postulate here that such an environment is a part of the skills themselves. That is, representationalism might originate as a positive evolutionary adaptation only to the extent that its skills are varied among individual members and these skills are selected by the natural-historical environment as more or less fit. The only natural-historical environment directly available to select among representational skills is the indirect one of representationalism itself, or—in the context of human beings possessing those skills—the abstraction of *self*.[7]

According to this model, symbol-transformational play functions in dialectical opposition to itself: as adaptive mechanism as well as environment in which that adaptive mechanism must adapt. This perspective echoes other insights into the dialectical nature of play...

> In addition to Bruner and his students, the two commentators who have probably come closest to discovering a dialectical role for play in the life cycle are Eibl-Eibesfeldt (1967: play as an experimental dialogue with the environment) and Sutton-Smith (1971: play as active exercise of voluntary control systems with disequilibrial outcomes). (Fagen, 1984, p. 167)

> Equally, the structure and function of the organism itself mutually shape each other. Just as the environment is structurally represented in the organism, so too does the adaptive functioning of the organism in the environment acquire a material representation in organismic structure; and just as organismic function is adapted to the environment, so too is organismic structure adapted to organismic function. (Sinha, 1984, p. 358)

This theoretical approach, if extended beyond the context of representationalism, might also be placed among those more recent attempts to address what seem to be directional (and thus anti-Darwinian) trends in natural evolution.

> There are indications that thermodynamic influences may operate beyond the random-generator, natural-selective level in giving the environment itself a formative role in self-

organization (Glansdorff & Prigogine, 1971; Ho & Saunders, 1979)—a notion quite incommensurable with even an expanded neo-Darwinism. (Wicken, 1984, p. 92)

But along this path, I am not, at the moment, prepared to blaze; therefore, the argument will remain restricted to the evolution of representationalism and, specifically, representational play.[8, 9]

The specific function I would set for play is this: to serve as a homeostatic mechanism increasing the variances of representationalism, not so much in genetic predetermination as in phenotypic expression. So that, in the absence of natural-historical pressures to evolve, representationalism might well evolve nevertheless, in response to those ecological pressures created by its own presence within the species: that is through play. This play mechanism would serve to increase combinatorially the formal processes of representationalism, but would not, in and of itself (at least not initially), assure that either survival benefits or survival negatives would be subsequently associated with these increasingly more combinatorially complex forms.

Thus, once the representational characteristics of the human brain were somehow minimally in place, play would serve as representational corollary to the random variations of physical sexual reproduction.

Observational and Theoretical Support for the Model

The common tendency for players to anthropomorphize the artificial intelligence of computer game opponents—a tendency I would characterize as the egoism of play, and, as such, not restricted to the play of computer games— seems rather odd until it is viewed within an evolutionary framework such as the one presented above. I could, for instance, refer to similar observations in a wide range of literature, perhaps exemplified by Piaget's observations of "egocentric" play.

Piaget's notion of egocentric play postulates an early state of cognition within which children are incapable of entertaining the notion that other minds exist in any form other than their own. That is, children under the ages of seven to eight are "permanently under the impression that they understand each other, and have no suspicion of the egocentric character of their thought" (Piaget, 1928, p. 207). This sort of egocentric thought might well occur among adults as well— though Piaget believes that such adult egocentric thought "impoverishes analysis and consciousness of self" (Piaget, 1928, p. 209) without subsequent reflection and progression beyond its limitations. Even at more advanced cognitive stages, however, the distinguishing characteristic of egocentrism remains the prioritization of satisfaction of thought over objectification of thought. And, should we, as Piaget does, postulate such an early stage of cognition wherein egocentrism is as pleasurable as it is unavoidable, then it is at least reasonable to expect the characteristics of that particular and pleasurable cognitive stage to recur during the phenomenon of play.

There are innumerable examples of egocentrism during computer game play. One is the consensual denigration of computer games that "cheat"—defined, in computer game player terms, as computer game opponents not having to abide by the same rules as their human counterparts. Thus, in the computer game *Civilization*, the game "cheats" insofar as playing pieces (boats, guns, etc.) controlled by the computer can move further and faster than those same pieces controlled by the human player. And, in the computer game *Master of Orion*, the game "cheats" insofar as computer opponents can utilize its playing pieces faster and at less cost than that incurred by the human player(s). These sorts of "cheats" are universally acknowledged as necessary to game play (to achieve proper balance between human and artificial intelligence), yet remain, simultaneously, a detriment to game play that would best and most enjoyably proceed without having to resort to such unfortunate kludges.

#: 640452 S4/Strategy Games
03-May-94 14:57:58
Sb: #640056-#MOO 1.4 idea
Fm: Lord Wynter 71524,624
To: Thomas M. Holsinger 73054,76

Hi a little off the subject. I've been reading the messages about the Masters of Magic game. Is there any chance that the AI will be better then that found in MOO?? I enjoyed MOO alot but found that choosing a harder level just ment the computer cheated, and gave your enemies more stuff then actually giving you better enemies. It was I thought a real let down, especially considering the weak AI.

   I look forward to the MOM (Masters of Magic) game but hope they have a better AI this time.

Wynter. (CompuServe Gamers Forum)

Similarly, whenever there is some doubt as to the actions and motives of computer game opponents (as occurs during "fog of war" or other hidden movement conditions), these actions and motives are initially assumed to be the actions and motives that would be most likely of human players in similar situations. Thus, there is the common reference to what the computer is "trying" to do, and how "dumb" or "smart" it is in the context of various game situations. These references occur among quite sophisticated computer game players, who are, undoubtedly, aware of the limitations of computer game opponents and, in fact, are quite capable of adopting game playing strategies that take full advantage of this or that non-human peculiarity in the game's artificial intelligence. Nevertheless, despite this knowledge of the computer game's inability to properly mimic human play behavior, it is apparently more pleasurable to play in ignorance than in possession of that knowledge. Those players who do find some way to beat or "cook" a computer game by adopting odd winning strategies—that would obviously never achieve similar success against a human opponent—point out such strategies as evidence of serious flaws in the game design. And, once discovered, these strategies make the game considerably less fun to play.

#: 127008 S3/War/Strategy Games
24-Jan-92 06:25:29
Sb: #126131-Civ government
Fm: Kelly Stanonik 70672,610
To: Joey Browning 76702,1365

I've changed the program so many times, it's hard to remember what the real program really does. The editor definitely gives a feeling of power, but not so much of accomplishment. Ignorance was a sort of bliss. But not when you're losing ALL the time....
(CompuServe Gamers Forum)

This phenomenon of assigning qualities of the self to play mates/objects— the egoism of play—has been noticed elsewhere as well, but its significance has been uncertain. Dennett (1981), for instance, recognized early the common attribution of human motives and desires to non-human mechanisms (such as computer game opponents)—but saw this as more fundamental to cognition in general than to play in specific. These attributions (e.g., a chess-playing computer likes to "get its Queen out early"—Dennett, 1981) seemed indicative of non-explicit mental representations— that is, representations that have no explicit tokening in the artificial intelligence routines producing the behavior that is so represented. Yet it remains unclear as to exactly why these commonplace, non-explicit representations would be of exactly the sort one would attribute to a *human being* exhibiting such behavior. It is also unclear, within these philosophy-of-mind debates, why such attributions would have such a large impact on the *pleasure* experienced during computer game play.

A somewhat similar issue arising in an entirely different context concerns the Vygotskian notion of zones of proximal development or "zo-peds" as fundamental to the learning process. Within this approach to child development, learning is understood as a process of movement between an "actual development level" and "potential development as determined through problem solving under adult guidance or *in collaboration with more capable peers*" (Vygotsky, 1978, p. 86; italics added). The characteristics of these "peers," of course, will vary in accordance with the learning child. In all such cases, however, learning occurs most readily in response to relatively small variations in the familiar context of the child's self (the "zone of proximal development").

Further, the entertainment one derives from literature, when placed in an information-theory context, shows patterns of self-reference similar to those encountered in play-based models of learning. Paulson (1991), for example, describes a model of cognitive growth in which cognitive processes are continuously (recursively) reorganized during successive readings of a difficult poem or passage of prose.

In the Paulson model, the complexities of literature are first recognized only as "noise" (abnormalities) in the communication channel. Confronted with this noise, cognition (from our point of view, simply "play") contextualizes this noise as complexity within existing self knowledge. During this contextualization (symbol-transformational) process, self knowledge is reorganized and extended into previously unknown realms. This reorganization and extension, however, occurs in incremental micro-stages that imply continual, slight variations in self. And this reorganization and extension only takes place wherein there is some recognizable and confrontational (oppositional) difference between complexity and noise, or between self and not-self.

Theoretical Implications of the Model

Why ever should any of this be so? That is, why should cognitive play (regardless of its conceptualization as learning or entertainment) most commonly and comfortably take place within the familiar context of self? The best sort of answer is, I would suggest, a natural-historical one describing the cognitive evolution of the species and involving, most particularly, the self-reflexive characteristics and skills of representationalism.

Ultimately, this answer would attempt to subsume the study of human physical play within the study of human mental play, and the study of human mental play within the study of cognitive evolution. It would represent a significantly different approach from most past investigations of play, since the study of evolution and the study of play have taken place most often in separate realms of theory and assumptions—to the detriment, it seems, of both.

Play theorists, in particular, have seldom considered play strictly within an evolutionary context.[10] Perhaps this is because many studies of human play have been anthropological in nature, and anthropological approaches often categorize play in accordance with the description found in Hunter's and Whiten's (1976) *Encyclopedia of Anthropology:* "The concept of play is never applied to behavior which meets individual or group survival needs" (p. 307).

There is also, of course, the widespread tendency to taxonomize play behaviors and then draw theoretical conclusions concerning play functions based on similarities among those behaviors—as documented in Schwartzman (1978) and Chick (1989). This has led over time to the implicit and widespread assumption that play is most fundamentally a physical activity; thus we associate play more often with the characteristics of the child who is physically active than with the characteristics of the adult who is not.

These sorts of misconceptualizations regarding play seem to parallel those found in some aspects of learning theory, which has become synonymous in many contexts with a theory of child development. In contrast to Piagetian notions, recent research efforts (see Sternberg, 1990) indicate that learning strategies and intellectual development continue beyond the physical maturation process. Likewise, play theorists (Sutton-Smith, Bateson) have begun to question the boundaries and limitations established by past social-scientific theories of play—particularly confining and defining play "as contributing to child development in one way or another" (Sutton-Smith & Kelly-Byrne, 1984, p. 308). In opposition to this trend, Csikszentmihalyi & Csikszentmihalyi (1988) have located play-like phenomena ("flow") within a variety of human experiences; and Bateson (1994) has been influential in particularizing play as a representational (framing) mechanism operating within an ecological context.

Contrary to Bateson, evolutionists have also infrequently considered play as a critical factor influencing the development and maintenance of higher-level cognition. While cognitive evolution remains a matter of great interest (and great mystery—see Eccles, 1989) to many evolutionists, it is hard to find any reference to play *per se* in their work. There are, however, some interesting corollaries—particularly in evolutionary biology. "Generativity," for instance, is very frequently mentioned as a unique and distinguishing characteristic of human cognition, particularly regarding high-level cognitive skills such as language. Corballis (1991) postulates a "GAD" (generative assembling device) somewhere within the left hemisphere of the human brain. This would, assumedly, be equivalent to a representational characteristic (or genotype) of what I have been calling "play."

Similarly, Edelman's (1989) theory of "neural Darwinism" assumes a high degree of human brain plasticity that would allow generative assembling devices (of whatever various sorts) to have a significant effect on brain structure and function.

> ...there is a semantic bootstrapping via linkage of phonological and lexical systems to already existent conceptual systems.... The theory holds that both during evolution and in the individual, concepts precede language and meaning. They are driven by the perceptual apparatus and are constructed by the brain as it models its own classes of activity. (Edelman, 1989, p. 247)

And, paralleling the notion developed in this essay that the rapid cognitive evolution of the recent hominid line is the result of the playful combination of a finite number of pre-existing representational characteristics of the human brain (Gazzaniga, 1992), and other selection theorists argue that evolution as a whole results from "the organism searching its [preexisting] library of circuits and accompanying strategies for ones that will best allow it to respond to the challenge" (p. 4). Likewise, Trehub (1991) proposes "an essentially deterministic cognitive model" (p. 297) of the brain, yet recognizes the importance of invention as "arguably the most consequential characteristic that distinguishes humans from all other creatures."

Further defining "search strategies" and "invention" and the elusive characteristics of generativity and creativity that distinguish human cognition might well benefit from the insight of Bateson (1991, 1979, 1972) and others who have begun to outline the representational characteristics and transformational processes of play and how those processes might contribute to what Eccles (1989, p. 240) labels "genetic dynamism ... whereby the hominid brain inevitably develops further and further beyond natural selection."

SUMMARY

This chapter is, in several senses, a discontinuous one, leaping from head-bone to neck-bone and so on without all considerations due many intervening complications. Let us at least review the bones of the argument to see how they might, in absence of the flesh yet to be added, dance and wiggle in a somewhat appealing way.

Here are the sticks that connect the figure:

• Play is a representational process.
• Representational characteristics (intentionality) are the basis of advanced (human-like) cognition.
• Representational characteristics evolved as a result of neurophysiological variations (increased complexities) in the physical organism.
• Once representational characteristic are present in the physical species, the skills associated with those representational characteristics *that are significantly different from non-representational skills* are not bound by the ecological context of that physical species.
• Evolution cannot occur without a bound ecological context.
• Representationalism serves as its own ecological context.
• Within the ecological context of representationalism, play both varies and tests representational skills.
• "Successful" representational variations produced by and within play may or may not have survival value within a natural-historical context.
• "Successful" representational variations produced within play that do have survival value proliferate within the ecological context of the physical species. (e.g., as the "magical" self, or the "religious" self, or the "scientific" self, or the "playful" self).

Thus, this version of the evolution of representationalism need assume no "stages" in the promulgation of representational skills, but might very well assume some sort of stages in the physical manifestation of those skills in the surrounding environment—resulting in what appears to be the choppy and discontinuous evolution of the more recent hominid line.

This approach does not attempt to undermine culture-based theories concerning the uses and functions of play. Rather it would attempt to provide the outline for the neurophysiological process of play necessary to assure the continued variety and generativity of human thought. This is, in that sense, an attempt to discover *a priori* evidence for play—play as a representational process—prior to and still beyond all artifacts of culture.

NOTES

[1] This assumes that the mind is most appropriately characterized as an "intentional system" (Dennett, 1981). See Dennett (1981) and Fodor (1990) for a more detailed description of the differences between representational and non-representational philosophies of mind.

[2] It has been pointed out to me that the basis of this chapter is similar to that of Miller (1973). I agree with this assessment.

Indeed, the conclusions of Miller (1973)—"we can begin to see that the pleasure of *Funktionlust* can be as clearly adaptive as the gratification pleasures of eating or sex" (p. 96)— are strikingly similar to my own. However, the Miller essay does not, as this chapter does, deal with the peculiarly dialectic characteristics of representational skills, preferring instead to emphasize the adaptive functions of play as manifest (most often if not always) in the refinement and perfection of existing physical skills. In this respect, Miller's approach is perhaps more similar to that of Fagen (see references cited) than my own.

3 Species variation in Darwinian evolution is a stochastic process, resulting from the random sexual combination and recombination of various genotypes or hereditary potentials. The physical and observable manifestation of these hereditary potentials is called a phenotype; and, to serve as the basis for natural selection, a genotype's phenotype(s) must directly affect the organism's survival potential—that is, the phenotype(s) in question must either make the organism more or less fit within its natural-historical environment.

This relationship—between hereditary and survival potentials—closely parallels the relationship between what I am calling an organism's characteristics and its skills. That is, a phenotype is normally considered in the context of all possible genetically and environmentally influenced expressions of a single genotype. Likewise, each characteristic of an organism entails a large array of potential survival skills. For instance, the long neck of the giraffe allows the giraffe to feed from tall edible-leaf-bearing trees and to cross deep rivers without having to swim—both potential survival skills. However, the possession of these skills, either singularly or in array, does not entail a singular characteristic. In the case of the giraffe, for instance, these same skills might have resulted from having wings instead of a long neck.

In this chapter, for simplicity's sake alone, I will tend to talk about characteristics and skills more often than genotypes and phenotypes. However, this discussion does not attempt to exclude certain behavioral "skills" (instincts) as genotypical, nor certain "characteristics" of organisms as phenotypical, in the broader sense. The idea here is merely to concentrate on the *relationship* between species characteristics that are genetically determined and species survival skills that result directly from those particular characteristics.

4 This conclusion is similar in most respects to "the law formulated by Copes [that] states that only non-specialized organisms are able to evolve further." (Devillers & Chaline, 1993, p. 163). See also the framework necessary for "organic selection," as defined by James Mark Baldwin and as espoused in Russell (1978) and Sinha (1984).

Connected to this point is another concerning the Hardy-Weinberg principle, which simply states that, in the absence of natural selection, genotype frequencies will remain constant from one generation to the next. Thus, dominant genes (called "normalities" later in this essay) will not displace recessive genes ("abnormalities") during random sexual reproduction.

5 This is, at first glance, in contradiction to the seemingly more popular perspective of species evolution based on the "survival of the fittest"—rather than, as this example supposes, the increasingly random propagation of the "unfit." But then the unit of analysis in classical evolution theory has always been unclear, ranging in various discussions from gene to community. See the discussion in Hull (1984), pp. 24–30, on different conceptualizations of "species."

6 Even given a social species whose survival potential as a group is enhanced by communication among its individual members (skills that representational characteristics seem particularly suited to provide), there is no obvious need to adopt overly complex representational systems to enhance those communications—thus the chemicals of the ants and those wiggly dances of the bees.

7 Or, in other words, if we did not play 'against' the self, we would not play at all. And

playing then becomes that which is, simultaneously, defined by the self (i.e., adapted to self) and outside its boundaries (i.e., beyond the limits of the representational skills used to construct self).

[8] The argument also, of course, is oriented toward the psychological development of the species and does not directly consider social and culture influences on cognitive evolution. It would be an assumption of this model, however, that social-cultural influences do not qualify as a species-independent mechanism of natural selection and thus serve rather to confine and normalize, rather than extend and abnormalize—as does the proposed mechanism of play.

Note that also, because I am, in this particular context, limiting the argument to representational skills and, simultaneously, assuming the presence of some extrinsic representational medium (pictorial, linguistic, cultural, etc.) that communicates "successful" representational combinations to subsequent generations, there is somewhat less necessity to justify allusions to a Lamarckian process wherein somatic change induces genetic change.

[9] And the particularization of this approach within the boundaries of representationalism distinguishes it from others similarly concerned with the evolutionary function(s) of play. Fagen (1984, 1981), for instance, shares many of the same goals of this chapter, but does not define, as this essay does, play most fundamentally as a cognitive, representational, symbol-transformation process and does not, therefore, distinguish cognitive play as an evolution mechanism significantly different from its behavioral manifestations.

Though there are important insights in Fagen's analysis...

> Let us suppose ... that the physical environment is not a given, fixed set of quantities but that it is only defined and becomes meaningful as an individual's experience with it develops or brings our certain salient qualities in relation to that individual.... The result is not merely familiarity but, more important, flexibility. By this I mean the ability to experience the spatial environment using varying frames of reference which are, at least in part, socially defined; and the ability to manipulate and shape one's own and others' active formulations of space and of the physical relationships within actively defined space. (Fagen 1984, p. 165)

...these are interpreted solely in the context of play motivating behavior. Fagen, for instance, hopes for "more tangible manifestation" of "ecological dialectics" that are currently "abstract and philosophical" (1984, p. 167). There is no discussion, as there is here, concerning the representational nature of play and how unavoidably "tangible" manifestations of cognitive play might well tend to bind that play to the non-representational, physical environment of the species and thus necessarily reduce (in order to avoid disastrous physical consequences) the variations of representational skills constructed through play.

[10] As already mentioned, Fagen (1984, 1981) is a notable exception in this regard, but his work, though influential and insightful, considers the play of animals in general and does not deal with the apparent discontinuity (see the discussion in Burghardt, 1984, pp. 7–8) between, for instance, reptiles and mammals—much less among various orders of primates.

REFERENCES

Bateson, G. (1991). *Sacred unity: Further steps to an ecology of mind.* New York: HarperCollins.

Bateson, G. (1979). *Mind and nature.* New York: Dutton.

Bateson, G. (1972). *Steps to an ecology of mind.* New York: Ballantine.

Bickerton, D. (1990). *Language and species.* Chicago: University of Chicago Press.

Bruner, J. S. (1972). Nature and uses of immaturity. *American Psychologist, 27,* 687–708.

Campbell, J. H. (1985). An organization interpretation of evolution. In D. J. Depew & B. H. Weber (Eds.), *Evolution at a crossroads: The new biology and the new philosophy of science* (pp. 133–167). Cambridge: MIT Press.

Chick, G. (1989). On the categorization of games. *Play & Culture, 2,* 283–292.

Corballis, M. (1991). *The lop-sided ape.* New York: Oxford University Press.

Csikszentmihalyi, M., & Csikszentmihalyi, I. S. (Eds.). (1988). *Optimal experience.* New York: Cambridge University Press.

Dennett, D. (1981). *Brainstorms.* Cambridge, MA: MIT Press.

DePryck, K. (1993). *Knowledge, evolution, and paradox: The ontology of language.* Albany: State University of New York Press.

Devillers, C., & Chaline, J. (1993). *Evolution: An evolving theory.* New York: Springer-Verlag.

Eccles, J. (1989). *Evolution of the brain.* New York: Routledge

Edelman, G. M. (1989). *The remembered present.* New York: Basic Books.

Eibl-Eiblesfeldt, I. (1967). Concepts of ethology and their significance in the study of human behavior. In H. W. Stevenson, E. H. Hess, & H. L. Rheingold (Eds.), *Early behavior: Comparative and Developmental approaches.* New York: Wiley.

Fagen, R. (1984). Play and behavioral flexibility. In P. K. Smith (Ed.), *Play in animals and humans* (pp. 159–173). New York: Basil Blackwell.

Fagen, R. (1981). *Animal play behavior.* New York: Oxford University Press.

Fodor, J. (1990). *A theory of content and other essays.* Cambridge, MA: MIT Press.

Gardner, H. (1983). *Frames of mind.* New York: Basic Books.

Gazzaniga, M. S. (1992). *Nature's mind.* New York: Basic Books.

Glansdorff, P., & Prigogine, I. (1971). *Thermodynamic theory of structure, stability and fluctuations.* New York: Wiley and Sons.

Gould, S. J. (1977). *Ontogeny and phylogeny.* Cambridge, MA: Harvard University Press.

Ho, M. W., & Saunders, P. T. (1979). Beyond neo-Darwinism—an epigenetic approach to evolution. *Journal of Theoretical Biology, 78,* 573–591.

Hull, D. L. (1984). Historical entities and historical narratives. In C. Hookway (Ed.), *Minds, machines and evolution: Philosophical studies* (pp. 17–42). Cambridge: Cambridge University Press.

Hunter, D. E., & Whitten, P. (1977). *Encyclopedia of anthropology.* New York: Harper & Row.

Levinton, J. S. (1992, November). The big bang of animal evolution. *Scientific American,* pp. 84–91.

Mayr, E. (1991). *One long argument: Charles Darwin and the genesis of modern evolutionary thought.* Cambridge, MA: Harvard University Press.

Miller, S. (1973). Ends, means, and galumphing: Some leitmotifs of play. *American Anthropologist, 75*(1), 87–98.

Myers, D. (1991). Computer Game Semiotics. *Play & Culture, 4* (4), 334–345.

Paulson, W. (1991). Literature, complexity, interdisciplinarity. In K. N. Hayles (Ed.), *Chaos and order* (pp. 37–53). Chicago: University of Chicago Press.

Piaget, J. (1928). *Judgment and reasoning in the child.* New York: Harcourt, Brace and Company.

Russell, J. (1978). *The acquisition of knowledge.* London: Macmillan.

Sinha, C. (1988). *Language and representation: A socio-naturalistic approach to human development.* New York: New York University Press.

Sinha, C. (1984). Biosocial evolution. In M. W. Ho & P. T. Saunders (Eds.), *Beyond neo-Darwinism: An introduction to the new evolutionary paradigm* (pp. 331–362). London: Academic Press.

Sternberg, R. J. (1990). Metaphors of the mind: Conceptions of the nature of intelligence. New York: Cambridge University Press.

Sternberg, R. J. (1988). *The triarchic mind: A new theory of human intelligence.* New York: Viking.

Sutton-Smith, B. (1971). Conclusion. In R. E. Herron & B. Sutton-Smith (Eds.), *Child's play.* New York: Wiley.

Sutton-Smith, B., & Kelly-Byrne, D. (1984). The idealization of play. In P. K. Smith (Ed.), *Play in animals and humans* (pp. 305–322). New York: Basil Blackwell.

Trehub, A. (1991). *The cognitive brain.* Cambridge, MA: MIT Press.

Vygotsky, L. S. (1978). *Mind in society: The development of higher psychological process.* (M. Cole, V. John-Steiner, S. Scribner, & E. Souberman, Eds.). Cambridge, MA: Harvard University Press.

Wicken, J. S. (1984). On the increase in complexity in evolution. In M. W. Ho & P. T. Saunders (Eds.), *Beyond neo-Darwinism: An introduction to the new evolutionary paradigm* (pp. 89–112). London: Academic Press.

part II
Traditional Play

Part II

Introduction

Alan Aycock

The study of children's play in comparative settings is both theoretically and method-ologically problematic, particularly when comparisons are global in scope. Each of the articles in this section illustrates the use of a different strategy to frame its comparison: Renson's article is the most abstract, Nwokah and Ikekeonwu the least, while Tudge, Lee, and Putnam's article lies somewhere in between.

Renson's account of the fate of traditional games in an era of globalization remains at a broad level of analysis to show the insufficiency of popular (or scholarly) stereotypes of traditional adaptation to modern circumstances. Renson initially counterposes traditional games such as crossbowing, largely maintained as a cultural relic that recalls medieval guild settings, to games such as judo that are transformed into the homogeneous paradigm of international sport. He suggests that an intermediate state of transnational gaming comparable to "glocalization" (the global plus the local) combines international recognition of traditional games with expressions of regional ethnic identity: a current instance would be bowling, whose diversity is celebrated in many international arenas under the aegis of a single organization.

By contrast, Nwokah and Ikekeonwu produce complex codings and voluminous data which attempt to retain much of the sense of local sociocultural context despite the comparison of apparent antitheses such as Indiana and south-eastern Nigeria. These codings include observations of physical movement, materials used in play, adherence to rules, weather and playing surface. The results are cross-tabulated and examined for level of unexpected statistical significance, for example, the greater reliance of "Hoosier" children on manufactured materials in their play, and the strong tendency of Igbo children to penalize losers formally. While Renson's chapter stresses theorizing over data, Nwokah and Ikekeonwu reverse this emphasis.

The third strategy of global comparisons is to attempt, as Tudge, Lee, and Putnam do in their study of four sites (two in South Korea and two in North Carolina), to identify middle-range variables such as class and gender that mediate the particularities of sociocultural context on the one hand, and the abstractions of national culture on the other. Systematic spot observations of the play ecologies at each site challenge some findings about play and national culture, such as the standard view of Korean children as less independent and self-directed than American children. More significant in my view is the authors' observation that heterogeneity is to be found not only across cultures but within them—for example, working-class children may express quite different play values from middle-class children of the same national culture. This to my mind is a caveat well taken, yet not sufficiently acknowledged in play literature.

4

The Cultural Dilemma of Traditional Games

Roland Renson

GLOBALIZATION VERSUS LOCALIZATION

Compared to modern sports, that is to say the highly standardized Olympic disciplines that are practiced in many parts of the world, traditional sports and games tend to be confined to a limited geographical area and are therefore often referred to as "national" or "local." They function as symbols of ethnic or regional identity and are therefore called "folk games." Both the macroscopic scale of modern sports on the one hand, and the microscopic scale of traditional games on the other, provide an interesting sociological test case for confronting the antithesis of globalization versus localization. The most common interpretation of globalization is the idea that the world is becoming more uniform and standardized through a technological, commercial and cultural synchronization, emanating from the West. Nederveen Pieterse (1994, p. 161) has therefore quite pertinently remarked that this process should rather be called Westernization and not globalization. Other more mediagenic terms such as Coca-colanization and McDonaldization, have been used to describe what Archer (1991, p. 133) has qualified as a growing world-wide interconnectedness of structure, culture and agency. With regard to the globalization of modern sports, terms such as recolonization or neo-colonization (Eichberg, 1984; Renson, 1992) have been uttered.

However, this globalization, which had led to a parallel de-differentiation of traditional boundaries, seems to go hand in hand with a simultaneous regeneration or reconstruction of particular traditional forms of life (Smart, 1994, p. 152). Friedman (1990) has called the idea that globalization is creating a single world society, a contentious idea, for it masks the forms of ethnic and cultural fragmentation that are increasingly becoming a feature of global reality.

Globalization can indeed mean the reinforcement of both supranational and subnational regionalism. Globalization encourages macro-regionalism, which, in turn, encourages micro-regionalism. The "New" Europe of 1992 has marked the beginning of a frontierless economic community (see Tiryakian, 1994) but at the same time the voices of regional cultural identity are loudly heard. Symptomatic for this tandem operation of *glocalization*, with the slogan "Think global, act locally" (Nederveen Pieterse, 1991, p. 165) are the two European seminars on traditional games of which the first one was organized in Vila Real (Portugal) in 1988 and the second in Leuven (Belgium) in 1990 (Committee for the Development of Sport, s.a.; De Vroede & Renson, 1991).

Globalization is further closely linked with postmodernism. Probably the best way to try to understand the "condition of postmodernism" is by contrasting it to "modernism." Friedman (1988) defined modernity as a structure of power and control; culture as a set of constraints, opposed to nature and repressive of nature. The postmodern configuration—on the contrary—encompasses both culture and nature, it is dedicated to both libido and "sagesse," to the polymorphous perverse as well as the deeper wisdom of the primitive. Via its absolute relativism, it praises the value of all culture and all nature. This set of oppositions is represented in the following model (Friedman, 1988, p. 450):

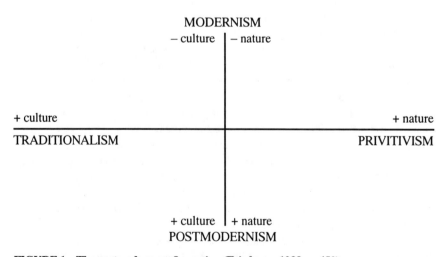

FIGURE 1.   The postmodern configuration (Friedman, 1988, p. 450).

This model offers an interesting framework to confront the globalization of culture with the cultural pluralization of the world, or within the scope of this chapter, the confrontation of modern sports versus traditional games in a postmodern perspective. Although the traditional sports and games are at the origin of almost all modern sports, they are too often treated as the Cinderellas of modern sport (Renson, 1992). In contrast to the international breakthrough of the modern sports movement around the turn of the century, local traditional sports and games gradually came to be regarded as the anachronistic remnants of a static and rustic pre-industrial society. The origins and development of modern sports has been explained in the maelstrom of the major sociological theories of Karl Marx (a.o. Wohl, 1973), Max Weber (Lüschen, 1967) and Norbert Elias (Dunning, 1971; Stokvis, 1979). All these theories are—to a certain extent—pillars of the paradigm of modernity, which has prevailed in sociology in general, as well as in the sociology of sport. An eminent example is Allen Guttmann's analysis, entitled *From Ritual to Record* (1978), of the nature and genesis of modern sports. More recently, the concept of *sportification* has been put forward. Sportification is depicted as a universal hegemonic trend of standardization and globalization of sport practices, thus affecting and repressing the regional differentiation of traditional games (Eichberg, 1991; van Bottenburg, 1994). Eichberg (1991) has called the resurgence of traditional games "a revolution of body culture" and a symptom of the transition from modernization to postmodernity:

> The "post-modern" and post-sportive tendencies are not at all unequivocal.... But the configuration of sportive modernity is in question ... the tendencies in Western Europe towards autonomy on smaller regional levels are not accidental and not without a larger societal perspective in the political field as well as in the fields of games and body culture. (Eichberg, 1991, p. 124)

TRADITION IN TRANSITION

Coming to terms with the dialectics between modernity and postmodernity, between culture and nature, between globalization and localization, between modern sports and folk games, it must be said that the results of a recent social analysis of the social profile of the participants in traditional games provoked a lot of question marks (Renson, De Cramer, & De Vroede, 1994). These participants in traditional games may, indeed, be local heroes, but the cultural stereotype of these "folk-gamesters" is that of an elderly rustic working class male, practicing his favorite game in a country pub, while sipping a beer in a cloud of tobacco smoke. Also the subtitle of this publication was challenged: "beyond the stereotype...." Indeed, for three out of the four assumptions, the stereotype of the practitioners of traditional games was confirmed: elderly lower class males. Only one popular belief was contradicted: folk games are much more frequently observed in urban areas than in the typical rural milieu.

These sociographic data seem to push folk games more in the corner of a "residual anachronism" than in the direction of "postmodern innovation." From another perspective, however, these folk gamesters can be idealized as the unconscious horticulturists of the patrimony of play and sportive pluralism. Although this sounds very nice, especially to a sports historian and anthropologist of play, it might be a (post)modern fairy tale. According to the social law of imitation of Tarde (1895) and the law of "prestigious imitation" of Mauss (1960), folk games have indeed little or no chance to become cultural trend-setters or sport fashion models.

When seen in the light of the Friedman model (see introduction), folk games definitely represent the cultural and traditionalist dimension within the so-called postmodern "mélange." *Tradition* was defined by Droysen (1868) and Bernheim (1889) as the conscious process of preserving something for posterity. This differs from *relic*, which is a remain that was not consciously intended. Many traditions are, moreover, not very ancient but they are in fact often quite recently invented, as shown by Hobsbawn and Ranger (1992).

This incites us to look closer at the cultural significance of traditional games in present day society. In an earlier account on the "traditionalist" renascence of sports, games, dance and recreation forms, we have put forward two possible cultural strategies: *conservation* versus *innovation*. The first one is retrogressive and is embodied, for instance, by the Society for Creative Anachronism (in the U.S.), where medieval tournaments and other activities are re-enacted. The second one is retro-progressive and consists of a return to the roots of play forms to enrich the quality of present day life; this approach might therefore be qualified as "diachronic creativity" (Renson, 1984).

Cheska (1987), on the other hand, has distinguished three different modes of cultural adaptation within the traditional games scene: (1) *revival* of ethnic opposition to the dominant culture; (2) *survival* as alternative ethnic values in a current society; (3) *revisal* (revision) as incorporating ethnic values within the dominant culture.

Einarsson (1991) encounters in the world of traditional wrestling two opposite attitudes: cross-cultural *cooperation* versus cultural *isolation*. The first trend is represented by the glima-wrestlers from Iceland, who have sought membership in the International Federation of Celtic Wrestling as well as in the Fédération Internationale de Lutte Amateur (FILA). The second trend is exemplified by the isolation on principle of Switzerland's Schwingen and Austria's Ranglen.

Eichberg (1991) sees three possible scenarios for traditional games, which are to some extent paraphrases of the foregoing ones: (1) *sportification* (modernization); (2) *pedagogization* (functionally used as pedagogical instruments); (3) *folklorization* (preservation via isolation and representation).

Tiryakian (1994, p. 143) has pointed out that the period of transition and flux we are in, alternating between order and disorder, between features of globalization and local reactions to globalization, between differentiation and de-differentiation, is witness to a set of dialectical relationships that do not culminate in any linear direction. Therefore, one of the major problems for sociology to study comparatively is that of recasting *identity*, personal and collective, individual and national. Traditional games can become salient emblems of local or ethnic identity and should therefore appear on the sociological radar screen.

THREE DIFFERENT STRATEGIES

In an attempt to summarize and reintegrate the different cultural meanings of traditional games and to confront these with the theories of postmodernism, we would like to present the following synthesis (see Table 1). Three different strategies or modes of cultural adaptation of traditional games to (post)modern society can be identified, each with particular sociocultural characteristics.

Exteriorization implies that folk games follow the path of modern sports with all the consequences of globalization and de-differentiation which leads to a revision of their original structures and functions. This is the case with most modern sports, which have become worldwide standardized activities. These sport activities are often revised to meet the needs of international competitions and they are absorbed under umbrella organizations with an almost exclusive monopoly, e.g. the International Olympic Committee, the FIFA (Fédération Internationale de Football Association), the FINA (Fédération Internationale de Natation Amateur) and so forth.

An example of this process of sportification has recently been given in a case study of the All Japan Judo Federation (Saeki, 1994). It showed a conflict between the value-oriented traditional structure of the All Japan Judo Federation (AJJF) and the goal-oriented rational and modern approach of the All Japan Student Judo Federation (AJSJF). This resulted in the organizational reformation of the AJJF, which transformed this federation into a modern competitive sport organization.

TABLE 1.
Three Different Strategies or Modes of Cultural Adaptation of Traditional Games to (Post)Modern Society

Strategy or Mode of Cultural Adaptation	Sociocultural Characteristics
Exteriorization	Globalization
	De-Differentiation
	Sportification
	Revisal
	Absorption
Mediorientation	Glocalization
	Hybridization
	Pedagogization
	Revival
	Cooperation
Interiorization	Localization
	Differerntiation
	Folklorization
	Survival
	Isolation

Interiorization, on the other hand, is characterized by "couleur locale" (localization), differentiation and folklorization, with the aim of preserving the survival of traditional games via cultural isolation. Tangible examples here are, for instance, two "traditionalist" regional federations of shooting guilds in Flanders, the Dutch speaking part of Belgium. The members of the High Guild Council of the Kempen and of the Guild Council of Brabant dress up in so called "traditional" style, that is, nineteenth-century Sunday clothes, and cling to the art of the crossbow or longbow. Thus they shoot at targets or at the "popinjay" on top of a tall mast. They refuse to consider these practices as sport, but rather as a continuation of the ancient shooting guild traditions (Renson, 1976). Moreover, they stress that their "esprit" of christian brotherhood together with their particular guild dances, banquets and pageants are not compatible with the secular and mundane character of modern sport.

Between these two opposite strategies of exteriorization and interiorization, we propose the new concept of *mediorientiation.* This third and centralist strategy can be characterized by globalization and hybridization and results from a pragmatic approach. It means that traditional forms of games are revivified via their pedagogization and through cooperation with similar local or international organizations. The game known as *road bowls* or *bullets* in Ireland, *klootschieten* in the Netherlands and *Bosseln* or *Klootschiessen* in East Frisia (Germany), is an interesting example both of the expression of regional ethnic identity and of the growing international awareness of traditional games. In 1969, these three independent "clans" of bowling enthusiasts joined together to form the International Bowlplay Association (IBA). They meet and compete at international get-togethers without giving up their local identity and play particularities.

A similar case is the international meetings between the adherents of traditional "handball," which bring together handball players from Belgium, Frisia (The Netherlands), the North of France and the North of Italy. Although each of these regions play a different version of the game, the players compete in an annual encounter where the different types are represented on an equal footing. Unfortunately, the Belgian ballplayers have recently withdrawn their participation for "official" financial reasons (Jespers, De Vroede, & Renson, 1994, p. 77).

These three different strategies are presented here as paradigmatic simplifications of possible cultural adaptations of traditional games to the exigencies of (post)modern society. They should not be interpreted as rigidly separated categories but rather as a complex continuum with several intermediate solutions. Their theoretical nature requires a verification through cross-cultural empirical observations of the adaptation patterns of traditional games within diverging cultural contexts. Nevertheless they seem to offer some structural guidance for understanding the past, present and future of games in pre-industrial, industrial and post-industrial societies.

All in all, I would like to end this contribution by a critical remark on the issue of postmodernity. While trying to link traditional games with concepts of postmodernism, I have the impression that postmodernism is often more a theoretical discourse than a reality, sometimes even more a rhetoric than a real discourse. I wonder therefore—very much in the same line of thought as Bauman (1988)—whether post-modernism is not just a new ideology and a new jargon, invented by the generation that failed to change the world in 1968?

REFERENCES

Archer, M. S. (1991). Sociology for one world: Unity and diversity. *International Sociology*, 6(2), 131–147.

Bauman, Z. (1988). Is there a postmodern sociology? *Theory, Culture & Society*, 5, 217–237.

Bernheim, E. (1889). *Lehrbuch der historischen methode und der geschihtsphilosophie*. Leipzig: Duncker.

Cheska, A. T. (1987). Revival, survival and revisal: Ethnic identity through "traditional games." In G. A. Fine (Ed.), *Meaningful play, playful meaning* (pp. 145–153). Champaign, IL: Human Kinetics.

Committee for the Development of Sport, (1988). *Seminar on traditional games*, (Vila Real, Portugal). Vila Real: Direcção-Geral dos Desportos.

De Vroede, E., & Renson, R. (Eds.). (1991). *Proceedings of the second European seminar on traditional games*. (Leuven, Belgium, 1990) Leuven: Vlaamse Volkssport Centrale.

Droysen, J. G. (1868). *Grundriss der Historik*. Leipzig: Veit.

Dunning, E. (1971). *The sociology of sport*. London: Cass.

Eichberg, H. (1984). Olympic sport—Neocolonialization and alternatives. *International Review for Sociology of Sport*, 19(1), 97–105.

Eichberg, H. (1991). A revolution of body culture? Traditional games on the way from modernization to postmodernity. In J. J. Barreau & J. Jaouen (Eds.), *Eclipses et renaissance des jeux populaires* (pp. 99–129). (Rencontre internationale de Berrien 1990), s.l.: Institut Culturel de Bretagne.

Einarsson, T. (1991). An attempt to describe some facts from traditional wrestling over the world. In J. J. Barreau & G. Jaouen (Eds.), *Eclipses et renaissance des jeux populaires* (pp. 28–40). (Rencontre internationale de Berrien 1990), s.l.: Institut Culturel de Bretagne.

Friedman, J. (1988). Cultural logics of the global system: A sketch. *Theory, Culture & Society*, 5, 447–460.

Friedman, J. (1990). Being in the world: Globalization or localization. *Theory, Culture & Society*, 7, 2–3.

Guttmann, A. (1978). *From ritual to record: The nature of modern sports*. New York: Columbia University Press.

Hobsbawn, E., & Ranger, T. (1992). *The invention of tradition*. Cambridge: Cambridge University Press.

Jespers, J., De Vroede, E., & Renson, R. (1994). Jeux et sociétés; Les sociétés des jeux. *Sport* (Bruxelles), 37(2), 74–81.

Lüschen, G. (1967). The interdependence of sport and culture. *International Review of Sport Sociology*, 2, 127–141.

Mauss, M. (1960). *Sociologie et anthropologie*. (Bibliothèque de sociologie contemporaine). Paris: PUF.

Nederveen Pieterse, J. (1994). Globalisation as hybridisation. *International Sociology*, 9(2), 161–184.

Renson, R. (1976). The Flemish archery gilds: From defense mechanisms to sports institution. In R. Renson, P. P. De Nayer, & M. Ostyn (Eds.), *The history, the evolution and diffusion of sports and games in different cultures* (Proceedings of the 4th internat. HISPA seminar; Leuven 1975) (pp. 135–159). Brussel: BLOSO.

Renson, R. (1984). The 'traditionalist' renascence: The revival of traditional forms of sports, games, dance and recreation around the world. In U. Simri, D. Eldar, & S. Lieberman (Eds.), *Health, physical education, recreation and dance education in perspective* (Proceedings of the 26th ICHPER World Congress; Wingate Institute 1983) (pp. 149–159). Wingate Institute: Emmanuel Gill.

Renson, R. (1992, December). Save our sports. *The Unesco Courier, 45*, pp. 41–45.

Renson, R., De Cramer, E., & De Vroede, E. (1994, July). Local heroes: Beyond the stereotype of the participants in traditional games. *International Review for the Sociology of Sport, 32*(1), 59–68.

Saeki, T. (1994). The conflict between tradition and modernization in a sport organisation: A sociological study of issues surrounding the organization reformation of the All Japan Judo Federation. *International Review for the Sociology of Sport, 29*(3), 301–315.

Smart, B. (1994). Sociology, globalisation and postmodernity: Comments on the sociology for one world' thesis. *International Sociology, 9*(2), 149–159.

Stokvis, R. (1979). *Strijd over sport.* Deventer: Van Loghum Slaterus.

Tarde, G. (1895). *Les lois de l'imitation: Étude sociologique.* Paris: Alcan.

Tiryakian, E. A. (1994). The new world and sociology: An overview. *International Sociology, 9*(2), 131–148.

Van Botttenburg, M. (1992). *Verborgen competitie.* Amsterdam: Bakker.

Wohl, A. (1973). *Die gesellschaftlich-historischen grundlagen des bürgerlichen sportes.* Köln: Pahl-Rugenstein.

5

A Sociocultural Comparison of Nigerian and American Children's Games

Evangeline E. Nwokah
Clara Ikekeonwu

Studies of children's social play and games in Middle Eastern and African communities have produced varied findings with game-playing described as non-existent, accepted or openly encouraged. Children have been portrayed as passive, quiet observers of adult activity who did not initiate individual or group play (Ammar, 1954; Feitelson, 1954). Levine and Levine in Kenya (1963) noted that children not only showed a lack of play but adults actively tried to prevent and discourage them from playing. In contrast, Fortes (1938) stressed that the concept of play in Taleland, Ghana was well-defined and clearly recognized. Many play events emerged as a "side-issue" of children's practical chores and activities. During the 1970s there was an upsurge of interest in anthropological studies of children's play and games (Feitelson, 1977; Leacock, 1971; Schwartzman, 1977, 1978; Sutton-Smith, 1986), but direct comparisons between the characteristics of children's games in two or more different cultures are limited (Bloch, 1989; Eifermann, 1968; Linaza, 1981), as reviewed by Salamone (1989). Even less common are cross-cultural studies of African versus non-African games (Bloch, 1989; Durojaiye, 1977).

Previous descriptions and mention of games in West and Central Africa (Beart, 1955; Centner, 1962; Schwartzman, 1978; Schwartzman & Barbera, 1976) reveal a rich but only partially documented source of children's activities in such a vast continent. Beart's detailed elaboration of games focused mainly on French-speaking West African countries including Senegal, Dahomey, and Niger, and Centner's work was based only in Central Africa. More recently there have been further attempts to compile detailed documentation of games of various ethnic groups in West and Central Africa (Bloch, 1989; Cheska, 1987; Pardo de Leon, 1989; Salomone, 1978) with increasing emphasis on the social context in which the games occur. Bloch (1989) found that by five to six years of age, Senegalese children's play was almost exclusively social, usually in same sex groups, and took place outside nearby houses rather than indoors like most American children's games. Girls' play groups tended to consist of babies and same age or younger age children, and boys' play groups of same age or older children.

Certainly, there is considerable evidence that the structure of games reflects the preoccupations and values of the society in which they occur, that games are social contexts for cultural learning (Borman & Lippincott, 1982) or microcosmic events that help to instill and fortify that culture's value system (Brown, 1974). For example, African-American children's games in slave times had a striking lack of elimination of players, and few combative activities, reflecting a need for solidarity (Wiggins, 1985). Eifermann's (1968) analysis of games revealed the expression of cooperation and egalitarianism in Kibbutz children's games with a preference for as few overprivileged or underprivileged participants as possible. More specifically, a categorization of games as those of physical skill, strategy and chance was used to suggest a possible relationship between types of games played and differences in the society's cultural and technological complexity (Roberts, Arth & Bush, 1959; Roberts, Sutton-Smith, & Kendon, 1963) and types of games and variations in child-rearing methods (Roberts & Sutton-Smith, 1962). In the Roberts and associates' studies a sampling of African societies was included along with other societies such as the Maori of New Zealand and various Native American groups. Despite later critiques of these proposals (Cheska, 1987; Chick, 1984; Chick, 1989; Eifermann, 1968; Linaza, 1981; Rich, 1978) the view of games as "an active ingredient of society" (Townsend, 1978) reflects the need for further investigation of game-playing differences between different cultural and social groups. We argue that only by a detailed analysis of all aspects of a game such as its length, presence of competition (Borman & Lippincott, 1982), materials used, sex and age grouping, can we begin to see to what extent games reflect aspects of the culture and differ from those in other cultures.

PREVIOUS STUDIES OF NIGERIAN GAMES

Nigeria, a country of over 88 million people, has three major language groups, Hausa, Yoruba, and Igbo, the latter with a roughly estimated 9,200,000 number of speakers (Brann, 1979; Nwokah, 1988). (The controversial 1991 Nigerian census listed the

Igbo population at 15 million.) There have been some specific studies of Nigerian children's play and games (Cheska, 1987; Durojaiye, 1977; Olofson, 1977; Peshkin, 1972; Salamone, 1978; Uka, 1966; Zarslarsky, 1973) but these have tended to focus on Hausa or Yoruba games. Anthropological descriptions of everyday life in various Nigerian ethnic groups sometimes briefly mention play in children (Basden, 1921, 1938; Bascom, 1969; Ekwueme, 1977; Leiber, 1971; Uchendu, 1965) and similar references are made in a few novels (Emecheta, 1980; Ike, 1973; Soyinka, 1981). Basden's (1921,1938) descriptions are limited to bow and arrow shooting, wrestling, okwe (mancala), and the use of a spring board by boys, and finger string games and oga (step dancing) by girls. Uchendu (1965) mainly describes a game of nsa (finding a ring in the sand) and Leis (1972) attempts a detailed discussion of play groups of different ages in Ijaw society. He observed the notable lack of toys in games and the use of usually uncarved pieces of wood by girls to represent dolls. Durojaiye (1977) emphasizes the importance of rhythm, repetition and sound in Nigeria and Uganda using several examples of games with variations seen in England and United States. Salamone and Salamone (1991) include in their discussion of three games in Ibadan, Oyo state, Nigeria, a description of sin-san (called "oga" in Igbo) that includes rhythm and step and dance movements. An example of rhythm and rhyme is a game in the Ijaw district of Nigeria, where children place their fists alternately, one on top of another to form a tower but a rhyme about a blacksmith banging on his anvil accompanies the game (Durojaiye, 1977).

Salamone (1978) has focused on children's games in Yauri, Northern Nigeria as a reflection of the organization of adult society including age grouping, interethnic relations and sex differentiation. One of the most popular girls' games he describes is (in Hausa) Sunana Bojo Ne (my name is Bojo) but the most common traditional boys' games are ring toss, snail shell game (alkwato), and zulli. Both the ring toss game and zulli involve punishment, with the last one to score "ragged rather unmercifully" in ring toss and in zulli, the most unsuccessful child, whose " point of the shell does not come upwards when spun," puts his hand, palm downwards, on the pile of sand and each of the others in turn "hits it hard three times with his fist."

The aim of the present descriptive study was to extend the current limited documentation of Nigerian children's games by examining those in the south-eastern or Igbo-speaking region of Nigeria. The project also looked at commonalities and differences between two contrasting cultures by using the same methodology to collect information on games in a suburban area of Lafayette, Indiana. Finally, possible relations between cultural socialization of children and social expectations are proposed that might be reflected in the content and structure of the games.

Method

Children's games were observed and described by trained senior undergraduate observers using methodology adapted from Eifermann's Hebrew University of

Jerusalem games research. "Spot observations" were conducted and if games occurred in the groups of children observed, these were recorded using pre-designed forms and recording information described below. No particular time of day was designated, but the observers were encouraged to choose times when social games were most likely to occur. Each assistant was responsible for the observations in one locality that was their home area where residents were familiar with them, to reduce the effect of stranger presence. The principal investigator was inconspicuously present for some observation sessions. Seven locations in southeastern Nigeria and seven locations in Lafayette, Indiana were chosen, with a total of 89 observations in Nigeria and 66 observations in the United States. The data collection in the United States commenced 15 months after the completion of the data collection in Nigeria. Observers were instructed not to record any repeated games in each location unless there were variations of the same game. They could include games that were interrupted or finished prematurely provided that at least half of the game appeared completed.

Games were defined as a type of social play, but considered to be more formal, conventionalized events with a clear beginning and end, and a structure that consists of moves in a particular sequence determined by an apparent set of procedures or rules (Duncan & Farley, 1990; Fogel, Nwokah, & Karns, 1991; Garvey, 1977). This definition is similar to that of Cheska (1978, 1987) who stated that a game must contain the elements of participants, opponents or sides; organized procedure, a fixed sequence of action or plot; and outcome, resolution or end result. According to Cheska, a game should also have the characteristics of pleasurable, voluntary, engrossing, with spatial and temporal limits which set it aside from other activities. Contrary to the view that games must always have a winner, competition, two or more sides, criteria for determining the winner and agreed upon rules (Roberts, Arth, & Bush, 1959), Cheska (1987) has argued that games can be competitive and/or cooperative where players work together toward a particular outcome. In the present study, role play, constructive play and formal team sports were not included.

The localities of the observations in Nigeria are shown in Figure 1 in Imo, Anambra and Abia States. They were Ugiri (Mbano); Umuogu; Ihiala; Aboh; Orji; Umezukwu; and Ugiri (Ikeduru). Ugiri is labeled only once on the map as the two villages are both not far from Owerri. All places listed were in rural and mostly forested or semiforested areas. The localities of the observations in United States were within the suburban area of Lafayette, Indiana.

The Nigerian games in this chapter are referred to mainly as "Igbo" to specify the ethnic group and culture/language studied. The American games are referred to mainly as "Hoosier" because although this label has been sometimes used in a derogatory manner implying rural and uneducated, it is a traditional term still used for native Indiana people and Indiana culture.

Each observation was coded with the date and weather condition as rain, drizzle, windy, snow, cold, warm, hot, and so forth. The latter categories were not mutually exclusive and several descriptions could be circled. The surface was coded as stony,

FIGURE 1. Localities of Nigerian observations.

concrete, indoors, bush, sand or grass. The observer recorded the time the game began, the time the game ended and how the game ended as: children quarrelled, adult intervened, new game, weather changed, tired, new children joined, or other. The number of participants, their ages and whether they were male or female was coded. There were 12 categories for type of physical movement, five for voice and nine for type of body contact with another child. Adherence to rules, whether the game had a declared winner and/or loser, taking turns, award for winner, and penalty/punishment for loser were also included in the data collected. Finally, the name of the game, materials used if any, and a full description of the game, completed the coding sheet.

A later analysis used an adaptation and elaboration of Roberts, Arth, and Bush's (1959) and Roberts and Sutton-Smith's (1962) subdivisions within the classes of physical skill, strategy and chance to categorize the attributes of each game. The nine categories were physical skill (fine motor); physical skill (fine motor) and strategy; physical skill (fine motor), strategy, and chance; strategy and chance; chance only; physical skill (gross motor); physical skill (gross motor) and strategy; physical skill (gross motor), strategy and chance; singing and verbal. The three main differences between this categorization scheme and that of Roberts, Arth, and Bush's (1959) were the co-occurrence of features such as physical skill and strategy for the same game instead of looking for the dominant feature; the use of categories to refer to the internal structure of games rather than only what determines the outcome; and the use of "chance" to refer to the influence of "luck" on the outcome as well as guesses or the use of a randomization artifact such as a die. Two coders independently scored each game as one of the nine categories. An example of a game involving physical skill (fine motor) and strategy in the Hoosier data was Pick-up sticks, and an example of a game involving physical skill (gross motor), strategy and chance in the Igbo data was Oku na-agba-n'ugwu (There is a fire on the mountain). In the latter game, a double circle is formed with each person having a partner behind them. A lead singer starts the song "There is fire on the mountain, run, run, run." During the singing the partners run round the circle until the singing stops with the refrain "oku ogbachaala" (the fire is out). Then they must run back to their places in a clockwise direction only. The last person to return to their position is penalized by staying in the center, singing and clapping and then carried shoulder high around the compound as an offender. Using our categorization of features, the cessation of singing affects the position of the person in relation to their original place (luck/chance). He/she must speedily find a way back (physical skill) while avoiding other runners and finding the best way of returning (strategy).

RESULTS

Most of the observations of games of Hoosier children were made in the afternoon (48.5%) but most of the observations of Igbo children's games were made in the morning (42.7%) (X^2 = 5.37, 1 df, p < .068) as it was often too hot to play in the afternoon. About 25 percent of game observations for both groups were in the early evening (after 4 p.m.). Significantly more Igbo games (86.5%) were played outdoors than Hoosier games (28.8%) (X^2 = 53.57, 1 df, p<.000). Environmentally, the Igbo games occurred mostly on sand, sometimes grass or bush whereas the American games were on stony ground, grass or concrete. Seven of the American games occurred in snow. Observers listed the weather as "cold" for 36.4 percent of the Hoosier observations and 27 percent of the Igbo observations but as "hot" for 15.2 percent of Hoosier and 60.7 percent of Igbo games. However, it should be noted that there was a different concept of "cold" between the two cultures with above 55°F still being considered "cold" in Nigeria. It was also just as likely to be windy in both cultures but more likely to be raining or drizzling during the observations of Hoosier games.

Of the 89 Igbo games, 51 were mixed sex play groups, 16 had female players only and 22 had male players only. Of the 66 American games, 25 were mixed sex groups, 12 had females only and 29 had males only. There was no significant difference between the ages of the oldest children in playgroups of the two cultures, (Igbo mean = 8.33 years; Hoosier mean = 8.17 years). However, there was a significant difference in the ages of the youngest children between the two cultures (Igbo mean = 5.31 years: Hoosier mean = 6.08 years, Mann Whitney $U = 2363$, $z = -2.10$, $p < .03$). This meant that the age range of the play groups was significantly broader for the Igbo (range = 3.03 years) than the American (range = 2.11 years) (Mann-Whitney $U = 2234$, $p < .01$). Play group size was also significantly larger for the Igbo children (mean = 8.25 children) than Hoosier children (mean = 3.01 children) (Mann-Whitney $U = 1544.5$, $p < .0001$).

Within the games themselves, American children were significantly more likely to use man-made materials than natural materials ($X^2 = 39.25$, 1 df, $p < .0001$). However, 47.2 percent of the Igbo games used no materials at all and this was also true of 22.7 percent of the Hoosier games. Man-made materials were used in 74.2 percent of Hoosier games and 15.7 percent of Igbo games but natural materials were used in 29.2 percent of Igbo games compared with 3 percent of American games. A combination of man-made and natural materials were found in the Igbo games only (7.9%). A list of the Igbo items is given in Table 1. Man-made materials in the Hoosier games were

TABLE 1.
Types of materials used in Igbo games.

Manmade Materials	Natural Materials
Cellophane and paper bags	Bamboo sticks
Nails	Banana leaves
Rubber-coated wire	Stones, pebbles and gravel
Local broomsticks	Palm fronds
Plastic, rubber and steel balls	Orange peel
String	Water
Cans	Sand
Milk cans	Palm kernels
Thread	Ube (Nigerian pear)
Pen tops	Cassava leaves
Rope	Crushed and whole leaves
Battery covers	Ugba (oil bean)
Beer and soda bottle tops	Rubber tree seeds
Whot cards	Sticks
Empty sugar packets	
Pieces of glass	
Empty washing powder packets	
Broken pottery	

objects like cloth, string, pinata, bicycles, toy trains and cars, board games such as Garfield and Candyland, a painted box, benches and a basketball.

Games were coded as to whether they appeared governed by clear and definite rules. Although 65 percent of Igbo and 68 percent of Hoosier games had well-defined rules, there was a much stricter adherence to the specified rules among Igbo children (94.8%) than Hoosier (58.3%) (X^2 = 21.7, 1 df, $p<.000$). The Hoosier children were more likely to argue for a change of rules during play or one child would actually change the rules of the game.

A compilation of examples of different games played by the Igbo children in Nigeria and the Hoosier children in the United States are given in Table 2 and a detailed description of some of the Igbo games is presented in the appendix.

Game length was highly variable for both cultures with a similar average length (Igbo mean = 31 mins, s.d. = 30.36; Hoosier mean = 24 mins, s.d. = 23.72)

Within the games, 57.6 percent of Hoosier had no gross motor physical activity but only 32.6 percent of Igbo games lacked such activity. Igbo games were significantly more likely to involve physical movement (X^2 = 9.64, 1 df, $p<.001$). This type of activity was primarily running but also jumping, throwing, catching, kicking, wrestling, hitting and touching for both cultures. In addition, Igbo games included hand-clapping, dancing, climbing, carrying, swimming and pulling.

Igbo games were also found to have a wider range of vocal use than Hoosier games. The voice was used for speaking, singing, yelling and whispering as an integral part of the game. 21.3 percent of Igbo games involved singing but singing was observed in only one of the Hoosier games.

The need for speaking as part of a game was similar for both cultures (Igbo 14.6%, Hoosier 18.2%) and this meant that giving a verbal suggestion, comment or response was an integral part of the game. For the Igbo games, this was often a spoken rhyme of dialogue. In the Igbo games, this might be a rhyme for the loser or a rhyme that accompanies the activity of the game. For example, in the game onye aririo (the beggar), the children formed a circle linking hands together. One person went inside the circle as the child of the woman beggar who wants to cook and has been sent to beg

TABLE 2.
Examples of Igbo and Hoosier Games.

Igbo	*Hoosier*
Oga (hand-clap and step chance)	Bicycle racing
Oro (hide and seek)	Checkers
Aku-ala (land nuts)	Hide and find
Swehi (hopscotch)	Alligator
Ogu oboku (duck fight)	Tag
Itu okwe (throw seeds)	King of the mountain
Agu na aturu (leopard & sheep)	Blind man's bluff
Ozu nwa bekee (corpse of European)	Red rover
Oku na-agba n'ugwu (fire on mountain)	Car race

for ingredients from the women neighbors. The child moved from one person to another asking "Nne m si m nata go ose" (My mother says to get ——— [pepper or salt, crayfish, etc.] from you). The answer given was either an excuse or an insult, calling the child's mother lazy, a beggar or a fool. Having been round the circle, the child tried to break out of the ring by chopping his/her hands down on the others' joined hands, and complaining:

"Ndi i uzo m si ala ye?" (Where do I go through?)

The group replied:

"Nne gi wu onye asisio o!" (Your mother is a beggar!)

The child continued around the circle with the call and response until breaking a pair of joined hands free and running off with everyone in pursuit. If the child had been caught, he/she would have been paraded and carried around as a thief.

There were numerous reasons why a game ended. These were primarily adult intervention, introduction of a new game, play time ended, quarreling, children were tired, a child was hurt, new children joined in, the play group moved to a new venue, mealtime or the children were distracted perhaps by some activity in the environment. The most common reason in both cultures was adult intervention. For the Hoosier children, the second most likely cause of game cessation was quarrelling and disagreement but for the Igbo children, the cause was significantly more likely to be due to fatigue and feeling tired than quarrelling (X^2 = 3.74, 1 df, $p<.053$).

The conclusion of any game in both cultures nearly always had a focus on either a winner or a loser. In a large group, the remainder who did not win could be considered losers, and vice versa, even though they were seldom labelled as such in the game. A few games had the potential for a winner or loser but none was declared. This was usually because the game had to end prematurely. For example, an informal game of football (soccer) was set up by two Igbo boys who made two younger children stand still as goal posts. However, these older boys were also responsible for attending to a baby so when the baby cried they had to go and look after it without completing their game. Some types of games comprised short cycles of winning and losing that could continue indefinitely. If these were played without keeping an overall score, then when the game finished, there was no declared winner or loser. For example, in the game oso-elu (racing on trees), only played by boys, one child climbed up in a grove of closely standing trees where it was possible to move from one tree to another without coming down. He called "Chuwa m ni" (come after me) to others on the ground. When someone touched him, he lost and that person moved off and was chased.

No significant difference was found between the cultures on the number of games declaring a winner. About half of the Igbo games had a declared winner and 36 percent of the Hoosier games. The same trend was found for the existence of a focus on

TABLE 3.
Penalties in Igbo and Hoosier children's games.

Igbo		Hoosier
Mild	• losing one's turn • losing a point • disqualified from game • must sing solo game song • captured by the opposing team • sent to center of ring to sit down	• playing "dead" for a set time • run around the circle again • miss a turn • out of the game
Harsh	• being carried around shoulder high as an offender/loser/thief (in one game, the group sings "throw away a cruel child, tomorrow one will be born") • 10 strokes of a pen on the back of the hand • hit on the head • dumped on a heap of refuse • the others hit the loser on the back of the hand	

losers, with 64 percent of Hoosier games with no declared loser and about 50 percent of Igbo games with no declared loser. A major difference was found in the competitive aspect of the games. Igbo games were six times more likely to have a penalty for the loser than in the American games (Igbo 39%, Hoosier 6.9%) ($X^2 = 16.96$, 1 df, $p<.00004$). Examples of typical penalties are shown in Table 3.

Because of the small numbers of games in each of the nine categories, the games for the two cultures were compared by using the largest categories and collapsing fine motor and gross motor physical skill into one category. There was no significant difference in the categories of games between the two cultures (physical skill: Hoosier 48.5%, Igbo 39.4%; physical skill and strategy: Hoosier 19.7%, Igbo 18%; and physical skill, strategy and chance: Hoosier 18.2%, Igbo 31.5%). Even when the games of physical skill were subdivided into fine motor and gross motor, the fine motor skills games still constituted 9 percent of Hoosier games and 7 percent of Igbo games. The gross motor skill games constituted 39 percent of the Hoosier games and 32 percent of the Igbo games. The main difference between the cultures was that the Igbo games of chance consisted only of guessing games and the Hoosier games of chance only of games using a die. An example of an Igbo game of chance was Nna m ogada. One person made a big circle in the sand, divided it into four parts and drew a circle in each. The next person had to guess which circle had been chosen while singing the song, "Nna m Ogada nye m ola m o" (My father Ogada. Give me my ring please). "O bu nke a" (Is it this one?) "Oloo" (No). "O bu nke a" (Is it this one?) "E" (Yes). If a person was wrong, he lost a turn.

DISCUSSION AND CONCLUSIONS

The information obtained on children's games in Indiana and Imo, Abia and Anambra states of southeastern Nigeria display a rich repertoire of this type of play behavior in both cultures. Using Avedon's (1971) components of a game as purpose, rules of game, roles of participants, participant interaction patterns, number of players, environmental requirements, physical settings, equipment, and pay-off, the major differences between the two cultures center on the last five components.

The number of children in a play group was larger for the Igbo games and this was partly because younger siblings were often included. Also the lack of traffic and structure of several houses in a compound, created easier access to a mutually agreed play area for a larger number of children. Duru (1980) noted that " children move freely from one compound to another and often eat and sleep as a group rather than in their respective compounds." The Hoosier play groups usually included neighborhood friends living on the same street. The smaller Hoosier play groups might partially explain why there was more flexibility on rule changing within a game that would require agreement by a smaller number of children than with the Igbo play groups.

Environmental requirements and physical setting would be expected to influence the types of games played and when the games were played. The fact that Igbo observers recorded more games in the morning was not surprising as children were discouraged from playing out in the midday/afternoon sun. The terrain for game playing was also expected to be mainly sand and bush and outdoors and many chores such as fetching firewood, carrying water, and watching siblings were outdoor activities that could be combined with game-playing as Bloch (1989) had observed. Some games such as okwe ala or nsa required being able to draw in the sand, or hide objects in the sand. These kinds of games were not found in the Hoosier data. However, when the games were categorized as reflecting physical skill, strategy, or chance, physical or environmental differences appeared to have little effect and the distribution was similar for both cultures.

A striking cultural difference was found in the number of adaptations of man-made and natural materials used by the Igbo children. Historically, throughout the world, children have utilized any available items for play such as the wrapping of bottle corks for balls in Denmark in the early 1900's (Anderson & Mitchell, 1978), round fruits for soccer balls in Central Africa (Centner, 1962) and the use of orange peel or pieces of broken glass for hopscotch by Appalachian children in the United States (Borman & Lippincott, 1982). Nevertheless, the authors were not expecting to find such a range of materials in the Igbo games. It should be noted that some of the seeds and leaves were seasonal just as games involving mud sliding would only be found during the rainy season. Further studies would be needed to consider the time of the year as an influencing factor on types of games played.

The final structural element of a game involves the issue of "payoff" and rewards/punishments for winners and losers. The two cultures were very similar regarding winners but differ in the degree of "punishment" for the loser. Physical admonishments and teasing in game songs do reflect the society's harsh use of ridicule, threats, scolding and caning if necessary in the socialization of children's learning of immediate obedience, appropriate greetings and behavior in the presence of adults, and limited questioning of authority (Durojaiye, 1975). Children's aggression is encouraged in the peer-group context but not if the children are of different sizes or from the same kindred (Duru, 1980). Punishment for losers, such as hitting the back of the hand, are not limited to the Igbo-speaking area of Nigeria. Salamone (1978) found similar procedures in Yauri games and Olofson's description of the Hausa game in Nigeria wasan hula (the cap game) shows that if the boy being chased falls or forgets his place, he continues to receive blows by the other children until he is back in position. Other Hausa games involve beating and even a rhyme including the phrase "he will be beaten severely with kicking and punching." Similar outcomes for girls' games can be found in West Africa, such as the simultaneous pinching of one girl while on the ground by the other girls in the group, during the game of seho falo in Dakar, Senegal (Beart, 1955). Olofson argues that roughness of play in games teaches the child emotional self-control in public even if in pain or disoriented, and that the competition in games encourages the child to have a competitive spirit. By being "it," a loser or outcast, the child is taught that only by the person's own efforts can they overcome the odds to be reinstated into a social group. While we should not be overzealous in trying to find direct links between games and adult behavior that the game teaches, many African societies are highly achievement-oriented, with collective rather than individually based values. Succeeding within the group and not bringing shame to parents and kinsmen (Duru, 1980) is therefore an important aspect of child upbringing, and appears to be an underlying focus of many games. The physical and verbal threats in games are similar to cultural management strategies in the upbringing of children described by Whittemore (1988) in his study of the Mandinka of Senegal.

Rather than looking for adult values that may be socialized through children's games, it may be more useful to use the data as a microcosmic reflection of various themes of cultural significance in everyday life and the kinds of interactive behaviors that are socially acceptable. For example, nwudo (tug of war) was accompanied by a song with a repeated refrain referring to "Child of peace, may the child whom the mother says should live for a long time, may he live." This reflects a social concern for high mortality during the first and second years of life. Kpum-kpum-o-ogene, where the penalty refrain as listed in Table 3 is to throw away a cruel child, reflects how a family can eventually disown any child who becomes a shame to them. Akpankoro, popular among girls, where everyone tries to sit down first at the end of the song, used a refrain that included reference to her waterpot and my waterpot, as watercarrying is an essential part of everyday activities. The leopard and the sheep is a popular game emphasizing the importance of protecting the goats and the sheep in a family from attack by larger animals. Finally some games of skill, such as epele played by boys, are an early introduction to a game of calculation and logic that may be a training for later male games such as Nigerian draughts. The dance/step games of girls prepare them for the complex songs and dances women perform within the various women's groups on social and important occasions.

The most popular of these games among girls, known as oga, requires particular mention. It has several versions and is even played in Equatorial Guinea by Fang girls (Pardo de Leon, 1989). Cheska (1987) has listed oga or ampe (Ghana) as simply being a game of rhythm but we argue that this is a game of physical skill and strategy because the girl must maintain the rhythm and steps but pick a particular move at each key time point. It is the girls with additional skills who learn to pick subtle cues from the leg movements of the leader in order to anticipate the leader's next likely move.

The issue of frequency of games of strategy in relation to African cultures has been dealt with extensively elsewhere (Cheska, 1987; Townshend, 1978) and the findings of the present study suggest little difference between Igbo and Hoosier games using an adapted classification. Further studies using Cheska's (1987) more detailed type of classification or Opie and Opie's (1969) system may yield different information. A detailed description of the Hoosier games is not given as some of these are described elsewhere such as red rover (Opie & Opie, 1969) and in studies of American children's games (Parrott, 1972; Sutton-Smith & Rosenberg, 1961; Mergen, 1991). Other games such as Candyland are commercialized and well-known.

Some important cross-cultural differences have been shown in this paper as well as the need for continued documentation of African children's games as these traditions become rapidly eroded by a preference for foreign or "overseas" pastimes and activities. Age-related changes in game preferences and participation, historical patterns of change, and analysis between cultures of games that are closely similar are areas that should be considered for future investigation.

ACKNOWLEDGMENTS

This data was collected as part of a project on the language and play of Igbo-speaking children partially funded by a University of Nigeria Senate research grant #0044182 to the first author. The authors are grateful to the children and families who participated in the study and to the Nigerian and American research assistants. Thanks are also due to Patricia Tirado for Spanish text translation and to Connie Wiemann for her discussions and assistance with the statistical analysis. Comments on Igbo children's games were contributed by G. Nwoazuzu, Department of Linguistics & Nigerian Languages, University of Nigeria, Nsukka. The authors would also like to thank Prof. Garry Chick, University of Illinois, for his criticisms and suggestions on the final draft of the paper. A preliminary version of this paper was presented at the International Society for the Study of Behavioral Development XIth Biennial Meeting, Minneapolis, July 1991.

APPENDIX

Igbo Children's Games

Oro (hide and seek)

A large circle is drawn in the sand and the chaser stays inside it. He/she calls out to the other children to hide and then comes out of the circle and starts chasing them. Any child who runs into the circle is safe but if touched outside the circle by the chaser, he/she takes over as chaser and the game is repeated. Oro is played by both males and females.

Okpasa (if it touches)

A small plastic ball is used for this game. Three boys move along the road with one boy at the back and two in front. The two boys in front must move skillfully to avoid the ball touching them each time it is kicked. If the ball touches anyone, that person takes over the kicking position and the game continues until the destination is reached. Only males play this game and it is sometimes performed while doing chores such as carrying water or firewood.

Oga (hand-clap and step chance)

Six possible moves form the basis of this game. These are legs apart, left leg forward or backward, right leg forward or backward and legs together. One person is designated the leader and one or more girls face the leader At a signal they begin clapping, dancing and hopping to a rhythm or song. At regular intervals that coincide with a clap, each girl must select one of the six moves. If the move matches the move chosen by the leader, that girl becomes the leader and scores a point. The players continue until someone reaches a previously agreed score. Only females play this game.

Swehi (hopscotch)

A popular game with girls. A large rectangle is drawn in the sand and partitioned into six "houses." A stone or green leaves crushed into a ball are used, and thrown into one of the houses. The girl must hop from 1 to 6 without jumping into the house where the object landed. She continues this play until number 6 has been mastered. Then she faces away from the houses and throws the object over her shoulder or head to land in a free box not owned by another child. This becomes her house and she is the only person who can land on it. If the object lands on a line while being tossed, that girl is out of the game. Drawings will eventually be made in each of the houses.

Okwe ala, ala-nchoro or aku-ala (seeds in the ground)

Also known as mancala in other parts of Africa.

Twelve holes are dug in the sand and there are 48 seeds. There are two rows of six holes. The holes are called "ulo" or houses. At the beginning of the game the houses are shared by all players. The game starts by one child emptying one of his houses and redistributing the seeds that were in there, moving from the left or right and dropping the seeds into each consecutive hole until the last one falls in an empty hole. The other players take turns to repeat this action but if at any time the last seed enters a hole that has three seeds, he or she is able to keep the seeds and this counts as one house. The game ends when one person has won 12 houses.

Agu na aturu (the leopard and the sheep)

The game is played by both male and female players. The children form a circle and one person stays inside as the sheep and another stays outside as the leopard. The leopard makes every effort to break in the circle to "eat" the sheep and, if successful, then becomes the sheep in the next round. This game is played with a call and response song with a solo and chorus.

Ogu obogwu (duck fight)

Two children pose as ducks and squat facing each other. They leap with two legs and their hands spread vertically. They begin to fight and pounce at each other's hands and head. Whoever falls with his backside touching the ground, loses a point. The game is played by male children.

Nsa (thread in sand)

A knot is made out of a thread and buried in a heap of sand. Children take turns to find the knot and the winner is the person who scores the highest.

Kota onye tara gi okpo (can you find the person who knocked you on the head?)

One child is "blinded" by another who keeps his/her hands firmly over the child's eyes. Another child comes and hits him/her on the head and goes back to their place. The "blinded" child is then allowed to look and guess who hit them. If correct, that child takes the place of the "blinded" child.

Oku-ube (pear game)

The game is usually played by boys. A Nigerian pear or oil-bean is tossed to the ground by one child and another child aims his fruit to try to hit it. If he succeeds, he obtains the fruit, but if he fails, the other child picks up his own fruit and tries to hit that of his opponent.

REFERENCES

Ammar, H. (1954). *Growing up in an Egyptian village.* London: Routledge and Kegan Paul.
Anderson, R. T., & Mitchell, E. M. (1978). Play and personality in Denmark. In M. Salter (Ed.), *Play: Anthropological perspectives.* New York: Leisure Press.
Avedon, E. M. (1971). The structural elements of games. In E. M. Avedon & B. Smith (Eds.), *The study of games.* New York: Wiley.
Barker, R. G., & Wright, H. F. (1955). *Midwest and its children.* New York: Harper and Row.

Bascom, W. (1969). *The Yoruba of Southwestern Nigeria.* New York: Holt, Rinehart and Winston.

Basden, G. (1921). *Among the Ibos.* Cass.

Basden, G. (1938). *Niger Ibos.* Cass.

Beart, C. (1955). *Jeux et jouets de l'Ouest Africain.* II Dakar, Senegal: IFAN.

Bett, H. (1929). *The games of children. Their origin and history.* London: Methuen.

Bloch, M. N. (1984). Play materials: considerations from a West African setting. *Childhood Education, 60*(5), 345–348.

Bloch, M. (1989). Young boys' and girls' play at home and in the community: A cultural-ecological framework. In M. N. Bloch & A. D. Pellegrini (Eds.), *The ecological context of children's play* (pp. 120–154). Norwood, NJ: Ablex.

Borman, K. M., & Lippincott, N. T. (1982). Cognition and culture: Two perspectives on "Free play." In K. M. Borman (Ed.), *The social life of children in a changing society* (pp.132–142). Hillsdale, NJ: Lawrence Erlbaum.

Brann, C. M. B. (1979). A typology of language education in Nigeria. In W. C. McCormack & S. Wurm (Eds.), *Language and society: Anthropological issues.* The Hague: Mouton.

Brown, W. (1974). Cultural learning through game structure: A study of Pennsylvania German children's games. *Pennsylvania Folklife, 23*(4) 2–11.

Centner, T. (1962). *L'enfant Africain et ses jeux.* Elisabethville: CEPSI.

Cheska, A. T. (1978). Native American games as strategies of societal maintenance. In E. Norbeck & C. R. Farrer (Eds.), *Forms of play of native North Americans.* St. Paul: West Publishing Co.

Cheska, A. T. (1987). *Traditional games and dances in West African nations.* Schorndorf, Germany: Verlag.

Chick, G. (1984). The cross-cultural study of games. *Exercise and Sports Science Reviews, 12,* 307–337.

Chick, G. (1989). On the categorization of games. *Play and Culture, 2,* 283–292.

Duncan, S., & Farley, A. M. (1990). Achieving parent-child coordination through convention: Fixed- and variable-sequence conventions. *Child Development, 61,* 742–753.

Durojaiye, M. O. A. (1975). *New introduction to educational psychology.* London: Evans Brothers.

Durojaiye, S. (1977). Children's traditional games and rhymes in three cultures. *Educational Research, 19*(3), 223–226.

Duru, M. S. (1980). *Socialization among the Igbo: An intergenerational study of cultural patterns, familial roles and child rearing practices.* Doctoral dissertation, University of Maryland.

Eifermann, R. K. (1968). *School children's games.* U.S. Dept. of Health, Education, and Welfare Final Report Contract No. OE-6–21–010.

Ekwueme, L. N. (1977). *Igbo performing arts.* Paper presented at Workshop on Igbo culture, University of Nigeria, Nsukka.

Emecheta, B. (1980). *The moonlight bride.* Oxford: Oxford University Press.

Feitelson, D. (1954). Patterns of early education in the Kurdish community. *Mergamot, 5,* 95.

Feitelson, D. (1977). Cross-cultural studies of representational play. In B. Tizard & D. Harvey (Eds.), *Biology of play.* London: Heinemann.

Fogel, A., Nwokah, E., & Karns, J. (1991). Parent-infant games as dynamic social systems. In K. B. MacDonald (Ed.), *Parents and infants playing.* Albany, N.Y.: Suny Press.

Fortes, M. (1938). Social and psychological aspects of education in Taleland. *Supplement to Africa, xi,* 4.

Garvey, C. (1977). *Play.* Cambridge, MA: Harvard University Press.

Ike, C. (1973). *The potter's wheel*. Glasgow: Fontana.

Lancy, D. F. (1977). The play behavior of Kpelle children during rapid cultural change. In D. F. Lancy & B. Tindall (Eds.), *The study of play: Problems and prospects* (pp. 84–91). New York: Leisure Press.

Leacock, E. (1971). At play in African villages. *Natural History, 6*, 60–65.

Leiber, J. W. (1971). *Ibo village communities*. Occas. Pub. no. 12, Institute of Education, University of Ibadan, Nigeria.

Leis, P. (1972). *Enculturation and socialization in an Ijaw village*. New York: Holt, Rinehart, & Winston.

Levine, R. A., & Levine, B. B. (1963). Nyansango: A Gusii community in Kenya. In B. Whiting (Ed.), *Six cultures*. New York: Wiley.

Linaza, J. (1981). *The acquisition of the rules of games by children*. Doctoral dissertation, Oxford University.

Mergen, B. (1991). Ninety-five years of historical change in the game preferences of American children. *Play and Culture, 4*, 272–283.

Nwokah, E. (1988). The imbalance of stuttering behavior in bilingual speakers. *Journal of Fluency Disorders, 13*, 357–373.

Olofson, H. (1977). Vertigo and social structure: Notes on Hausa children's play. In P. Stevens, Jr. (Ed.), *Studies in the anthropology of play; papers in memory of B. Tindall*. New York: Leisure Press.

Opie, I., & Opie, P. (1969). *Children's games in street and playground*. Oxford: Clarendon Press.

Pardo de Leon, P. P. (1988). Juegos de los ninos Fang. *Africa 2000, 37*–42.

Pardo de Leon, P. P. (1989). Personal communication.

Parrott, S. (1972). Games children play: Ethnography of a second grade recess. In J. Spradley & D. McCurdy (Eds.), *The cultural experience: Ethnography in complex society* (pp. 207–226). Chicago: Science Research Associates.

Peshkin, A. (1972). *Kanuri schoolchildren: Education and social mobilization in Nigeria*. New York: Holt, Rinehart and Winston.

Rich, G. (1978). Games and values in Iceland. In M. Salter (Ed.), *Play: Anthropological perspectives* (pp. 113–126). New York: Leisure Press.

Roberts, J. M. (1978). Comment on "Games of strategy: A new look at correlates and cross-cultural methods." In H. B. Schwartzman (Ed.), *Play and culture. Proceedings of the association for the Anthropological Study of Play*. New York: Leisure Press.

Roberts, J. M., Arth, M. J., & Bush, R. R. (1959). Games in culture. *American Anthropologist, 61*, 579–2605.

Roberts, J. M., & Sutton-Smith, B. (1962). Child training and game involvement. *Ethnology, 1*(2), 166 -185.

Roberts, J., Sutton-Smith B., & Kendon, A. (1963). Strategy in games and folktales. *Journal of Social Psychology, 61*, 185 -199.

Salamone, F. A. (1978). Children's games as mechanisms for easing ethnic interaction in ethnically heterogeneous communities—a Nigerian case. *Ethnicity, 5*, 203–212.

Salamone, F. A. (1989). Anthropology and play: A bibliography. *Play and Culture, 2*, 158–181.

Salamone, F., & Salamone, V. A. (1991). Children's games in Nigeria redux: a consideration of the uses of play. *Play and Culture, 4*, 129–138.

Schwartzman, H.B. (1977). Works on play: A bibliography. In P. Stevens (Ed.), *Studies in the anthropology of play: Papers in memory of B. Allan Tindall*. Cornwall, NY: Leisure Press.

Schwartzman, H. B. (1978). *Transformations: The anthropology of children's play.* New York: Plenum.

Schwartzman, H. B., & Barbera, L. (1976). Children's play in Africa and South America: A review of the ethnographic literature. In D. F. Lancy & B. A. Tindall (Eds.), *The study of play: Problems and prospects.* New York: Leisure Press.

Seagoe, M. V. (1970). An instrument for the analysis of children's play as an index of the degree of socialization. *Journal of School Psychology, 8*(2),139–144.

Soyinka, W. (1981). *Ake. The years of childhood.* New York: Random House.

Sutton-Smith, B. (1986). The fate of traditional games in the modern world. *Association for the anthropological study of play newsletter, 12*(2), 8–13.

Sutton-Smith, B., & Roberts, J. M. (1970). The cross-cultural and psychological study of games. In G. Luschen (Ed.), *The cross-cultural analysis of games.* Champaign, Illinois: Stipes.

Sutton-Smith, B., & Rosenberg, B. G. (1961). Sixty years of historical change in the game preferences of American children. *Journal of American Folklore, 74,* 17–46.

Townshend, P. (1978). Games of strategy: A new look at correlates and cross-cultural methods. In H. B. Schwartzman (Ed.), *Play and culture. Proceedings of the Association for the Anthropological Study of Play* (pp. 217–225). New York: Leisure Press.

Uchendu, V. C. (1965). *The Igbo of Southeast Nigeria.* New York: Holt, Rinehart and Winston.

Uka, N. (1966). *Growing up in Nigerian culture.* Occasional Pub. no. 6, Institute of Education, University of Ibadan, Nigeria.

Whittemore, R.D. (1988). *Child caregiving and socialization to the Mandinka way: Toward an ethography of childhood.* Doctoral dissertation, University of California, Los Angeles.

Wiggins, D. K. (1985). The play of slave children in the plantation communities of the Old South, 1820–60. In N. Ray Hiner & J. M. Hawes (Eds.) *Growing up in America: Children in historical perspective* (pp. 173–190). Chicago: University of Illinois Press.

Zaslarsky, C. (1973). *Africa counts: Number and pattern in African culture.* Westport, CT: Lawrence Hill.

6

Young Children's Play in Socio-Cultural Context: South Korea and the United States

Jonathan Tudge
Soeun Lee
Sarah Putnam

INTRODUCTION

In this chapter we examine some aspects of children's play in cultural context. Our assumption is that development occurs differently in different cultural contexts, and that these differences are at least as important as similarities that exist across cultural contexts. Our definition of "culture" is one that includes a set of values, beliefs, practices, institutions, and tools that differentiate one group from another, and which are passed on (or co-constructed anew) from generation to generation. Cross-cultural developmental psychologists and cultural anthropologists typically make this clear by focusing on groups that are maximally different, contrasting (for example) members of a schooled society with those where there is no formal schooling, or distinguish development in a technologically simple (non- or semi-industrialized) culture either implicitly or explicitly with development in their own culture of origin (Tudge, Putnam, & Sidden, 1993). As Bornstein recently pointed out, with reference to cross-cultural comparisons:

"Not unexpectedly, the modal comparison is with U.S. samples" (1991, p. 7).

The best example of a study of young children's social ecologies—the activities in which they engage, the settings in which they are situated, and the company they keep is that of B. Whiting and her colleagues in the "Six Cultures" study (Whiting & Whiting, 1963) and its more recent incarnation (Whiting & Edwards, 1988). They and their colleagues used very similar observational methods to collect data on children in 13 different communities, from the United States (Orchard Town, New England), Mexico, Philippines, Okinawa, Liberia, India (3 communities) and Kenya (5 communities), and also gathered much less extensive spot observational data on children in four more communities in Kenya, Guatemala, Peru, and the United States (Claremont).

All but two of the communities are drawn from non- or semi-industrialized societies, with six different communities drawn from rural Kenya. By contrast, the United States features as the sole exemplar of a technologically complex society. Whiting and Edwards pay relatively little attention to the Claremont sample, not surprisingly given that only eight observations were collected on each of 17 children, which means that Orchard Town represents the primary example of children who are being reared in an industrialized, schooled society. To what extent is this sample representative of such societies? Rather poorly, we think, on at least two grounds.

First, there is no reason to believe that children's activities or parent-child relationships in the United States are typical of those experienced by families with different cultural norms but similar levels of industrialization in Asia, for example (Befu, 1986; Choi, Kim & Choi, 1993; Hsu, 1985; Tobin, Wu, & Davidson, 1989; Stevenson, Azuma, & Hakuta, 1986; Stevenson & Lee, 1989; Yi, 1993) or the former Soviet Union (Bronfenbrenner, 1970; Liegle, 1975; Mace & Mace, 1963; Tudge, 1973).

Second, there is little reason to believe that even within the United States there is homogeneity across all sub-cultural groups or within the same cultural group across time. Orchard Town, the primary representative of a community in an industrialized society, was homogeneous (as all the communities were supposed to be) and consisted of white families in which all had professional or self-employed fathers and mothers who did not work outside the home. The data were gathered in the mid-1950s, when the norm, at least for Anglo-American two-parent families, was for the mother to stay at home with her young children. Whiting and Edwards make no reference to the passage of time (for example, that currently in the United States it is far less likely for women to stay at home) or to the fact that a community from different socioeconomic, ethnic, or racial background (in the 1950s or currently) might have provided evidence for a quite different set of experiences between parents and children (Dunn, 1988; Dunn & Wooding, 1977; Heath, 1983; Kohn, 1977; Kohn & Schooler, 1983; Ogbu, 1980).

In this chapter we would like to take the argument one step further. We want to argue that differences in relation to the social stratification system (social class) are cultural differences, at least to the extent that members of different social classes have distinctive sets of values and beliefs which are carried forward from generation to generation. To what extent is there good evidence for this position? Work on social class differences in childrearing practices goes back a good way (Bronfenbrenner, 1958; Bronfenbrenner & Crouter, 1983; Lynd & Lynd, 1929; Miller & Swanson, 1958), but the most extensive work on parental values as a function of social class has been carried out by the sociologist Melvin Kohn, with his colleagues (Kohn, 1977, 1979; Kohn & Schooler, 1983; Kohn & Slomszynski, 1990). Kohn and his colleagues, after conducting extensive interviews with parents in this country and abroad (examples include Italy, Poland, Taiwan, and Japan), has concluded that while parents from many walks of life share certain values about their children and beliefs about childrearing, parents who work in the professional sphere (whose jobs are substantively complex, and who are likely to work with people rather than objects) are more likely to encourage self-direction and initiative in their children than are parents whose jobs are non-professional. The typical distinction that Kohn had in mind was between a manager and a line worker in a factory.

While Kohn and his colleagues were able to make a strong case for the connection between workplace experiences and childrearing values, they paid only minimal attention to childrearing practices themselves. Somewhat surprisingly, few studies have tried to establish the next link in the causal chain stretching from workplace experiences to parental values to parental childrearing beliefs to childrearing practices, although data gathered by Luster and his colleagues (Luster, Rhoades, & Haas, 1989) nicely support Kohn's thesis. (Some supporting evidence is also provided by Burns, Homel, & Goodnow, 1984; Goodnow & Collins, 1990.)

In this chapter we examine young children's naturally occurring play in four different cultural contexts, focusing primarily on the types of play in which they engage and their partners in play. Our position, in line with that taken by several scholars (Schwartzman, 1978, 1986; Slaughter & Dombrowski, 1989; Sutton-Smith, 1983), is that while young children's play may be universally found, its nature varies from culture to culture, in response to specific cultural constraints and differential degrees of encouragement.

Although many cross-cultural studies focus on societies or groups that are maximally different, we argue that potential confounds are best avoided by focusing on groups that are similar on many criteria (Bornstein, Tal, & Tamis-Lamonda, 1991). Our participants are drawn from four cultural communities (i.e., "groups of people having some common local organization and similarities in values and practices," Rogoff, Mistry, Göncü, & Mosier, 1991, p. 174), two of which are from a city in South Korea, and two from a city in North Carolina. The two cities are of medium size, with similar cultural and educational amenities, and lie on the same latitude. Clearly, however, they also differ greatly in terms of language, history, traditions, and values, for example, independence and interdependence (Triandis, 1993). Following Kohn, in both cities participants were drawn from two groups—one in which the parents work in the professional sphere (middle class) and one where the parents are working class.

METHODS

Families were asked to keep their daily routines unchanged as much as possible during the observation period. We used modified spot observations (Ellis, et al., 1981; Munroe & Munroe, 1971; Rogoff, 1978; Whiting & Edwards, 1988) to observe each child. Following a period of acclimatization, observations occurred over a period of six days, in blocks of two hours each on the first two days and the last day, and four hours each on the other days for a total of 18 hours over the course of one week, distributed so as to cover each child's waking hours. This yielded approximately 180 observations on each child. The children were followed wherever they went during each block; they wore a wireless microphone (audible only to the data gatherer) to allow us to overhear conversations without being too intrusive. Observations were continuous (to provide information on the context of the events) but the spot observations focused on what occurred during a 30-second "window" every five and-a-half minutes. The timing of the window was signaled to the data gatherer, audible only to her, from an endless loop tape recording. We focused on:

1. the activities available to the child (i.e., those within easy ear- or eye-shot);
2. whether the child was involved in those activities;
3. if the child were involved, his or her role, who initiated the activity, who initiated the child's involvement, and the partners (if any);
4. if there was one or more partner, their relationship to the child (related or not, age, gender) and their role in that activity;
5. the number and type of people potentially available to be partners, the presence of parents, and the location of the action.

On the final day of observation, the child's activities were videotaped for two additional hours, to allow for assessment of reliability and for more detailed analyses of processes of interaction, but data derived from the videotapes were not included in this chapter.

The activities of interest were of four main types, each of which were subdivided further, and comprised lessons (four categories), work (five categories), conversation (three categories), and play, the focus of this presentation. We had 10 categories of play, but for the purposes of this chapter they have been grouped into four—pretend (including emulation of adult roles), play with academic objects (playing with or looking at objects such as books, numbers, and so on, but without being asked for or given information about them, which would constitute an academic lesson), watching a performance (which was almost always watching TV), and other play (which included play with toys and other objects designed primarily for children, play with objects designed for adults, play with objects from the natural world, and play with no objects, such as rough and tumble play, chasing, etc.).

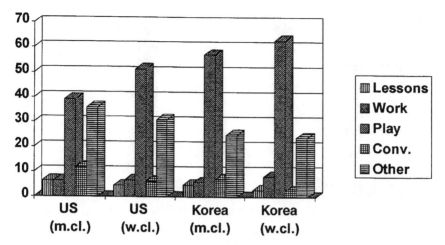

FIGURE 1. Children's activities (% of total activities).

PARTICIPANTS

The participants comprised 32 children (20 from the U.S. [11 females], 12 from Korea [6 females]), aged between 28 and 45 months. In both countries, the cities were very similar in terms of size, cultural and educational amenities, and presence of a sufficient number of adults who worked in the professional sphere and those whose jobs were non-professional. In each city, families termed middle class consisted of at least one parent with a college degree whose occupation, by Hollingshead criteria, was professional (range 7–9 Hollingshead ranking). Working class families were those in which neither parent had a college degree, and whose occupations were non-professional (range 2–5 Hollingshead ranking). In both countries the median family income was quite different between the two social class groups, although U.S. families typically earned a good deal more (in dollar terms) than their Korean counterparts. Participants were recruited from birth records in the United States, and by word of mouth in Korea (access to birth records not being possible there). Data were gathered by natives of their respective countries, all of whom had been trained by the first author.

RESULTS

A total of 5,725 observations were coded, in which the target children were engaged in a total of 6,751 different activities. As can be seen in Figure 1, children in each of the four communities were far more likely to be observed in play than in any other type of activity.[1] This was particularly true of the children in the Korean communities, although in both countries the working class children were somewhat more likely to

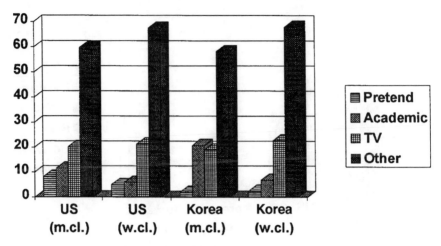

FIGURE 2. Types of play (% of total play).

be observed in play than their middle class counterparts. (It should be pointed out that some, although not all, of the greater observation of play in Korea may be explained by the fact that they were less likely to be observed in the "other" category, which included eating, sleeping, dressing, and so on.)

As can be seen from Figure 2, "other" play (play with toys, with objects from the adult world, with objects from the natural world, or with no object at all) comprised the largest proportion of these children's play. Expressed as a proportion of all play, the results were very similar in the two countries, with working class children engaged in other play more than their middle class counterparts. The amount of TV watching was also very similar. We shall focus more on the remaining two categories of play—pretend and play with academic objects.

On average, as can be seen in Figure 3, children in the two Korean communities were more likely to play with academic objects than were their counterparts in the United States. However, the bulk of this cross-cultural difference is explained by the middle class Korean children. In both countries, middle class children were more likely than their working class counterparts to play with academic objects, but this difference was far more apparent in Korea. By contrast, children in the U.S. communities were more likely to engage in pretend play.

Breaking these data down by gender, it is apparent that in both countries middle class girls were more likely than middle class boys to be engaged in play with academic objects, although this was not true of the working class children (see Figure 3). It is interesting to note, by way of contrast, that in our U.S. communities there was a very clear distinction between both class and gender in terms of academic lessons (differentiated from play with academic objects by virtue of either the child requesting information, being asked a question, or being proffered information about some

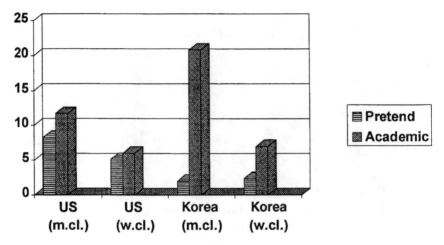

FIGURE 3. "Sophisticated" play (% of total play).

academic object). In the U.S. communities middle class children were more likely than working class children to engage in academic lessons, and boys in both communities were more likely than girls to be engaged. In Korea, middle class children were also more likely than their working class counterparts to engage in academic lessons, but in both groups girls engaged in more such lessons than did boys. Interestingly, the four groups of children engaged in approximately the same equivalent proportions of academic lessons.

In terms of cross-cultural comparisons, we found very interesting similarities in terms of the relative frequencies with which children were engaged in different types of play as well as some interesting differences. Most striking were the within-societal differences as a function of social class, differences that were mirrored across societies. As we mentioned above, Kohn has found strikingly similar social class differences across an array of societies. Critical to Kohn's analysis, however, is the view that middle class parents are more likely than their working class counterparts to socialize their children to become self-directed and exert initiative; by contrast, Kohn has argued, working class parents are more likely to stress obedience and conformity in their children.

To what extent did these children exercise differential amounts of self-direction in play, as measured by their initiation of play (either alone or in collaboration with a partner), and by their initiation of involvement in play (irrespective of whom initiated the play itself)? Across all categories of play, children in each community were most likely to initiate play themselves, as is displayed in Figure 4. (Initiation of involvement in play was even more likely under their own direction—in each community more than 90% of all such initiation was under the direction of the children themselves.) Ignoring social class, the U.S. children were more likely than those in Korea

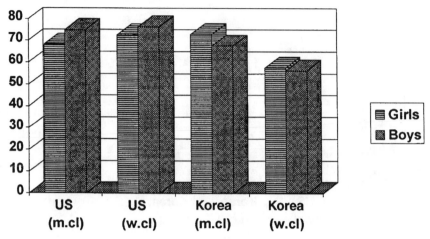

FIGURE 4.   Initiation of play by child alone or with a partner (in %).

to initiate play themselves or with a partner, but the cross-societal differences were primarily a function of within-society social class variations; Korean working class children were less likely to initiate than children in the other three groups, as displayed in Figure 4. In Korea, middle class children were more likely to initiate play than working class children, but there was no clear difference in the United States. In the United States, boys were more likely than girls to initiate play themselves or in conjunction with another person, but this tendency was reversed in Korea.

This pattern of results hardly fits the model of middle class children's parents' greater encouragement of self-direction in their children. However, play is an activity that is perhaps more likely to be under children's own direction than other activities in which children could be involved. It is therefore worth pointing out some comparisons with other activities. For example, we have argued elsewhere that middle class US children were more likely than their working class counterparts to initiate both lessons and work (Tudge, Putnam, & Sidden, 1993, 1994; Tudge & Putnam, 1996). As displayed in Figures 5 and 6, on average children in the U.S. communities were more likely than those in Korea both to initiate lessons and initiate their involvement in lessons. In both countries, however, children in the middle class communities were much more likely to exercise this type of self direction than their counterparts in the working class communities.

Finally, we wish to discuss some data regarding the children's partners in play. As shown in Figure 7, in all communities the mother was the single most likely partner in their children's play. This is not surprising, given that she was available to the children far more than any other single person, particularly in Korea and in the middle class U.S. community where many of the mothers were not employed outside of the home. What is somewhat surprising, however, is that the Korean children were observed playing alone almost as much as their U.S. counterparts were. Koreans,

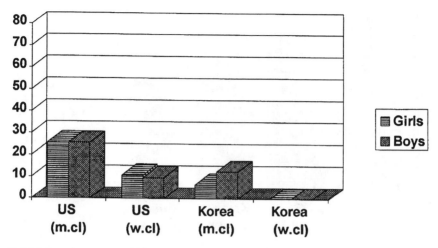

FIGURE 5. Initiation of lessons by child alone or with a partner (in %).

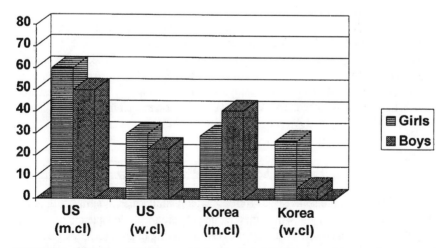

FIGURE 6. Initiation of involvement in lessons by child alone or with a partner (in %).

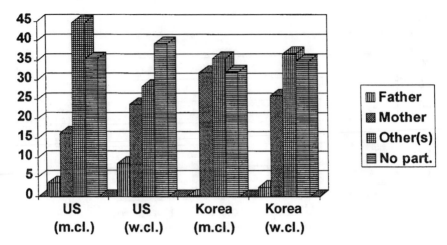

FIGURE 7.   Partners in play (% of observations of play).

compared to people living in the United States, are more likely to stress interdependence and collectivism than independence and individualism (Choi, Kim, & Choi, 1993; Hsu, 1985). We therefore had expected that the Korean children would have played alone a good deal less than those in the United States. There is some evidence, however, that the degree of stress on interdependence is declining, particularly among the middle class, who are more influenced by Western culture (Cha, 1994; Kagitcibasi, 1989; Yi, 1993).

This finding is yet more noteworthy when we examine the role taken by the mother in the four communities. Mothers were observed engaging with their children far more in Korea than in the United States (439 observations vs. 383 observations, but these 439 observations were taken from data on 12 children rather than the 20 children observed in the U.S.). However, their engagement was far more likely to be passive (as an observer) than as an active participant in play. In the United States middle class community it was particularly striking that when mothers were engaged with their children in play they took a very active role. This finding nicely parallels research on U.S. middle class mothers' greater active participation in their infants' play (Göncü & Mosier, 1991; Haight, 1994; Lewis & Wilson, 1972).

CONCLUSION

It is clear that there are some striking cross-cultural similarities in terms of both the amount and types of play in which these young children were involved. Play, as one might expect from a group of two- to four-year-olds living in most societies, occupied a good proportion of their time. Along with the cross-societal similarities, however,

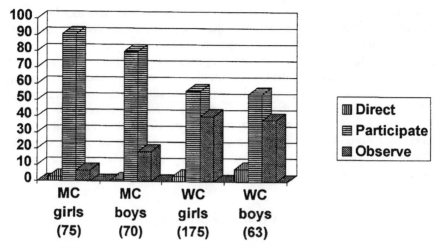

FIGURE 8. Mother's role in play in U.S. (% of engagement).

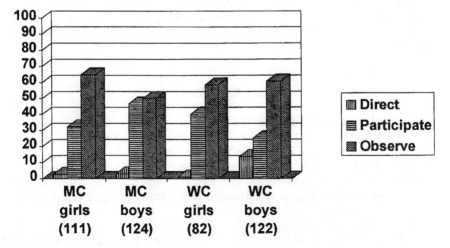

FIGURE 9. Mother's role in play in Korea (% of engagement).

are within-society differences as a function both of social class and gender. In contrast to many cross-cultural studies, which for the most part deal with between-culture differences, we have argued that it is as important to take into account within-culture differences. Being raised as a Korean or a U.S. citizen is indeed likely to be associated with learning through participation in somewhat different sets of activities, learning different values and beliefs, and coming to see the world in somewhat different ways. These children's play, and the ways in which their partners play with them, both reflect cultural differences and serve to recreate them. Nonetheless, neither the United States nor Korea are homogeneous societies; focusing on social class and gender revealed striking differences within each society, some of which (particularly associated with class) were mirrored in each society.

ACKNOWLEDGMENT

A version of this chapter was presented as part of a symposium entitled "The pretend play of cultures: Cultures of pretend play" (Artin Göncü and Ageliki Nicolopoulou, Chairs) at the biennial meeting of the Society for Research in Child Development, Indianapolis, April 1, 1995. The authors would like to express their deep appreciation to all of the children and families who gave so generously of their time, to Judy Sidden, who collected part of the data, and who collaborated in the design of the coding scheme used in this study.

NOTE

[1] We wish to point out that our intention is not to generalize from any "sample" to a wider population, for our participants in this research constituted the population of children (at least of those whose parents agreed to participate) of the requisite age and background from the four communities of interest. Inferential statistical tests are therefore not appropriate and have not been performed.

REFERENCES

Befu, H. (1986). The social and cultural background of child development in Japan and the United States. In H. Stevenson, H. Azuma, & K. Hakuta (Eds.), *Child development and education in Japan* (pp. 13–27). New York: Freeman.

Bornstein, M. H. (Ed.). (1991). *Cultural approaches to parenting.* Hillsdale, NJ: Erlbaum.

Bornstein, M. H., Tal, J., & Tamis-LeMonda, C. S. (1991). Parenting in cross-cultural perspective: The United States, France, and Japan. In M. H. Bornstein (Ed.), *Cultural approaches to parenting* (pp. 69–90). Hillsdale, NJ: Erlbaum.

Bronfenbrenner, U. (1958). Socialization and social class through time and space. In E. E. Maccoby, T. M. Newcomb, & E. L. Hartley (Eds.), *Readings in social psychology.* New York: Holt, Rinehart and Winston.

Bronfenbrenner, U. (1970). *Two worlds of childhood: USA and USSR.* New York: Russell Sage.

Bronfenbrenner, U., & Crouter, A. C. (1983). The evolution of environmental models in developmental research. In P. H. Mussen (Ed.), *Handbook of child psychology, Vol. 1: History, theory, methods* (pp. 357–414). New York: Wiley.

Cha, J.-H. (1994). Aspects of individualism and collectivism in Korea. In U. Kim, H. C. Triandis, C. Kagitcibasi, S.-C. Choi, & G. Yoon (Eds.), *Individualism and collectivism: Theory, methods, and applications* (pp. 157–174). Newbury Park, CA: Sage.

Choi, S., Kim, U., & Choi, S. (1993). Indigenous analysis of collective representations: A Korean perspective. In U. Kim & J. W. Berry (Eds.), *Indigenous psychologies: Research and experience in cultural context* (pp. 193–210). Newbury Park, CA: Sage.

Dunn, J. (1988). *The beginnings of social understanding.* Cambridge, MA: Harvard University Press.

Dunn, J., & Wooding, C. (1977). Play in the home and its implications for learning. In B. Tizard & D. Harvey (Eds.), *Biology of play* (pp. 45–58). London: Heinemann Medical Books.

Ellis, S., Rogoff, B., & Cromer, C. (1981). Age segregation in children's social interactions. *Developmental Psychology, 17,* 399–407.

Göncü, A., & Mosier, C. (1991, April). Cultural variations in the play of toddlers. Paper presented at the biennial meetings of the Society for Research in Child Development, Seattle, WA, USA.

Goodnow, J., & Collins, W. A. (1990). *Development according to parents: The nature, sources, and consequences of parents' ideas.* Hillsdale, NJ: Erlbaum.

Haight, W. (1994). Pretend play: A cultural and developmental phenomenon. In A. Alvarez & P. del Rio (Eds.), *Explorations in socio-cultural studies, Vol. 4: Education as cultural construction* (pp. 53–60). Madrid: Fundacion infancia y aprendizaje.

Heath, S. B. (1983). *Ways with words: Language, life, and work communities and classrooms.* Cambridge: Cambridge University Press.

Hsu, F. L. K. (1985). The self in cross-cultural perspective. In A. J. Marsella, G. de Vos, & F. L. K. Hsu (Eds.), *Culture and self* (pp. 24–55). London: Tavistock.

Kagitcibasi, C. (1990). Family and socialization in cross-cultural perspective: A model of change. *Nebraska Symposium on Motivation, Vol 37.* Lincoln: University of Nebraska Press.

Kohn, M. L. (1977). *Class and conformity: A study in values,* 2nd Ed. Chicago: University of Chicago Press.

Kohn, M. L. (1979). The effects of social class on parental values and practices. In D. Reiss & H. Hoffman (Eds.), *The American family: Dying or developing?* (pp. 45–68). New York: Plenum.

Kohn, M. L., & Schooler, C. (1983). *Work and personality.* Norwood, NJ: Ablex.

Kohn, M. L., & Slomszynski, K. M. (1990). *Social structure and self-direction: A comparative analysis of the United States and Poland.* Oxford: Basil Blackwell.

Lewis, M., & Wilson, C. D. (1972). Infant development in lower-class American families. *Human Development, 15,* 112–127.

Liegle, L. (1975). *The family's role in Soviet education.* New York: Springer.

Lynd, R. S., & Lynd, H. M. (1920). *Middletown: A study in modern American culture.* New York: Harcourt, Brace, & World.

Mace, D., & Mace, M. (1963). *The Soviet family.* Garden City, NY: Doubleday.

Miller, D. R., & Swanson, G. E. (1958). *The changing American parent: A study in the Detroit area.* New York: Wiley.

Munroe, R. H., & Munroe, R. L. (1971). Household density and infant care in an East African society. *Journal of Social Psychology, 83*, 3–13.

Ogbu, J. (1979). Social stratification and the socialization of competence. *Anthropology and Education Quarterly, 10*, 3–20.

Rogoff, B. (1978). Spot observation: An introduction and examination. *The Quarterly Newsletter of the Institute for Comparative Human Development, 2* (2), 21–26.

Rogoff, B., Mistry, J., Göncü, A., & Mosier, C. (1991). Cultural variation in the role relations of toddlers and their families. In M. H. Bornstein (Ed.), *Cultural approaches to parenting* (pp. 173–183). Hillsdale, NJ: Erlbaum.

Schwartzman, H. G. (1978). *Transformations: The anthropology of children's play*. New York: Plenum.

Schwartzman, H. G. (1986). A cross-cultural perspective on child-structured play activities and materials. In A. W. Gottfried & A. C. Brown (Eds.), *The contribution of play materials and parental involvement to children's development* (pp. 13–29). Lexington, MA: Lexington Books.

Slaughter, D. T., & Dombrowski, J. (1989). Cultural continuities and discontinuities: I mpact on social and pretend play. In M. N. Bloch & A. D. Pellegrini (Eds.), *The ecological context of children's play* (pp. 282–310). Norwood, NJ: Ablex.

Stevenson, H. W., Azuma, H., & Hakuta, K. (Eds.). (1986). *Child development and education in Japan*. New York: Freeman.

Sutton-Smith, B. (1983). Commentary on social class differences in sociodramatic play in historical context: A reply to McLoyd. *Developmental Review, 3*, 1–5.

Tobin, J. T., Wu, D. Y. H., & Davidson, D. H. (1989). *Preschool in 3 cultures*. New Haven, CT: Yale University Press.

Triandis, H. C. (1993). Collectivism and individualism as cultural syndromes. *Cross-Cultural Research, 27*, 155–180.

Tudge, J. R. H. (1973). *The moral aspect of socialization in the Soviet Union: Its development in theory and practice*. Unpublished master's thesis, Oxford University, England.

Tudge, J. R. H., & Putnam, S. A. (1996). The everyday experiences of North American preschoolers in two cultural communities: A cross-disciplinary and cross-level analysis. In J. Tudge, M. Shanahan, & J. Valsiner (Eds.), *Comparisons in human development:Understanding time and context* (pp. 252–281). New York: Cambridge University Press.

Tudge, J. R. H., Putnam, S. A., & Sidden, J. (1993). Preschoolers' activities in socio-cultural context. *Quarterly Newsletter of the Laboratory of Comparative Human Cognition, 15*, 71–84.

Tudge, J. R. H., Putnam, S. A., & Sidden, J. (1994). The everyday activities of American preschoolers: Lessons and work in two socio-cultural contexts. In A. Alvarez & P. Del Rio (Eds.), *Perspectives in socio-cultural research, Vol 4: Education as cultural construction* (pp. 109–120). Madrid: Fundacion Infancia i Aprendizaje.

Whiting, B. B. (1963). *Six cultures: Studies of child rearing*. Cambridge, MA: Harvard University Press.

Whiting, B. B. & Edwards, C. P. (1988). *Children of different worlds: The formation of social behavior*. Cambridge, MA: Harvard University Press.

Yi, S. H. (1993). Transformation of child socialization in Korean culture. *Early Child Development and Care, 85*, 17–24.

part III
Children's Play

Part III

Introduction

Garry Chick

The chapters that follow deal with the degree to which children differ in playfulness on an individual basis. That play differs cross-culturally, intraculturally, and individually—though it is a human universal—should surprise no one. However, this circumstance presents researchers with a predicament, especially since there are no obvious and accepted units by which play can be measured and, thus, meaningfully compared among contexts (Chick & Barnett, 1995). The chapters in this section contribute to the solution of this dilemma.

Lynn Barnett carefully reviews literature dealing with "the playful child," observing in the process that virtually all research dealing with the phenomena has demonstrated that play is important in the development of the young child. A substantial part of the literature that she reviews suggests that playfulness may be regarded as an aspect of the child's personality, unique to the individual but related to a constellation of other personality traits. In her chapter, Barnett attempts, first, to gather data in support of the idea that playfulness may differ on an individual basis among young children and, second, to explore the role of playfulness in anxiety reduction. Using the Children's Playfulness Scale, which she developed, Barnett collected data on the playfulness of one hundred and twenty two children who averaged just under 45 months of age. Children who fell into the upper quintile on the playfulness measures were labeled high playfulness while those who were in the lowest quintile were labeled low playfulness. She also collected data on anxiety experienced by the children after seeing a short film. Half of the children, in a no anxiety condition, saw a film where Lassie and her master, Cory, parachuted from a disabled airplane with Lassie falling into a raging river and Cory being knocked unconscious. The two were soon happily reunited. The other half of the children, the anxiety condition, did not see the resolution of the situation (though they did later, after the data collection). Children were then permitted to play with a number of toys in a solitary play situation, during and after which anxiety data was again collected. Analyses indicated that children in the anxiety condition did, in fact, exhibit higher anxiety than those in the no anxiety condition. Second, children in the high anxiety/low playfulness group had a higher level of anxiety following the play session than children in the other three groups. Third, children in the high anxiety group had a dramatic decrease in their level of anxiety after being allowed to play with the high anxiety/high playfulness group exhibiting a significantly larger decrease than the high anxiety/low playfulness children. Barnett's results support the notion of playfulness as a useful construct and the utility of the Children's Playfulness Scale in measuring it. In addition, her results strongly suggest that playful children are more able to restore their emotional equilibrium through play when stressors are present in their environment.

Cosby Steele Rogers, James Impara, Robert Frary, Teresa Harris, Amy Meeks, Susan Semanic-Lauth, and Mary Ruth Reynolds take a different tack in measuring playfulness. They are concerned that definitions of playfulness based on work by Lieberman (1965, 1967, 1977) may not adequately characterize the concept inasmuch as her work focused on play behaviors rather than on personality disposition. Hence, using a sample of 892 children and dispositional criteria for playfulness provided by Rubin, Fein, and Vandenberg (1983), Rogers, Impara, Frary, Harris, Meeks, Semanic-Lauth, and Reynolds developed the Child Behaviors Inventory, a 28-item trait-rating scale for measuring playfulness in children. Analysis of the psychometric properties of the inventory yielded two factors, playfulness and externality. Correlations with age, gender, and grade in school were negligible and internal consistency, inter-rater reliability, and construct validity were established. The authors found that playfulness was related to certain temperament measures as well as to some Type A behaviors. The authors conclude that playfulness appears to be a valid construct and that it appears to be distinct from external dependency. They judge the Child Behavior's Inventory to be a reliable and valid instrument for measuring children's disposition to play.

Bundy and Clifton explore the construct validity of the Children's Playfulness Scale using Rasch analysis, an alternative to the more typical factor analysis method of construct validity assessment. With Rasch analysis, construct validity is examined through rankings of item difficulty and subject ability. For a measure to be valid, items should discriminate between subjects of varying ability and subjects should score as expected on items of varying difficulty. The subjects in this study included 89 children who averaged about 61 and a half months of age. Nine of these children were enrolled in special education classes but were no more than moderately impaired in any domain. Rasch analysis suggested that three of the twenty items used from the scale (it actually has 23; three were omitted for various reasons) appear not to be part of a unidimensional scale of playfulness. In addition, Bundy and Clifton observe that the validity of the Children's Playfulness Scale may be questionable for children with disabilities (though Barnett, in her chapter, indicates that her samples have not included children with cognitive, emotional, or physical disabilities so she does not assume that the scale is valid for such individuals). These concerns aside, Bundy and Clifton indicate that the Children's Playfulness Scale is a valid means for assessing playfulness.

Unfortunately, while each of the chapters on playfulness provides information on the validity of the construct, as well as evidence for the validity of its measurement by either the Children's Playfulness Scale or the Child Behaviors Inventory, there is no data yet available on the degree of association between the two scales. Hence, the degree to which they may be measuring the same construct is unknown.

O'Brien, Boatwright, Chaplin, Geckler, Gosnell, Holcombe, and Parrish address the issue of how positioning equipment, apparatus that is is designed to provide handicapped children with support for proper body position, improved a child's ability to play. It has been generally assumed that the quality of life of a handicapped child is enhanced through play but there is no previous research on how positioning equipment improves play skills. O'Brien and her colleagues surveyed parents of children, most of whom had either cerebral palsy or spina bifida, concerning their views on the value of positioning equipment. A large majority of parents indicated that positioning equipment had a positive effect on the play skills of their children. Given that the equipment also made it easier to feed, transport, and care for their children, it lowered the stress levels in parents' lives as well.

REFERENCES

Chick, G. E., & L. A. Barnett (1995). Children's play and adult leisure. In A. D. Pellegrini (Ed.), *Play as multi-disciplinary inquiry: Essays in honor of Brian Sutton-Smith* (pp. 45-69). New York: Cambridge University Press.

Lieberman, J. N. (1965). Playfulness and divergent thinking: An investigation of their relationship at the kindergarten level. *Journal of Genetic Psychology, 107*, 219-224.

Lieberman, J. N. (1967). A developmental analysis of playfulness as a clue to cognitive style. *Journal of Creative Behavior, 1*, 391-397.

Lieberman, J. N. (1977). *Playfulness: Its relationship to imagination and creativity.* New York: Academic Press.

Rubin, K. H., Fein, G. G., & Vandenberg, B. (1983). Play. In E. M. Hetherington (Ed.), P. H. Mussen (Series Ed.), *Handbook of child psychology: Vol. 4. Socialization, personality, and social development* (pp. 693-774). New York: Wiley.

7

The Adaptive Powers of Being Playful

Lynn A. Barnett

INTRODUCTION

Virtually all of the research efforts over this century have successfully demonstrated that play is important to the young developing child. The exact nature of the way in which play serves a functional, utilitarian, or evolutionary role has been the topic of multitudes of studies and reams of paper. Collectively, we can now agree that play is worthy of study in its own right, and that the child's very survival would be severely disadvantaged should play be dramatically constrained or its natural "life" drastically altered.

THE PLAYFUL CHILD

A great deal of the research on children's play has employed an observational approach to cataloging play. Play has been defined according to observable categories of behavior that conform to specific behavioral definitions (cf. Corrigan, 1987; Enslein & Fein, 1981; Hart & Sheehan, 1986; Krasnor & Pepler, 1980; Mounts & Roopnarine, 1987; Parten, 1932; Roper & Hinde, 1978; Rubin, 1977, 1982; Smilansky, 1968; Smith, Takhvar, Gore & Vollstedt, 1985). Detailed ethnographic accounts utilize underlying structures, features, or delimiting characteristics in the facial, postural, gestural or bodily expressions of the child (cf. Blurton-Jones, 1967,

Crook & Goss-Custard, 1972; Eibl-Eibesfeldt, 1970; Kerr, 1976; Krasnor & Pepler, 1980; Loizos, 1967; McGrew, 1972; Reynolds, 1976; Smith, 1978; Smith & Connolly, 1972). Detailed naturalistic observations have been collected in home bedrooms, living rooms, and dens, backyards, school yards, alleys, playgrounds, sand lots, ball fields, camp grounds, swimming pools, video arcades, toy stores, and so forth, as well as in experimental play areas, laboratory settings, and child centers (cf. Barnett & Kruidenier, 1981; Bates, Benigni, Bretherton, Camaioni, & Volterra, 1979; Brown, Brown, & Reid, 1992; Bruner, 1974; Carvalho, Smith, Hunter, & Costabile, 1990; Doyle, Connolly, & Rivest, 1980; Dunn & Wooding, 1977; Fein, 1975; Fein & Apfel, 1979; Fein & Robertson, 1975; Fenson & Ramsay, 1980; Henninger, 1980; Labov, 1972; McLoyd, 1982; Nicolich, 1977; Rheingold & Cook, 1975; Richardson & Simpson, 1982; Riessman, 1964; Rosenblatt, 1977; Sanders & Harper, 1976; Watson & Fischer, 1977). We have chronicled the play choices, behaviors, and interactions of children in spontaneous, controlled, and manipulated environments (cf. Beller, Zimmie, & Aiken, 1971; Caldera, Huston, & O'Brien, 1989; Chaille, 1978; Connolly, Doyle, & Reznick, 1988; Creasey & Myers, 1986; Giddings & Halverson, 1981; Huston-Stein, Freidrich-Cofer, & Susman, 1977; Johnson, Ershler, & Bell, 1980; Kinsman & Berk, 1979; McLoyd, 1983; Pellegrini, 1985, 1986, 1987; Tizard, Philips, & Plewis, 1976) and with or without adults, parents, peers, supervisors, teachers or unfamiliar others (cf. Berenbaum & Hines, 1992; Berndt & Heller, 1986; Costabile, Smith, Matheson, Aston, Hunter, & Boulton, 1991; Eckerman & Stein, 1990; Fagot, 1984; Ruble, Balaban, & Cooper, 1981; Schwartz & Markham, 1985). Videotapes and observational records of children with and without toys, play structures, visual cues, or manipulable furniture or large equipment abound (cf. Almqvist, 1989; Andreas, 1969; Barnett & Wade, 1979; DiPietro, 1981; Gramza, 1970; Gramza & Scholtz, 1974; Gramza & Witt, 1969; Gramza, Corush, & Ellis, 1972; Kline & Pentecost, 1990; McLoyd, 1986; Tracy, 1987).

With this vast encyclopedia of play descriptions, it is a bit surprising to see relatively more attention focused on what the child does, rather than on the child herself and, by extension, what she brings to the environment. Sporadically throughout our literature are the suggestions by several noted authors that play be better viewed from the point of view of the player and that the environment is only of secondary and relatively minor importance.

There is evidence that young children maintain a characteristic and consistent approach, structure, and content in their behavioral repertoire (Wolf & Grollman, 1982) and that reliable and discernible characteristic features persist across a wide variety of situations, processes, and tasks (Ward, 1966, 1968; Witkin, Dye, Paterson, Goodenough, & Karp, 1962; Witkin, Goodenough, & Karp, 1967). In addition, it has been shown that each child has a unique play style, which has been linked to other personality descriptors and attributes. For example, playful sounds, playful activities, and playful interactions have been described across contexts with young infants (Papousek, Papousek, & Harris, 1987). Observational research on the incidence and appearance of imaginative play has shown that same-age peers express their imaginative play in different but consistent ways (Matthews, 1977). Some children exhibited an "imaginative predisposition" that has led them to demonstrate more symbolic play across a variety of situations than their less imaginative peers (Hudson, 1966; Minuchin, Biber, Shapiro, & Zimiles, 1969; Singer, 1973). Winner, McCarthy, Kleinman, and Gardener (1979) generated longitudinal data demonstrating that individual children differ in their expression of make-believe during spontaneous play. Also, longitudinal data from Harvard Project Zero detailed the similarity in play elements that children show from their first through their sixth birthdays (Wolf & Grollman, 1982).

Freud (1955) early presumed the relationship between play and personality, regarding the child's play as expressive of personality patterns and internal desires. Similarly, Linton (1945), Centner (1962), and Schwartzman (1978) spoke about the "playful child," emphasizing the child's natural qualities which are imposed upon any situation. Berlyne (1969) regarded play as a part of a comprehensive model of personality. Dansky and Silverman (1975) demonstrated that there is a "playful set" that can be detected in associative fluency assessments of young children.

Several authors have also speculated on the existence of a playful personality trait. Cattell (1950) and Meehl, Lykken, Schofield, and Tellegen (1971) included a playful factor as part of their respective personality inventories. Their research showed that playfulness in preschool children was captured in a "surgency" factor, related to the attributes of cheerful, joyous, humorous, witty, and energetic. Cattell's (1979) "siza-affectia" factor included the playful attributes of being good natured, laughing readily, and liking to participate with people.

Other researchers sought to more directly establish a playful characterization as a component of the child's personality. Singer and Rummo (1973) factor analyzed preschool teachers' ratings and found that three major factors resulted, one of which was playfulness. The corresponding attributes that carried similar high loadings on the playfulness factor were imaginativeness, humorous and playful attitude, emotional expressiveness, curiosity, openness, novelty-seeking, and communicativeness. Singer and her colleagues (Singer & Singer, 1978; Singer, Singer, & Sherrod, 1980) collected behavioral observations of play to examine various common factors as well as their underlying correlates. Their research supported the existence of a playfulness factor and found that children who scored high on the playfulness factor also were high on positive affect, showed high levels of physical activity, were very imaginative and social in their play, and were more verbal than their less playful preschool peers. Singer, Singer, and Sherrod (1980) recorded each child's behavior at several points in time, to explore the temporal stability of this playfulness factor. They found that the playfulness factor was significantly (but rather modestly) stable over a one-year period of time ($r = +.29, p < .05$).

Rogers, Meeks, Impara, and Frary (1987) demonstrated a relationship between the child's play and other personality dimensions, such as approachability, adaptability, persistence, aggression, impatience, competitiveness, and dependence. Barnett (1991b) found that playfulness was related to other individual descriptive characteristics, such as bright, active, aggressive, cheerful, confident, curious, dependent, imaginative, impulsive, mischievous, and responsible. The playfulness quality was not related to the attributes of affectionate, attractive, considerate, cute, disruptive, docile, obedient, temperamental, and truthful. Barnett (1991b) also found that the attributes related differentially to five components of the playfulness quality. Athey (1984) demonstrated a positive correspondence between the young child's play activities and his style of leadership, followership, cooperation, competition, teamwork, perseverance, flexibility, toughness, altruism, idealism, self-concept, emotional stability, freedom to move, power, listlessness, trust, verbal and communicative ability, object manipulativeness, autonomy, guilt, openness to new experiences, independence, initiative, indignation, comprehension, intelligence, social ability, fantasy predisposition, humor, abstraction, symbolism, creativity, problem-solving ability, exuberance, coordination, skill level, maturity, and interest in exploration.

This literature suggests that there might exist a more general playful personality trait or style that transcends situations, contexts, tasks, and materials. It would predispose the child to a certain mode of play interactions which would be fairly consistent across settings, objects, and play partners, and at the same time represent a unique representation of that individual at that point in developmental and experiential time. There is much to be gained from considering play as an integrated and necessarily complementary part of the child's self. The above evidence suggests that play is very much a part of the "inner self" of the child—it may be regarded as an aspect of the child's personality—unique to that individual but integrated into a larger interrelated coherent system. The issue now remains of how to capture this playful characterization through an appropriate and efficient means of measurement.

Lieberman's work (1965, 1966) represents one of the earliest efforts to define and delineate the essence of this general playfulness quality. From her investigations of preschool teachers' ratings of the children in their classroom, she hypothesized the existence of five components of a playfulness quality: physical spontaneity, social spontaneity, cognitive spontaneity, manifest joy, and sense of humor. Barnett and Kleiber (1982, 1984) were able to replicate Lieberman's original conceptualization of the five playfulness qualities, and support the general playfulness factor. However, they also demonstrated significant psychometric problems with the instrument, illustrated differential relationships of the five playfulness components with gender, and found that playfulness ratings were confounded with intelligence and creativity. Lieberman's (1977) own later efforts to replicate and extend her playfulness inventory were largely unsuccessful, and suggested that further refinement and testing were necessary.

In a series of studies, Barnett (Barnett,1990, 1991a, 1991b) attempted to further explore the meaning and conceptualization of the playfulness construct, as well as to refine its measurement. She confirmed the existence of the playfulness quality, illustrated its component characters, and demonstrated a reliable and valid way to capture its essence. In addition, she showed that playfulness as a construct held consistently as descriptive of a child across response types, raters, situations, and time. Playfulness is made up of five component and distinguishable dimensions of cognitive spontaneity, social spontaneity, physical spontaneity, manifest joy, and sense of humor. Each of these dimensions can be reliably and validly measured, and as well, a generalized playfulness quality can be isolated and defined. The method of measuring the playfulness factor and its five component dimensions is reliable and valid, and correlates with behavioral measures and two other play inventories and observational classification systems.

PLAY AND EMOTIONAL DEVELOPMENT

Although researchers seemed to lag behind, from rather early on, clinicians viewed a child's play as an integrated extension and rich pictorial of the self—a vivid reflection of the child's personality, dreams, fantasies, wishes, traumas, conflicts, emotions, and construction and representation of his world. Sigmund Freud (1953, 1955) regarded play as serving a central role in enabling children to deal with life circumstances, and he used this notion as the basis for his analysis of adult reactions to trauma and the functioning of the ego in attempting to master life events. Jung also drew on young children's pretend play and early on reported cases of what would later come to be called *play therapy*. Vygotsky (1976) similarly believed in the adaptive function of fantasy play in helping children cope with frustrations: "play occurs such that the explanation of why a child plays must always be interpreted as the imaginary, illusory realization of unrealizable desires" (p. 538). Many other noted therapists (cf. Erikson, 1940, 1950; A. Freud, 1965; Klein, 1955; Waelder, 1933) wrote at length about the importance of play in offering a window into the child's unconscious, and the often troubling and conflicting emotions which are present there. Anna Freud (1965) wrote about play and the fantasies underlying play as among the principal "items of childhood behavior" which are used to understand a child's unconscious:

> The well-known sublimatory occupations of painting, modeling, water, and sand play point back to anal and urethral preoccupation. The dismantling of toys because of the wish to know what is inside betrays sexual curiosity. It is even significant in which manner a small boy plays with his railway: whether his main pleasure is derived from staging crashes (as symbols of parental intercourse); whether he is predominantly concerned with building tunnels and underground lines (expressing interest in the inside of his body); whether his cars and buses have to be loaded heavily (as symbols of his pregnant mother); or whether speed and smooth performance are his main concern (as symbols of phallic efficiency). (A. Freud, 1965, p. 19)

The young child poses a dilemma for a therapist because of his inability to articulate crises and traumas, as he struggles to adequately represent his experiences. As Winnicott (1986) noted:

> Psychotherapy takes place in the overlap of two areas of playing, that of the patient and that of the therapist. Psychotherapy has to do with two people playing together. The

corollary of this is that where playing is not possible then the work done by the therapist is directed towards bringing the patient from a state of not being able to play into a
state of being able to play. (p. 38)

It is assumed that the psychologically healthy child is able to use play to organize,
articulate, and master those important aspects of his life that would otherwise cause
strain, and that play is the medium through which a child's inner world can be seen
and better understood. It seems reasonable, then, to postulate that children use play
more actively and intentionally to manipulate a distressing environment to bring about
resolution and harmony.

Waelder (1933) more explicitly described play under stressful circumstances, indicating that through pretend play, children attempt to understand and control their
highly charged emotions, they seek to repeat negative experiences in order to make
them more predictable and hence controllable, and they seek, enact, and rehearse
solutions to resolve conflicts. He suggested that there are three related processes that
children employ to accomplish these purposes: first, play serves a cathartic function
to organize and express negative emotions in an acceptable way; second, children
invent characters and themes to distance themselves from the anxiety and fear associated with a strange event (Bettelheim, 1975); and third, the child gains control over
the conflict-arousing situation by actively controlling its course rather than being the
passive recipient (Erikson, 1950; Geer, Davison, & Gatchel,1970).

There have been some efforts to experimentally test the notion that play figures
prominently and actively in the emotional adjustment of young children to the distress, conflict, and trauma posed by their environment. Gilmore (1966) conducted
three studies to systematically examine the relationship between anxiety and play in
hospitalized school-aged children. He first compared the play of hospitalized and
nonhospitalized children in the duration of play they showed with different types of
toys and in their verbalized toy preferences. He found that the hospitalized children
showed more play and expressed more preferences for hospital-related toys than did
the nonhospitalized children. However, it was not clear that the play and preference
differences could be directly attributed to the hospital children being more anxious
and distressed. In a second study, Gilmore manipulated the anxiety level of school-
aged children by giving them the opportunity to join a special club with a painful initiation ritual. The initiation ritual contained either a bright light (visual anxiety
group) or a loud noise (auditory anxiety group), and a control group was included
that had no initiation procedure. After being told about the initiation, the children
were allowed to play with a variety of toys, some of which had loud sounds, or bright
lights. Results indicated that the auditory initiation children played more with auditory toys, but there was no difference in play preferences between the visual initiation group and the control condition. In a third study, Gilmore added an auditory
control group which was told that there would be a loud noise in the initiation ceremony, but that it would be pleasant to hear. The findings indicated that all groups
showed a preference for the visual over the auditory toys; Gilmore concluded that

the auditory group was highly anxious, and that there is a curvilinear relationship between anxiety and toy preference.

Gilmore conducted two follow-up studies (Gilmore, Best, & Eakins, 1980) in which he induced test anxiety in school-age children and again examined their toy preferences. Three anxiety conditions were included (high, medium, low) by varying the instructions to the children about how important a geography test was that they were going to take. In the second study, intelligence and need achievement test scores were also taken on the children. The children were given a variety of jigsaw puzzles with which to play, that differed in terms of their difficulty and their relevance to the geography test. The authors found that as anxiety levels increased, the children's preferences for puzzle difficulty increased, but these results were dependent on intelligence and need achievement. Gilmore and his colleagues interpreted these findings to indicate that the brighter, more achievement-oriented children reacted differentially to the stress, which in turn, increased their preference for a challenging puzzle in the high test anxiety condition.

Barnett and Storm (1981) explored the relationship between play and anxiety with preschool children. A high anxiety group viewed a clip from a *Lassie* movie in which the dog gets into a dangerous situation with apparently no chance of survival. A control group viewed the same movie but with a happy resolution at the end. The salience of the theme across the movie conditions was thus held constant, a point of criticism in the earlier Gilmore research. Following the movie condition, the children were allowed the opportunity for free play, with some of the toys available to them related to the theme of the movie (Lassie toy dog, helicopter, etc.). Physiological and behavioral measures of anxiety were taken at three points in time during the study: at the start of the study to establish a baseline for each child and familiarize them with the procedure, following the movie to confirm the distressing (and nondistressing) manipulations, and also immediately upon conclusion of the play session. The results indicated that the children in the experimental group were significantly more anxious at the conclusion of their film presentation than the control group. The data also showed that the experimental group returned to their baseline anxiety level after the play session. In addition, children in the experimental group played longer with the Lassie dog, and boys in the experimental group showed more pretense and thematic play.

In a follow-up study, Barnett (1984) attempted to replicate these findings in a more naturally occurring anxiety-invoking situation. Anxiety levels of the children were assessed as they separated from their mother on the first day of preschool; these scores were then used to place the children into high and low anxiety groups. One-fourth of the children in each anxiety condition were allowed a period of free play in a social setting (other children present), one-fourth were allowed to play alone (solitary play), one-fourth listened passively to a story read aloud to them in a group setting (no play–social) and the remaining one-fourth in each anxiety group listened to the story alone (no play–solitary). Anxiety measures were taken again at the conclusion of the play or story session. The findings indicated that the highly anxious children in the free play condition showed a greater decrease in anxiety than their comparable peers in the story conditions. In addition, the children in the high anxiety condition showed more pretend play than any other play form. The conclusions from these two studies are that play serves an important function in the child's emotional development by actively allowing her to imaginatively engage with his environment to reduce the stressors impinging upon her. In addition, the opportunity for solitary play is important as the data indicated that the presence of other children appeared to have an inhibiting effect on the child's ability to reduce her anxiety.

Watson (1994) also attempted to experimentally demonstrate a link between anxiety and pretend play in preschool-age children. In his three studies, young children listened to a tape recording of *Hansel and Gretel*, accompanied by scary music and sound effects. Observers watched the children while they were listening to the tape, and divided them into low, medium, and high anxiety groups based on their reactions. Each child was then left alone in a room and told he could play with one of four sets of toys: high fantasy toys relevant to the tape theme, high fantasy toys irrelevant to the theme of the tape, low fantasy toys relevant to the tape, or low fantasy toys irrelevant to the tape (low fantasy toys are coloring sheets and markers). Results showed no relationship between anxiety and the incidence of pretend play among the children; however, the medium anxiety subjects did show more relevant play than other forms of play and more than the high and low anxiety subjects. In the second study, procedures were essentially similar, with the addition of an anxiety-reduction measure computed before and after the play session. The second study produced nonsignificant findings: no relationship between anxiety and pretend play was found. In study three, a larger sample size was used and mothers were allowed to stay in the room with their child. A doctored version of the *Hansel and Gretel* story was used in the following way: children in the high anxiety condition saw the actual story, those in the low anxiety group saw a film about a witch who tried to frighten people but instead made them laugh, and in the nonanxiety condition the children saw an amusing film about a monkey. A free play session again followed the manipulations; one of the four toy sets from the previous study was present in the play room. The findings from this latter study were mixed: no relationships between anxiety (film type) and preferred toy, degree of fantasy play shown, or relevance/irrelevance of the toys was evident. In addition, the children in the high anxiety condition showed the greatest reduction in anxiety but they also had the most room to move scores. No relationship between changes in anxiety and amount or type of pretend play was observed. The author concluded further research was needed to more empirically and systematically test the relationship between children's play and anxiety.

FOCUS OF THE STUDY

The present study attempts to pull these literatures together. There is some preliminary evidence that a general playfulness trait can be posited, at least for young children. And similarly, there is also some preliminary experimental evidence that suggests that play helps the young child to neutralize or work through sources of distress posed by her environment. While some of the scant research in this latter area has not provided clear and conclusive findings, it can be argued that, following the first line of inquiry, the focus should have been on measures of the child's playful qualities and not on attempting to define and measure specific observable behaviors labeled pretense play. Thus, the research presented here will attempt to first, gather additional data to further confirm the existence of the playfulness quality; and second, to explore further the role of play in anxiety reduction by defining play as a characteristic of the child with no attempt to categorize or chart observable behaviors (and thereby make inferences as to whether or not they constitute play).

METHOD

Children

One hundred and twenty-two children, from three local day care centers, were participants in this study. The children ranged in age from 30.3 months to 62.8 months at the time of data collection (M age = 44.67 months); 58 children were male and 64 were female. The children were all attending their respective day care center full-time, were of normal intelligence (both verbal and nonverbal), and from intact homes (both parents in the home throughout the course of the study). The children were all of middle socio-economic status; none of the children were receiving any type of financial assistance to attend their day care program. Parental consent was obtained prior to all children participating in the study.

Instrumentation

Playfulness

The Children's Playfulness Scale (Barnett, 1990, 1991a, 1991b) was used as the primary measure of playfulness in this study. The scale comprises 23 items, in Likert-type format using a five-point response scale: "sounds exactly like the child," "sounds a lot like the child," "sounds somewhat like the child," "sounds a little like the child," and "doesn't sound at all like the child." The 23 statements are presented, and the rater is asked to indicate the extent to which the statement is characteristic of the child being rated by selecting one of the five responses. The instructions are standardized and printed at the top of the form; several of the items are inverted in wording to minimize the appearance of a response set.

Measures of Anxiety

Two primary measures of anxiety were taken, following from previous research (Barnett & Storm, 1981; Barnett, 1984). The first was the Palmar Sweat Index (PSI), which has been found in previous research to be a reliable indicator of changes in anxiety in young children (cf. Dabbs, Johnson, & Leventhal, 1968; Harrison &

MacKinnon, 1966; Johnson & Dabbs, 1967; Martens, 1969a, 1969b). Administration of the PSI involves cleaning the child's ring finger to remove excess sweat and dirt, coating the finger with a black ink-type chemical solution, putting a piece of cellophane tape over the coated finger after allowing the solution a minute to dry, and then pulling the tape off with the solution adhering to the tape. The tape is then put on a glass slide, enlarged fifteen times, a 36-cell grid is superimposed, and the number of white dots (active sweat gland secretions) are counted and recorded.

The second measure of anxiety was a paper and pencil test (PPT). Each child was shown a sheet of paper with five faces shown in an ordinal position from top to bottom. The face at the top had a wide grin, while the one at the bottom showed a distinct frown. Each child was asked to describe the faces in a familiarization session to determine that he understood the meaning, range, and positional ranking of the faces. The child was instructed to color the face that showed his feelings right at the moment during the actual testing sessions.

PROCEDURES

Following parental permission, day care classroom teachers were each asked to complete the Children's Playfulness Scale (CPS) on the children in their room for whom consent had been given. They were individually shown the form, given a sample child to evaluate, and questions were discussed and answered. The teachers were each told to complete the forms without conferring with anyone else, and to rate only the children they felt they knew well. They were given two weeks to complete and return the form directly to the experimenter.

After all of the CPS forms were returned, preliminary analyses were conducted on the CPS data to explore its measurement properties and seek to demonstrate the scale to be reliable and valid. Once it was determined that the playfulness ratings could be used and that the teachers were in agreement with each other in their playfulness rating of the children, the mean rating scores were then used to determine high and low playfulness groups. For the playfulness composite data, as well as for the five individual dimension mean scores, the upper and lower quintiles were determined. Children who fell within the upper quintile on all six calculations were labeled High Playfulness and those who consistently fell within the lower quintile on all six distributions were called Low Playfulness. Of the initial 122 children, 21 (14 boys and 7 girls) comprised the High Playfulness group, and 14 (5 boys and 9 girls) were in the Low Playfulness group. One-half of each of the boys and girls in each of the Low Playfulness and High Playfulness groups was randomly assigned to the experimental treatment (movie manipulation).

An experimenter then went to each of the children's classrooms to conduct a familiarization session. She showed all of the children how their finger would be wiped off, how the "black ink" would be applied, and how it would then be magically removed with a piece of tape. Each of the children had a turn at trying out the ink procedure and several asked to repeat it two or more times. These scores were obtained as a baseline measure for each child. The following day, the experimenter visited the classroom, accompanied the specially designated individual child to a small area in a nearby room, and collected the PSI data (to obtain an individual baseline score and to ascertain that the child was not anxious). The child was then told she would be viewing a short movie about a dog named Lassie, and the movie was started. When the film was over, the experimenter came over to the child, collected the PSI data, and administered the paper and pencil test. Following this, the child was taken to an adjoining room where she was told she could play with anything in the room in any way he chose. The toys in the room were the following: Lassie toy dog, stuffed poodle dog, two wooden puzzles (one with a dog on it), three cans of play-dough, helicopter, boat, dishes and cups, boy doll, girl doll, wooden blocks, Legos, and Sesame Street sewing cards.

After the first four minutes of the play session, the experimenter entered the room and asked the child if she would agree to allow the experimenter to "play the ink-tape game" (i.e., obtain the PSI data). At that time, he was also asked to "color the face to show how he feels right now" (PPT data). When the play session was over, the child was again asked to provide the PSI data and complete the pencil and paper test. She was escorted back to her classroom by the experimenter and thanked for her participation.

All behavior during this session was videotaped through a one-way mirror in the play room; none of the children were aware of the camera or monitor in the adjoining room. The play session was solitary play since previous research (Barnett, 1984) indicated that social play (the presence of others) had an inhibiting effect on the child's ability to reduce his level of distress/anxiety. These observational data are not included in this presentation of the findings.

The concluding portion of the *Lassie* film differed for one-half of the children. The film clip opens with Lassie and Cory (her master) flying in a small plane in an electrical storm. The storm forces Cory to parachute from the plane holding Lassie in his arms. Cory lands on a rocky cliff, falls, is knocked unconscious, and Lassie tumbles down the cliff into the raging river below. At this point, the film clip ends for the Anxiety Condition. The No Anxiety Condition viewed the same film with an additional 30-second scene in which Lassie crawls out of the water onto a sandy bank where Cory is waiting to dry her off and hug her. Following the play session for the Anxiety Condition, the children were each shown the additional film segment with the happy resolution where Lassie is reunited with her master.

ANALYSIS AND RESULTS

Measuring Playfulness

A minimum of two playfulness ratings from the CPS were obtained for each participant in the study. In every classroom, there was at least two full-time teachers, and in a few classrooms three or more teachers provided CPS ratings on the children. Correlations were computed on these multiple teacher ratings for each child in each classroom, using the individual item responses. All correlations were highly statistically significant (all $p < .001$ or better), and none were below $r = +.922$. Thus, in all subsequent analyses, a mean teacher rating per item was used for each child.

Cronbach alpha reliability estimates of internal consistency were calculated for each of the five playfulness dimensions, as well as for the global playfulness composite. These internal consistency reliability measures were all statistically significant (all $p < .001$ or better), indicating the five playfulness dimensions were again found to be supported by the individual items within them. The alpha coefficients for the dimensions were as follows: physical spontaneity $r = +.87$, social spontaneity $r = +.82$, cognitive spontaneity $r = +.77$, manifest joy $r = +.80$, and sense of humor $r = +.72$. The overall playfulness composite produced an alpha reliability coefficient of $r = +.81$.

The next step in this process was to explore the validity of the CPS using the mean item ratings as input data. A principal-components factor analysis with the squared multiple correlation for each as the communality estimate was adopted. This procedure explored the general validity of the scale by calculating the individual factor patterns and determining the extent to which the scale structure was maintained across the schools. Similar findings were obtained across the three schools under study. The factor structure for each showed that six dominant factors emerged from the sample solution. These factors accounted for over 72 percent of the common variance. The first six factors in each solution were then rotated using the varimax criterion. Factor-scoring weights were then used to calculate regression estimates for the component playfulness dimensions. These estimated factor scores were then correlated with the individual playfulness item scores. The results indicated that the anticipated convergent/discriminant item/factor pattern did emerge. Inspection of the playfulness factors shows that the individual playfulness items are highly correlated with their appropriately corresponding regression-based factor scores. That is, the convergent correlations are all high (ranging from .60 to .86), and simultaneously, the discriminant correlations are all low (ranging from −.01 to .12).

Additional factor analyses were undertaken to demonstrate the validity of the individual items on the CPS. Again, the item scores used in the analysis were the mean teacher ratings for each of the schools that participated in the study. The mean item scores were factor analyzed using the principal-components factor analysis with squared multiple correlations as the initial communality estimates for each school sample data set. The composite findings of the factor analyses indicate that the six factors accounted for most of the common variance in each of the solutions: 75.90 percent in one school, 77.14 percent in the second school, and 71.24 percent in the third school. All of the items showed consistently strong primary loadings (all above .65) on their corresponding factor as well as low secondary loadings on the other playfulness factors (all below .31). (The results of all of the factor analyses and regression analyses are not reproduced here for the sake of brevity; they are readily available from the author upon request.)

Playfulness and Anxiety

The first step in our experimental exploration of the relationship between playfulness and anxiety was to determine that the children were all equivalent at the start of the study. To accomplish this, three separate 2×2 (all possible two-factor combinations of Playfulness × Anxiety Group × Gender) within-subject factorial designs were subjected to analysis of variance (ANOVA) procedures using the PSI as the dependent variable. These were calculated, rather than using one three-factor design because of the small cell sizes when all three factors were included simultaneously. Results indicated no significant differences as a function of any of the main effects or interactions. Regardless of level of playfulness, boys and girls were equal in their anxiety level before the start of the movie manipulation; no differences in experimental groups were evident prior to the manipulation. (Further analyses explored the role of gender, but since no significant effects were ever obtained, they are omitted from the following narrative.)

The introduction of the movie manipulation was intended to create anxiety in one group, and not in the other. To validate this experimental manipulation, a 2×2 (Playfulness × Anxiety Group) ANOVA was computed on the PSI data collected immediately following the movie. Results indicated a significant Anxiety Group main effect ($F = 7.14$, $df = 1,31$; $p < .015$); cell means showed that the children who viewed the high anxiety movie (unresolved *Lassie* film clip) had a significantly higher anxiety level than the No Anxiety condition at the conclusion of their respective movie (see Figure 1). Thus, the films were having the intended effect. In addition, playfulness levels did not produce differential reactions ($p > .05$).

The actual test of the hypothesized effect of play in the reduction of anxiety involved examining the PSI data directly following the play session. The post-play PSI data was subjected to ANOVA procedures using a 2×2 factorial design (Playfulness × Anxiety Group). The results of the analysis indicated a signficant Playfulness × Anxiety Group interaction ($F = 5.88$, $df = 1,31$; $p < .03$). Scheffe post-hoc tests indicated that the children in the High Anxiety/Low Playfulness Group had a higher level of anxiety following the play session than the children in the other three groups. There was no difference in PSI data between any of the low anxiety children and the High Anxiety/High Playfulness Group (see Figure 1).

Additional analyses employed PSI difference scores to examine changes in anxiety between the start (post-movie manipulation) and conclusion of the play session. A 2×2 ANOVA (Playfulness × Anxiety Group) explored the extent to which the children actually decreased their anxiety levels after being afforded an opportunity to play, and whether their ability to do so was differentially effected by levels of playfulness or the content of the movie they viewed. The findings indicated that the children in the Low Anxiety Group showed no change in PSI anxiety levels from the post-film to post-play periods. In contrast, a significant main effect of Anxiety Group ($F = 10.27$, $df = 1,31$; $p < .001$) showed that the high anxiety children demonstrated a dramatic decrease in their PSI level after being allowed the opportunity to play. In addition,

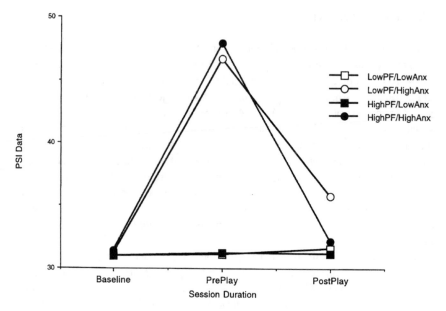

FIGURE 1. Cell means for playfulness × anxiety group across session for PSI data.

Scheffe post-hoc tests conducted on the significant Anxiety Group × Playfulness inter-action ($F = 7.41$, $df = 1,31$; $p < .017$) indicated that the High Anxiety/High Playfulness Group reduced their anxiety level more dramatically across the session than the High Anxiety/Low Playfulness Group. Figure 1 illustrates these data and graphically depicts the changes across time and differences between the playfulness and anxiety groups.

It was also of interest to examine the results from the pencil and paper test. While unarguably not a measure of anxiety, the ratings do provide some indication of the level of distress the child is feeling. Data analyses identical to those indicated above with the PSI scores were also computed for the PPT data. The results with the PPT data virtually mirrored those obtained with the PSI data, indicating that the PSI data does in fact provide a measure of the distress the child is experiencing, and it is relat-ed to his anxiety level.

Preliminary analyses with gender first nested within playfulness and then within anxiety group also yielded no PPT differences (all $p > .05$). Boys and girls through-out the study appeared to react similarly to the experimental manipulations, and play-fulness did not differentially effect boys in a manner different than the girls.

As with the PSI data, it was first important to demonstrate that the children were all comfortable and relatively happy at the start of the study. A 2×2 (Playfulness × Anxiety Group) ANOVA was conducted on the baseline PPT data col-lected before the movie was introduced. The results of the analysis indicated no dif-ferences in PPT between any of the children, including those high or low in the playfulness quality ($p > .05$).

The film manipulations produced the desired experimental effects on the children: results of the ANOVA on post-film (pre-play) PPT data showed the High Anxiety Group was indeed more distressed than the Low Anxiety Group ($F = 7.76$, $df = 1,31$; $p < .01$); differences due to playfulness were negligible ($p > .05$). Further analyses of the PPT data following the play session showed the children were all at about the same level—no differences were found between the feelings reported by the children as a function of the anxiety manipulation or playfulness ($p > .05$). This was a bit surprising considering the PSI data which indicated the High Anxiety/High Playfulness Group was more anxious than the others following the play session. It appears that while these children may have shown higher physiological anxiety scores, they were not feeling measurably more distressed (at least as shown on a five-point "face" scale).

Finally, when changes in PPT were examined across time, the effects of anxiety again were demonstrated ($F = 12.49$, $df = 1,31$; $p < .001$). The High Anxiety children showed a drastic reduction in their reports of feeling distressed after being allowed the opportunity to play, whereas the Low Anxiety children were consistently happy from pre- to post-play times. Figure 2 graphically depicts this data, illustrating changes in the PPT data across time, and in group and manipulation comparisons.

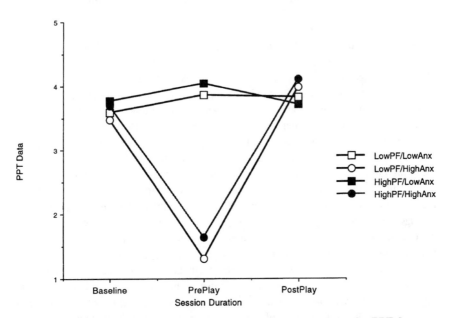

FIGURE 2.   Cell means for playfulness × anxiety group across session for PPT data.

DISCUSSION AND CONCLUSIONS

This research attempted to address two questions. The first was to provide data to (hopefully) advance yet another step in an ongoing exploration of the playfulness construct. The study gathered data to reflect on the generalizability of the playfulness construct, and to further probe its reliability and validity qualifications.

Three additional samples of preschool children provided data on the use of the Children's Playfulness Scale to both define and measure playfulness. Playfulness is conceived as a relatively stable measure of the extent to which a child consistently demonstrates what the previous observational literature has labeled playful behaviors. These consist of the physical dimension wherein we witness the energy expenditure and physical challenge and risk elements (physical spontaneity), the fine motor manipulations and symbolic activity as in imaginary themes and roles and the use of pretense (cognitive spontaneity), the cooperative and competitive interactions with others and the apparent ease or lack of it as well as the leader-follower characterization (social spontaneity), the affective quality so evident in the spontaneity and exuberance of various play interactions both alone and with others (manifest joy), and the verbalizations and mimicry and imitative rhyming that has so often been noted in play sessions (sense of humor).

The data reflected favorably on the existence of a general playfulness quality, on its five component dimensions as noted above, and on our ability to successfully capture it, at least with the children within the age range collected here. In conjunction with previous research (Barnett, 1990, 1991a, 1991b), the Children's Playfulness Scale does appear to be a reliable and valid indicator of a child's playful quality.

The playfulness data reported here derived from teacher ratings at three different schools, with children ranging in age from about two to six years. While this is an age range that has been the subject of a great deal of empirical attention, it also has unique play characteristics as has been noted by many observers. There are few who would question the differences in the play of a toddler compared to a kindergartner, yet while their behavioral manifestations differ, their levels of playfulness might well be comparable. The data presented here represent a wide age range (for the play literature, at least), but we intentionally made no effort to separate the children into age groups. It was of interest, rather, to explore differences as a function of the playful character of the child, rather than as a function of what the specific toy is that he chooses or what he specifically does with it. When the children were divided into quintiles based on their playfulness ratings, we did examine these quintiles to determine if children of one age were more likely to be represented at a certain place on the distribution. There were no discernible age clusters anywhere along the playfulness continuum. Further research is clearly warranted to more directly test this hypothesis.

A second question to which we directed our attention in this research was to explore the way in which playfulness operates within the child, particularly within one important arena. Play as a mainstay in the psychological treatment of young children has a long history. The play of troubled children has been shown to be highly disorganized, vague, and primitive at times; and at other times, there is minimal make-believe or sociodramatic play (cf. Hellendoorn, 1994; McConkey, 1994; Mogford-Bevan, 1994; Scarlett, 1994; Singer, 1994; Slade, 1994; Smilansky, 1968). Perhaps children who are more playful are more effective and efficient at dealing with problems and distress in their environment. This was the thrust of the present investigation: to explore the role of playfulness in helping the child adjust his environment to reduce the distressing effects of an anxiety-invoking event.

Preliminary support was found for the notion that playful children might manage their environment through play to achieve a desirable emotional state. The playful preschool children in this study showed themselves to be quite effective at restoring a happy equilibrium when their environment posed a source of distress. While play again showed itself to be a powerful way to reduce anxiety (all of the anxious children returned to baseline comfort following play), the more playful children achieved this to a greater extent than the less playful children.

This appears to the author to be a compelling finding, and one that holds promise for continued examination of the role of play in the child's development. If we believe that play is in some way preparatory for adulthood (or at least later childhood), then the playful quality is a highly adaptive one to have. If, rather, we are skeptical about the longer-term effects of play, then at least in the short term, a playful predisposition is eminently helpful to a content disposition.

It is not the intent of the author to suggest that the findings about the relationship between anxiety and playfulness should be extended to children with severe emotional, cognitive, affective, or physical problems. The only data that has been brought to bear on this relationship has been collected with a relatively homogeneous group of middle class, racially unbalanced, preschool children, who are functioning at a relatively normal level and fairly integrated into a day care system. This presents a fairly significant challenge to those interested in the playful characterization of a child, and extreme caution should be exercised in its generalization beyond the homogeneous group noted above.

All of the above still leaves us with the queasy feeling that there is much to learn, much to be done. If we confront these questions with the drive and the seriousness that play deserves, we should advance in our knowledge and understanding of so potentially rich a construct as playfulness.

REFERENCES

Almqvist, R. (1989). Age and gender differences in children's Christmas requests. *Play & Culture*, 2, 2–19.

Andreas, C. (1969). War toys and the peace movement. *Journal of Social Issues*, 25, 83–99.

Athey, I. (1984). Contributions of play to development. In T. D. Yawkey & A. D. Pellegrini (Eds.), *Child's play: Developmental and applied*. Hillsdale, NJ: Lawrence Erlbaum.

Barnett, L. A. (1984). Young children's resolution of distress through play. *Journal of Child Psychology & Psychiatry*, 25, 477–483.

Barnett, L. A. (1990). Playfulness: Definition, design, and measurement. *Play & Culture, 3,* 319–336.

Barnett, L. A. (1991a). The playful child: Measurement of a disposition to play. *Play & Culture, 4,* 51–74.

Barnett, L. A. (1991b). Characterizing playfulness: Correlates with individual attributes and personality traits. *Play & Culture, 4,* 371–393.

Barnett, L. A., & Kleiber, D. A. (1982). Concomitants of playfulness in early childhood: Cognitive abilities and gender. *Journal of Genetic Psychology, 141,* 115–127.

Barnett, L. A., & Kleiber, D. A. (1984). Playfulness and the early play environment. *Journal of Genetic Psychology, 144,* 153–164.

Barnett, L. A., & Kruidenier, W. P. (1981). The effects of encapsulation on preschool children's imaginative play. *Journal of Leisure Research, 13,* 323–336.

Barnett, L. A., & Storm, B. (1981). Play, pleasure, and pain: The reduction of anxiety through play. *Leisure Sciences, 4,* 161–175.

Barnett, L. A., & Wade, M. G. (1979). Children's play and the processing of information: An integrative study. *Leisure Sciences, 2,* 13–38.

Bates, E., Benigni, L., Bretherton, I., Camaioni, L., & Volterra, V. (1979). *The emergence of symbols: Cognition and communication in infancy.* New York: Academic Press.

Beller, E. K., Zimmie, J., & Aiken, L. (1971). *Levels of play in different nursery settings.* Liege, Belgium: International Congress of Applied Psychology.

Berenbaum, S. A., & Hines, M. (1992). Early androgens are related to childhood sex-typed toy preferences. *Psychological Science, 3,* 203–206.

Berlyne, D. E. (1969). Laughter, humor, and play. In G. Lindzey & E. Aronson (Eds.), *The handbook of social psychology* (Vol. 3). Reading, MA: Addison-Wesley.

Berndt, T. J., & Heller, K. A. (1986). Gender stereotypes and social influence: A developmental study. *Journal of Personality and Social Psychology, 50,* 889–898.

Bettelheim, B. (1975). *The uses of enchantment: The meaning and importance of fairy tales.* New York: Knopf.

Blurton-Jones, N. G. (1967). An ethological study of some aspects of social behavior of children in nursery school. In D. Morris (Ed.), *Primate ethology.* London: Weidenfeld & Nicholson.

Blurton-Jones, N. G. (1972). Categories of child-child interaction. In D. Morris (Ed.), *Ethological studies of child behaviour.* Cambridge, England: Cambridge University Press.

Brown, R. M., Brown, N. L., & Reid, K. (1992). Evidence for a player's position advantage in a videogame. *Perceptual and Motor Skills, 74,* 547–554.

Bruner, J. S. (1974). Child's play. *New Scientist, 62,* 126–128.

Caldera, Y., Huston, A., & O'Brien, M. (1989). Social interactions and actions and play patterns of parents and toddlers with feminine, masculine and neutral toys. *Child Development, 60,* 70–76.

Carvalho, A. M. A., Smith, P. K., Hunter, T., & Costabile, A. (1990). Playground activities for boys and girls: Developmental and cultural trends in children's perceptions of gender differences. *Play & Culture, 3,* 343–347.

Cattell, R. B. (1950). *Personality.* New York: McGraw-Hill.

Cattell, R. B. (1979). Personality and learning theory: Vol. 1. The structure of personality in its environment. New York: Springer.

Centner, T. (1962). *L'enfant africain et ses jeux.* Elisabethville, Zaire: CEPSI.

Chaille, C. (1978). The child's conceptions of play, pretending, and toys: Sequences and structural parallels. *Human Development, 21*, 201–210.

Connolly, J., Doyle, A-B., & Reznick, E. (1988). Social pretend play and social interaction in preschoolers. *Journal of Applied Developmental Psychology, 9*, 301–313.

Corrigan, R. (1987). A developmental sequence of actor-object pretend play in young children. *Merrill-Palmer Quarterly, 33*, 87–106.

Costabile, A., Smith, P. K., Matheson, L., Aston, J., Hunter, T., & Boulton, M. (1991). Cross-national comparison of how children distinguish serious and playful fighting. *Developmental Psychology, 27*, 881–887.

Creasey, G., & Myers, B. (1986). Video games and children: Effects on leisure activities, schoolwork, and peer involvement. *Merrill-Palmer Quarterly, 32*, 251–261.

Crook J. H., & Goss-Custard, J. D. (1972). Social ethology. In P. H. Mussen & M. R. Rosenzweig (Eds.), *Annual review of psychology,* (Vol. 23). Palo Alto, CA: Annual Reviews, Inc.

Dabbs, J. M., Johnson, J. E., & Leventhal, H. (1968). Palmar sweating: a quick and simple measure. *Journal of Experimental Psychology, 78*, 347–350.

Dansky, J. L., & Silverman, I. W. (1975). Effects of play on associative fluency in preschool-aged children. *Developmental Psychology, 9*, 38–43.

DiPietro, J. (1981). Rough and tumble play: A function of gender. *Developmental Psychology, 17*, 50–58.

Doyle, A. B., Connolly, J., & Rivest, L. (1980). The effect of playmate familiarity on social interactions of young children. *Child Development, 51*, 217–223.

Dunn, J., & Wooding, C. (1977). Play at home and its implications for learning. In B. Tizard & D. Harvey (Eds.), *The biology of play*. London: William Heinemann Medical Books.

Eckerman, C. O., & Stein, M. R. (1990). How imitation begets imitation and toddlers' generation of games. *Developmental Psychology, 26*, 370–378.

Eibl-Eibesfeldt, I. (1970). *Ethology: The biology of behavior*. New York: Holt, Rinehart & Winston.

Enslein, J., & Fein, G. G. (1981). Temporal and cross-situational stability of children's social and play behavior. *Developmental Psychology, 71*, 760–761.

Erikson, E. H. (1940). Studies in the interpretation of play: (1) Clinical observations of play disruption in young children. *Genetic Psychology, 22*, 563–564.

Erikson, E. H. (1950). *Childhood and society*. New York: Norton.

Fagot, B. I. (1984). Teacher and peer reactions to boys' and girls' play styles. *Sex Roles, 11*, 691–702.

Fein, G. G. (1975). A transformational analysis of pretending. *Developmental Psychology, 11*, 291–296.

Fein, G. G., & Apfel, N. (1979). Some preliminary observations on knowing and pretending. In N. Smith & M. Franklin (Eds.), *Symbolic functioning in childhood*. Hillsdale, NJ: Lawrence Erlbaum.

Fein, G. G., & Robertson, A. R. (1975). Cognitive and social dimensions of pretending in two-year-olds. ERIC Document Reproductive Service No. ED 119806.

Fenson, L., & Ramsay, D. (1980). Decentration and integration of the child's play in the second year. *Child Development, 51*, 171–178.

Freud, A. (1965). *Normality and pathology in childhood*. New York: International Universities Press.

Freud, S. (1953). Analysis of a phobia in a five year old boy. In *Collected papers, Volume III*. London: Hogarth.

Freud, S. (1955). Beyond the pleasure principle. In J. Strachey (Ed.), *The standard edition of the complete psychological works of S. Freud, Vol. VXIII*. London: Hogarth and the Institute of Psychoanalysis.

Geer, J. H., Davison, G. C., & Gatchel, R. I. (1970). Reduction of stress in humans through nonveridical perceived control of aversive stimulation. *Journal of Personality and Social Psychology, 16*, 731–738.

Giddings, M., & Halverson, C. F. (1981). Young children's use of toys in home environments. *Family Relations, 30*, 69–74.

Gilmore, J. B. (1966). The role of anxiety and cognitive factors in children's play behavior. *Child Development, 37*, 397–416.

Gilmore, J. B., Best, H., & Eakins, S. L. (1980). Coping with test anxiety: Individual differences in seeking complex play materials. *Canadian Journal of Behavioural Science, 12*, 241–254.

Gramza, A. F. (1970). Preferences of preschool children for enterable play boxes. *Perceptual and Motor Skills, 31*, 177–178.

Gramza, A. F., & Scholtz, J. G. L. (1974). Children's responses to visual complexity in a play setting. *Psychological Reports, 35*, 895–899.

Gramza, A. F., & Witt, P. A. (1969). Choices of colored blocks in the play of preschool children. *Perceptual and Motor Skills, 29*, 783–787.

Gramza, A. F., Corush, J., & Ellis, M. J. (1972). Children's play on trestles differing in complexity: A study of play equipment design. *Journal of Leisure Research, 4*, 303–311.

Harrison, J., & MacKinnon, P. C. B. (1966). Physiological role of the adrenal medulla in the palmar anihidrotic response to stress. *Journal of Applied Psychology, 21*, 88–92.

Hart, C., & Sheehan, R. (1986). Preschoolers' play behavior in outdoor environments: Effects of traditional and contemporary playgrounds. *American Educational Research Journal, 23*, 668–678.

Hellendoorn, J. (1994). Imaginative play training for severely retarded children. In J. Hellendoorn, R. van der Kooij, & B. Sutton-Smith (Eds.), *Play and intervention*. Albany, NY: State University of New York Press.

Henninger, M. L. (1980). Free play behaviors of nursery school children in an indoor and outdoor environment. In P. F. Wilkinson (Ed.), *In celebration of play*. New York: St. Martin's Press.

Hudson, L. (1966). *Contrary imaginations*. New York: Schocken.

Huston-Stein, A., Friedrich-Cofer, L., & Susman, E. J. (1977). The relation of the classroom structure to social behavior, imaginative play, and self-regulation of economically disadvantaged children. *Child Development, 48*, 908–916.

Johnson, J. E., & Dabbs, J. M. Jr. (1967). Enumeration of active sweat glands: A simple physiological indicator of psychological changes. *Nursing Research, 16*, 273–276.

Johnson, J. E., Ershler, J., & Bell, C. (1980). Play behavior in a discovery-based and a formal education preschool program. *Child Development, 51*, 271–274.

Kerr, M. K. (1976). *Patterns of social group structure, interpersonal spacing and behavior in young children*. Unpublished doctoral dissertation, University of Minnesota.

Kinsman, C. A., & Berk, L. E. (1979). Joining the block and housekeeping areas. *Young Children, 35*, 66–75.

Klein, M. (1955). The psychoanalytic play technique. *American Journal of Orthopsychiatry, 25*, 223–237.

Kline, S., & Pentecost, D. (1990). The characterization of play: Marketing children's toys. *Play & Culture, 3*, 235–255.

Krasnor, L. R., & Pepler, D. J. (1980). The study of children's play: Some suggested directions. In K. H. Rubin (Ed.), *Children's play*. San Francisco: Jossey-Bass.

Labov, W. (1972). *Language in the inner city: Studies in the black English vernacular*. Philadelphia: University of Pennsylvania Press.

Lieberman, J. N. (1965). Playfulness and divergent thinking: An investigation of their relationship at the kindergarten level. *Journal of Genetic Psychology, 107*, 219–224.

Lieberman, J. N. (1966). Playfulness: An attempt to conceptualize a quality of play and of the player. *Psychological Reports, 19*, 1978.

Lieberman, J. N. (1977). *Playfulness: Its relationship to imagination and creativity*. New York: Academic Press.

Linton, R. (1945). *The cultural background of personality*. New York: D. Appleton Century.

Loizos, C. (1967). Play behavior in higher primates: A review. In D. Morris (Ed.), *Primate ethology*. Chicago: Aldine.

Martens, R. (1969a). Palmar sweating and the presence of an audience. *Journal of Experimental Social Psychology, 5*, 371–374.

Martens, R. (1969b). The palmar sweat print technique. Internal report, Children's Research Center, University of Illinois, Urbana, IL.

Matthews, W. S. (1977). Modes of transformation in the initiation of fantasy play. *Developmental Psychology, 13*, 211–216.

McConkey, R. (1994). Families at play: Interventions for children with developmental handicaps. In J. Hellendoorn, R. van der Kooij, & B. Sutton-Smith (Eds.), *Play and intervention*. Albany, NY: State University of New York Press.

McGrew, W. C. (1972). *An ethological study of children's behavior*. London: Academic Press.

McLoyd, V. (1982). Social class differences in sociodramatic play: A critical review. *Developmental Review, 2*, 1–30.

McLoyd, V. (1983). The effects of the structure of play objects on the pretend play of low-income children. *Child Development, 54*, 626–635.

McLoyd, V. (1986). Scaffolds or shackles? The role of toys in preschool children's pretend play. In G. Fein & M. Rivkin (Eds.), *The young child at play: Reviews of research*, (Vol. 4). Washington, D.C.: National Association for the Education of Young Children.

Meehl, P. E., Lykken, D. T., Schofield, W., & Tellegen, A. (1971). Recaptured-item technique (RIT): A method for reducing somewhat the subjective element in factor naming. *Journal of Experimental Research in Personality, 5*, 171–190.

Minuchin, P., Biber, B., Shapiro, E., & Zimiles, H. (1969). *The psychological impact of school experience*. New York: Basic Books.

Mogford-Bevan, K. P. (1994). Play assessment for play-based intervention: A first step with young children with communication difficulties. In J. Hellendoorn, R. van der Kooij, & B. Sutton-Smith (Eds.), *Play and intervention*. Albany, NY: State University of New York Press.

Mounts, N., & Roopnarine, J. (1987). Social-cognitive play patterns in same-age and mixed-age preschool classrooms. *American Educational Research Journal, 24*, 463–476.

Nicolich, L. M. (1977). Beyond sensorimotor intelligence: Assessment of symbolic maturity through analysis of pretend play. *Merrill-Palmer Quarterly, 23*, 89–99.

Papousek, M., Papousek, H., & Harris, B. J. (1987). The emergence of play in parent-infant interactions. In D. Gorlitz & J. F. Wohlwill (Eds.), *Curiosity, imagination, and play: On the development of spontaneous cognitive and motivational processes*. Hillsdale, NJ: Lawrence Erlbaum.

Parten, M. B. (1932). Social participation among preschool children. *Journal of Abnormal and Social Psychology, 27*, 243–269.

Pellegrini, A. D. (1985). The narrative organization of children's fantasy play: The effects of age and play context. *Educational Psychology, 5*, 17–25.

Pellegrini, A. D. (1986). Play centers and the production of imaginative language. *Discourse Processes, 9*, 115–125.

Pellegrini, A. D. (1987). The effect of play context on the development of children's verbalized fantasy. *Semiotica, 65*, 285–293.

Reynolds, P. (1976). Play, language, and human evolution. In J. Bruner, A. Jolly, & K. Sylva (Eds.), *Play: Its role in development and evolution*. New York: Basic Books.

Rheingold, H., & Cook, K. V. (1975). The contents of boys' and girls' rooms as an index of parents' behavior. *Child Development, 46*, 459–463.

Richardson, J. G., & Simpson, C. G. (1982). Children, gender, and social structure: An analysis of the contents of letters to Santa Claus. *Child Development, 53*, 429–436.

Riessman, F. (1964). The overlooked positives of disadvantaged groups. *Journal of Negro Education, 33*, 225–231.

Rogers, C. S., Meeks, A. M., Impara, J. C., & Frary, R. (1987). Measuring playfulness: Development of the child behaviors inventory of playfulness. Paper presented at the Southwest Conference on Human Development, New Orleans.

Roper, R., & Hinde, R. A. (1978). Social behavior in a play group: Consistency and complexity. *Child Development, 49*, 570–579.

Rosenblatt, D. (1977). Developmental trends in infancy play. In B. Tizard & D. Harvey (Eds.), *The biology of play*. London: William Heinemann Medical Books.

Rubin, K. H. (1977). Play behaviors of young children. *Young Children, iii*, 16–24.

Rubin, K. H. (1982). Social and social-cognitive developmental characteristics of young isolate, normal, and sociable children. In K. H. Rubin & H. S. Ross (Eds.), *Peer relationships and social skills in childhood*. New York: Springer-Verlag.

Rubin, K. H., Fein, G. G., & Vandenberg, B. (1983). Play. In E. M. Hetherington (Ed.), *Handbook of child psychology: Vol. 4. Socialization, personality, and social development*. New York: Wiley.

Ruble, D., Balaban, T., & Cooper, J. (1981). Gender constancy and the effects of sex-typed televised toy commercials. *Child Development, 52*, 667–673.

Sanders, K. M., & Harper, L. V. (1976). Free play fantasy behavior in preschool children: Relations among gender, age, season, and location. *Child Development, 47*, 1182–1185.

Scarlett, W. G. (1994). Play, cure, and development: A developmental perspective on the psychoanalytic treatment of young children. In A. Slade & D. P. Wolf (Eds.), *Children at play: Clinical and developmental approaches to meaning and representation*. New York: Oxford University Press.

Schwartz, L. A., & Markham, W. T. (1985). Sex stereotyping in children's toy advertisements. *Sex Roles, 12*, 157–170.

Schwartzman, H. B. (1978). Transformations: *The anthropology of children's play*. New York: Plenum.

Singer, D. G., & Rummo, J. (1973). Ideational creativity and behavioral style in kindergarten aged children. *Developmental Psychology, 8*, 154–161.

Singer, D. G., & Singer, J. L. (1978). Some correlates of imaginative play in preschoolers. Paper presented at the meeting of the American Psychological Association, Toronto.

Singer, J. L. (1973). *The child's world of make-believe*. New York: Academic Press.

Singer, J. L. (1994). The scientific foundations of play therapy. In J. Hellendoorn, R. van der Kooij, & B. Sutton-Smith (Eds.), *Play and intervention.* Albany, NY: State University of New York Press.

Singer, J. L., Singer, D. G., & Sherrod, L. R. (1980). A factor analytic study of preschooler's play behavior. *American Psychology Bulletin, 2,* 143–156.

Slade, A. (1994). Making meaning and making believe: Their role in the clinical process. In A. Slade & D. P. Wolf (Eds.), *Children at play: Clinical and developmental approaches to meaning and representation.* New York: Oxford University Press.

Smilansky, S. (1968). *The effects of sociodramatic play on disadvantaged children: Preschool children.* New York: Wiley.

Smith, P. K. (1978). A longitudinal study of school participation in preschool children: Solitary and parallel play reexamined. *Developmental Psychology, 14,* 517–523.

Smith, P. K., & Connolly, K. (1972). Patterns of play and social interaction in preschool children. In N. Blurton-Jones (Ed.), *Ethological studies of child behaviour.* Cambridge, England: Cambridge University Press.

Smith, P. K., Takhvar, M., Gore, N., & Vollstedt, R. (1985). Play in young children: Problems of definition, categorization, measurement. *Early Child Development and Care, 19,* 25–41.

Tizard, B., Philips, J., & Plewis, I. (1976). Play in preschool centers: II. Effects on play of the child's social class and of the educational orientation of the center. *Journal of Child Psychology and Psychiatry, 17,* 265–274.

Tracy, D. M. (1987). Toys, spatial ability, and science and mathematics achievement: Are they related? *Sex Roles, 17,* 251–260.

Vygotsky, L. (1976). Play and its role in the mental development of the child. In J. Bruner, J. Jolly, & K. Sylva (Eds.), *Play: Its role in development and evolution.* New York: Basic Books.

Waelder, R. (1933). The psychoanalytic theory of play. *Psychoanalytic Quarterly, 2,* 208–224.

Ward, W. C. (1966). *Creativity and impulsivity in kindergarten children.* Unpublished doctoral dissertation, Duke University, Durham, NC.

Ward, W. W. (1968). Reflection-impulsivity in kindergarten children. *Child Development, 39,* 867–874.

Watson, M. W. (1994). The relation between anxiety and pretend play. In A. Slade & D. P. Wolf (Eds.), *Children at play: Clinical and developmental approaches to meaning and representation.* New York: Oxford University Press.

Watson, M. W., & Fischer, K. W. (1977). A developmental sequence of agent use in late infancy. *Child Development, 48,* 828–836.

Winner, J., McCarthy, M., Kleinman, S., & Gardener, H. (1979). First metaphors. *New Directions in Child Development, 1,* 29–41.

Winnicott, D. W. (1986). *Playing and reality.* New York: Tavistock.

Witkin, H. A., Dye, R. B., Paterson, H. F., Goodenough, D. R., & Karp, S. A. (1962). *Psychological differentiation.* New York: Wiley.

Witkin, H. A., Goodenough, D. R., & Karp, S. A. (1967). Stability of cognitive style from childhood to young adulthood. *Journal of Social Psychology, 1,* 291–300.

Wolf, D., & Grollman, S. H. (1982). Ways of playing: Individual differences in imaginative style. In D. J. Pepler & K. H. Rubin (Eds.), *The play of children: Current theory and research.* Basel, Switzerland: Karger AG.

8

Measuring Playfulness: Development of the Child Behaviors Inventory of Playfulness

Cosby S. Rogers, James C. Impara, Robert B. Frary,
Teresa Harris, Amy Meeks, Susan Semanic-Lauth,
and Mary Ruth Reynolds

Playfulness is a psychological construct involving individual differences in the disposition to play. The Child Behaviors Inventory of Playfulness was constructed as a brief trait-rating instrument suitable for use with parents and teachers who have received no specialized training. This chapter summarizes the psychometric properties of the Child Behaviors Inventory and the outcomes of studies on the concurrent relationships of playfulness to other variables.

One of the first to develop an instrument to measure playfulness was Lieberman (1965, 1967, 1977), who defined playfulness as physical, cognitive and social spontaneity, manifest joy, and humor. Her research reports indicated that playfulness in children is a unitary behavioral dimension across the physical, social, and cognitive domains (Lieberman, 1977). However, methodological flaws limited the conclusions that could be drawn from her work. Though other researchers have provided data which evidence the existence of playfulness as a stable personality trait (e.g., Singer & Rummo, 1973; Singer, Singer, & Sherrod, 1980), only one line of research has followed directly from the pioneering work of Lieberman (Barnett, 1990, 1991a, 1991b). Using Lieberman's definition of playfulness, Barnett (1990) developed a methodologically improved measure of the construct. Though Barnett's carefully constructed new measure of playfulness was reliable, it was limited by the fact that the definition of playfulness, borrowed from Lieberman, may have failed to adequately define the construct. Lieberman's definition focused on play behaviors rather than on the personality dispositions. Moreover, many of the behaviors rated on the scale are known to vary systematically by gender and age rather than by individual differences in personality dispositions.

An interest in defining play has led to more specific definitional criteria (Krasnor & Pepler, 1980; Rubin, Fein, & Vandenberg, 1983; Smith & Vollstedt, 1985) than were extant when Lieberman presented her definition. Rubin and associates (1983) distinguished the play dispositions according to criteria related to (a) motivation source, (b) orientation to goals, (c) degree of domination by stimuli, (d) degree of non-literality, (e) rule boundedness, and (f) degree of active involvement. Krasnor and Pepler (1980) suggested combining four criteria to define play: (a) flexibility, (b) positive affect, (c) intrinsic motivation, and (d) nonliterality. They proposed that, although all criteria might not be met simultaneously, behaviors are more likely to be regarded as play as the number of criteria present increases.

Smith and Vollstedt (1985) studied the usefulness of dispositional criteria for defining play using the criteria from Krasnor and Pepler (1980) plus the criterion of domination by means from Rubin and associates (1983). Although no single criterion predicted play with certainty, observers using the five criteria generally agreed on which behaviors were play. Operationally defined dispositional criteria appear to provide a reliable and valid definition of play.

If playfulness is a personality disposition trait, then a trait-rating instrument, completed by persons knowledgable of a child's behaviors across multiple contexts, could provide data which is reliable but less time-consuming than laboratory observation. This article summarizes the development of such a trait-rating instrument designed to measure individual differences in playfulness as a personality disposition. The dispositional criteria provided by Rubin and associates (1983) served as the definition of playfulness for the present study because of its comprehensive theoretical and empirical base.

METHOD

The Child Behaviors Inventory of Playfulness was developed by generating a pool of items, evaluating content validity of the items, assessing the factor structure, and evaluating the scale for reliability and validity.

SUBJECTS

Parents and teachers of 892 children (preschool–grade 4) provided data that were used for the construction and validation of the Child Behaviors Inventory. The 892 children

TABLE 1.
Description of Samples

Sample	N	Grade Range	Raters
1	47	Preschool	Teacher ($n = 4$)
2	36	Preschool	Teacher ($n = 2$)
			Mothers ($n = 36$)
			Fathers ($n = 36$)
3	48	Preschool	Mothers ($n = 48$)
			Fathers ($n = 36$)
4	382	K-4	Teachers ($n = 51$)
			Mothers ($n = 382$)
5	296	K-4	Teachers ($n = 19$)
			Student Teachers ($n = 19$)
6	83	K-4	Teachers ($n = 9$)
Total	892		

comprised six independent samples (Table 1). Sample 1 included 47 university laboratory preschoolers who were rated by teachers, and Sample 2 included ratings from teachers, mothers, and fathers of 36 other university laboratory preschoolers. A subsample of the laboratory children (Sample 2) was rated separately by both the teacher from a morning session and the teacher from the afternoon session. Sample 3 included ratings by both mothers ($n= 48$) and fathers ($n= 36$) of 48 non-university preschool children. Sample 4 included 382 school-age children in grades kindergarten through four who were rated independently by mothers and by teachers. Sample 5 included 296 subjects from kindergarten through grade four, rated by both a student teacher and by the student teacher's cooperating teacher who observed the children in the same context on a daily basis. Sample 6 comprised ratings made by the teachers of 83 school children (kindergarten through grade four).

ITEM CONSTRUCTION AND REVISION

Items for the trait-rating scale were solicited from sixteen scholars, well-known for their contributions to research and theory in the area of play. Five of the scholars responded with items for each of the six criteria outlined by Rubin and associates (1983). A total of 63 items comprised the original pool. To assess content validity, 16 other well-known scholars were asked to rate each item for its conceptual relationship to the criterion it was intended to measure. Eight scholars responded, rating items on a continuum from 1 (not a good measure at all) to 5 (measures the concept very well). Any item receiving a mean rating of two or below was discarded and several items were eliminated on the basis of qualitative comments by the scholars. Items were randomly ordered and printed with instructions for rating children on each behavior on a scale from "1" (very uncharacteristic) to "5" (very characteristic).

TABLE 2.
Rotated Factor Pattern and Item Means and Standard Deviations for all Samples Combined (Mothers' Ratings, $N = 467$)

Item	Factor 1	Factor 2	Mean	SD
PLAYFULNESS:				
Always has ideas of things to do	.54		4.07	0.83
Explores different ways	.52		3.54	0.98
Invents new games	.67		3.98	1.03
Uses things in own way	.37		4.18	0.83
Enjoys learning new skills	.46		4.40	0.85
Works well on his/her own	.42		4.01	0.99
Enjoys doing things/no purpose	.39		3.79	1.00
Has fun doing things/doesn't worry how well they turn out	.31		3.51	1.19
Gets involved in activity/hard to get to quit	.50		3.85	1.06
Starts activities for own enjoyment	.63		4.29	0.79
Pretends a lot	.45		3.82	1.20
Plays eagerly	.56		4.49	0.72
Plays intently	.61		4.43	0.79
Invents variations on stories	.48		3.54	1.18
Rearranges situations to come up with novel ones	.64		3.44	1.07
Creates own way to do things	.48		3.61	1.01
Is imaginative	.67		4.40	0.80
Uses toys/objects in unusual ways	.50		3.63	1.07
Finds unusual things to do with common objects	.66		3.71	1.03
Identifies with many characters	.55		3.66	1.05
Gets so involved/forgets what is going on	.42		3.68	1.17
EXTERNALITY:				
Uses props in typical ways		.51	3.29	0.94
Once goal is achieved, stops		.42	3.22	1.08
Needs reinforcement to continue activities		.49	2.84	1.26
Asks many questions about what to do		.62	3.44	1.29
Seeks approval frequently		.66	3.65	1.14
Looks to others to tell him/her what to do		.68	2.65	1.20
Uses toy/objects in way they were designed to be used		.53	2.67	1.21

Note: Response options ranged from 1: very uncharacteristic to 5: very characteristic.

RESULTS

The results describe the psychometric properties of the inventory, factor patterns, and means and standard deviations for items. Internal consistency reliability estimates are presented along with subscale means and standard deviations. Interrater reliability and construct-related validity are reported. A brief overview of concurrent validity findings is also presented.

FACTOR STRUCTURE

Factor analysis was used to investigate the underlying structure of the scale. The matrix of intercorrelations among the maternal ratings of 467 children (all samples combined) was subjected to a principal components extraction of roots Inspection of the scree plot of the resulting eigen values led to the conclusion that two factors (accounting for 31% of total variance) could account for the underlying structure. Thus, the six criteria defining play disposition proposed by Rubin and associates (1983) were not confirmed empirically as separate factors. A varimax rotation was performed on the two factors of this study and the resulting factor loadings with absolute values greater than .3 indicated that the two-factor solution was a parsimonious solution that included all items. A higher factor loading criterion would have resulted in three factors, thus reducing the parsimony. Inspection of the factor loadings led to the following characterization of the factors. Factor one, playfulness is characterized by 21 of the 28 items (Table 2). The remaining items comprise factor two, externality. Externality appears to measure a tendency to be affected by environmental factors such as dependency on other people for direction and non-flexible uses of objects in the environment. A second analysis, based on teacher ratings in all samples combined (N= 844), resulted in a similar factor structure with the exception of six items (Table 3). In contrast to the factor analysis of the parents' responses, one item loaded on neither factor, two loaded on the opposite factor and three loaded on both factors.

ITEM AND SUBSCALE MEANS AND STANDARD DEVIATIONS

Means for individual items on the playfulness factor (Tables 2 and 3) ranged from 3.44 to 4.49 when mothers were raters, indicating that most mothers perceived children as being generally playful. Ratings made by teachers were slightly lower, with mean ratings ranging from 3.08 to 3.89 for individual items related to playfulness. Item means on the externality factor ranged from 2.65 to 3.65 when mothers were raters and from 2.83 to 3.26 when teachers were raters, indicating that children, and quite possibly raters, are also affected by their environment (Tables 2 and 3). Standard deviations indicate that there is moderate variability, supporting the construct of indi-

TABLE 3.
Rotated Factor Pattern and Item Means and Standard Deviations for all Samples Combined (Teachers' Ratings, $N = 844$)

Item	Factor 1	Factor 2	Mean	SD
PLAYFULNESS:				
Always has ideas of things to do	.71		3.55	1.06
Explores different ways	.69		3.17	1.01
Invents new games	.75		3.12	1.08
Uses things in own way	.59		3.44	0.95
Enjoys learning new skills	.44	−.47	3.77	0.98
Works well on his/her own		−.67	3.58	1.19
Enjoys doing things/no purpose	.38	−.45	3.28	1.04
Has fun doing things/doesn't worry how well they turn out	.36	−.34	3.34	1.07
Gets involved in activity/hard to get to quit	.57		3.19	1.09
Starts activities for own enjoyment	.69		3.57	0.99
Pretends a lot	.69		3.18	1.10
Plays eagerly	.57		3.89	0.92
Plays intently	.58		3.78	0.98
Invents variations on stories	.76		3.28	1.05
Rearranges situations to come up with novel ones	.79		3.11	1.01
Creates own way to do things	.76		3.19	0.99
Is imaginative	.76		3.56	1.02
Uses toys/object in unusual ways	.67		3.10	0.93
Finds unusual things to do with common objects	.74		3.08	0.95
Identifies with many characters	.72		3.11	0.90
Gets so involved/forgets what is going on	.62		3.09	1.10
EXTERNALITY:				
Uses props in typical ways[1]			3.26	0.97
Once goal is achieved, stops		.31	3.10	0.97
Needs reinforcement to continue activities		.73	3.06	1.22
Asks many questions about what to do		.73	2.94	1.17
Seeks approval frequently		.75	3.04	1.21
Looks to others to tell him/her what to do		.69	2.83	1.20
Uses toy/objects in way they were designed to be used	−.32		3.12	0.91

[1] Loading less than .3 on both factors

126

TABLE 4.
Subscale Means and Standard Deviations for All Samples Combined

	Playfulness		Externality	
	M	SD	M	SD
Teacher (N = 844)	3.35	.67	3.05	.67
Second Teacher (N=317)	3.34	.68	3.04	.69
Mother (N = 467)	3.90	.52	3.11	.68
Father (N = 72)	3.92	.40	2.86	.56

Note: Second teachers included preschool teachers for an afternoon session in Samples 1 and 2 and student teachers in Sample 5.

vidual differences in the disposition to play. Subscale means and standard deviations (Table 4) were, like the item means, positively skewed, reflecting that children are generally both playful and externally responsive. In general, teachers' ratings of playfulness were lower than those made by parents, perhaps reflecting a situational impact on the trait. Ratings of externality were lowest when made by fathers, slightly higher when by teachers, and highest on mothers' data, suggesting that the externally dependent behaviors are more likely to be displayed in the presence of persons to whom the child is likely to turn for comfort and security, that is, the primary attachment figure.

INTERNAL CONSISTENCY

Cronbach alpha coefficients were high (Table 5), ranging from .81 to .94, for the items that related to factor one, playfulness, and from .62 to .72 for the items that related to factor two, externality.

INTERRATER RELIABILITY

Interrater reliability was studied in five samples (see Table 6). Using sample five (Semanic-Lauth, 1986), 19 pairs of student teachers and their supervising teachers, each rated an equal number of boys and girls, randomly selected from class rolls (N = 296). Pearson coefficients were .60 ($p < .001$) for factor one, playfulness, and .37 ($p < .001$) for factor two, externality. With all samples combined, correlations between pairs of teachers, some who saw the child in different settings, were $r = .60$ ($p < .001$) for playfulness and $r = .42$ ($p < .001$) for externality. Correlations between 71 pairs of mothers and fathers, all parents of preschoolers, were lower ($r = .33$, $p < .01$) than these between teachers for playfulness but higher for externality ($r = .57$, $p < .001$). Correlations between ratings by 418 mothers versus those by teachers were substantially lower, $r = .12$ ($p < .05$) for playfulness, and $r = .11$ ($p < .05$) for externality.

Table 5.
Cronbach's Alpha Index of Internal Consistency for Each Sample

Sample	Rater	Scale	
		Playfulness	Externality
Sample 1:			
Preschool ($N = 47$)	Teacher	.92	.62
Sample 2:			
Preschool ($N = 36$)	Teacher	.93	.80
	Mother	.86	.72
	Father	.85	.57
Sample 3:			
Preschool ($N = 48$)	Mother	.82	.69
Preschool ($N = 32$)	Father	.81	.62
Sample 4:			
School Age ($N = 382$)	Mother	.87	.68
School Age ($N = 382$)	Teacher	.94	.69
Sample 5:			
School Age ($N = 296$)	Teacher	.93	.71
	Student Teacher	.93	.72
Sample 6:			
School Age ($N = 83$)	Teacher	.94	.72

TABLE 6.
Interrater Reliability: Pearson Correlation Coefficients

Sample	Raters	Pearson's r	
		Playfulness	Externality
2: Preschool ($N = 36$)	Mother vs. Father	.49**	.67***
2: Preschool ($N = 36$)	Father vs. Teacher	−.05	.21
2: Preschool ($N = 36$)	Mother vs. Teacher	−.10	.25
3: Preschool ($N = 36$)	Mother vs. Father	.14	.54**
4: School ($N = 382$)	Mother vs. Teacher	.12	.09
5: School ($N = 296$)	Teacher vs. Student Teacher	.60***	.37***
Combined Samples ($N = 317$)			
	Teacher vs. Second Teacher	.60***	.42***
Combined Samples ($N = 71$)			
	Mother vs. Father	.33**	.57***
Combined Samples ($N = 418$)			
	Mother vs. Teachers	.12*	.11*

Notes: *$p < .05$; **$p < .01$; ***$p < .001$

INTERSCALE CORRELATIONS

Correlations between the two subscales were moderately low ($r = -.37$) when teachers were raters and very low (indeed negligible) when mothers ($r = -.12$) or fathers ($r = -.13$) were raters. Interscale correlations in the case of teachers were negative, that is, children rated as more playful tended to be rated as less dependent on external factors. This interscale relationship in the case of teachers reflects the fact that three items had loaded on both scales. In other words, the factor structure underlying the teachers' ratings appears to be slightly different from that attributable to mothers' ratings. This outcome may reflect the fact that each teacher rated an average of 11 children, with the multiple ratings contributing to scale intercorrelations through a halo effect.

RELATIONSHIP TO OTHER VARIABLES

Behavioral ratings were examined to test for developmental and gender differences. All correlations between gender, age, grade, and the two factor scores were negligible (Table 7) with two exceptions. First, a low but significant correlation between age and playfulness indicated a tendency for older children to be rated as more playful by their mothers. A moderately low but significant negative correlation was found between age and externality when teachers were the raters. The direction of the correlation reflected a normal developmental trend, that is, with increasing age children were less externally dependent on objects and/or people.

TABLE 7.
Pearson Correlations of Factors With Gender, Age, and Grade for All Samples Combined

	Playfulness			Externality		
Rater	Gender	Age	Grade	Gender	Age	Grade
Teacher ($N = 843$)	.05	.04	−.06	.07	−.35***	.05
Second Teacher ($N = 317$)	.01	—	−.01	−.01	—	.05
Mother ($N = 467$)	−.04	.10*	−.04	.10	−.07	−.00
Father ($N = 72$)	−.03	.03	—	.21	−.02	—

Note: Second teachers include afternoon teachers in preschool Samples 1 and 2 and student teachers in Sample 5. All ratings obtained from fathers were on preschool children.
*$p < .05$
***$p < .001$

CONSTRUCT-RELATED VALIDITY

A subsample of Sample 1, comprised of 28 four-year-olds (mean age = 55.86 months, SD = 4.89), enrolled in a university laboratory school participated in an observational study of construct-related validity (Hawkins, 1987). Children were invited, individually, to participate in a semi-structured pretense scenario called "The Birthday Party." A trained student prompted and supported pretense episodes which were aided by some realistic and some ambiguous props. Sessions were videotaped for later coding.

Fourteen behaviors corresponding to items on the CBI subscales were observed. The ratio of the frequency of occurrence of each behavior to the amount of time in seconds the child was engaged in the birthday party scenario was computed. However, only the five behaviors that achieved interrater reliability of .90 or above were retained for comparison with the CBI. Reliably observable behaviors were categorized as either dependent behaviors (consisting of reality-based questions such as "What's that?", or "What do you do with this?") and pretense behaviors. Children spent varying amounts of time in the pretense scenario, and thus the rate of occurrence of specific behaviors (frequency/time) was used in analyses. Dependent behaviors were moderately and negatively correlated with playfulness (Table 8) but moderately positively correlated with externality. Three of the four pretense behaviors were significantly and positively correlated with playfulness but none were significantly related to externality.

TABLE 8.
Pearson Correlation Coefficients of Play Observations With Teacher Ratings on Playfulness and Externality

Pearson's r		
Variable	Playfulness	Externality
Dependent Behaviors:		
Reality-based questions	−.42**	.43**
Pretense:		
Dissimilar objects substituted for hat	.27*	−.13
Guests suggested	.41**	−.22
Makes replicas act	.26*	−.10
Names/uses suggested for J-shaped object	.15	−.10

Note: N = 28
* $p < .10$
** $p < .05$

CONCURRENT RELATIONSHIP TO OTHER TRAIT VARIABLES

Two other traits, temperament (Blevins, 1987) and Type-A behavior (Moore, 1985), were studied to assess their degree of association with the two factors of the Child Behaviors Inventory. It was predicted that more playful children would have easier temperaments and would be rated low on Type A behaviors.

TEMPERAMENT

Parents in Sample 3 (N's = 48 mothers, 48 fathers) completed the Behavioral Style Questionnaire (McDevitt & Carey, 1978) on temperament. Results (Table 9) indicated that high maternal ratings on the playfulness scale correlated with positive mood and increased persistence whereas high ratings on externality were associated with high intensity and negative mood. Playfulness was correlated with fathers' ratings of their children's, approachability, adaptability, and persistence, whereas fathers' ratings on externality were not significantly correlated with any of the temperament dimensions.

TYPE A BEHAVIOR

The common association among the subscales of the Matthews Youth Test for Health (MYTH-Form 0) (Matthews & Angulo, 1980) measure of Type A behavior in children and the CBI factors were studied by Moore (1985) using data from Sample 6

TABLE 9.
Pearson Correlations Between CBI and Temperament Ratings by Mothers and Fathers

Temperament Scale	Playfulness		Externality	
	Mother (N = 36)	Father (N = 36)	Mother (N= 36)	Father (N = 36)
Activity	−.05	−.25	.18	.17
Rhythmicity	.02	−.17	.01	−.18
Approachability	−.07	−.45**	−.04	−.04
Adaptability	−.24	−.49**	.23	−.14
Intensity	−.06	.19	.49**	.28
Mood	−.24	−.27	.42**	.15
Persistence	−.41**	−.44**	.20	.09
Distractibility	−.06	.03	.07	.16
Threshold of Responsiveness	−.08	−.04	.13	.19

Notes: Low scores on temperament scales reflect "easier" temperament traits.
**$p < .01$

($N = 83$), a predominately white middle class group of school age children. Playfulness was not related significantly to the impatience-aggression subscale on the MYTH ($r = .10$, ns) but, contrary to expectations, playfulness was correlated positively and significantly with the Type A subscale measuring competitiveness ($r = .59$, $p < .001$). Externality had a low but significant relationship to impatience-aggression ($r = .29$, $p < .01$) but was not related significantly to competitiveness ($r = -.15$).

DISCUSSION

The Child Behaviors Inventory of Playfulness appears to be a reliable and valid instrument for measuring the disposition of play in children. Items selected for the final version of the scale were judged to have content validity and to be easy for untrained adults to use. The item and scale means and standard deviations reflected variability, and thus a sensitivity to individual differences not explained by gender, age, or grade.

Although the item pool was constructed to represent six criteria for the disposition of play, those six dimensions did not represent separate factors. Rather, two factors emerged with one representing playfulness and one representing a dependency on external environmental support.

The presence or absence of specific criteria seems to coexist, supporting the notion that playfulness is a unidimensional trait in young children (Lieberman, 1977). This is congruent with Krasnor and Pepler's (1980) postulation that the more specific criteria that are found to be present, the more one can define a behavior as play. Smith and Vollstedt (1985) also found that when two or more specific criteria were present, an observational episode was likely to be judged as play. Therefore, it seems reasonable to conclude that playfulness is a personality trait that can be scaled.

Internal consistency reliability estimates were moderate to high for all samples. Interrater reliability for factor one, playfulness, was high when based on ratings from adults who observed children in the same setting, that is, student teachers and their supervising teachers, even if time of day observing varied. Teacher agreement on factor 2, externality, was moderate. Agreement between mothers and fathers was moderate for the playfulness factor but high for the externality factor. Agreement between mothers and teachers was low for both factors. These correlational patterns are reminiscent of interrater reliability ratings for temperament which have been found to be moderate when two parents or two teachers rate the child but low when ratings of parents and teachers are compared. This pattern suggests the hypothesis that individual differences in the play disposition interact with contextual factors to produce intraindividual variation.

Intercorrelations between the playfulness and externality subscales are low for data based on parental ratings indicating that the two scales on the Child Behaviors Inventory are indeed measuring different factors. However, playfulness and externality measures based on teachers' ratings are significantly intercorrelated, reflecting the differing factor structures discussed earlier.

Construct-related validity was suggested for the playfulness factor by significant correlations between teacher ratings' and behaviors observed by an independent observer outside the classroom and unfamiliar with the children. The validity of factor 2, externality, was supported by observations of conceptually related dependent behaviors. There is no theoretical reason to expect pretense to be related to external dependency and thus low correlations between those two factors were not surprising. Dependent behavior, manifested as reality-based questions, was significantly related to both scales of the CBI (negatively with playfulness, positively with externality). Externally dependent behaviors apparently depress the disposition to play.

No acceptable criterion was available for the assessment of concurrent validity, owing to the fact that no other instrument exists which is based on the same definition of the construct. However, studies of concurrent relationships with other logically-related trait variables provide useful and supportive information and some evidence related to construct validity. First, although most dimensions of temperament were not related to the CBI factors, moderate significant correlations between persistence and playfulness were found for ratings from both mothers and fathers. It is interesting to note that persistence in play has served as the operational definition of mastery motivation (Jennings, Harmon, Morgan, Gaiter, & Yarrow, 1979). Fathers who rated their preschoolers as more playful also rated them as approachable and adaptable on the temperament scale. Mothers who rated their preschoolers as more external also tended to rate their children as highly intense and as having more negative moods. It appears then that negative mood and high intensity of emotional responsiveness is linked with dependent behavior which in turn can be expected to have a depressing effect on play. This supports the notion that play occurs in conjunction with a positive emotional state (Rubin et al., 1983), rather than as a criterion for defining play as Lieberman (1965, 1977) and Krasnor and Pepler (1980) have suggested.

Play scholars have emphasized that the context for play must include a physically and emotionally safe environment (Rubin et al., 1983) and stress is generally considered to be a deterrent to play. Thus, we expected Type A behaviors in general to be associated with low playfulness and high externality. Although highly external children were more impatient-aggressive, playful children were highly competitive. These results point to the need to clarify the nature of the hypothesized stress-related health risks thought to be associated with competitiveness. Particularly, researchers need to address the source of motivation associated with competitiveness, that is, is it intrinsically motivated and competency-based or extrinsically motivated and performance based (Dweck & Elliott, 1983)? The pattern of results in this study seem to indicate that playfully competitive individuals may engage in competition "just for the fun of it" rather than in a spirit of aggression.

In summary, playfulness appears to be a valid construct which can be reliably measured and which is distinct from external dependency. Playfulness is associated with easy temperament but only on a few dimensions, and the dimensions of significance vary depending on whether ratings are obtained from mothers or fathers. Future research is needed to assess the distinguishability of playfulness from other positive traits.

REFERENCES

Barnett, L. A. (1990). Playfulness: Definition, design, and measurement. *Play and Culture, 3,* 319–336.

Barnett, L. A. (1991a). The playful child: Measurement of the disposition to play. *Play and Culture, 4,* 51–74.

Barnett, L. A. (1991b). Characterizing playfulness: Correlates with individual attributes and personality traits. *Play and Culture, 4,* 371–393.

Blevins, T. (1987). *Dispositions of play: Correlates of temperament.* Unpublished manuscript. Virginia Polytechnic Institute and State University, Blacksburg, VA.

Dweck, C. S., & Elliott, E. S. (1983). Achievement motivation. In E. M. Hetherington (Ed.), P. H. Mussen (Series Ed.), *Handbook of child psychology: Vol. 4. Socialization, personality, and social development* (pp. 643–691). New York: Wiley.

Hawkins, M. R. (1987). *Construct-related validity of the Child Behaviors Inventory of playfulness in children.* Unpublished manuscript. Virginia Polytechnic Institute and State University, Blacksburg, VA.

Jennings, K. D., Harmon, R. S., Moran, G. A., Gaiter, J. L., & Yarrow, L. J. (1979). Exploratory play as an index of mastery motivation: Relationships to persistence, cognitive functioning, and environmental measures. *Developmental Psychology, 15,* 386–394.

Krasnor, L. R., & Pepler, D. J. (1980). The study of children's play: Some suggested future directions. In K. H. Rubin (Ed.), *New directions in child development: Children's play* (pp. 85–95). San Francisco: Jossey-Bass.

Lieberman, J. N. (1965). Playfulness and divergent thinking: An investigation of their relationship at the kindergarten level. *Journal of Genetic Psychology, 107,* 219–224.

Lieberman, J. N. (1967). A developmental analysis of playfulness as a clue to cognitive style. *Journal of Creative Behavior, 1,* 391–397.

Lieberman, J. N. (1977). *Playfulness: Its relationship to imagination and creativity.* New York: Academic Press.

Matthews, K. A., & Angulo, J. (1980). Measurement of the Type A behavior pattern in children: Assessment of children's competitiveness, impatience-anger, and aggression. *Child Development, 51,* 466–475.

McDevitt, S. C., & Carey, W. B. (1978). The measurement of temperament in three- to seven-year-old children. *Journal of Child Psychology and Psychiatry, 19,* 245–253.

Moore, A. J. (1985). *Childrearing practices associated with playfulness and Type A behavior in children.* Unpublished master's thesis. Virginia Polytechnic Institute and State University, Blacksburg, VA.

Rubin, K. H., Fein, G. G., & Vandenberg, B. (1983). Play. In E. M. Hetherington (Ed.), P. H. Mussen (Series Ed.), *Handbook of child psychology: Vol. 4. Socialization, personality, and social development* (pp. 693–774). New York: Wiley.

Semanic-Lauth, S. (1986). *Interrater reliability for the Child Behaviors Inventory of playfulness in children.* Unpublished manuscript. Virginia Polytechnic Institute and State University, Blacksburg, VA.

Singer, D. G., & Rummo, J. (1973). Ideational creativity and behavior style in kindergarten-age children. *Developmental Psychology, 8,* 154–161.

Singer, J. L., Singer, D. G., & Sherrod, L. R. (1980). A factor analytic study of preschoolers' play behavior. *Academic* Psychology Bulletin, 2, 143–156.

Smith, P. K., & Vollstedt, R. (1985). On defining play: An empirical study of the relationship between play and various play criteria. *Child Development, 56,* 1042–1050.

9

Construct Validity of the Children's Playfulness Scale

Anita C. Bundy
Jeanne L. Clifton

INTRODUCTION AND REVIEW OF LITERATURE

In summarizing the play literature, Rubin, Fein, and Vandenberg (1983) described an approach to the study of play that emphasized children's disposition toward play. Adopting this approach, recent theorists and researchers (Barnett, 1990, 1991a, 1991b; Bundy, 1991, 1993; Lieberman, 1977) have elected to study the construct of playfulness in particular. Although these authors agree that a playful approach to tasks may be more important than engagement in any particular play activity, they disagree on exactly how to conceptualize and assess playfulness. The present study was designed to explore playfulness through an examination of the construct validity of the Children's Playfulness Scale (CPS; Barnett, 1990).

The CPS was based on the early work of Lieberman (1977). Drawing from play literature and her own preliminary, observational studies of how children play, Lieberman developed the Playfulness Scale for children to be rated by teachers or caretakers. This scale consists of five main subscales comprised of two items each and designed to tap the quality and quantity of a child's physical spontaneity, manifest joy, sense of humor, social spontaneity, and cognitive spontaneity during play.

Accepting Lieberman's conceptualization of playfulness as a unitary dimension with these five underlying components, Barnett (1990) drafted her own 25-item play-fulness scale. Like Lieberman, Barnett designed items to assess the child's playful-ness in each of these five developmental domains. She also employed a 5-point scale for item ratings. Barnett, however, developed statements rather than questions for her items, and she adapted the response scale so that the five rating points were labeled identically for each statement. This 25-item draft was then reviewed for face and con-tent validity by two panels of individuals knowledgeable in child development and research design. Based on their suggestions and the results of a pilot test, two items were dropped, resulting in the 23-item Children's Playfulness Scale (CPS).

Barnett (1990, 1991b) conducted extensive testing of her scale's construct validity based on CPS scores of children in different environments (same raters, different children in each setting). These data were analyzed and found to be adequate using factor analy-sis, descriptive statistics, and Cronbach alpha reliability estimates of internal consistency.

Traditionally, factor analysis has been used to examine construct validity (Rogers, 1987). Factor analysis identifies factors within a scale by examining groupings of highly correlated items. Convergent (within factor) correlations indicate whether or not items within a factor are tapping the same dimension of a construct. Discriminate (between factor) correlations indicate whether or not each factor measures a distinct dimension or a construct. The construct validity of a multi-dimensional scale is sup-ported by relatively high convergent correlations and relatively low discriminate cor-relations. The construct validity of a unidimensional scale, however, is supported when all items load heavily on one factor. Likewise, Cronbach's alpha provides infor-mation about a scale's internal consistency reliability based on inter-item correlations. This statistic "evaluates the ability of items to reliably separate people by ability level" (A. G. Fisher, 1993, p. 327). Therefore, high alpha reliabilities also support a scale's construct validity. The drawbacks with these traditional statistics include the follow-ing: interval treatment of ordinal data (W. P. Fisher, 1993), sample-dependent corre-lations (A. G. Fisher, 1993), limited information about why items fail to contribute to a construct, and a large sample requirement (Gliner, 1992).

Rasch analysis (Wright & Linacre, 1992), on the other hand, involves a logarithmic conversion of data to an equal-interval linear scale. This transformation allows for detailed, sample-free analysis of the difficulty calibration and discrimination of each test item (A. G. Fisher, 1993). This information is helpful in determining why certain items fail to contribute meaningfully to the construct being measured. As opposed to tradition-al psychometrics, Rasch analysis examines construct validity based on rankings of item difficulty and subject ability. When test items discriminate as expected between subjects of varying ability (internal validity) and when subjects score as expected on items of vary-ing difficulty (person response validity), the "validity of the test as a measure of the con-struct is supported" (Rogers, 1987, p. 24). In other words, if 95 percent of items and subjects fit the Rasch model, the scale can be thought to have construct validity. Finally, Rasch analysis can be used to examine data from a relatively small sample.

Although Barnett concluded that the CPS has adequate construct validity, other research introduces additional questions. For instance, Metzger (1993) studied the construct validity of the Test of Playfulness (ToP; Bundy, 1992). The ToP differs from the CPS in at least two important ways. First, it is an observational scale. Second, it is based on a different conceptualization of playfulness. While Lieberman and Barnett developed their scales to reflect the domains in which playfulness could be manifest, Bundy developed her scale to reflect three criteria *contributing to* playfulness: intrinsic motivation, internal control, and suspension of reality (Neumann, 1971). Nonetheless, the ToP included 15 items drawn from the CPS, thought to represent both conceptualizations of playfulness. Using Rasch analysis to evaluate validity of the ToP, Metzger suggested that the following items from the CPS failed to contribute to a unidimensional construct of playfulness: "is physically active during play," "assumes different character roles," "uses unconventional objects in play," and "laughs at jokes or funny stories."

In a related study, Li, Bundy, and Beer (1995) examined whether or not Taiwanese adults valued playfulness as it is expressed by the items on the CPS. Their findings suggested that the item "gently teases others in play" did not seem to fit a unidimensional construct of playfulness (at least for Taiwanese adults).

Given two studies in which CPS items failed to contribute to a unidimensional construct of playfulness , further research seems necessary to examine the construct validity of the CPS. Furthermore, Barnett's construct validity studies included only typically-developing children. While there is a dearth of research regarding the play and playfulness of children with disabilities, there is increasing legally- and ethically-driven interest in this area. In one summary of the literature, Muñoz (1986) described the play of children with disabilities as generally less spontaneous and less interactive than that of children without disabilities. However, Clifford and Bundy (1989) suggested that children with disabilities may express playfulness differently than other children. Clearly, Barnett's findings must be replicated in studies that incorporate children with disabilities before the CPS is adopted as a valid measure of playfulness for all children.

For these reasons, we selected Rasch analysis to examine the construct validity of the CPS. We addressed the following research questions:

1. Can the internal validity of the CPS as a unidimensional construct be demonstrated by fit of at least 95% of items to the Rasch measurement model?
2. Can person response validity of the CPS be demonstrated by fit of at least 95 percent of children to the Rasch measurement model?

METHOD

Subjects

The subjects for this study were 89 children (49 males, 40 females), ranging in age from 15 to 118 months (M = 61.6). These predominantly Caucasian children were generally from middle SES families across the United States and the Toronto area.

Of the 89 subjects, 80 were children whose parents and teachers expressed no concerns about any area of the child's development. The other 9 children, all independently-ambulatory and verbally able to communicate their needs, were enrolled in special education classes. Based on observation, these 9 children were no more than moderately-impaired in any domain. The subjects were rated by their parents or teachers/day care providers on a slightly modified version of the CPS. The subjects and raters were recruited through personal acquaintance of the research team involved in this project. All subjects participated voluntarily.

Instrumentation

Of the 23 CPS items, 20 were selected for use in our study. Two items ("stays with one activity rather than changes activities during play" and "is restrained in expressing emotion during play") were excluded because they were inversely coded. Another item ("assumes different character roles in play") was eliminated due to an error in reproducing scoring sheets. Each item was scored on a 5-point rating scale indicating the degree to which that item's description characterized the child being rated (0 = "doesn't sound at all like the child," 1 = "sounds a little like the child," 2 = "sounds somewhat like the child," 3 = "sounds a lot like the child," and 4 = "sounds exactly like the child").

Procedure

This project was done as part of a larger study of playfulness that included videotaped observation of play. Parents were asked to complete the CPS (or give permission for the child's teacher/day care provider to complete) based on their previous experience with the child. During taping, consenting parents (teachers/day care providers) were verbally instructed to complete the CPS form in another room and to return it directly to the investigator at the end of the session. In this investigation, we will focus only on data from the CPS.

Data Analysis

To obtain information about the construct validity of the CPS, the data were analyzed using Rasch analysis (Wright & Linacre, 1992). Two assumptions apply to the use of Rasch analysis in this investigation. First, a highly playful child has a greater probability of getting a higher rating on any given item than does a less playful child. Second, any child has a greater probability of getting a higher rating on an easier item than on a harder one. When both of these assumptions are met, a subject or an item is said to "fit" the Rasch model. The higher the proportion of items and children that fit the model, the greater the probability that the scale represents a single unidimensional construct.

Results and Discussion

BIGSTEPS program (Wright & Linacre, 1992) was used to examine the children's scores on the modified CPS. These data were analyzed according to item difficulty and children's playfulness. In this case, "more difficult" refers to items for which children tended to receive lower scores (i.e., less characteristic of the child). "Less difficult" refers to items for which children tended to receive higher scores (i.e., more characteristic of the child). The item calibration scores are reported in logits (log-odds probability units) in Table 1. High positive logit measures are indicative of more difficult items. For example, #17 "gently teases others while at play" (1.08 logits ± .11) was found to be the most difficult item, whereas #12 "expresses enjoyment during play" (−.99 logits ± .17) was found to be the least difficult item.

Construct validity of the modified CPS was examined in two ways: scale validity and person response validity. These are discussed below.

Scale Validity

The fit of the items to the Rasch measurement model was examined to investigate whether or not the CPS reflects a unidimensional construct of playfulness. The CPS was defined by the calibrations of the 20 items along an equal-interval linear contin-

TABLE 1.
Item Calibrations

Calibration (Logit)	Error (Logit)	Infit MnSQ	Std.t	Outfit MnSq	Std.t	Item #, name
1.08	.11	.91	−.6	.88	−.8	17, teases
.90	.11	.92	−.5	.86	−.9	18, funny stories
.60	.11	1.30	1.9	1.45	2.5	9, leadership
.54	.11	1.02	.2	1.11	.7	8, shares
.23	.12	.80	−1.3	.81	−1.1	7, cooperative
.20	.12	1.31	1.9	1.26	1.4	20, clowns
.19	.12	1.23	1.4	1.12	.7	16, joking
.19	.12	.65	−2.5	.60	−2.6	6, initiates
.13	.12	.99	.0	.91	−.4	5, responds
.13	.12	1.35	2.1	1.43	2.2	11, unconventional
−.09	.13	1.00	.1	.92	−.4	4, runs
−.13	.13	1.07	.5	1.00	.1	19, laughs
−.15	.13	1.21	1.3	1.07	.4	10, invents
−.18	.13	1.21	1.2	1.20	1.0	3, not quiet
−.35	.14	1.17	1.0	1.47	2.0	1, coordinated
−.40	.14	.84	−.9	.86	−.6	13, exuberance
−.55	.15	.99	.0	1.04	.2	15, sings
−.57	.15	.92	−.4	.85	−.7	2, active
−.78	.16	.51	−3.1	.52	−2.4	14, enthusiasm
−.99	.17	.61	−2.3	.59	−1.8	12, enjoyment

uum. An item's failure to fit the Rasch model suggested that the item did not fall along this continuum. That is, the item failed to contribute meaningfully to the construct of playfulness. Item misfits occurred, for example, when less playful children obtained high scores on difficult items or when easy items were not easier for all children.

The outfit and infit statistics were examined for each item to ascertain the item's fit to the Rasch model. Outfit refers to whether or not children at the extremes of the play/non-play continuum (the highly playful or unplayful children) scored as expected on the item. Infit, on the other hand, refers to whether or not the moderately playful children obtained an expected progression of moderate scores on the item. Both outfit and infit are represented by mean square standardized residuals (MnSq) and standardized t values. The desired MnSq value is 1.00, and the desired t value is 0. If the item's MnSq is larger than 1.00 ($t>0$), the item performs erratically. If the item's MnSq is less than 1.00 ($t<0$), the item is too predictable or too perfect. In this case, erratic scoring is of greater concern than scoring that is too predictable. No standard criteria exist to determine how much deviation from these desired values is acceptable. It is commonly acknowledged, however, that an item is presumed to fit the Rasch model if simultaneously its MnSq values are 1.40 or more and its t values are 2.00 or more or if MnSq values are less than 0.6 and t values simultaneously are less than –2. Therefore, these values were selected as cutoffs in this investigation.

As reported in Table 1, the analysis revealed that 3 (15%) of the 20 items had both MnSq values greater than 1.40 and t values greater than 2.00, suggesting that they performed erratically. Thus, only 17 (85%) of the 20 items fit the Rasch measurement model. This percentage is less than the desired 95 percent fit of the items. Thus, the internal validity of the CPS as a whole is not as good as hoped for or as suggested by earlier studies. These results may have differed, however, had children been rated on all 23 of the original CPS items. At any rate, the seven items which fit the model seem to represent a unidimensional scale of playfulness according to Barnett's conceptualization.

The three items which failed to fit in this investigation included one item from the physical spontaneity category (#1 "movements are generally well-coordinated during play activities"), one item from the social spontaneity category (#9 "assumes a leadership role when playing with others"), and one item from the cognitive spontaneity category (#11 "uses conventional objects in play"). In general, these items failed to fit because they performed erratically in terms of scoring.

For example, item #11 "uses unconventional objects in play" was only moderately difficult (.13 logits ± .12), yet several rather playful children received unexpectedly low scores on this item. This item also failed to fit the model in Metzger's (1993) investigation of the playfulness construct defined by the ToP (Bundy, 1992), which included items from the CPS. In this same study, however, a similar ToP item (not included on the CPS), "uses conventional objects in unconventional ways" did fit the model. As Metzger suggested, perhaps it is more indicative of playfulness when children use any object creatively than when they use strictly unconventional objects in play. This shift in emphasis fits with the conceptualization of playfulness as a disposition rather than as a specific act (Barnett, 1990, 1991a, 1991b; Bundy, 1991, 1993;

Lieberman, 1977). Therefore, Barnett could perhaps reword this item so that it captures the quality of creativity without being so narrow in focus.

Item #9 "assumes a leadership role when playing with others" also performed erratically in our study. In this case, several highly playful children scored unexpectedly low on this item and several unplayful children scored unexpectedly high. This item also presented a paradox for Li and associates (1995) in their investigation of Taiwanese parents' values regarding playfulness. Specifically, the leadership item was the least valued of the 21 CPS items that fit the Rasch measurement model in their investigation. Furthermore, it was the only item in the social spontaneity category that was not highly valued by these parents. Li and associates suggested that this finding may have been a reflection of ambivalent attitudes toward leadership in Taiwan. However, because this item failed to fit in our investigation as well, it may be that leadership is viewed by adults across cultures as outside the construct of playfulness. Leadership may in fact be more a reflection of dominance or social competence (LaFreniere & Stroufe, 1985; Pettit, Bakshi, Dodge, & Coie, 1990) than of playfulness.

Finally, item #1 "movements are generally well-coordinated during play activities" also appears to be outside the construct of playfulness as defined by Barnett. Although this item was relatively easy (-.35 logits ± .14), several highly playful "typical" children and one highly playful child enrolled in special education scored unexpectedly low on this item. This item's failure to fit suggests coordination is not perceived as part of playfulness even for typically-developing children. This finding is particularly relevant, however, to the assessment of playfulness in children with disabilities. For example, having a physical disability such as cerebral palsy will impede a child's ability to move with coordination while playing. The question is whether or not that child is any less playful because of this impairment. Perhaps such children compensate for their poor motor abilities by expressing their playfulness in different ways (Clifford & Bundy, 1989). Therefore, valid assessments of playfulness for children with disabilities, in particular, should exclude such items.

Person Response Validity

We also analyzed the playfulness scores to determine the extent to which individual children fit the Rasch model. A child's failure to fit the measurement model indicates that his or her response pattern was erratic (i.e., the child tended to receive uncharacteristically low scores on easy items or uncharacteristically high scores on hard items). In this case, outfit refers to whether or not the child scored as expected on the easiest or most difficult items. Infit, on the other hand, refers to whether or not the child's scores progressed as expected on the moderately difficult items. The criteria for children fitting the model were identical to the criteria set for item fit (MnSq 1.40, t 2.00).

In the present investigation, seven (8%) of the 89 children had MnSq values greater than 1.40 and t values greater than 2.00, indicating erratic scoring and failure to fit. Thus, 92 percent of the children who participated in this study fit the Rasch measurement model. This percentage is slightly less than the desired 95 percent. Upon closer examination, however, three (43%) of the seven misfitting children were children with special needs. In fact, 33 percent of the children with special needs who were rated on the CPS failed to fit the model. Only four (5%) of the typically-developing children misfit for a total fit of 95 percent for these children. In other words, person response validity was adequate for the typically-developing children alone but not for the total sample including children enrolled in special education.

As noted earlier, children who failed to fit the model scored higher than expected on more difficult items while scoring lower than expected on relatively easier items. This unexpected scoring was particularly prevalent with the three children enrolled in special education who failed to fit the model. For example, one of these children received the highest score possible on difficult items #9 "assumes a leadership role when playing with others" and #17 "gently teases other while at play," yet received the lowest score possible on much easier items #5 "responds easily to others' approaches during play" and #19 "laughs at humorous stories." Perhaps, due to the nature of this child's disability, he was better able to initiate than to respond during play. Likewise, another child enrolled in special education received average scores on most items, but received the lowest score possible on relatively easy items #1 "movements are generally well-coordinated during play activities" and #4 "runs (skips, hops, jumps) a lot in play." Perhaps a physical disability impeded physical expressions of playfulness for this child. Conversely, another child enrolled in special education received the highest score possible on each of the items in the physical spontaneity category, yet received the lowest score possible on all items requiring speech, including one of the easiest items, #15 "sings and talks while playing."

We further analyzed the person response validity of the CPS by investigating potential associations between a child's failure to fit the Rasch model and his or her gender, age, rating source (parent vs. teacher/day care provider), and special education status. No significant relations were found between failure to fit and gender, age, or rating source (all $p > .05$). We did, however, find a significant positive relationship between a child's being enrolled in special education and failure to fit, X^2 $(1, N = 89) = 8.96, p < .005$.

We also examined potential associations between a child's overall CPS score and his or her gender, age, rating source, and special education status. No significant difference was found between playfulness scores of children rated by parents ($M = 2.46$) vs. those rated by teachers/day care providers ($M = 2.36$). Likewise, there was no significant difference between the playfulness scores of males ($M = 2.46$) vs. females ($M = 2.40$) on the CPS. Barnett (1991a) did find a significant difference between playfulness scores for males and females in the physical spontaneity, cognitive spontaneity, and manifest joy dimensions. Because we did not analyze these dimensions individually, any potential differences may have canceled each other out.

Our analysis did reveal, however, that typically-developing children scored significantly higher on overall playfulness ($M = 2.53$) than did children enrolled in special education ($M = 1.59$), $t(87) = 2.40, p < .02$. We also found a statistically significant positive correlation between age and playfulness scores, $t(87) = .39, p < .001$. Barnett

(1991a) also found significant effects for age in the social spontaneity, cognitive spontaneity, and sense of humor dimensions. Therefore, these results are not surprising.

Interestingly, when item calibrations within each of the five domains were averaged in the present study, the domains differed significantly in terms of difficulty, $F(4, 15) = 8.70, p < .01$. For example, manifest joy ($M = -.68$) was found to be the least difficult domain. Next, physical spontaneity ($M = -.30$), cognitive spontaneity ($M = -.01$), and social spontaneity ($M = .33$) were found to be moderately difficult domains. Finally, although the calibrations of its individual items spanned a wide range, sense of humor ($M = .45$) was found to be the most difficult domain (see Figure 1).

In general, with the exception of the three items noted, the CPS appears to be valid for typically-developing boys and girls between 15 and 118 months (1.3 and 9.8 years)

Calibrations (in logits)

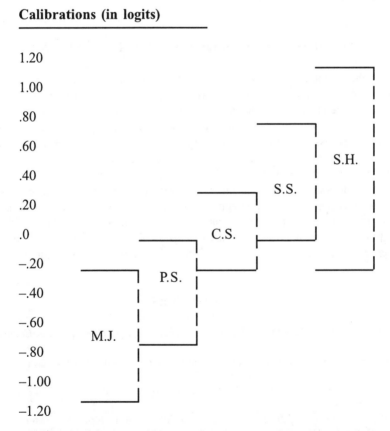

FIGURE 1. Range of calibration scores among items in Barnett's five domains of playfulness (The higher the score, the more difficult the item. M.J. = manifest joy; P.S. = physical spontaneity; C.S. = cognitive spontaneity; S.S. = social spontaneity; S.H. = sense of humor).

based on both parent and teacher ratings. The validity of the CPS for children with disabilities, however, is questionable because of the large percentage of such children who failed to fit the model. Additionally, our results indicating lower playfulness scores for children enrolled in special education suggest either (a) these children actually are less playful than the typically-developing children tested, (b) the CPS items were in some way biased against the children enrolled in special education, or (c) children with disabilities score in diagnostically-significant ways on the CPS.

Perhaps as Clifford and Bundy (1989) suggested, children with disabilities often compensate for deficits by expressing playfulness in different ways. If this is the case, playfulness assessments that are to be used with this population must look beyond typical developmental expressions of playfulness. Rather, these assessments must tap the essential components of playfulness that all children are capable of expressing, regardless of developmental disruptions.

CONCLUSIONS AND IMPLICATIONS FOR FUTURE STUDY

Clearly the advantage of the CPS is its simplicity. Furthermore, it is efficient and cost-effective for professionals to use because it requires no direct observations of the child. It can be filled out by parents and teachers who know the child personally.

The scale's construct validity, however, based on item and person response validity is slightly less than desired. Modifying the scale to exclude the three misfitting items would potentially enhance its construct validity. The fact that a significant number of children with disabilities failed to fit is of great concern, however, particularly to professionals who would be using the CPS with this population. It appears that the CPS, with its emphasis on expressions of playfulness in five developmental domains, has construct validity for children without disabilities but may not for those with disabilities. Clearly, further research, based on large samples of children with disabilities, is needed investigate the validity of the CPS for a wide spectrum of children.

REFERENCES

Barnett, L. A. (1990). Playfulness: Definitions, design, and measurement. *Play & Culture, 3,* 319–336.

Barnett, L. A. (1991a). Characterizing playfulness: Correlates with individual attributes and personality traits. *Play & Culture, 4,* 371–393.

Barnett, L. A. (1991b). The playful child: Measurement of a disposition to play. *Play & Culture, 4,* 51–74.

Bundy, A. C. (1991). Play theory and sensory integration. In A. G. Fisher, E. A. Murray, & A. C. Bundy (Eds.), *Sensory integration: Theory and practice* (pp. 46–68). Philadelphia: F. A. Davis Company.

Bundy, A. C. (992). *Test of playfulness.* Unpublished scale, University of Illinois at Chicago. Department of Occupational Therapy, Chicago.

Bundy, A. C. (1993, March). Assessment of play and leisure: Delineation of the problem. *The American Journal of Occupational Therapy, 47*(3), 217–222.

Clifford, J. M., & Bundy, A. C. (1989). Play preference and play performance in normal boys and boys with sensory integrative dysfunction. *Occupational Therapy Journal of Research, 9,* 202–217.

Fisher, A. G. (1993, April). The assessment of IADL motor skills: An application of many-faceted Rasch analysis. *The American Journal of Occupational Therapy, 47*(4), 319–329.

Fisher, W. P., Jr. (1993, April). Measurement-related problems in functional assessment. *The American Journal of Occupational Therapy, 47*(4), 331–338.

Gliner, J. A. (1992). *OT 650-B: Clinical research.* Unpublished manuscript, Colorado State University, Department of Occupational Therapy, Fort Collins, CO.

LaFreniere, P. J., & Stroufe, L. A. (1985). Profiles of peer competence in the preschool: Interrelations between measures, influence of social ecology, and relation to attachment history. *Developmental Psychology, 21,* 56–69.

Li, W., Bundy, A. C., & Beer, D. W. (1995). Taiwanese parental values toward an American evaluation of playfulness. *Occupational Therapy Journal of Research 15,* 237–258.

Lieberman, J. N. (1977). *Playfulness: Its relationship to imagination and creativity.* New York: Academic Press.

Metzger, P. (1993). *Validity and reliability of a test of playfulness.* Unpublished master's thesis, University of Illinois at Chicago, Chicago.

Muñoz, J. P. (1986). The significance of fostering play development in handicapped children. In An American Occupational Therapy Association Monograph, *Play: A skill for life* (pp. 1–11). Rockville, MD: The American Occupational Therapy Association.

Neumann, E. A. (1971). *The elements of play.* New York: MSS Information.

Pettit, G. S., Bakshi, A., Dodge, K. A., & Coie, J. D. (1990). The emergence of social dominance in young boys' play groups: Developmental differences and behavioral correlates. *Developmental Psychology, 26*(6), 1017–1025.

Rogers, J. C. (1987). Selection of evaluation instruments. In L. King-Thomas & B. J. Hacker (Eds.), *A therapists guide to pediatric assessment* (pp. 3–33). Boston: Little, Brown.

Rubin, K. H., Fein, G. G., & Vandenberg, B. (1983). Play. In P. H. Mussen (Ed.), *Handbook of child psychology (4th ed.): Vol 4. Socialization, personality and social development* (pp. 693–774). New York: Wiley.

Wright, B. D., & Linacre, J. M. (1992). *BIGSTEPS: Rasch analysis for all two-facet models* (Computer program). Chicago: MESA.

10

The Impact of Positioning Equipment on Play Skills of Physically Impaired Children

Jane O'Brien, Tonya Boatwright, Jennifer Chaplin,
Charlene Geckler, Doug Gosnell, Jenni Holcombe,
and Kelsey Parrish

Positioning equipment prescribed frequently by health care providers helps to improve the play skills of children with disabilities. It is often assumed by professionals that improving a child's ability to play will enrich the quality of life of the child and family. However, no research has been conducted showing that the use of positioning equipment improves play skills thus enhancing the quality of life of disabled children and their families.

Positioning equipment is designed to provide children with support, safe and proper positioning, so that they are capable of manipulating objects with their upper extremities and carrying out activities of daily living (i.e., feeding, dressing, toileting, and bathing) and play. It assists children with physical impairments in moving throughout the environment. The equipment facilitates normal development and decreases muscle abnormalities. Positioning equipment includes toilet seats, bath chairs, car seats, feeder seats, toddler chairs, infant seats, prone standers, specialized strollers and crawlers.

Presently, studies address the orthopedic benefits of the positioning equipment and neglect to discuss the issue of play and quality of life for children and families. No research has been conducted examining how proper positioning improves a child's ability to play.

Research conducted in 1992 (Chapmon, Cromartie, Dickey, Heaitley, Mills, O'Brien,& Parker, 1992) at the Medical University of South Carolina indicated that the quality of life of families was increased with the use of the positioning equipment. The study defined quality of life as "one's view of their life satisfaction" and looked at how parents viewed the positioning equipment in making self care skills easier. Results of this study reported improved ability of the parent to care for the child, improved ability of the child to interact and play and increased independence of the child in performing self care tasks (Chapmon et al., 1992). However, the sample size of the study was small; and the data was collected via second hand informant; therefore, the results are questionable. Little emphasis was placed on the importance of the positioning equipment in increasing the child's play skills.

Since play is crucial to the social and psychological development of children, further research is required on how health professionals can assist children with handicaps in improving their ability to play. It is assumed by health care professionals that positioning equipment provides children with proper seating to manipulate objects with their hands, thus improving their ability to play, yet this has never been examined. The purpose of this study was to document the parent's view of the effectiveness of positioning equipment on improving their child's play skills.

POPULATION

The population for this study was families residing in the Low Country region of South Carolina with a family member between the ages of one to 11 years diagnosed with a physical impairment. These children were receiving occupational and/or physical therapy at the Vince Moseley Center, Medical University Hospital, Charleston County Schools, or Home Health agency.

LITERATURE REVIEW

Occupational therapists play a vital role in improving the quality of life for disabled children and their families. This is accomplished through direct intervention, home programs, family intervention, family education and the prescription of positioning equipment. The equipment prescribed by therapists improves the child's position so various skills can be performed with ease. Once the child is in a more functional position, self care (i.e., feeding, dressing, bathing, and toileting) and play skills are improved. For example, children who do not have enough truncal control to sit up on their own can sit up and play with toys while positioned in a specialized chair. Children who would otherwise spend the day lying on their back are able to sit in special seats and use their hands to operate simple toys. However, there has been no research conducted concerning the important link between the use of positioning equipment and its effects on improving the play skills, thus quality of life of children with disabilities and their families.

Callahan (1988) reported that when family members learn that one of their children is disabled, they often feel confined to a questionable future and a life they did not choose. At the same time, they must learn how to give the child special care that he/she needs. This may involve special medical treatment, increased time and energy for parenting, added expenses, and adapting to the play needs of the child.

When children have decreased play skills and an inability to care for themselves due to a disabling condition, the family members experience a decrease in their quality of life (Callahan, 1988; Wallande, Pitt, & Millins, 1990). For example, a higher degree of psychological distress has been found in mothers of disabled children as compared to mothers of normal children (Wallande, Pitt, & Millins, 1990). This can be attributed in part to the fact that mothers of disabled children spend more time on physical daily care of their children and less time in play and leisure activities. These mothers may not be able to go to work outside the home, which may cause financial problems for the family. They may also feel isolated from society. Many mothers of disabled children experience feelings of guilt due to their resentment of the added responsibility of the disabled child (Wallande, Pitt, & Millins, 1990).

One study revealed that families with a disabled child reported less satisfaction in their lives because of the greater time demands and lower incomes due to the expense of the disabled child (Dunst, Trivette, & Cross, 1985). Other problem areas identified are the limited free time for family members, added child care responsibilities that make daily living stressful, and feelings of helplessness and frustration (Harris & McHale, 1989; Anderson & Hinjosa, 1984). These factors interfere with the quality of social interaction and play.

The amount of time that families with a disabled child spend engaging in physical care is greater than the time required to care for a normal child. The increased time spent on physical care of the disabled child places greater demands on parents resulting in less time to play with their children. Time spent on self care activities is not as playful because of the physical requirements. Therefore, the families' quality of life is strained. By decreasing the burden of providing daily care to a disabled child family members are able to engage in more play activities (Johnson & Dietz, 1985).

Since play is the primary role of childhood (Kielhofner, 1985), it is crucial that health professionals concerned with improving the quality of life of children with special needs address play. Research has shown that children with special needs play more passively secondary to decreased physical capabilities (Brooks-Gunn & Lewis, 1982). Is this truly play if the child is not actively involved? Although the definition of play is continually being debated, one recurring theme is that play is characterized by active involvement of the player (Rubin, Fein, & Vandenburg, 1983). If positioning equipment can provide children with the support they need to be more independent in play, then health care professionals are truly making a difference in children's and families' lives.

This study seeks to document the effect of positioning equipment on improving the play skills of children with special needs. This study suggests that improving the play skills of children with special needs and decreasing the stress involved in daily care activities improves the quality of life of the children and their families. Results of this study provide professionals with insight to more effectively meet the needs of children with special needs and their families.

METHODOLOGY

A survey (Appendix A) was designed to document the parent's view of the effect the positioning equipment made in improving the play skills of the child. The study set out to answer the questions "Does positioning equipment improve the child's play skills?" and "Does positioning equipment improve the parents ability to care for their child?"

Therapists in the community asked parents to participate in the study and provided researchers with the names and phone numbers of those who agreed to participate. Team members contacted 30 parents and set up individual appointments convenient for the parents. The survey consisting of 10 Likert Scale questions was administered to the parents. The Likert Scale is a 5-point rating system, with 1 being the lowest rating, 5 being the highest, and 3 being average. 5 open-ended questions were answered during the interview by the parent. Completion of the survey and interview implied consent for inclusion in the study.

SAMPLE SELECTION

The participants in this study were parents of children between the ages of 1 and 11 years who received occupational and/or physical therapy in the Low Country of South Carolina. The parents agreed to be interviewed and complete a survey. Only members of the research team had access to the names and medical history of the children. Selections of the children were made at random and not based on sex, race, ethnic group, or religion.

RESULTS

The completed surveys were gathered from the parents and responses were prepared for data analysis using P-Edit, a test editor. Descriptive statistics were used to analyze the data.

Thirty surveys were completed. Demographic information revealed the primary respondents were married ($n = 19$) mothers ($n = 18$) an average age of 30 who had completed high school ($M = 12.33$). The employment status of the respondents showed that an equal number were unemployed as were employed ($n = 14$) while two respondents worked part time. The gross yearly income average for all respondents was $18,000.

The children were mostly white males ($n = 21$) ranging between 1 to 11 years of age with the average age being 4 years old. The most prevalent diagnoses were cerebral palsy ($n = 14$) and spina bifida ($n = 3$). The most common pieces of equipment used were: Rifton chair ($n = 10$); Prone Stander ($n = 9$); Corner Seat ($n = 5$); Zippie Wheelchair ($n = 5$); Feeder Seat ($n = 4$) and Bath Seat ($n = 3$). The major purpose of the equipment was reported as: Positioning ($n = 23$); Feeding ($n = 15$); Play ($n = 13$); Bathing ($n = 3$); and Mobility ($n = 3$).

The question "Did the positioning equipment improve the parent's ability to care for the child?" was supported by the following data. Of the parents ($n = 15$) who stated the major purpose of the equipment was to improve feeding skills, 73.3 percent rated it as excellent; 20 percent rated it as very good; and 7 percent rated it as good. Of the parents ($n = 23$) who stated the major purpose for the equipment was to improve positioning, thus improving self care skills, 34.7 percent rated it as excellent; 30 percent rated it as very good; 17 percent rated it as good; and 9 percent rated it as fair. Of the parents ($n = 3$) who stated the major purpose for the equipment was to improve bathing, 67 percent rated it as excellent; and 33 percent rated it as very good. According to this data, the positioning equipment was very good to excellent at improving the parent's ability to feed, position, and bathe their child.

In further support of this data, the top three responses to the open-ended question, "What do you like most about the equipment?" were that it makes feeding, transporting, and taking care of the child easier. Informal conversations with the parents revealed that by improving these aspects of daily living skills, the use of the positioning equipment decreased the stress level in their lives significantly. Parents reported the time saved and ease in caring for their children dramatically improved the atmosphere in the household. "Did the positioning equipment improve the child's play skills?" was addressed in three specific responses. Of the parents ($n = 13$) who stated the major purpose of the equipment was to improve play skills, 77 percent rated it as excellent; 15 percent rated it as very good; and 7 percent rated it as fair. When describing their interaction with their child while using the equipment, 43 percent of the parents reported the interaction as excellent; 39 percent reported it as very good; and 18 percent reported it as good. To further support this data, 92 percent of the parents reported the equipment improved the ability of the child to entertain him/herself.

DISCUSSION AND IMPLICATIONS

This study confirmed that there is a significant impact upon play skills of children with physical impairments through the use of positioning equipment as viewed by their parents. Since daily living skills were accomplished easier per report from the parents, one may assume parents had both more time to play with their child and reduced stress in their lives. This is further supported by 92 percent of the responses ranging from excellent to very good to the direct question "Did the positioning equipment improve the child's play skills?"

Play allows children to explore, learn, and interact with their environment and others. A child's quality of life depends largely on his/her play skills. Children with physical impairments are not able to play in the same manner as their normal peers. If positioning equipment provides children with stability and motor skills necessary to play, then it is truly enriching their quality of life. This study confirmed that the positioning equipment had a positive impact on the child's quality of life through enhancing their play skills.

This research validates the use of the equipment in improving both the children's and families' quality of life. Not only does the positioning equipment improve the children's quality of life through improving their ability to play more effectively, but it also improves the quality of life for the parents by making daily living activities easier for the parents. This allows parents more free time to interact playfully with their child.

The results of this study support what health professionals have assumed to be true, but have failed to examine; improved positioning increases a child's ability to play and decreases the stress involved in performing daily living activities, therefore enhancing the quality of life for the child and family. For example, parents of disabled children frequently report difficulty in feeding their children. Often mealtime lasts for over one hour and the child is positioned awkwardly on their lap. A specialized chair with added support helps the child sit upright independently. This makes mealtime more enjoyable for both the child and family. Furthermore, parents reported to the researchers that children played more with their brothers and sisters when he/she was sitting upright.

While other studies focus upon the orthopedic benefits of positioning equipment, this study stresses the benefits of positioning equipment on the child's quality of life. Health professionals should not overlook the other advantages (i.e., improved play skills) obtained through the use of positioning equipment. As this study concludes, specialized positioning equipment positions the child so that he/she is able to play.

The information gained from this study can be used by health care providers to enhance the quality of life of children with special needs and their families. Further research is recommended regarding the methods to evaluate the impact made upon the quality of life of the children and families they treat. Further identification of factors influencing the quality of life in the family of children with disabilities would be beneficial to health care providers.

APPENDIX: QUALITY OF LIFE

Child's Initials
Researcher _____
Date _____
Address _____
Telephone # _____
Therapist_____

I. CAREGIVER

a) Relation to Child: _____

b) Age: _____

c) Gender: _____ Female _____ Male

d) Marital status: _____ Married

_____ Not Married (single, divorced, separated)

e) Circle highest grade completed in school:

6 7 8 9 10 11 12 (or GED) 13 14 15 16 17 18

f) Work status: _____ employed full-time

_____ employed part-time

_____ unemployed

g) Gross monthly income (including all types of aid):

_____ $ 0.00–500.00

_____ $ 501.00–1000.00

_____ $1001.00–1500.00

_____ $1501.00–2000.00

_____ $2001.00–2500.00

_____ $2501.00–3000.00

_____ $3001.00–up

II. CHILD

a) Age: _____

b) Gender: _____ Female

_____ Male

c) Race: _____ Afro-American

_____ Caucasion

_____ Hispanic

_____ Other, please specify_____

d) Diagnosis: _____

1) List type(s) of adaptive equipment received.

1._____

2._____

3._____

4._____

2) What was the major purpose(s) of each piece of adaptive equipment?

1._____

2._____

3._____

4._____

3) Overall, how would you rate the equipment in serving its intended purpose (Circle one)

1. *Purpose*

Excellent	5
Very Good	4
Good	3
Fair	2
Poor	1

2. *Purpose*

Excellent	5
Very Good	4
Good	3
Fair	2
Poor	1

3. *Purpose*

Excellent	5
Very Good	4
Good	3
Fair	2
Poor	1

4. *Purpose*

Excellent	5
Very Good	4
Good	3
Fair	2
Poor	1

4) How would you rate the following factors?

1. *Convenience*

Excellent	5
Very Good	4
Good	3
Fair	2
Poor	1

2. *Convenience*

Excellent	5
Very Good	4
Good	3
Fair	2
Poor	1

3. *Convenience*

Excellent	5
Very Good	4
Good	3
Fair	2
Poor	1

4. *Convenience*

Excellent	5
Very Good	4
Good	3
Fair	2
Poor	1

1. *Time Saving*

Excellent	5
Very Good	4
Good	3
Fair	2
Poor	1

2. *Time Saving*

Excellent	5
Very Good	4
Good	3
Fair	2
Poor	1

3. *Time Saving*

Excellent	5
Very Good	4
Good	3
Fair	2
Poor	1

4. *Time Saving*

Excellent	5
Very Good	4
Good	3
Fair	2
Poor	1

1. *Portable*

Excellent	5
Very Good	4
Good	3
Fair	2
Poor	1

2. *Portable*

Excellent	5
Very Good	4
Good	3
Fair	2
Poor	1

3. *Portable*

Excellent	5
Very Good	4
Good	3
Fair	2
Poor	1

4. *Portable*

Excellent	5
Very Good	4
Good	3
Fair	2
Poor	1

1. *Lightweight*

Excellent	5
Very Good	4
Good	3
Fair	2
Poor	1

2. *Lightweight*

Excellent	5
Very Good	4
Good	3
Fair	2
Poor	1

3. *Lightweight*

Excellent	5
Very Good	4
Good	3
Fair	2
Poor	1

4. *Lightweight*

Excellent	5
Very Good	4
Good	3
Fair	2
Poor	1

1. *Size*

Excellent	5
Very Good	4
Good	3
Fair	2
Poor	1

2. *Size*

Excellent	5
Very Good	4
Good	3
Fair	2
Poor	1

3. *Size*

Excellent	5
Very Good	4
Good	3
Fair	2
Poor	1

4. *Size*

Excellent	5
Very Good	4
Good	3
Fair	2
Poor	1

5) How would you best describe your interaction with your child while using this equipment?

Fun and Enjoyable	5
Relaxed	4
Neutral-okay	3
Difficult	2
Tense and Stressful	1

6) What did you like most about the adaptive equipment?
   1) _____
   2) _____
   3) _____
   4) _____

7) What did you like least about the adaptive equipment?
   1) _____
   2) _____
   3) _____
   4) _____

8) Did the equipment increase the child's ability in areas of feeding, dressing, bathing, or toileting? (explain how)

_____
_____

9) How has the use of this equipment changed your feelings about what your child can do? (please explain).
   (ex. "Now he can feed himself," "I can take her anywhere")

   play: _____
   feeding: _____
   self-care:_____
   daily-routine: _____

10) Explain how the use of the equipment helped you with your daily routine?

_____
_____

11) How did the positioning equipment effect your child's play?

_____
_____

12) Would you recommend this equipment to other parents in your same situation?

yes _____

no _____

13) Please include any additional information you would like to share with us concerning your feelings toward the use of this equipment.

_____

_____

14) Do you see any difference in family interactions with others that you would attribute to the use of the equipment?

_____

_____

_____

15) Please share any feelings or experience you have regarding the funding of necessary equipment for your child? (ex. "my insurance wouldn't cover it," "it would take too long to get it approved").

_____

_____

REFERENCES

Anderson, J., & Hinojosa, J. (1984). Parents and therapist in a professional partnership. *American Journal of Occupational Therapy, 38*, 452–462.

Brooks-Gunn, J., & Lewis, M. (1982). Development of play behavior in handicapped and normal infants. *Topics in Early Childhood Education, 2*, 14–27.

Callahan, D. (1988). Families as care givers: the limits of morality. *Arch Phys Med Rehabilitation, 69*, 323–327.

Chapmon, S., Cromartie, K., Dickey, L., Heaitley, R., Mills, C., O'Brien, J. & Parker, H. (1992). *Positioning equipment: Its impact on the parent and child.* Unpublished manuscript, Medical University of South Carolina, Occupational Therapy Educational Program, Charleston, SC.

Dunst, C. J., Trivette, C. M., & Cross, A. H. (1985). Mediating influences of social support: Personal, family, and child outcomes. *American Journal of Mental Deficiency, 90*, (4), 403–417.

Harris, V. S., & McHale, S. M. (1989). Family life problems, daily care giving activities, and the psychological well-being of mothers of mentally retarded children. *American Journal of Mental Retardation, 94*(3), 231–239.

Johnson, C. & Deitz, J. (1985). Time use of mothers with preschool children: a pilot study. *American Journal of Occupational Therapy, 39*, 578–583.

Kielhofner, G. (Ed.) (1985). *A model of human occupation: Theory and application.* Baltimore: Williams & Wilkins.

Rubin, K., Fein, G., & Vandenberg, B. (1983). Play. In P.H. Mussen (Ed.) *Handbook of child psychology (4th ed.): Vol.4. Socialization, personality and social development* (pp. 693–774). New York: Wiley.

Wallande, J. L., Pitt, L. C., & Mellins, C. A. (1990). Child functional independence and maternal psychosocial stress as risk factors threatening adaptation in mothers of physically or sensorially handicapped children. *Journal of Consulting and Clinical Psychology, 58*(6), 818–824.

part IV

Playful Primates

Introduction

Garry Chick

Play is common among the young of most mammalian species. There are intraspecies differences in the forms of play but it is one of the very few forms of behavior that is not universally subjected to the Cartesian dichotomization of humans and animals, that is, us versus them. Further, playfulness in animals correlates well enough with factors such as relative brain size, length of lifespan, and reliance on learning versus instinct that it does not seem to be either evolutionarily accidental or a byproduct of something else. Yet, though it seems certain that mammalian play is the result of natural selection and thus has adaptive consequences, those consequences are not at all obvious at this time (Boulton & Smith, 1992). The two chapters that follow deal with the play of a relatively distant primate relative of humans, the rhesus monkey, and that of our closest primate relative, the chimpanzee. Though neither deals directly with the adaptive functions of play, studies like these contribute to the knowledge base that furthers our understanding of why play is so widespread among primates, including humans, and mammals more generally.

In the first chapter, Rosemary Bolig, Cristofer Price, Peggy O'Neill-Wagner, and Stephen Suomi determine whether the frequency of play and exploratory behavior of young rhesus monkeys is stable and consistent and whether it is related to reactivity level, a temperament dimension. They also evaluate the interactions of context, whether the animal is free ranging or confined indoors, age, and the influences of social and situational stressors, on play. Reactivity, a characteristic style of responding to demand, change, and challenge, is commonly used to used to predict behaviors in both humans and nonhumans.

Bolig, Price, O'Neill-Wagner, and Suomi find that variability in both play and environmental exploration are great among rhesus monkeys and that apparent individual differences most often failed to persist over time. Animals that were either high or low reactors were more likely than moderate reactors to change in play frequency but only in the free ranging condition. Reactivity level did predict variability in both indoor and outdoor environmental exploration and indoor self-play. Environmental exploration may be related to reactivity level for one-year-olds while social play may be related to reactivity for two-year-olds, although the latter finding may reflect a gender rather than reactivity effect (females were high reactors while males were low reactors). A variety of possible explanations are offered for these results. This study demonstrates the potential productivity in looking at observable temperament variables in conjunction with environmental conditions, age, and gender in the study of play among nonhuman primates.

In the second chapter, Drummer, Cunningham, and Sughrue evaluate play behavior with respect to the estrus cycle of an adolescent chimpanzee, Julie, at the Knoxville Zoological Gardens. This study is part of a larger project dealing with the social integration of two infant chimpanzees into an existing group at the Zoo. Drummer, Cunningham, and Sughrue found that Julie exhibited social play almost exclusively during estrus. The authors do not speculate on the reasons for this but do suggest directions for future research that will help elucidate the effects of estrus on other social behavior, such as grooming and proximity.

REFERENCE

Boulton, M. J., & Smith P. K. (1992). The social nature of play fighting and play chasing: Mechanisms and strategies underlying cooperation and compromise. In J. H. Barkow, L. Cosmides, & J. Tooby (Eds.), *The adapted mind* (pp. 429–444). New York: Oxford University Press.

11

Reactivity and Play and Exploration Behaviors of Young Rhesus Monkeys

Rosemary Bolig, Cristofer S. Price,
Peggy L. O'Neill-Wagner, and Stephen J. Suomi

INTRODUCTION

Exploration and play of both non-human and human primates have been found to be influenced by age, gender, situational variables, contextual factors, social rank, and early childrearing experiences (Baldwin, 1986; O'Neill-Wagner, Bolig, & Price, 1994; French, 1981; Pellegrini & Perlmutter, 1989; Suomi & Harlow, 1978). Although individual differences in exploration and play have been studied, they have not typically been related to specific temperament dimensions. Highly reactive children, however, have been rated low on such measures as "is curious and explorative" and "is resourceful in initiating activities" (Suomi, 1987). Certain forms of human play (e.g., solitary-functional) have also been related to rankings of hyperactivity-distractibility (Pellegrini & Perlmutter, 1989). Play levels of nine-month-old rhesus monkeys have been found to be predictive of home-cage reactivity at 18 and 30 months (Higley, 1985).

Play and exploration are particularly characteristic behaviors of young primates and are generally observable in a variety of contexts when specific conditions such as toys and freedom from excessive anxiety are present. Play, often preceded by exploration, increases in intensity and duration during infancy, becomes more complex in early childhood, and decreases in middle childhood. Gender differences in frequency and patterns also appear during early childhood.

Play behavior appears important for normal development among primates. However, the exact function play serves is still in question. Among researchers of human play, there are two primary views: that play serves a direct function in development, and that play serves a primary expressive function and indirect influence on development (Johnson, Christy, & Yawkey, 1987). Nonhuman primate play researchers primarily cite socialization or behavioral flexibility functions, although over 28 functions have been suggested (Poirier, Bellisari, & Haines, 1978). Despite the lack of consensus on the functions of play, when young are deprived of play or the conditions necessary for play, it becomes clear that the *absence* of play is related to poor social skills, anxiety, depression, and for humans, cognitive and academic difficulties (Smilansky, 1968; Suomi & Harlow, 1976).

Among human young, play behavior is a developmental phenomenon, shifting from object manipulation (exploration), to transformation, to independence, to internalized fantasy, while simultaneously shifting from self-play to play with others (Johnson et al., 1987). In addition to age, gender, and social class differences, a number of individual differences have been determined. Emmerick (1964) and Jennings (1975) described an object-versus-people orientation. Degree of field independence/dependence has also been found to be related to object- or people-orientation. Coates, Lord, and Jakabouics (1975) found field-dependent children more people-oriented and field-independent children to be more object-oriented. Liebermann (1977) defined a "playfulness" dimension of personality, which was correlated with divergent thinking as well as mental and chronological age. Dansky and Silverman (1975) found that preschool players, as opposed to nonplayers, scored significantly higher on tests of divergent thinking. A fantasy-making predisposition has also been suggested (Singer, 1975). High fantasy children have been found to have greater imaginativeness, positive affect, concentration, social interaction, and cooperation during free play than low-fantasy children (Johnson et al., 1987). High fantasy has also been found to be associated with impulse control and delay of gratification (Singer, 1968). Correlations with situational anxiety and play have also yielded significant results: the more anxious children are, the less they play.

In addition to these broad dimensions across all forms of human play, individual differences within forms have also been studied. Through their study of symbolic play, Wolf and Grollman (1982) delineated two styles: object-independent/fantasy and object-dependent/transformational. These styles have also been found to be stable over time. "Patterns" and "dramatics" have also been found to have differing underlying mental structures (Wolf & Gardner, 1979). Style of play with objects has also been characterized by tempo (e.g., number of actions, changes, and combinations) (Fein, 1979) or elaborations, complexity, and persistence (Johnson et al., 1987).

As with human's play, nonhuman primates' play and exploration varies by age and gender, and proceeds from self to increased social play. But dominance rank as well as species differences have also been found (Baldwin, 1986). For example, subordinate males are more likely to touch unknown objects, but are less systematic in their exploration than dominant males (McGuire & Raleigh, 1986). Infants of subordinate females play less frequently than the infants of dominant mothers (Gard & Meier, 1977).

However, despite attempts to account for the differences in exploration and play through these previously cited factors (e.g., age, gender, social/dominance rank, situation, and individual differences in styles or tempo), not all the variance in play has been accounted for either human or nonhuman primates. But certain dimensions of temperament have been found to be related to characteristic styles of reacting to change, demand, or challenge. Temperamental inhibition in humans (Kagen, Reznick, & Snidman, 1986) and reactivity in nonhuman primates (Higley & Suomi, 1989; Suomi, 1987) have been related to degree of inhibition, withdrawal, anxiety and relaxation, and spontaneity when presented with novel stimuli. Highly reactive monkeys or behaviorally inhibited children are, for example, more inhibited in their exploration of new environments and less playful following exploration than their less inhibited/reactive counterparts (Higley, 1985). These patterns, which appear to become stable after infancy in humans and after six to eight months in rhesus monkeys are assessable under duress (Kagen, 1982; Suomi, 1987), but may be observable in behaviors responsive to the day-to-day developmental demands (Champoux, 1988).

Is the quantity of exploration and play related to temperamental reactivity differences that mediate the experience of young monkeys and children? To what degree does context, such as whether confined indoors or permitted to be outdoors or in, interact with reactivity systems to influence play or environmental exploration (Stevenson-Hinde, 1986)? The purposes of this exploratory study were to determine: (1) the nature and degree of individual variation in the exploration and play of young rhesus macaques and whether this variation is stable over time; (2) whether subjective assessments of temperamental reactivity were related to differences in frequency of exploration and play behaviors; (3) whether subjectively assessed reactivity level interacts with environment to influence play/environmental exploration frequency; (4) whether reactivity level is expressed through different behaviors at different ages; and (5) whether situational/social stressors affect the play and exploration of high, moderate, and low reactive monkeys differently.

METHODS

The subjects of this study were 12 rhesus monkeys followed from infancy through three years of age, when the most play is exhibited, with rapid decline thereafter. The troop was a captive group of animals of four generations, the original animals having been surrogate-raised. These animals were observed utilizing a focal animal system from two to five times per week over a four year period in two conditions: semifreeranging and confined, each for approximately one-half year. When confined, animals were located in one of two large enclosures (i.e., mesh corncrib with plexiglass

TABLE 1.
Subject Characteristics and Tempermental Reactivity Ratings

	OBS1	OBS2	OBS3	AGREE		SEX	MAT	BIRTH
Evan	2	3	2	67%	2	M	MO	5/1/84
Linda	3	3	3	100%	3	F	MO	3/9/84
Hershey	2	1	3	—	-	M	SU	3/28/84
Taurus	2	3	2	67%	2	M	MO	5/3/85
Tanker	3	3	2	67%	3	M	SU	5/21/85
Billy	2	3	2	67%	2	M	MO	3/8/86
Muffin	2	2	2	100%	2	F	MOL	5/22/86
Pearl	3	2	3	67%	2	F	SU	4/5/86
Trout	1	1	1	100%	1	M	SU	5/12/87
Kiwi	3	3	3	100%	3	F	SU	6/26/87
Bardot	2	2	3	67%	2	F	MO	4/12/88
Lily	2	3	3	67%	3	F	MO	4/3/88
Schlim	1	2	-	—	-	M	MOL	3/23/88
Orbit	1	1	1	100%	1	M	SU	5/2/88

and barn); when free, animals had access to the enclosures as well as five acres of grassland, pond, and trees. The total troop had from 19 to 25 members during the time the data for the present analyses were collected.

The subjective reactivity assessment was completed by three observers (Bolig, Price, O'Neill, & Suomi, 1992). Subjects were ranked as high, moderate, or low on reactivity, based on personal assessments. High reactivity was defined as "least likely to approach new stimuli, most anxious, most socially inhibited, and least likely to attempt challenging situation" (Suomi, 1987). For the animal to be classified, acceptance was set at agreement between two of the three observers. Of the 14 age-eligible animals, 12 were included in this analysis. One animal was not included as one observer failed to classify him; the other was omitted because there was no agreement among observers (see Table 1). There was 100 percent agreement on six animals, and 67 percent agreement on eight. In no instance was the dissenting category more than one category in difference.

RESULTS

Prediction of Behaviors by Reactivity Level

In order to determine whether variability in nonsocial play, social play, initiating and receiving play, and environmental exploration, was predicted by subjectively-rated reactivity level, regression analyses were employed. For each behavior, first age and gender, and then reactivity level were entered as predictors. Reactivity level was found to be a significant predictor in indoor self-play ($p = .05$) and indoor environmental exploration was associated but only at the $p = .07$ level. As animals increased in reac-

TABLE 2.
Multiple Regression Analyses

	Model 1	Model 2
SOCIAL PLAY		
OUTDOOR	R2 = .31	R2 = .34
	Age = −.31, p.004	Age = −.29, p.006
	Sex = −.64, p.006	Sex = −.51, p.05
		React = −.60, p.76
INDOOR	R2 = .53	R2 = .58
	Age = −.50, p.02	R2 = .55, p.0001
	Sex = −1.62, p.001	Sex = −1.97, p.0001
		React = .35, p.26
NONSOCIAL PLAY		
OUTDOOR	R2 = .36	R2 = .36
	Age = −30, p.0001	Age = −31, p.0006
	Sex = −.06, p.70	Sex = −.06, p.78
		React = −.05, p.74
INDOOR	R2 = .50	R2 = .36
	Age = −.78, p.0001	Age = −.89, p.0001
	Sex = −.31, p.23	Sex = −.62, p.06
		React = .36, p.13
ENVIRONMENTAL EXPLORE		
OUTDOOR	R2 = .06	R2 = .14
	Age = −.27, p.15	Age = −.04, p.84
	Sex = .05, p.90	Sex = .61, p.21
		React = −.73, p.04
INDOOR	R2 = .09	R2 = .19
	Age = −.75, p.12	Age = −.38, p.44
	Sex = −.28, p.71	Sex = .49, p.59
		React = −1.28, p.07

tivity, they decreased in exploration, while increasing in self-play. Likewise, environmental exploration while freeranging was also predicted by reactivity level ($p = .04$). Environmental exploration, unlike social and nonsocial play, was not influenced by age and gender. The amount of variability in any of the other behaviors in either the confined or free condition were not predicted by reactivity level.

Stability Across Development

In order to determine stability in social and nonsocial play, initiating and receiving social play, and in environmental exploration, correlational analyses across ages were conducted. Because previous examination of similar data found the confined or semi-freeranging contexts to be important in the frequency of play behaviors (O'Neill-Wagner, Bolig, & Price, 1994), especially for males, separate correlations for these two conditions were conducted.

Only for the ages from one-to-two-years of age was environmental exploration during the outdoor condition found significant ($r = .89$, $p = .0068$). For social play while outdoors, again for the one-to-two-year-olds, the relationship approached significance ($r = .84$, $p = .099$). But when indoors, there was a highly significant relationship in social play for animals from two-to three-years ($r = .84$, $p = .008$). In nonsocial play, or its three subtypes (i.e., self-, apparatus, locomotion), there was little stability in animals' relative frequency over time. The only exception was in self-play which approach significance indoors from one-to two-years ($r = .66$, $p = .11$), and outdoors from infancy from one-to two-years ($r = .61$, $p = .08$).

Analyses for Instability

From these analyses, the least stable time was from infancy to one year of age and again from two- to three-years. The greatest stability was from one to two years, as found in environmental exploration, social play, and self-play (See Table 2), although social play in the confined condition was highly stable from two to three years. Efforts to determine why there was so little stability over time included: exploration of the degree of variance and changes in rank (e.g., highest to lowest frequency of each selected behavior) related to reactivity level.

Analyses of Variability

The reason the amount of between-subject variability was investigated was that if there had been little between subject variability in infants and one-year-olds, then it wouldn't have been surprising if there was change in rank frequency time. If all means clustered at infancy and at one year, any change in rank would not indicate major actual change. If the amount of between-subject variation was high, however, actual change may have occurred. In this case, it is of interest that an individual who played a lot more than age mates as an infant may actually be a relatively low frequency player as a one-year-old. Thus, between-subject variability did not explain lack of relationship between one age group and the next.

Analysis of Rank Change

In exploration of whether reactivity influences changes in relative rank over time, a series of individual graphs and tests of significance were conducted. For each age group for each behavior subjects were ranked from highest to lowest frequency. If an individual was ranked highest at infancy, but was ranked third as a one-year-old, then the subject decreased in rank. The relationship of reactivity level to direction and degree of rank change was also investigated. Outdoors, those who did change in position *in general* were the high and low reactors, who usually increased in frequency, while the moderate reactors tended to decrease somewhat. On average, the high reactors increased in rank, while low reactors decreased, and moderates tended to remain the same. Indoors, reactivity level didn't appear to explain degree or direction of rank changes.

To further explore whether reactivity level was related to degree of change from one age group to the next, a series of 1-Factor ANOVAS were performed. For each animal, the difference from one age to the next was calculated for each behavior. Analysis of variance was used to test whether high, moderate, or low reactors differed significantly in mean difference from one age group to another. In no case was there a significant relationship between reactivity level and mean differences from one year to the next. However, across play and exploration behaviors in the outdoor condition there was a tendency for either high or low reactors to have greater differences from infancy to one year and from one year to two years than did the moderate reactors. By two to three years, there was no trend apparent by reactivity level. Indoors, there were no apparent trends related to reactivity level.

TABLE 3.
Means & Correlations Between Ages

	Infants	0 to 1	Ones	1 to 2	Twos	2 to 3	Threes
NS Play							
Out	1.03	−.08	1.28	−.05	.58	−.10	.22
In			2.75	.23	1.69	.37	.92
Social Play							
Out	1.42	.01	1.94	.67**	1.33	−.10	.53
In			2.49	.66*	2.72	.84****	1.45
Environmental Explore							
Out	2.79	.36	2.30	.89****	2.82	.43	2.07
In			3.42	.59*	3.33	−.37	2.88

**** $p < .01$
*** $p < .05$
** $p < .10$
* $p < .15$

Reactivity at Different Age Levels

In order to determine whether reactivity level influences any of the selected behaviors in a non-linear fashion, that is, interacts uniquely at different ages, analysis of variance was performed on each group in both the free and confined conditions.

Infants: Free

For infants ($n = 8$), with outdoor data only, reactivity level did not significantly influence any of the behaviors.

One Year-Olds: Confined and Free

For one-year-olds ($n = 10$) in the freeranging condition, environmental exploration was found to differ significantly by reactivity level ($p = .05$). Low reactors ($M = 4.475$) and moderate reactors ($M = 1.837$).

In the confined condition, environmental exploration was not significant, although there was a similar trend ($p = .11$) to that observed outdoors. Receive play ($p = .07$) was of border-line significance in confinement; moderates received the most play ($M = 1.40$), with low reactors ($M = 1.03$) and high reactors ($M = 0.89$) less. Apparatus play during confinement ($p = .08$) also approached significance, with low reactors ($M = 2.47$) engaging in the most, followed by high reactors ($M = 2.28$) and moderate reactors ($M = 1.56$).

Two-Year-Olds: Confined and Free

Two-year-olds in the outdoor condition socially played significantly different by reactivity level ($p = .03$), with low reactors ($M = 2.38$) playing significantly more than the moderates ($M = 1.31$) and highs ($M = 1.12$). When social play was broken down into "initiating" ($p = .04$) and "receiving" ($p = .06$) both were significant and in the same direction: i.e., low reactors both initiated ($M = 1.04$) and received ($M = 1.22$) more social play than the moderates (receive, $M = .575$; initiate, $M = .615$) and high reactors (receive, $M = .495$; initiate, $M = .495$).

In the confined condition, only receiving play approached significance ($p=.09$), but for initiate play and overall social play, the trend was for low reactors to play the most, followed by moderate reactors, and then the high reactors.

Three-Year-Olds: Confined and Free

For three-year-olds, with no low reactors, there were no significant differences in either the confined or free conditions for highs versus moderates.

Although these findings may be reflecting gender differences as well as reactivity level differences, because the proportion of males was progressively less from highs to lows, these data do suggest that within age reactivity—if it affects behaviors at all—may not affect one behavior consistently throughout development. For example, environmental exploration seems to be most affected in one-year-olds, while social play is most affected in two-year-olds.

Effect of Situational and Social Stressors

Since it did appear that the reactivity level of rhesus monkeys might differently affect stability at particular developmental periods and in different contexts (i.e., confined or free), the next question was whether there might likewise be more vulnerability to particular stress events (i.e., mothers' sexual consort, and transitions from outdoor to in and vice versa) related to reactivity level.

Adjustment: Free to Confined and Confined to Free

The test was whether for the two weeks after confinement there was a difference in mean frequency of behaviors by reactivity level for one-to two-year-old females and for one- to three-year-old males. There were two individuals for each reactivity level. But the low reactors were both males and the high reactors both females.

For initiating play, the low reactors ($M = 1.875$) played significantly ($p = .04$) more during the transition from free to confined than did either the moderates ($M = 0.50$) or high reactors ($M = 0.00$). Similarly, for social play, the low reactors ($M = 5.75$) played significantly more ($p = .03$) than the highs ($M = 0.75$) or moderates ($M = 0.88$). Reactivity level was not found to affect any other behaviors during the adjustment from free to confinement. But low reactors were both males and highs were females; previous analyses found that males social play significantly more than females under stable conditions.

In the adjustment period from confined to free, high reactors ($M = .25$) played on apparatus significantly ($p = .05$) more than did the moderate ($M = .00$) or low ($M = .00$) reactors. None of the other behaviors were found to be influenced by reactivity level.

Maternal Consort

Another potentially stressful condition that was tested was when mothers were in breeding consort. When a mother's in consort she may alter interactions with her offspring, since her attention may be on establishing or maintaining relations with selected males. Also, with an adolescent or adult male in closer proximity than in other circumstances, offspring may be more threatened. Although infants would most likely be affected, in this sample there were insufficient numbers to be tested. Instead, one- and two-year-olds were studied.

Utilizing data for individuals only during times their mothers were consorting, a *t-test* was employed to compare mean frequencies of behaviors of one-year-old low reactors to high reactors, and two-year-old low reactors to high reactors. There were two subjects per group.

Among the one-year-olds, only for environmental exploration was there a significant difference ($p = .05$) with low reactors ($M = 2.37$) exploring more during the stressful condition than the high reactors ($M = 0.56$). While both explored less, the difference was greatest for the high reactors. Across the outdoor condition, however, low reactors ($M = 4.48$) environmentally explored more than the high reactors

(M = 3.82), but only approaching significance (p = .07). For the two-year-olds, there were no significant differences found in any of the behaviors during maternal consort. (Since environmental exploration did appear to be the behavior most influenced by reactivity level, and/or in interaction with stress events, environmental exploration was examined of the few (n = 3) infants who had been categorized as high, moderate, and low reactors. In all cases, environmental exploration was repressed, but did not seem to interact with reactivity level).

DISCUSSION

Although there is great variability in the exploration, play, and initiating or receiving play of infant rhesus monkeys, individual differences generally failed to persist over time. By three years of age, there was far less variability, and animals had often changed relative positions in frequency. The period from one to two years was somewhat more stable, especially in environmental exploration, but there was also stability from two-to-three-years in social play.

However, there was some evidence that animals that were rated as high or low temperamental reactors were more likely to change in frequency of play or environmental exploration when freely ranging outdoors than were the moderate reactors. When confined, there were no discernible patterns of change in play or environmental exploration related to reactivity level. Reactivity level was also predictive of variability in both indoor and outdoor environmental exploration, and indoor self-play. An interaction between age and reactivity level implies that environmental exploration for one-year-olds and social play for two-year-olds are the behaviors most reflective of reactivity level. Stress events did not significantly influence play or environmental exploration by reactivity level, but there were trends indicating that high reactors may change most and that environmental exploration might be more influenced than play.

Among human infants, high reactors have been found to be most stable from two days to two months (Lewis, Worobey, & Thomas, 1989). In these data, it appears that the play frequency of high and low reactors, at least outdoors, is more likely to change than that of moderate reactors. This discrepancy is perhaps explained by intensity of emotional reaction measured by Lewis and associates (1989), rather than frequency of behaviors studied herein (Stevenson-Hinde, 1986). Intensity of play, measured by duration or tempo, may be a better indicator of reactivity level than frequency alone. Stevenson-Hinde, Stillwell-Barnes, and Zunz (1980) also found that individual differences, assessed through various tests also failed to correlate from one age to the next. In their study, only males' behavior in testing correlated with subjective ratings of their behavior within the colony. But it was the "excitable" as opposed to the "confident" males who fared better in the testing situations.

Previous analyses have demonstrated that one-to-three-year-olds rhesus males and one-year-old females play significantly more frequently in the confined than in the freeranging condition (O'Neill-Wagner et al., 1994). An alternative explanation for this phenomenon to that of increased density, contact or fewer choices than when outdoors was that of increased stress, with play serving as a coping mechanism. (Two-year-old females and older females may use other means to cope, such as grooming). But from these data, in which the relationships between play behaviors when animals are confined and reactivity levels were less strong and stable than when animals were freeranging, confinement may be less stressful than hypothesized. If reactivity level is best determined in situations of demand (Suomi, 1987), then it would seem that it would have been in the confined condition that individual differences would be most evident. Confinement of these animals did, however, limit contact between age mates and separated families so that dominance relationships may have been different than when freeranging. Self-play while indoors was, however, related to reactivity level, with more reactive animals engaging in greater amounts. Self-play, perhaps like solitary play among humans, may be a less developmentally appropriate response to stress than increased social play.

Nevertheless, there is some support for the contention that environmental exploration rather than play may be the behavior that is most indicative of reactivity level, especially for one-year-olds. Or, environmental exploration is most easily determined by frequency alone. In these data, only environmental exploration was significantly related to reactivity level in both conditions, there was greater stability in environmental exploration than in play behaviors, and exploration was not influenced by age and gender. However, for two-year-olds, social play appears to be most related to reactivity level, and social play was stable from two- to three-years of age. But since social play has been found in other analyses to be influenced by gender, and in these data high reactors were female and low reactor males, these results may reflect a gender rather than a reactivity effect.

Another explanation includes the possibility that the assessment made by the observers was inaccurate: with a small number of subjects even the misclassification of one animal could alter results. However, subjective assessment does appear to be a valid means of capturing emotionality (Stevenson-Hinde et al., 1978; 1980), and previous comparison of subjective assessment of reactivity with personality traits had found convergent validity (Bolig et al., 1992). Variability in subjective personality assessment has also been linked to differences in physiological assessments (Raleigh, McGuire, & Brammer, 1989). The small number of subjects is also of concern since there was little that was consistent. Finally, it is possible that differential patterns of play, combining frequency and duration, may be most illustrative of reactivity level. It is possible, for example, that high reactors may have play episodes of shorter duration than do low reactors.

REFERENCES

Baldwin, J. (1986). Behavior in infancy: Exploration and play. In J. Baldwin (Ed.) *Comparative primate biology, vol. 2a: Behavior, conservation, and ecology.* New York: Alan R. Liss, Inc.

Bolig, R., Price, C. S., O'Neill, P. L., & Suomi, S. J. (1992). Subjective assessment of personality traits and reactivity level of rhesus monkeys. *International Journal of Primatology*, *13*, 287–302.

Champoux, M. (1988). Behavioral development and temporal stability of reactivity to stressors in mother-reared and nursery/peer-reared rhesus macaque (*Macaca mulatta*) infants. *Infant Behavioral Development*, *11*, 367–371.

Coates, S., Lord, M., & Jakavovics, E. (1975). Field independence-dependence, social-nonsocial play and sex differences in preschool children. *Perceptual and Motor Skills*, *40*, 195–202.

Dansky, J., & Silverman, I. (1975). Play: A general facilitator of associative fluency. *Developmental Psychology*, *11*, 104.

Emmerich, W. (1964). Continuity and stability in early social development. *Child Development*, *35*, 311–332.

French, J. (1981). Individual differences in play in macaca fuscata: The role of maternal status and proximity. *International Journal of Primatology*, *2*, 237–246.

Gard, G., & Meier, G. (1977). Social and contextual factors of play behavior of sub-adult rhesus monkeys. *Primates*, *18*, 367–377.

Higley, J. (1985). *Continuity of social separation behaviors in rhesus monkeys from infancy to adolescence.* Unpublished doctoral dissertation. University of Wisconsin, Madison, WI.

Higley, J., & Suomi, S. (1989). Temperamental reactivity in non-human primates. In G. Hohnstamm, J. Bates, & M. Rothbart (Eds.), *Temperament in childhood.* New York: John Wiley.

Jennings, K. (1975). People versus object orientation, social behavior, and intellectual abilities in preschool children. *Developmental Psychology*, *11*, 511–519.

Johnson, J., Christie, J., & Yawkey, T. (1987). *Play and early childhood development.* Glenview, IL: Scott, Foresman, and Co.

Kagen, J. (1982). Heart rate and heart rate variability as signs of temperamental dimension in infants. In C. Izard (Ed.), *Measuring emotions in infants and young children* (pp. 36–66). New York: Cambridge University Press.

Kagen, J., Reznick, J., Snidman, N. (1986). Temperamental inhibition in early childhood. In R. Plomin & J. Dunn (Eds.), *The study of temperament.* Hillsdale, NJ: Erlbaum.

Lewis, M., Worobey, J., & Thomas, D. (1989). Behavioral features of early reactivity: Antecedents and consequences. In M. Lewis & J. Worobey (Eds.), *Infant stress and coping.* San Francisco: Jossey-Bass, Inc.

Lieberman, J. (1977). *Playfulness: Its relationship to imagination and creativity.* New York: Academic Press.

McGuire, M. & Raleigh, M. (1986). Behavioral and physiological correlates of ostracism. *Ethology and Sociobiology*, *7*, 197–200.

O'Neill-Wagner, P. L., Bolig, R., & Price, C. S. (1994). Do play activity levels tells us something of psychosocial welfare in captive monkey groups? *Communication and Cognition*, *27*, 261–272.

Pellegrini, A., & Perlmutter, M. (1989). Classroom contextual effects of children's play. *Child Development*, *25*, 289–296.

Poirier, F., Bellisari, A., & Haines, L. (1978). Functions of primate play behavior. In E. Smith (Ed.), *Social play in primates* (pp. 143–167). New York: Academic Press.

Raleigh, M., McGuire, M., & Brammer, G. (1989). Abstract: Subjective assessment of behavioral styles. *American Journal of Primatology*, *18*, 161–162.

Singer, J. (1961). Imagination and waiting ability in young children. *Journal of Personality, 29,* 396–413.

Smilansky, S. (1968). *The effects of sociodramatic play on disadvantaged preschool children.* New York: Wiley.

Stevenson-Hinde, J. (1986). Behavioral inhibition: Issues of context. In J. Resnick (Ed.), *Perspectives on behavioral inhibition* (pp. 125–138). New York: Academic.

Stevenson-Hinde, J., Stillwell-Barnes, R., & Zunz, M. (1980). Individual differences in young rhesus monkeys: Consistency and change. *Primates, 21,* 498–509.

Suomi, S. (1987). Genetic and maternal contributions to individual differences in rhesus monkey biobehavioral development. In (Ed.), *Prenatal development: A psychobiological perspective.* New York: Academic Press, Inc.

Suomi, S. & Harlow, H. (1976). Monkeys without play. In J. Bruner, A. Jolly & K. Sylva (Eds.), *Play: Its role in development and evolution.* New York: Basic Books.

Wolf, D. & Gardner, H. (1979). Style and sequence in early symbolic play. In M. Franklin & N. Smith (Eds.), *Symbolic functioning in children.* Hillsdale, NJ: Erlbaum.

Wolf, D. & Grollman, S. (1978). Ways of playing: Individual differences in imaginative style. In D. Pepler & K. Rubin (Eds.), *The play of children: Current theory and research.* Basel, Switzerland: Karger, AG.

12

Social Play and Estrous Cycle: The Relationship Between Social Play and Estrous Cycle in a Captive Adolescent Female Chimpanzee (Pan troglodytes)

Lisa Drummer New, Daniel S. Cunningham,
and Karen Sughrue

Awareness of a species biological and behavioral patterns can help animal managers with husbandry decisions such as proper housing conditions, diets, and social groupings. These considerations are necessary to maintain physically and psychologically healthy animals that display species appropriate behavior. For chimpanzees, play is one behavior that can serve as an indicator of well being. Therefore, knowledge of the characteristics of play and how it is measured can be of use in applied settings.

Unfortunately, another species appropriate behavior in chimpanzees is agonism toward unfamiliar conspecifics (Goodall, Bandora, Bergmann, Busse, Matama, Mpongo, Pierce, & Riss, 1979). This can pose problems in a captive setting as chimpanzees are often transferred between facilities and subsequently introduced to established social groups. Introductions without careful planning can result in overly aggressive and/or fearful behavior. These reactions can be altered in degree or form if the individuals involved are in estrus. For these reasons, data on individual behavioral characteristics and normal biological rhythms can provide useful information for how and when to attempt an introduction.

Estrus is the periodic state of sexual excitability during which the females of most mammalian species are willing to mate and are capable of being impregnated. Estrus has characteristic morphological, hormonal, and behavioral qualities. With chimpanzees, the females estrogen level peaks as her anogenital area swells (Nadler, Graham, Gosselin, & Collins, 1985). Maximal swell is an indication of ovulation and serves as a visual cue of sexual receptivity to potential mates (Pusey, 1990). Such morphological and hormonal changes affect not only the individual female's behavior, but also the behavior of conspecifics (Shefferly & Fritz, 1992; Wallis, 1992; Pusey, 1990). These characteristics indicate that estrus state may be an important condition for animal managers to consider when planning an introduction strategy.

The information that is available on the behavioral changes associated with estrus indicates that adolescent chimpanzee females during estrus exhibit different behavior than do their adult counterparts. For example, adolescents frequently solicit copulation from males of all ages, even infants (Nishida, 1983). More experienced females, on the other hand, solicit copulation less frequently (Pusey, 1990; Wallis & Lemmon, 1986). Although throughout adolescence play frequencies decrease, adolescent female behavior during peak estrus is often described as curious and playful (Pusey, 1990; Hayaki, 1985). Nishida (1983) reports that this playfulness during estrus is frequently directed towards infants and juveniles.

This chapter investigates whether the sociosexual patterns observed in other adolescent females are also characteristic of the adolescent female at the Knoxville Zoo. This information is particularly useful from an applied perspective, as the ability to predict the subjects behavioral changes can provide objective information on the most appropriate time to introduce her to two unrelated infant males with the greatest level of success. If this females play behavior increases during estrus, then we might predict that the same behavior would occur, after familiarization, toward the two male infants.

METHODS

This investigation is part of a larger project involving the social integration of two infant chimpanzees into an existing group at the Knoxville Zoological Gardens.

Subjects

The subjects of the larger introduction project are six chimpanzees housed in two groups (Table 1). The first group comprises two mother daughter dyads. The two infant males comprise the second group.

TABLE 1.
Chimpanzee subjects at the Knoxville Zoo

NAME	SEX	AGE CLASS	DOB	ORIGIN
Debbie	female	adult	27/02/1971	pet
Moms	female	adult	1962	unk
Julie	*female*	*adolescent*	*28/03/1986*	*Knox. Zoo*
Kerry	female	juvenile	19/03/1988	Knox. Zoo
Mugsy	male	infant	21/06/1990	W.Way Sta
Lu	male	infant	24/11/1990	Lowry Prk.

For this investigation, we focused on an eight year old adolescent, Julie, and whether her behavior changed with state of estrus.

Housing

The subjects are housed in a facility designed specifically for great apes with specialized features to accommodate introductions (McMillan, Drummer, & Fouraker, 1992).

Observational Methods

Data were collected using momentary time sampling of state behavior, with frequency recording of certain event behavior. The sampling interval was set at 15 seconds and each subject was observed for 132 intervals (i.e., 32 minutes).

The six chimpanzees of the project were randomly chosen for observation, therefore the data for each subject represent a random sample of observation periods. Sixty-four days of observational data were collected for Julie encompassing the time period of April 15, 1993 to February 8, 1994. Observations took place between 9:00 a.m. and 2:00 p.m. Observers were rigorously trained for data collection, with an inter-observer reliability requirement of 80 percent or better for each dependent variable.

Variables

The independent variable in this investigation was the anogenital swell condition of the adolescent female, Julie. Daily records from caretaker staff were collected for the swell state of all females. The data were collected as being In Swell or Out of Swell. The larger introduction project investigates over 20 state and six event behavioral categories. Dependent variables of interest for this project were: social play, locomotor play, social groom (both active and receptive), object manipulation, and social proximity. Data were collected so that when an individual was engaged in any social activity, the identity of the other participant was recorded as well.

Social play was defined as nonaggressive interactions between two or more individuals that are often accompanied by a play face and raspy panting. Examples of social play included any occurrence or combination of tickling, wrestling, biting, sparring, chasing, butting, kicking, dragging, and so forth.

RESULTS

Social play presented itself as a unique variable in this data set. The same four females live together on a continual basis, and the adults seldom play. In fact, there were no instances of play recorded for the adults in the data set. Therefore, Julie had a reciprocal play relationship with the juvenile female Kerry. This was the case for no other

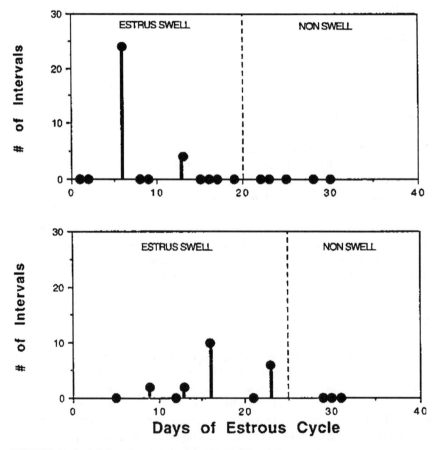

FIGURE 1.   Social play data in two of Julie's estrous cycles.

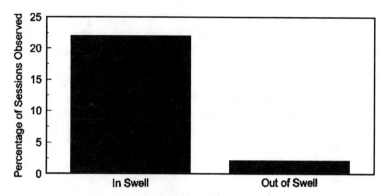

FIGURE 2. Occurrence of social play for sessions observed *in swell* and *out of swell.*

TABLE 2.
Occurrence of social play for sessions observed
in swell and *out of swell*

	In swell	*Out of swell*
Play	18	1
No play	64	50

Notes: Chi-square = 10.26
d.f. = 1
$p < 0.005$

TABLE 3.
Average number of intervals per observation session while *in swell* and
out of swell for social play

Dependent variable	*In swell*	*Out of swell*	*Probability*
Social play	1.867	0.020	0.001*

variable in the data set, since all four females engaged in social grooming and social proximity.

Due to the reciprocity of the play relationship and the specificity with which the data were collected, we combined the social play data for both Julie and Kerry to more accurately reflect true frequencies of play.

Julie exhibited social play almost exclusively while in swell. Figure 1 illustrates the number of intervals of play per observation day during one complete estrous cycle. The number of sessions where social play occurred based on whether Julie was In Swell or Out of Swell is illustrated in Figure 2. The percentage of days In Swell when play occurred is 21.95 percent, whereas the same statistic for Out of Swell and occurrence of social play is 1.96 percent. This was significant using a chi square test (Table 2).

The frequency of social play based on whether Julie was In Swell or Out of Swell was also significant using a Wilcoxon rank sums test (Table 3). Note that even though significant, the average number of intervals of play per observation session was still low: In Swell = 1.867; Out of Swell = 0.02. No other behavior observed changed with respect to estrus.

CONCLUSIONS

Our investigation indicated that social play for the adolescent female chimpanzee at the Knoxville Zoo significantly increases while she is in swell. Julie's increase in play while in estrus coupled with the high frequencies of play displayed by the infants, suggests that this period of Julie's cycle is an appropriate time for her introduction to the infants.

Although the results pertain only to this adolescent female chimpanzee, the findings are consistent with the literature. Her low frequencies of social play support other findings that also document low levels of play in adolescent chimpanzees (Pusey, 1990; Hayaki, 1985). Her increase of playful behavior toward the juvenile female while in estrus is also consistent. Nishida (1983) includes invitation and enticement, tickling, and rough and tumble play in his definition of alloparental or aunting behavior. This incorporation of social play, along with his observation that alloparental behavior increases during estrus, provides further support for our findings.

The results on locomotor and object play are also consistent with the literature in that play frequency, overall, is at low levels in adolescents (Pusey, 1990; Hayaki, 1985). Our findings that grooming and proximity do not change with estrus condition are inconsistent with the literature (Wallis, 1992; Pusey, 1990). This is likely a result of the focal animals social environment. Julie has access only to other females at a time in her development when emigration to other groups is likely and her interest in males is high. Previous research on behavioral correlation with estrus state is primarily restricted to male-female interaction (Shefferly & Fritz, 1992; Wallis, 1992). This is because nonrelated females in wild groups rarely have close and long term bonds and therefore female-female interactions are rarely recorded.

These findings raise some interesting areas for future research, specifically with the individual chimpanzees at the Knoxville Zoo, and on a broader scale. For example, it will be useful to investigate whether the relationship between social play and estrus state is generalizable to other captive and wild adolescent female chimpanzees.

For the adolescent female at the Knoxville Zoo, it will be interesting to investigate whether her frequency of play behavior changes with access to more than one play partner, especially males. And finally, future research will examine whether other social behavior that Julie displays, such as grooming and proximity, is affected by estrus state while in the presence of males.

REFERENCES

Goodall, J., Bandora, A., Bergmann, E., Busse, C., Matama, H., Mpongo, E., Pierce, A., & Riss, D. (1979). Intercommunity interactions in the chimpanzee population of the Gombe National Park. In D. A. Hamburg & E. R. McCown, (Eds.), *The great apes* (pp. 13-53). Menlo Park, CA: Benjamin/Cummings.

Hayaki, H. (1985). Social play of juvenile and adolescent chimpanzees in the Mahale Mountains National Park, Tanzania. *Primates, 26*, 343–360.

McMillan, G., Drummer, L., & Fouraker, M. (Eds.). (1992). *Findings from the chimpanzee enclosure design workshop* (39 pp.).

Nadler, R. D., Graham, C. E., Gosselin, R. E., & Collins, D. C. (1985). Serum levels of gonadotropins and gonadal steroids, including testosterone, during the menstrual cycle of the chimpanzee. *American Journal of Primatology, 9*, 273–284.

Nishida, T. (1983). Alloparental behavior in wild chimpanzees of the Mahale Mountains, Tanzania. *Folia Primatologica, 41*, 1–33.

Pusey, A. E. (1990). Behavioural changes at adolescence in chimpanzees. *Behaviour, 115*, 203–245.

Shefferly, N., & Fritz, P. (1992). Male chimpanzee behavior in relation to female anogenital swelling. *American Journal of Primatology, 26*, 119–131.

Wallis, J. (1992). Chimpanzee genital swelling and its role in the pattern of sociosexual behavior. *American Journal of Primatology, 28*, 101–113.

Wallis, J., & Lemmon, W. B. (1986). Social behavior and genital swelling in pregnant chimpanzees (Pan troglodytes). *American Journal of Primatology, 10*, 171–183.

part V

Resistant Play

Part **V**

Introduction

Margaret Carlisle Duncan

The three chapters that form this section resonate with themes of resistance, struggle, and subversion. Steven J. Jackson's chapter focuses on the "play" of significance that occurs in the construction of a Canadian identity. Jackson argues that national identity is a process and a "terrain of struggle" where contradictory and competing meanings vie for acceptance. Focusing on the 1988 televised Olympic Games and the broadcasters' discourse that constructed them, Jackson delineates three major categories of signification: stereotypical images of Canada (as an exotic, foreign, northern wilderness), identity out of difference (in particular, Canada as different from the United States), and Canada tells its own story (positive representations by Canadians of Canada as multicultural, yet egalitarian and unified).

Jackson concludes that the struggle among these categories of meaning to ultimately define Canada's national identity and to differentiate it from the United States is part of a larger hegemonic process that repositions and stabilizes Canada in relation to the United States. Thus, each type of discourse preserves certain interests, while relegating others to the margins.

Becky Beal analyzes skateboarding as a form of play that resists daily norms and relations in mainstream American culture. In this ethnographic study conducted in Northern Colorado, Beal describes how a subculture of skaters inverted dominant (bureaucratic, capitalist) social relations and exposed the contradictions in the "American Dream." Beal argues that, unlike traditional sport which embodies bureaucratic structures such as competition, hierarchy, discipline, and obedience to authorities, skateboarding is cooperative, nonhierarchical, self-directed, and intrinsically motivated. Because skaters challenged many mainstream values through their play, their style, their attitudes, and their dress, they provoked a sometimes hostile and often disapproving reaction from the public. Skaters were quite conscious of their behavior as resistant, were able to critique dominant bureaucratic values, and took pride in their creative, nonconformist play. Yet, ironically, these same skaters seemed to be largely unaware of the privilege that accrued to them as (mostly) white middle-class males. Thus, as Beal argues, her study of skaters reveals the contradictions inherent in the American Dream.

Like Beal, Margaret Carlisle Duncan studied the ways in which a playful subculture resisted some of the mainstream values of larger society. In this case, Duncan analyzed the discourse of female martial artists who, while committed in many ways to *Tae Kwon Do*, simultaneously enjoyed parodying the seriousness of their sport. Employing Bahktin's notion of heteroglossia, Duncan argues that scholars must preserve a multiplicity of voices when studying sport culture.

Duncan focused on the subversive humor used by a small group of women at her *do jang*. For example, one woman delighted her group by doing a comical Bruce Lee imitation. Another mockingly intoned the lines of a poem that students were required by the Grandmaster to recite at testing. Instead of uttering the real words, however, she substituted obscenities at crucial points in the verses. By contrast, very few men were observed to use oppositional humor against the enterprise of the martial arts; in fact, they accorded *Tae Kwon Do*, its rituals, ceremonies, and heroes, the utmost respect and reverence. Duncan argues that oppositional communities, such as this subculture of women, have interesting ways of resisting certain elements of the institution of sport that would otherwise oppress them, either literally or symbolically. Such subversive humor enables women to enjoy what is otherwise a profoundly masculinist undertaking.

13

The 49th Paradox: The 1988 Calgary Winter Olympic Games and Canadian Identity as Contested Terrain

Steven J. Jackson

INTRODUCTION

For many the mention of Canada often conjures up images of a large, cold, mountain and snow covered wilderness, populated by moose and protected by Mounties; a country where reserved, bilingual, and, generally speaking, friendly people eat back bacon, drink Molson and Labatts, and watch Hockey Night in Canada (or more recently their beloved Blue Jays) when they aren't hunting and fishing. These images, sometimes produced by Canada itself, and sometimes by others wishing to capture the essence of "Canadiana," have come to embody a major problematic faced by Canada as a nation, that is, its identity. However, as this chapter reveals, the very assumption that there is *a* Canadian identity waiting to be discovered only serves to confuse the issue.

One aspect of this problem is highlighted in Richard Gwyn's (1985) book *The 49th Paradox*. Gwyn's title is an insightful turn of a phrase in reference to the fact that the 49th parallel, which acts as the continental divide between Canada and the United States, is much more than a symbolic geographic marker. His analysis states that while historically the Canadian identity has been defined by, and indeed has survived by, aspiring to no more than a "not-American" status, this is no longer the case. Rather, he suggests that the 49th paradox lies in the fact that Canadians, while being fully "North" American, are distinctive from those who live in the United States. In his words:

> two nations have evolved that are utterly alike in almost all of their externals and yet are utterly unlike in their political cultures so that they are as distinct from each other as are the Germans from the French, say even though both are Europeans. (Gwyn, 1985, p. 11)

Gwyn further asserts that as economic distinctions between the two countries diminish, through accords such as the Canada-U.S. Free Trade Agreement (F.T.A.), the more important it will be to emphasize the political differences.

The aim of this study is to show that a 49th paradox continues to exist, that is, that the Canadian identity continues to be constructed "out of difference" to the United States. The focus will be on the nature and extent to which Canadian identity served as a contested terrain of meaning between particular interest groups during the 1988 Calgary Games. Among the most powerful of those interest groups were the Canadian State and The American Broadcasting Corporation (ABC) whose $309 million bid guaranteed them various rights and privileges which undoubtedly influenced how Canada would be represented both domestically and internationally.

Three specific categories of analysis are used to trace a particular set of discursive practices in order to highlight the ideological and often contradictory meanings associated with the construction of a national identity. These categories include: Stereotypical Images, The 49th Paradox (constructing identity out of difference), and Canada Tells Its Own Story. It is asserted that while economic and political processes and structures are indeed important for the analysis of the 49th paradox their influence upon, and their relations to, the cultural realm should not be ignored.

CONCEPTUALIZING IDENTITY

Given the diverse set of meanings which the concept of "identity" has assumed within various fields of study it is important to first establish its conceptual basis within this analysis. Canada's national identity, similar to any other identity, is socially constructed. That is, it is subject to various historical, political, and cultural struggles and processes which affect both its dominant and residual meanings. More specifically, identity can be conceptualized in two interrelated ways.

First, identity can be conceptualized with respect to its ability to ideologically construct the nation out of both similarity and difference. Hargreaves (1982, p. 80) for example, has noted how the process works in two directions:

> One is to mark us off from the "others"—foreigners, strangers, aliens—it identifies and values what is unique to us. The other is to draw us together, to unite us in the celebration, maintenance and furtherance of "our" way of life.

This view suggests that we tend to define ourselves and the groups (including nationalities) to which we belong in terms of the assumed shared meanings, symbols, and experiences which link us together. At the same time we differentiate between our shared meanings, symbols, and experiences and those of others; that is, identity out of difference. Second, identity is interpreted with respect to the meanings, politics, and effects which contribute to, are embodied in, and arise from our collective definition both self- and other-imposed.

To this extent, McArthur (1986) asserts that identity is not an essence but a process and hence offers the opportunity for social change. Furthermore, McArthur notes that:

> National identity comes to be seen, therefore, not as a set of eternal, mosaic tablets, but as a terrain of struggle where, to be sure, certain regressive and politically disabling discourses may currently be in hegemony but which require constant reutterance and rearticulation to sustain that hegemony. Crucially, that hegemony is open to challenge by a counter-hegemony offering new definitions of national identity. (1986, p. 132)

Thus, according to McArthur, identity is not an innate constant but a historical product open to change, not carved in stone but rather a "terrain of struggle." In addition, he suggests that identity can be located within the current ongoing discourse of hegemony: a set of conditions whereby particular alliances of dominant groups and individuals exercise control over subordinate groups and individuals, not through coercion, but by winning and shaping consent "ideologically." This process is accomplished by dominant interest groups such as the state, which work to make any hierarchies appear legitimate and natural. However, McArthur is quick to note that the hegemonic process is never complete, that an identity is continually subject to challenges, and in turn, rearticulations by the state. Major cultural events such as the Olympics provide an ideological site where these various struggles to define and represent particular images of a national identity occur.

The conceptualizations of identity presented underscore major problematics in the analysis of identity in general, and Canadian identity in particular. As previously explained, identity is constructed from both similarity and difference, and for Canada this has largely been endeavored within the context of its relationship with the United States. In addition, identity embodies the meaning, politics, and effects that arise from the process of identifying a nation and its people. The interaction of these two conceptualizations has produced a kind of paradox for the ongoing social construction of Canada by the state as will become evident when examining the Calgary Games. However, prior to proceeding to the analysis of the Games themselves, a brief contextualization of the problem of Canadian identity is provided.

THE PROBLEM OF CANADIAN IDENTITY IN CONTEXT

The problem of Canadian identity which is herein referred to is not a new one. The number of scholarly works which address the issue gives some indication of its historical importance if not its captivating significance to Canadians who have been described as "the world champions at collective self-analysis" (Gwyn, 1985, p. 188). Titles such as *The Canadian Identity* (Morton, 1972); *The Americanization of Canada* (Moffett, 1972); *Neighbours Taken for Granted* (Merchant, 1966); *Life with Uncle* (Holmes, 1981); *From Nation to Colony* (Scott, 1988); and *In the Eye of Eagle*, (Lisee, 1991) all tend to reflect a concern with Canadian identity. Moreover, each of these books implies a preoccupation with the relationship between Canada and the United States and its impact on the national identity.

In 1988, the problem of Canadian identity was resurrected anew. Concepts such as Canadian culture and identity became firmly established within the popular discourse. This seemingly unparalleled concern with the state of the nation arose in part as a response to debates surrounding the Canada-United States Free Trade Agreement (FTA). In brief, the goal of the FTA was to eliminate trade tariffs and to reduce any remaining barriers to commerce and investment.

The FTA highlights one aspect of the 49th paradox in the sense that it was one of the most controversial issues in recent history and was strategically employed by both major opposition parties (Liberals and New Democratic Party) to force the 1988 Canadian federal election. Yet, there was rarely a mention, let alone a debate, about this issue during the U.S. presidential race that same year.

It is important to understand the overall implications of the FTA and its relationship to defining Canadian national identity. While Canada and the United States have long engaged in the largest and most unrestricted trade of any two countries in the world, there has been an escalating fear on the part of many Canadians that the FTA will eventually lead to, not only economic domination, but also political and cultural domination by its southern neighbor. As one newspaper headline of the day put it: "Canadian Identity is Embedded in Free Trade Pact." And, as Canadian writer Pierre Berton (1987, p. 4) observed:

> The suspicion persists that Mr. Mulroney, who rose to prominence as the chief executive officer of an American-owned company, is quite prepared to bargain away some of those very aspects of our society that make us distinctive.

Consequently, Canadian sovereignty, the Canadian way of life, and Canadian culture, in essence, "the Canadian identity" was represented as being under threat of extinction.

The attitude expressed by some of the more conservative ranks of the "American" press and academia suggests that some of the perceived threat on the part of many Canadians is not unfounded. Consider, for example, the following comments which were cited in a late 1988 article entitled: "Come to Uncle" published in the right-wing American publication *The New Republic*:

> Canada needs us. Indeed it's hard not to suspect that in briefly threatening to reject this obviously sensible treaty, Canada—as is so often the case with stagy suicide attempts—was simply trying to draw attention to itself. The entire election was a cry for help.... It

doesn't take a Ph.D. in psychology to realize that Canadians' mock horror at the thought of becoming part of the United States actually masks a deep desire to do precisely that. They protest too much. Their lips say "no, no." but their eyes say "yes, yes." ... There is only one cure for this complex neurosis. We must purge it once and for all by giving Canadians what they secretly want. We must embrace them, adopt them, love them, annex them. In short, we must make Canada the 51st state. (1988, p. 4)

Undoubtedly intended to be tongue-in-cheek, the previous narrative is significant because it captures one of the prevailing moods represented within Canada during the FTA debates. In short, a mood which characterized the United States' desire to assimilate, merge, or otherwise incorporate Canada. Despite these indictments, however, it must be recognized that Canada and the United States have long engaged in the most unrestricted trade of any two countries in the world with an estimated annual exchange of $121 billion dollars worth of goods and services. In fact, 80 percent of trade between Canada and the United States was already "free" prior to the signing of the FTA. Such a contradiction has prompted critics such as Peter Brimelow to charge that the current popularization of Canadian nationalism and identification "is a fraud, designed primarily to benefit particular interest groups in Canada" (1986, p. 1). Where then does sport fit into this discussion?

SPORT AND CANADIAN IDENTITY

As a social and cultural practice, sport plays an interesting and important role in the lives of Canadians and in the construction of their identity. In 1967, a report of the *Task Force on Sport*, a part of the "Unity through sport" campaign of eventual Prime Minister Pierre Trudeau, "argued that sport was ... an effective antidote to economic and cultural domination by the United States" (Macintosh, Bedecki, & Franks, 1987, p. 74). In addition, Macintosh, and associates (1987) have suggested that sport: "has an important role to play in any government attempt to promote unity and a unique Canadian identity" (1987, p. 186) and, "in countering the threat to Canadian identity of the pervasive mass culture of the United States" (1987, p. 174). Yet, Canada has never been particularly successful in international sporting competition which is why specific events such as the Olympics assume such national significance.

In 1988, the Calgary Olympic Games served as one site within which to investigate the implications for the construction of Canadian identity in relation to the 49th paradox. Although the official "host" broadcaster for the Games was CTV (The Canadian Television Network), it was ABC who was the major media sponsor. Moreover, it is within some of the most key segments of the Olympics, such as the Opening and Closing ceremonies, which are not "officially" a part of the Games (Tomlinson, 1989), where ABC television was more likely to be exert greater influence and control. For example, Fotheringham (1988, p. 60) described how ABC decided what Canadian volunteers would wear during the Games because: "the camera knows what looks best against the snow." Furthermore, Taafe (1988, p. 8) argued that: "More than any previous Olympics, these Games have been tailor-made for U.S. television." Consequently, Canada's identity, could in part be represented and interpreted through "American" visual and narrative production.

THE 1988 CALGARY OLYMPIC GAMES

The Calgary Games were selected as a site for studying the social construction of Canadian identity for several reasons. First, the Olympic Games have become the world's most prominent media event (Gruneau, 1989). Thus, there is an opportunity to see how the media both constructed a nation and worked to position the millions of people who constitute its audience. Second, MacAloon (1984, p. 274) has noted that:

> the Olympic Games create a sort of hyperstructure in which categories and stereotypes are condensed, exaggerated, and dramatized, rescued from the taken for granted and made the objects of explicit and lively awareness for a brief period every four years.

If the basis of this increased transparency is true, then emerging struggles to represent Canadian identity within various economic, political, and cultural pressures should illuminate an immense range of compelling, and often contradictory, meanings and interpretations (Gruneau, 1989).

Finally, Jim McKay, an ABC sports broadcaster, announced at the very beginning of the Games that hosting the Olympics would lead Calgary and Canada "into a new era in its history." Assuming the validity of this statement then it must be understood that history is constructed not only by those of us in the audience, nor solely by the Games themselves, "history" is also being made by the media (Whannel, 1989). At this point I will turn to the three categories of analysis beginning with stereotypical images.

Stereotypical Images of Canada

Without fail, and from the opening shot until the closing ceremonies the most pervasive theme running through ABC's representation of Canada was northern wilderness. Even ABC's evening hosts: Frank and Kathy Lee Gifford speak to the audience from a position supposedly located within a rustic cabin. As noted in *Sports Illustrated* (1988, p. 16):

> The Giffords' homey set—constructed in the ABC compound in the Calgary Stampede Park and modeled after a Colorado dude ranch—features a cozy gas fire and a small library of books.

The result is that the audience is invited into ABC's home as if it were about to view a vacation video or slide show. Viewers are able to feel as if they were visiting an exot-

ic, distant, isolated, and *foreign* location but within the security of a "friends" home.
The characterization of this northern wilderness theme continued. At almost every
commercial and station break throughout the entire coverage of the Games, the view-
er is presented images of: mountains, snow, lakes, rivers, Mounties, Cowboys, Indians,
and animals, especially moose, bison, antelope, rams, and horses. The depiction of
"northern wilderness" is consistently tied to Canada's diverse and rugged geography.
Moreover, both Canadian and foreign writers and journalists have linked this to
Canadian identity. The comments of Johnson (1988) during his cross-Canada train ride
are quite revealing in this regard. Johnson (1988, p. 300), writing for *Sports
Illustrated*'s special Olympic preview edition, attempted to capture Canada's character
through his cross-Canada train ride as follows:

> The images and ideas you derive from looking out the window of a moving train during
> days and nights of travel are basically impressionistic, if not surreal. You are struck by an
> endless barrage of fleeting romantic notions. Such material, as a rule, is dubious as social
> research and useless for drawing scientific conclusions.... Yet traveling through Canada
> may be different. Everything about the country is, in one way or another, a result of its
> geography. Its culture, politics and economy are ruled by the sheer size and wildly diverse
> topography of the land.

Johnson admits that although a train ride to appreciate a nation's geography really only
provides "images," "impressions," and "fleeting romantic notions" about the character
of that country, *somehow* Canada is different. He notes that everything about Canada:
"its culture, politics, and economy *are ruled* by the size and diversity of its geography."
But, how is this different from any other country? There is no explanation provided.
The media, including foreign productions, can play a significant role in the stereotypical social constructions of a national identity. Although the following statement made
by Johnson (1988, p. 301) was not made specifically in relation to ABC's coverage of
the Calgary Games it is, nevertheless, appropriate here:

> Having seen only a slice of Canadian life via the one-eyed vision of TV most
> Americans will go on thinking of Canada as the place that sends down cold fronts and
> hockey players, while the U.S. comes back with acid rain, baseball and the old, insult-
> ing veil of ignorance.

Of course Johnson's remarks also point to some commonly held stereotypes that
Canadians have regarding Americans. For example, the fact that they are all responsible for acid rain and are completely ignorant about Canadian affairs. This of course is
not true either. The important point here is that although there are no "guarantees" that
a particular message sent by the media will be read by an audience in any pre-deter-
mined way, the message itself originates, is transmitted and understood within an existing system of signification with its own inherent limits and constraints. One major
constraint is a lack of information itself. Mahant and Mount (1987) for example, note
that the American media devote about two-tenths of one percent of space to anything

connected with Canada. The point is that it is difficult to form an educated opinion about something without any access to information about it.

Paramount among the stereotypical portrayals of northern wilderness were the images of cowboys and Indians. These appear to signify Canada's untamed and under-developed status in general and, in relation to the United States, in particular. Admittedly, Calgary does hold the annual "Stampede" complete with rodeo contests and covered-wagon races. Despite this identity's restricted tradition within "western" Canada, it is one that many foreigners seem to have about the nation as a whole. As Alan Fotheringham (1988, p. 68) observed:

> yes we must address the cowboys-and-Indians issue. No doubt those two billion viewers around the world are now convinced Calgarians ride a buckskin to work. No one would have any idea, from watching the coverage, that there is a little business called oil and gas going on in those towering towers. Bears and bighorn sheep and beating tom-toms make better television.

The "western" signification provides a basis for a duality of identity for both Calgary and Canada. In searching for unique features through which to represent Canada's identity, both Canadian and American media become overdependent upon cultural forms and practices which are not necessarily representative. Another common stereotype about Canada and Canadians is that they all go hunting and fishing. Needless to say, ABC television provided an extended story of Keith Jackson and Curt Gowdy going fishing on the Bow River. This in itself is perhaps not so unusual, but their presentation made it appear as if they were going fishing in downtown Calgary! Again, this is not to deny that it is possible for people to go fishing near downtown Calgary. Unfortunately, the story that ABC told was presented within a very restricted cultural context. For example, although we are to assume that their urban fishing expedition coincides with the Olympics in the month of February, the audience really has no idea when this particular segment was videotaped. Whannel (1984, p. 102) refers to the "story-telling" power of the media by stating that:

> the insistence that television does not simply cover events, but transforms them into stories—is to raise questions about the polarity between actuality and fiction. Television sport can clearly be seen in terms of dramatic presentation and analyzed as a form of narrative construction.

Thus, in the process of covering a sporting event, ABC "transformed" the Olympics into an extended story, a constructed narrative which inevitably became a story about Canada's identity. The images that ABC presents are indeed *real,* they do exist, but they may be misleading. This analysis does not focus upon the "effects" of such representations or mis-representations. However, there does seem to be a tendency on the part of many foreigners, including Americans, to believe that Canadians live in the wilderness of "the great white north." Refuting this stereotype however, Kilbourn (1988) notes that over 60 percent of Canada's 27 million people live in urban areas with populations of over 100,000 people. By comparison, less than 30 percent of Americans live in cities of this size (Kilbourn, 1988). In short, Canada as a whole is a much more urban, metropolitan-based nation which contrasts with its commonly held stereotype.

One final example provides a useful link between the discussion of stereotypes and the focus of the next section: "defining identity out of difference" or, as it is more generally referred to here, as defining identity within the 49th paradox. While Canada's stereotypical northern wilderness was being socially constructed at each of ABC television's commercial and station breaks, they employed a subtle yet common production technique to include their corporate sponsors.

It was commonplace to see Mounties or moose roaming through the wilderness as a backdrop to "IBM," "Coca-Cola," and other "official Olympic" sponsors' logos. Corporate America was superimposed onto the Canadian landscape with ABC's traditional "Olympic" theme music playing in the background. The practice was so routine and technically refined that it appeared "natural." Through its media production strategies ABC was able to achieve two self-serving yet conflicting goals. First, ABC was able to articulate the espoused tradition and ideals of the Olympics with various sponsors' commercial interests. And second, ABC was able to align itself with the economic basis of the American Dream while maintaining sufficient distance from corporate America to preserve a more honest and virtuous image.

In summary, ABC television utilized stereotypical images to socially construct the identity of both the city of Calgary and of Canada in general. However, it is apparent that some of these stereotypes are emphasized and perpetuated by the city and the nation itself. For the most part these images were consciously, deliberately, and intentionally constructed and transmitted. Significantly, many of these stereotypes become naturalized and taken-for-granted within both American and Canadian audiences. As a result they are often accepted without contestation despite the fact that they may alienate various segments of the population.

The 49th Paradox: Identity out of Difference

There are many examples of the 49th paradox in ABC's coverage of the Calgary games and these selections are necessarily selective. The first example is a very subtle one: Peter Jennings, best known as the anchor for ABC news, joined Jim McKay as a commentator for the opening ceremonies. The subtlety exists in that Peter Jennings is a Canadian, yet a highly recognizable Canadian to Americans. Two interrelated implications develop from Peter Jennings' selection as an Olympic host.

First, because he is the number one news anchor in the United States news media, Jennings is not only highly recognizable but highly respected. Moreover, upon learning that he is a Canadian, (is a fact which is difficult to ignore because it is repeated by Jim McKay) Jennings is granted instant credibility to offer his "innate," expert opinion about Canada and its identity.

For example, during the opening ceremonies the Mounties entered the Olympic stadium in a traditional formation known as the "musical ride." Each aspect of the

Mounties formation and dress is dramatically, and carefully, if not stereotypically, described by Jim McKay. Then, at a point when there was little action taking place, Jim McKay turns to Peter Jennings and says: "Well, Peter, this is your ... show." Although it is difficult to convey, McKay's meaning certainly implied that, given that Canada is Peter Jennings' place of birth, this legendary symbolic representation must really be an emotional experience for him. Responding as if he had little choice, Jennings replied: "Well, it is kind of moving," affirming both an identification with the Mounties and an affective response of pride to the them. This type of discourse underscores how American media are able to construct Canada's national identity through the use of traditional symbols. However, Berton (1987) has identified the contradictory nature of the use of the Mountie as a signification of Canadian identity by stating that:

> I didn't say you Americans invented the Mounties; I said you invented the image. As a result, we Canadians are almost as awestruck by the Mountie myth as you are. In fact, it's partly because you revere our Mounties that we also revere them; after all, the Mounties are something we've got that you haven't. (1987, p. 34)

Berton's (1987) remarks highlight several aspects of the 49th paradox including the fact that: (a) Canada does utilize the Mountie as a symbol of its national identity; (b) it has become an important symbol because it is something "different" from the United States; and, (c) the Mountie has gained it's national significance in part *from the United States*! The Mounties offer one example of what Hobsbawm and Ranger (1983) refer to as invented traditions. Invented traditions are cultural practices and symbols which serve to link the present with a "suitable past," often through a nostalgic, highly romanticized, and depoliticized view of history.

A second example of the 49th paradox concerns Peter Jennings' own efforts to define Canada and its uniqueness. He notes for example, that while culturally Americans have tended towards the "melting pot," Canadians have preferred cultural pluralism, popularly described as a "salad bowl." In another segment, Jennings offers an explanation of the Canadian system of government. Here, another twist is added concerning the 49th Paradox. Jennings notes that Canada is a constitutional monarchy, with a parliamentary system of government, run by the Prime Minister, and yet the head of state remains the Queen as represented by the Governor General of Canada. In addition to this, ABC provides a mini-segment of the playing of the national anthem which features, in order, "God Save the Queen" and then "O, Canada." Here, then Canada's identity is constructed not only out of difference to the United States but in relation to, and some would argue in subordination of, Great Britain.

One of the most intriguing examples of the 49th paradox (the defining of Canadian identity out of difference to the United States) came from ABC sports' Frank Gifford. Gifford identifies "the defining difference" between Canada and the United States as the fact that "Canadians are obedient, they don't J-walk, and they don't block up their streets with cars." Frank Gifford wasn't kidding, he meant what he said. More importantly, he had just told the American public as well as others what Canada's identity was.

A third and final example to illustrate the 49th paradox involved a long story that ABC presented concerning ice hockey. The audience is told from the start that Canadians of all ages, from all walks of life, and from all over the country "have found common ground on frozen ground." Hockey is described as "an obsession, a religion, a key part of Canadian society and its values." In an interview with a small town hockey coach we are told that "if it weren't for hockey in the community there would be virtually nothing for young people to do." It is implied that this is due to the fact that Canadian winters are long and cold. Unfortunately, there is very little socio-historical analysis offered. ABC offers no explanation as to why hockey, as opposed to other forms of play, games, sport, and leisure, is "the only thing" in Canada; nor does ABC offer any explanation as to why long, cold winters have predisposed hockey to be *the* sport in Canada but not in, for example, northern European countries, Scandinavia, or for that matter the United States.

In a summary statement ABC reporter Judd Rose delivers an illuminating commentary stating that: "Canada often has trouble figuring out what it stands for, but hockey is the very definition of Canada." In that one sentence ABC television had just told the world that Canada has an identity problem and then subtly bestows one upon it—"hockey."

Despite its shortcomings, ABC is not solely to blame for any *mis*representations of Canada's identity. There is no doubt the Canadian state held its own agenda during the Calgary Games.

Canada Tells its Own Story

Throughout the opening ceremonies the audience was directed to take notice of the number and diversity of cultural groups represented. The pervasive signification of "multiculturalism" illustrates how ABC's televised coverage was constrained by the structure and process of the ceremonies as an instrument of the state. Moreover, it underscores the negotiated nature of media representations.

Canada has long celebrated its multicultural diversity. Fleras (1991, p. 347) asserts that: "the ideals embodied by multiculturalism provide Canadians with certain signposts by which to sort out their national identity." Although it was not yet in effect at the time of the Olympics, it is interesting to note that Prime Minister Mulroney later passed the Multicultural Act of 1988, making Canada the world's first official multicultural nation. The significance of the Act is noted by Fleras (1991, p. 348):

> The Multicultural Act not only catapulted Canada into the forefront of global developments in race relations management, but also imbued multiculturalism with legal authority. Provisions of the Act sought to promote cultural identity and sharing, prevent discriminatory and racist behaviour, and enhance the full and equal participation of racial minorities within Canadian society.

Although he did not announce his election until October of 1988, Prime Minister Mulroney's introduction and implementation of the Act in July of 1988 was no doubt a strategic part of his future election campaign. The implementation of the Multicultural Act illustrates the hegemonic process in action. Recognizing the growing political power of the "third force" in Canada, the dominant alliance conceded a certain amount of decision making power enabling it to win back consent for the overall structure of relations as currently established.

Perhaps the most striking observation during the opening ceremonies was the disproportionate number of Native Indians, who are officially known and classified as *aboriginals* by the Canadian government. At one juncture an assembly of various tribes, cloaked in traditional dress, entered the stadium prompting ABC's Peter Jennings to inform the audience that: "there are more Native Indians now than there were in the time of Christopher Columbus." Jennings' remark may be an effort to try and minimize the historical tragedy of the Native Indian by emphasizing their relatively stronger numerical representation today. Not long thereafter Jim McKay puts forth the isolated statement that: "it is appropriate that the Games would begin with Native Indians." Curiously, no explanation is offered for this rather puzzling announcement. Is it appropriate because the Indians are Natives, the first dwellers of North America? Is it appropriate because there are so many Natives living in Canada, and they are a significant and highly valued part of its culture and identity? Or, is it appropriate because Native Indians provide one traditional stereotype within which Canadian identity can be socially constructed, offering a visible testimony to both the multicultural make-up of Canada and its democratic and egalitarian structure? While all three suggestions are possibilities it is the latter one which appears most reasonable in light of current evidence. Fleras (1991, p. 352) outlines the "hegemonic" value of stereotypes by alleging that:

> Stereotypes "sanitize" our perceptions of the world by glossing over what is troublesome about reality and transforming it into something cozy and comfortable. Majority apprehension of racial minorities is partly alleviated through perpetuation of these reassuring images. Racial minorities are rendered less threatening by framing them in familiar and comforting terms; this, in turn, diminishes their impact as a threat to the social fabric. Stereotypes also reassure the audience that potentially troublesome constituents are still "in their place."

There are 2,277 reserves where about half of Canada's 450,000 official or "status" natives reside in Canada. They are officially recognized by the Indian Act of 1951 and numerous other treaties providing special rights with respect to education, hunting, fishing, and so forth. However, their fate is still a tragedy and everyone knows it. Although public sympathy runs high, aboriginals are "usually" negatively represented in the media as: a threat to Canada's territorial rights, a risk to the social order, an economic liability, and/or a problem for the justice system (Fleras, 1991). Aboriginals or Natives are not only overrepresented within the Olympic Games, they are also portrayed in stereotypical terms. The result is that "white" Canadians (and others) are able to rationalize the tragedy of the Indians by pointing to their presence and inclusion within such an important event. Moreover, by overrepresenting Native Indians in the media, the possibility increases that the majority will underestimate the nature and extent of their social problems (Granzberg, 1989).

Canadians are particularly defensive about their position on Indian rights. They tend to point with pride at the fact that they never actually had a war with their Indians, whereas the Americans had a total of 69 with theirs (Newman, 1989). However, the view of many Native Indians is that the Canadian government, although professing their support of cultural diversity and autonomy, is really seeking to "detribalize" and assimilate them. As Marule (1991, p. 16) observes:

It is not known to what degree the Canadian government has been successful in its efforts to eliminate traditional Indian attitudes and values. It is assumed by many that very little remains of traditional Indian ideology and philosophy because the traditional Indian lifestyle is no longer in evidence; that is, we don't live in tepees anymore. This assumption holds that traditional values and beliefs changed when our lifestyles changed. Implicit in this assumption, also, is the notion that Indian culture must remain static to remain Indian. But the history of our people is a history of successful adaptations to change while countering oppression and resisting oppositions of undesired changes.

The charges of Canadian nationalists in fear of losing their unique identity at the hands of a foreign dominant culture take on a whole new perspective here. How can a society that proclaims its commitment to multiculturalism deny some of its members, its *original* members, the freedom to pursue their chosen cultural basis of existence? Marule (1991) certainly makes it clear that Natives do not wish to hold on to some traditional "image" or socially constructed identity which was not of their own choosing in the first place. Rather, there is a call for tolerance and understanding of the right to negotiate their own set of cultural values and beliefs and to adapt to social change as necessary. The Canadian Charter of Rights and Freedoms has guaranteed the Natives certain traditional rights. However, this must be understood within the larger socio-cultural context as an ongoing process of hegemony. Jhally (1989, p. 84) emphasizes the use of stereotypical images to reinforce assumed cultural differences stating that:

First "we" are separated from "them," the foreigners, through the use of stereotypical representations. "They" are different from us culturally and psychologically. Second, "we" who are separated from them are drawn together under the mythical sign of the "nation." This itself involves a two-step procedure. In the initial step our real differences (of class, ethnicity, religion, and so on) are dissolved to create a false unity of "nation."

Thus, the erasure of cultural differences between Canadians provides an ideological basis for the construction of an *"imagined nation."* Native Indians were also featured during the singing of the national anthem. A Shoshonee Indian, by the name of Daniel Tlen, had secretly been selected to sing the Canadian national anthem in his native tongue. During the performance the audience is presented with a shot of the Prime Minister along with an overlay of the Canadian flag signifying the state's commitment to its minorities. Following the Shoshonee version of the national anthem the audience then hears O'Canada sung in English and French simultaneously (the French was inter-mixed in between the English choruses). While many are duly aware that Canada is a *bi*lingual country, the audience may have been given the impression that Canada was now a *tri*lingual country. What is really striking about all of this is the fact that Daniel Tlen may have been the only one in McMahon stadium who understood the song. It seems doubtful that a literal translation is possible of Tlen's version into English. However, as an aboriginal he is at least entitled to legitimately sing: "O, Canada, our home and *native* land!" Reference has been made to the incorporation of multicultur-alism and of the Native case in particular but "cultural" minorities were not the only focus of identity construction within the Olympics.

The climax of the Olympic Games opening ceremonies is the arrival and lighting of the Olympic flame. In the case of the Calgary Winter Olympics the torch was deliv-ered by two former Canadian sport champions: a male (Ken Read) and a female (Cathy Priestner). There had been considerable build-up centering on the secret identity of the torch bearers and ABC's Jim McKay made no hesitation in declaring the gender-shared responsibility.

On their journey to the steps leading up to the Olympic flame the pair made a brief stop to let Canadian Rick Hansen, "The Man in Motion," the man who raised millions of dollars for spinal chord research and who is himself confined to a wheelchair, touch the Olympic torch (The representation of the disabled as a minority group reappears in a later ABC segment which examines some of the participants of the Winter Special Olympics and their link to the Calgary Games). Then, finally the pair of Olympic torch carriers passed off the torch to a young girl, Robyn Perry, who eventually lit the Olympic flame.

The process of lighting the Olympic torch provides several examples of the ideo-logical power of both sport and the media. The conscious decision to have a man and a woman carry the torch appears to signify Canada's stance of equality in relation to gender issues.

The choice of a young female to light the Olympic torch is also noteworthy. The rationale for this strategic choice is based on the same logic that incorporated other minority groups. Youth represents the promising future of Canada and its people. The selection of a young female reinforces the myth of equality within the power structure of Canadian social relations. Notably, both the female torch bearer and Olympic flame igniter were "white," Anglophone females. The dominant ethnic background of the female torch bearer is not surprising if we consider that the state had selected Canadian winter sport champions: there are very few other racial-ethnic groups represented on elite Canadian athletic teams especially in winter sports. Even francophone athletes are underrepresented within this category.

A final illustration of "Canada Telling Its Own Story" occurred in an interview between ABC's Peter Jennings and Canadian Prime Minister Brian Mulroney that took place just prior to the opening ceremony. The interview commenced with Peter Jennings mispronouncing the Prime Minister's name as "Munroney." Though he does not make the same mistake again, Jennings does not correct himself for the audience.

Later in the interview, and somewhat predictably, the Prime Minister is asked about what the games mean to Canada. Prime Minister Mulroney responds with various comments about the unified sense of pride he had witnessed on the part of all Canadians. However, Jennings pressed the Prime Minister about the nation's cohesiveness citing the longstanding sense of resentment that the west region holds toward the east. In response, Prime Minister Mulroney admits that the country "has had its problems: east and west, French and English, and the difficulties in having such a small population base in the second largest nation in the world." However, he talks about these as if they are in the past, as if they "used to be" problems, emphasizing that the Olympics serve to bring the nation together, providing unity, a consensus, and a sense of national pride.

How does one interpret these images and narrative of the story that Canada is trying to tell about itself through the Olympics? The emphasis on pluralism and multi-culturalism is difficult to ignore. The "salad bowl" image and signification of Canada was indeed presented. Arguably, however, catch-phrases like the "salad bowl" are clearly misleading. If, indeed, the multicultural constitution of Canada can be characterized as a salad bowl, then it is asserted that no matter how it is tossed there will always be something on the bottom. Moreover, it is important to recognize who actually "tosses" the salad. In other words, there will always be relations of power expressed in terms of domination and subordination.

The problem of constructing and representing a national identity presents a major ideological challenge for any state. In the case of the 1988 Calgary Winter Olympics the state was faced with selecting and displaying those aspects of culture which symbolized Canadian "uniqueness." However, in so doing, two important processes occur: (1) the state typically selected "positive" representations and symbols of sovereignty and in conjunction with this tended to portray the nation as a unified, consensual whole; and, (2) the state selectively articulated those contexts within which differentiations are made, typically in relation to another identity. The result is often a highly idealized, mystical, and even forged construction and interpretation of an identity.

Thus, there is an ongoing political struggle over the meaning of the Canadian identity, wherein the state (through its institutionalized political arm—the government) represents its own interests as "the national interests." The "effect" is often a masking and depoliticizing of the various Canadian "cultures" and their efforts to be recognized as legitimate formations within the Canadian social structure.

SUMMARY

This study set forth to examine the evidence of the continued existence of a 49th paradox in relation to the social construction of Canadian identity. More specifically, the present analysis examined the problem of Canadian identity within a particular structural relationship, that is, the "49th Paradox," within a specific cultural site, that is, the Olympic Games, and in a specific socio-historical context, 1988, the year of the

Calgary Winter Olympic Games, a Canadian Federal election, and the signing of the Canada-U.S. Free Trade Agreement.

Various political, economic and cultural forces combined to position Canadian identity as a contested terrain of meaning, a site of ideological struggle. Moreover, Canada's identity is continually constructed out of difference to the United States. Thus, Gwyn's (1985) argument that Canadian identity is no longer defined by, nor survives by, simply aspiring to a "not-American" status, is only partly true. The very dialectical nature of identity construction suggests that Canada will probably *always* define its identity out of difference to the United States.

ABC television, the Canadian state, and official Olympic sponsors operated within their own self-interests to produce an identity signifying diverse and often contradictory meanings. In particular, the Canadian state utilized the Calgary Olympics hegemonically to represent Canada as a multicultural, egalitarian, consensual whole by "incorporating the margins" and by ignoring existing sources of social conflict. However, since 1988 the Canadian state has been under increasing pressure to resolve emerging domestic political problems such as: The Meech Lake Accord, the Referendum on Quebec, new Native claims for self-government, and serious problems surrounding the economy linked to both the Canada-U.S. FTA and the more recent NAFTA (North American Free Trade Agreement which includes Mexico).

It is also important to note that ongoing sources of conflict between Canada and the U.S. were disregarded during the Olympics. There was a conspicuous absence of critical discourse related to such issues as: Free Trade, Acid Rain, The United States tapping of the Great Lakes, The United States' lack of recognition of Canada's sovereignty in the Northwest Passage, and, Canada's opposition to United States support of the Contras in Nicaragua, Star Wars deployment, and nuclear arms testing in the Arctic.

Global cultural events such as the Olympics provide an opportunity for the construction of what might be referred to as "tele-nations," that is, national political and cultural entities which are represented both domestically and internationally through the media. And, while such an apparatus has the potential to contribute to, and foster, a sense of cultural awareness and international understanding, it may also be used to serve the interests of those currently in power. Consequently, the Olympics are often used by the host state to construct a nation which the audience is encouraged to believe that it belongs to.

The globalization of economies and the cultural effects of the New World Order are only now beginning to appear. However, there is little doubt that the study of identity, national and other, will be the subject of passionate intellectual, political and popular discussion into the next decade. The elevated global stature achieved by the Olympics, particularly as a media event, is likely to maintain them as an important site for the analysis of the politics of identity.

Richard White's (1981, p. viii) observations regarding the ideological basis of identity construction provide a fitting end to this discussion. For purposes of illustration the liberty has been taken to substitute Canada for Australia in the following passage:

There are no prizes for getting it right. There was no moment, when for the first time, [Canada] was seen 'as it really was'. There is no 'real' [Canada] waiting to be uncovered. A national identity is an invention. There is no point asking whether one version of this essential [Canada] is truer than another because they are all intellectual constructs, neat, tidy, comprehensible—and necessarily false. They have all been artificially imposed upon a diverse landscape and population and a variety of untidy social relationships, attitudes and emotions. When we look at ideas about national identity, we need to ask, not whether they are true or false, but what their function is, whose creation they are, and whose interests they serve.

REFERENCES

Bale, J. (1986). Sport and national identity: a geographical view. *The British Journal of Sports History, 3*, 18–41.

Brimelow, P., (1986). *The patriot game*. Toronto: Key Porter.

Clarke, A. & Clarke, J. (1982). Highlights and action replays—ideology, sport and the media. In J. Hargreaves (Ed.), *Sport, culture and ideology* (pp. 62–87). London: Routledge and Kegan Paul.

Come to Uncle. (1988, December 12). *The New Republic*, p. 4.

Fleras, A. (1991). Beyond the mosaic: Minorities and the media in multiracial/multicultural society. In B. D. Singer (Ed.), *Communications in Canadian society* (pp. 344–367). Scarborough: Nelson Canada.

Fotheringham. A. (1988, February 22). For the glory of ABC and skippy. *Maclean's, 101*, (9), p. 60.

Fotheringham, A. (1988, February 29). The media children of the games. *Maclean's, 101*, p. 56.

Fotheringham, A. (1988, March). Team Calgary wins a gold medal. *Maclean's, 101*, p. 68.

Fotheringham, A. (July, 1989). Different—in a manner of speaking. *Maclean's*, p. 84.

Granzberg, G. (1989). Portrayal of visible minorities by Manitoba television: a summary of findings. *Currents, 5*, p. 25.

Gruneau, R., (1988). Notes on popular cultures and political practices. In R. Gruneau (Ed.), *Popular cultures and political practices* (pp. 11–32). Toronto: Garamond Press.

Gruneau, R. (1989). Television, the Olympics, and the question of ideology. In R. Jackson & T. McPhail (Eds.), *The Olympic movement and the mass media: past, present and future issues* (pp. 7.23–7.34). Calgary: Hurford Industries Ltd.

Gwyn, R. (1985). *The 49th paradox: Canada in North America*. Toronto: Totem Books.

Hobsbawm, E. & Ranger, T. (1983). *The invention of tradition*. Cambridge: Cambridge University Press.

Holmes, J.W. (1981). *Life with uncle*. Toronto: University of Toronto Press.

Jackson, S. J. (1992a). *Sport, crisis and Canadian identity in 1988: A cultural analysis*. Unpublished doctoral dissertation, University of Illinois, Urbana.

Jackson, S. J. (1992b). *Sport, crisis and Canadian identity in 1988: The issue of Americanisation*. Paper presented at The Americanisation of Culture Conference, University of Wales, Swansea, September 16–18.

Jhally, S. (1989). Cultural studies and the sports/media complex. In L. A. Wenner (Ed.), *Media, sports and society* (pp. 70–93). Newbury Park: Sage Publications.

Kilbourn, W. (1988). The peaceable kingdom still. *Daedalus, 117*, 1–29.

Lisee, J.-F. (1990). *In the eye of the eagle.* Toronto: HarperCollins Publishers.

MacAloon, J. J. (1984). *Rite, drama, festival, spectacle.* Philadelphia: Institute for the study of human issues.

Macintosh, D., Bedecki, T., & Franks, C.E.S. (1987). *Sport and politics in Canada.* Kingston: McGill-Queens University Press.

Marule, M. S. (1991). An Indian perspective on Canadian politics. In P.W. Fox & G. White (Eds.), *Politics Canada* (pp. 15–22). Toronto: McGraw-Hill Ryerson Ltd.

Merchant, L. (Ed.). (1966). *Neighbors taken for granted.* New York: Praeger.

Moffett, S.E. (1972). *The Americanization of Canada.* Toronto: University of Toronto Press.

Newman, P. C. (1989, July 3). Bold and cautious. *Maclean's*, pp. 24–25.

Scott, M. (1988). *From nation to colony.* Lindsay, ON: Tri-M Publishing.

Taafe, W. (1988, January 27). The $309 million games. *Sports Illustrated, 68*, (4), pp. 8, 21.

Taafe, W. (1988, February 29). They do run on. *Sports Illustrated, 68*, pp. 66–67.

Taafe, W. (1988, March 7). No gold for ABC. *Sports Illustrated, 68*, (10), p. 81.

Tomlinson, A. (1989). Representation, ideology and the Olympic Games: A reading of the opening and closing ceremonies of the 1984 Los Angeles Games. In R. Jackson & T. McPhail (Eds.), *The Olympic movement and the mass media: past, present and future issues* (pp. 7.3–7.11). Calgary: Hurford Industries Ltd.

Whannel, G. (1984). The television spectacular. In A. Tomlinson & G. Whannel (Eds.) *Five ring circus: Money, power and politics at the Olympic Games.* London: Pluto Press.

Whannel, G. (1989). History is being made: television sport and the selective tradition. In R. Jackson & T. McPhail (Eds.), *The Olympic movement and the mass media: past, present and future issues* (pp. 7.13–7.21). Calgary: Hurford Industries Ltd.

White, R., (1981). *Inventing Australia: Images and identity 1688–1980.* Sydney: George Allen & Unwin.

14

Symbolic Inversion in the Subculture of Skateboarding

Becky Beal

INTRODUCTION

Symbolic inversion has been used to analyze a variety of social rituals such as carnivals, religious holidays, as well as different forms of play (e.g., Babcock, 1978; King, 1982; Lincoln, 1989; McLaren, 1985; Sutton-Smith, 1983; Szala-Meneok, 1994), and is defined as, "any act of expressive behavior which inverts, contradicts, abrogates, or in some fashion presents an alternative to commonly held cultural codes, values, and norms be they linguistic, literary or artistic, or social and political" (Babcock, 1978, p. 14). Symbolic inversion has been studied in two different contexts. One context is in a culturally designated space which is separated from the everyday lives of people such as religious holidays or theater productions, and the other is within the everyday lives of people such as behavior in a classroom or in a subculture.

The implications for inversion occurring in each context are quite different because the ideological underpinnings of a society are either challenged or reinforced, and when they are challenged the societal response is often negative. For example, when inversions occur as part of everyday behavior it upsets what people take-for-granted as the ground rules of social interaction which, in turn, can cause people to react negatively to the inversion as if it is an abhorrence to the "natural" or "right" social behavior. Whereas, inversions that occur in segregated spaces do not disrupt the structure of people's everyday lives and, therefore, do not provoke the same degree of public disruption and disapproval.

This chapter will describe how the social practices of the subculture of skateboarding inverted mainstream values and how this daily inversion upset a number of taken-for-granted perceptions. It is my supposition that when symbolic inversion was ritualized into daily behaviors the dominant social relations became ridiculed or contradicted on an ongoing basis. In turn, the "normalcy" of dominant relations was challenged and people felt uncomfortable with this daily critique. More precisely, the subculture's inversion exposed some contradictions in the "American Dream" which led to an uneasy relation with the dominant culture.

SPORT AND THE AMERICAN DREAM

For many Americans, sport is symbolic of the qualities of American life because it represents achieving success through work hard, following the rules, competition, and delayed gratification. Sport is an apparent mirror of how American system works because it ostensibly is a sphere where individuals who live by the above standards and have the talent will climb the ladder of success. In this vein, sport has been touted as a means to "build character," especially the qualities of a good worker. These same characteristics have been described by researchers as the ideological underpinnings which help maintain and justify capitalism.

Capitalist Ideology and Sport Practices

Many researchers have described a dominant sport culture as one in which competition, extrinsic rewards, elitism based on skill, and specialization are central components (Donnelly, 1993; Stevenson, 1991). In addition, mainstream sport in North America has been associated with bureaucratic relations (Berlage, 1982; O'Hanlon, 1980; Whitson, 1984). It has been argued that these structures of sport in North America are connected with a capitalist ideology and, therefore, have reinforced the lived practices and experiences of capitalist relations (Bray, 1988; Foley, 1990; O'Hanlon, 1980; Whitson, 1984). The following are some studies which made the connection among culture, ideology, and capitalist relations.

O'Hanlon (1980) argued that mainstream sport is a significant avenue for youth to learn values and relations of corporate capitalism. For example, he asserted that youth learn that they need to prepare for a hierarchical society in which unequitable social benefits are justifiable through "fair" competition, and that youths are socialized to accept and give allegiance to rules which govern their competition for different positions within society. Whitson (1984) argued that mainstream sports have been framed in the value structures of advanced capitalism: discipline, control, accountability, and bureaucratic rationalization which has created a managerial level of "experts." Whitson claimed that this reaffirmation of capitalistic values outside of the work force had the effect of confirming those values as natural or as "common sense" which promotes the ideological basis of capitalism as normal.

Foley's (1990) *Learning Capitalist Culture: Deep in the heart of Tejas*, describes a variety of social practices, including high school football, and how they reinforce capitalist relations in a small town in Texas. Foley described how hegemony is lived: "The great ideological struggle in advanced capitalist societies is not only over explicit political ideologies but also over one's mode of identity expression" (p. 186). The rituals of expression are what he investigated and organized football was one ritual by which youths learned, lived, and supported capitalist relations: "Youths practice, learn, and anticipate their different class identities and roles through the way they play football, display peer status, and horse around in the classrooms" (p. 192).

In summary, the structure and relations of corporate bureaucracies are prevalent in mainstream North American sport. When popular cultural activities are structured by corporate bureaucratic social relations it helps to promote and legitimize the values and norms that underlie capitalism to the point where they are taken-for-granted. On the other hand, when physical activities are structured on other values and beliefs, if, in fact, those values are inverted, then it has the potential to challenge those assumptions and social relations.

PLAY: AN INVERSION OF SPORT

Although play may have some physical similarities to sport, many of the components of play invert the above mentioned components of American sport. Vital factors of play include intrinsic motivation, the freedom to start and stop at any point, the lack of rules and authority figures, and the lack of competition. (Figler & Whitaker, 1991) Several researchers (King, 1982; McLaren, 1985; Sutton-Smith, 1983) have analyzed how play can be used by children as a means of challenging dominant relations and the authority figures which uphold and impose those relations. The subculture of skateboarding shares the traits associated with play such as a flexible environment in which the participants are the authority, the motivation is primarily intrinsic, and where competition is not paramount.

METHODOLOGY

I used qualitative methods of observation, participant-observation, and semi-structured in-depth interviews to investigate the subculture of skateboarding in northeastern Colorado. My research began in June 1989, when I started observing skateboarders in Jamestown and Welton, Colorado at local hangouts, skateboard shops, and a locally sponsored skateboard exhibition.

My initial participants were children of my friends and employees at skateboard shops. I used a snowball style of sampling so these initial contacts led to many others. In addition, I met many participants by stopping them while they were skateboarding on the streets and asking if I could talk with them. (They call themselves "skaters," and the act of skateboarding they call "skating.") I met one female skater (a rarity) through mutual membership in a local feminist group. Over a two year period (1990–1992) I talked with 41 skaters, two skateboard shop owners, and several parents and siblings.

Of the 41 skateboarders, 24 I interviewed more than once, and six of those became my best informants for we cultivated a closer relationship which fostered more trust. This relationship consisted of continual feedback in which they checked the reliability of the information I was gathering and, in turn, I could continually refine and ask more pertinent questions. In addition, I spent over 100 hours observing skateboarders many of whom I had not interviewed (they were observed in public spaces). Thirty-seven of the 41 participants were male and four were female. In addition, all were anglo except two who were Hispanic males. The average age of those participating was 16, but ranged from 10 to 25 years. The participants had skateboarded for an average of four years, but the range of their participation was from one to 15 years. My most consistent contacts were from two friendship groups of skaters: the group from Jamestown was younger (ages 10 to 16 years) and included two Hispanic males; the second group was from Welton and was older (ages 15–25 years) and included a female.

After I finished gathering data, the information and analysis of their subculture was presented to approximately one third of the participants. Their comments served to reaffirm and fine tune my conclusions. They especially wanted me to note that, although they shared many norms and values, they did not share all values and, therefore, just because they were all skateboarders did not mean that they were all good friends.

It is necessary to elaborate on the above comment because there was not an ubiquitous skateboard subculture. In fact, there were a variety of subgroups who skateboarded. The two most basic distinctions are those who skated within corporate bureaucratic relations and those who inverted and subsequently challenged those relations. Obviously, I focused my study on those who challenged the relations, but even within that group their challenges were demonstrated through a variety of styles.

The term the skaters used to describe the skaters who lived corporate bureaucratic relations was "rats." Skaters defined "rats" as those who bought the commercially produced paraphernalia and plastered all their belongings with corporate logos. But, most distinctively, they were described as kids who aspired to skate professionally. There is a structured competitive outlet for skateboarders which is organized by the National Skateboard Association (NSA), a group managed mainly by volunteers but strongly supported by the skateboarding industry (NSA, 1990).

On the other hand, there was another group of skaters who resisted the professionalization of their physical activity. They denounced skateboarding as primarily a way to make a living, instead they used skateboarding as a way of living which they did by incorporating their interests with the commercially produced products. For example, they bought commercially produced skateboards (many tried to make their own but claimed they were not as good) but they decorated their boards with their own symbols and in a few cases that included poetry. They no longer bought the "right" clothes or commercially produced stickers, instead they were more innovative with their clothing and often created their own stickers leaving them where they skated. The style of expressing a way of living varied greatly, and the skaters classified each by an association with music or by the style of skating. Some of these included "hippies," "punks," "skinheads," "frat boys," "metalers" (i.e. heavy metal music), "rappers," and "old timers" (e.g. those who do slalom skating as opposed to "trick" skating).

This study concentrated on those who opposed the professionalization of their physical activity by inverting the dominant values of corporate bureaucracies. The common subcultural features will be the focus of the following discussion.

SKATEBOARDING AS SYMBOLIC INVERSION

The popular practice of skateboarding was structured quite differently from the corporate bureaucratic model of sport. Most significantly, skating was not extrinsically oriented. There was no end goal to achieve, nor to win. In fact, winning was nonsensical, because there was nothing to win. There were no exclusive positions, no championships, no elite standards. Therefore, there was little need to compete, and in fact, competitive attitudes were discouraged. At the heart of skateboarding was intrinsic motivation. People skated as a means to have fun or as a means to express themselves. Within this flexible structure, the athletes controlled their own physical activity and, in the process, their own bodies. The popular practice of skateboarding had no coaches, no rules, and no referees. The athletes created their own tricks and games, and they determined which tricks they practiced and how long. They also controlled their own dress, language, and style.

Specifically discussed will be the skaters' intentional inversion of normative standards as articulated by Grace, a 21-year-old skateboarder: skating demands people to "look at what's wrong with you and your society, not with us [skateboarders]." As the skateboarders often noted, skateboarding is not just an activity, but a lifestyle. Thus, their inversion was not separate event or ceremony, but a daily critique and alternative to mainstream relations. Therefore, the societal reaction to this daily inversion, which makes skateboarding virtually illegal, will also be addressed.

Participants as Experts

The most distinguishing characteristic in skateboarding is the participants' control over their physical activity as opposed to an institutionalized system controlled by an authority figure. The popular practice of skateboarding does not use rules, referees, coaches, or organized contests. This lack of formal structure leads to a very flexible environment where the participants not only control their physical activity, but engage in creative endeavors. Often, skaters create and name their own games and their own tricks. This control over their activity distinguishes the participants as the experts. The following comments illustrate the control, flexibility, and creativeness skaters demonstrated.

One formal question I asked skaters was to compare and contrast their experiences in organized sport with those in skateboarding, and I followed by asking which they prefer and why. A telling description of the difference is revealed in a conversation two brothers had:

Jeff: Skating is a lot less confined, people are open to new things when you skate. … I mean there's so many different types of skating, not just ramp skating, and you can take stuff from other things and put into another element, for instance take street tricks and put them on a ramp, so that's one thing I like about it just that it's interchangeable, you can do a lot of different things and people are always progressing.

Philip: Skateboarding is young and there are so many new tricks people are doing, it's not like baseball where all the rules have been set down.

Jeff: Well, there are no rules to skating.

Philip: When was the last time someone invented something in baseball?

This openness and flexibility of skateboarding was often contrasted to the regimented rules they experienced in other sports. Again, skaters consciously inverted mainstream values and relations. Craig stated that skating is different from organized sports because "it's not as military minded," "there are no manuals or no coaches," and you're "not part of a machine, [you] go at your own pace, to each his own." One woman skater, Kathleen, stated that in skating it is not just the control of the activity, but the control over one's body which is significant. She stated that there are "no referees, no penalties, no set plays, you can do it anywhere and there's not a lot of training, no strict regiment, you can eat whatever you want, and smoke."

This need to control their own physical activity was a way of ensuring that the only limits of skateboarding were each skater's which they specifically addressed. Paul claimed that in skating you "don't need uniforms, no coach to tell you what to do and how to do it." Philip added, "I quit football because I didn't like taking orders."

Most of the skating was not bound by rules; again, it was testing the limits and imagination of the skaters. A skating session often involved practicing certain techniques, finding fun places to skate, and trying to do new tricks on the new obstacles found. When skaters created more organized forms of games, they were the ones who decided the rules. Different groups of skaters created different games. Most of the games I saw or heard about incorporated risk-taking challenges. For example, follow the leader was a game in which a line of skaters followed the leader through various tricks and obstacles; when the leader made a mistake, or couldn't "land" a trick, then he/she would go to the back of the line and the next person would be the leader.

The lack of control by an authority was reflected in the lack of standardized criteria. Craig commented, "there is no such thing as a perfect '10' for a trick." Effort and participation were essential to skating, and not achieving some elite defined objective. These values and the ability to control their physical activity often lead to empowering feelings. Many skaters expressed this simply by stating that they loved to learn new tricks and enjoyed seeing themselves improve.

The following comments drew the connection more explicitly. Grace discussed how she didn't want skating to become a sport because she didn't want practices, coaches, and specific tricks to learn, "For who's to say what trick is better? I like to do stuff that feels cool, that gives me butterflies in my stomach." Eric stated "When you do a really good trick, it makes it seem like more things are possible," and his friend added that someone may get that same satisfaction in organized sport only if they are really good. Eric concluded by stating that "skating is more challenging (than organized sports); you see yourself improve, you amaze yourself."

Intentional Inversion

Rules established by an authority figure which limit the participants' creative use of skateboarding were open to contention. What I found particularly interesting was the resistance to the rules created by the National Skateboard Association (NSA). Part of the goal of the NSA is to promote skateboarding through the sponsorship of amateur competitions. In the summer of 1991 the Colorado Skateboard Association (an affiliate of the NSA) sponsored a series of eight amateur competitions. They created age and skill categories, and participants placed themselves within the appropriate category. Those who wanted to be judged had to pay an initial 40 dollar fee, and then 10 dollars more for each of the following competitions. The contest courses were created by local skateboard shops who individually sponsored the events. These contest courses usually consisted of ramps of various sizes and rails of varying heights to slide on. Each skater had two rounds of two minutes to impress the judges. The judges were the local skateboarding leaders, and they were often employed by the skate shop that was sponsoring the event.

Before each age and skill category was judged, the skaters were allowed to warm up on the courses. Only those about to compete were supposed to be warming up, yet many of the competitors as well as those who had not entered the contests skated during these warm-up periods. During one contest the CSA organizers tried to enforce that rule, so over the loud speaker they announced that anyone who skated out of turn would be disqualified. This did not stop anyone, but the volunteers went out on the course and actually wrote down the competitors' registration numbers (which they had to wear, and literally inverted by pinning them upside down) who warmed-up out of turn, and then announced over the loud speaker who was disqualified.

This attempt to disqualify skaters led to an argument which temporarily stopped the competition. A few of the skaters were debating with the CSA volunteers about the purpose of the competition. During this argument the announcer (who was a local skater) started to rap over the loud speaker, "You have all been D.Q.'ed," and went on with "D.Q., you went to Dairy Queen." In the mean time, the judges, volunteers, and contestants agreed that no one should be disqualified, but the volunteers asked that the skaters allow each other to have proper warm up periods. At the next contest (two weeks later) the announcer mockingly reminded everyone that they may be disqualified if they break the rules. This did not hinder the skaters from skating on the equipment during the warm-up periods.

In this instance the skaters challenged the rules which had limited the opportunities for the skaters during the amateur series. They ensured that everyone, even those who had not paid the contestant fees, would be able to skate during the non-competitive times. The purpose of the contest for the skaters and the purpose for the volunteers differed greatly. The volunteers took seriously the competitive face of the contest, but most skaters with whom I talked played that down. Instead, they enjoyed the opportunity to meet new people, see new tricks, to skate on new equipment, and to skate in new towns. Therefore, the rules created by an outside elite (CSA) were challenged, and the value of open participation as opposed to elite competition was reaffirmed. The emphasis on open participation and cooperation is another key element of the subculture, and one which inverts the mainstream value of competition.

Cooperation

A prevalent and significant characteristic of the popular practice of skateboarding is the lack of competition in the activity. Skateboarding's informal structure facilitates an environment where the emphasis is on the process of the activity and not the outcome. Therefore, motivation tends to be intrinsic as opposed to extrinsic. The lack of authority figures and their standardized goals promotes a non-competitive and cooperative environment. As Craig stated, "You never lose when you skateboard."

The vast majority of skaters described their sport as different from competition. Jeff stated: "I don't know if I would classify it (skating) as a sport. I suppose I just find sport as competition; unless you are on the pro circuit or amateur circuit you're not really competing against anybody." Pamela compared competitive sport with skateboarding:

> Soccer is a lot of pressure ... you have to be as good if not better than everybody else, you have to be, otherwise you don't play at all. Skating you can't do that, you just have to push yourself harder and harder ... swimming is just sort of there, you get timed, now for me you go against the clock, *now when you skate you don't go against anything, you just skate.* That's what it is.

Within the subculture there were some status differences, but they were not established through competition with others. The criteria for high status was two fold: One must be highly skilled and creative, and one must not use that skill to belittle others. Although there was a skill differentiation, it was not used to promote exclusivity from others. Status was gained primarily by promoting cooperation. Without those values, skaters were denied full skater status. This position was revealed by the responses to one of the questions I asked, what made a skater "cool" or "uncool." Overwhelmingly the response was that an uncool skater was competitive and exclusive. The reverse was true for a cool skater, someone who was supportive and does not show-off. Joe, a 12-year-old skater, described cool skaters as people who help each other out and don't put each other down, he claimed that everyone has to start at the beginning and skaters know that. Brian, a 13-year-old skater, elaborated on this:

> Well, we don't, we're not like competitive, like saying "I can ollie higher than you so get away from me," and stuff like that, we're like, we just want to do a few things people are doing, and skaters help out skaters … and if I were to ask a good skater like some people I can skate with, like Brad Jones, he's really good, he's probably the best skater I know in Welton, if I asked him he would like give me tips and stuff, you know, on how to do it, and that's just how we do it, we want to show other people how to skate, but if they aren't willing to try then they aren't worth showing how to do it.

Skaters did not appreciate those who tried to compete, for it contradicted the disposition of skating. As Jeff stated:

> Nobody really seemed to like competitive natures, for instance, me, Philip, and a couple of our friends all found that to be a really turn off. This guy would pull a really good trick and rub it in their faces. And then there's Hugh who can do stuff and he doesn't go, "oh wow, bet you can't," but he's fun to be with … and he encourages you so that's pretty cool.

My two years of observing skaters' interactions confirmed these statements. Skaters were very supportive with each other. It was common to see skaters who on their first meeting would encourage each other, give tips, and laugh at their own mistakes. It was a marked contrast to watching other more traditional sports being played by young people. For example, one day I passed a public tennis court where two pre-adolescent boys were playing tennis. They were yelling at each other about how good they were, and announcing how they were going to "kick" the other one's "ass." Unlike the skaters I observed, they did not stop to show each other tips on playing, support the good shots of the other, or laugh at each other. The significant aspect of this observation was the response I received when I relayed this to a group of skaters in Welton. One of the skaters, Doug, commented "That's because we don't skate *against* somebody; we skate *with* them."

Intentional Inversion of a Sporting Competition

Skaters mocked the mainstream emphasis on competition and winning. For example, Jeff and Philip shared with me an inside joke about dancing which they use to ridicule a win-at-all-cost attitude. Social dancing is usually considered an expressive form of physical activity; although there may be subtle forms of competition through competence, social dancing often is a means to have fun and socialize. Philip was a drummer in a local rock band. The type of music they played usually involved a pit which refers to a space where dancing is rough and there is a lot of physical contact. Philip: "and this guy walks by and he's wearing a Yankees hat and a Jordan T-shirt, typical jock looking guy, and he walks by and he leans over to his friend and he goes, 'Man, is there going to be a pit here, if there is, dude, I'm going to win.'" Both Philip and Jeff laughed, and Jeff stated, "The object is not to win." Their joke reflected their assumptions that not every physical activity had to be competitive or used as an arena to prove oneself through winning.

Intentional Inversion of Instrumental Social Relations and Extrinsic Motivation

Skaters were aware that their inversion of instrumentality was one reason that skateboarding was not overwhelmingly accepted. Many of the skaters observed and pointed out that people seem to be uncomfortable around skaters, or do not accept skating, precisely because it is not instrumental. Craig claimed that most people feel comfortable with organized and sanctioned sport which encourages competition and where the goal is concrete, where they know what is accomplished. He claimed that people don't like spontaneous sport, like skateboarding, in which unstructured and expressive human interaction is demanded.

Other skaters expressed similar reasons for the non-acceptance of skating. Sam, a 15-year-old, stated that people don't like skating because it's "dumb," not intellectually, but because it doesn't get you anywhere or serve a specific purpose. Specifically critiqued was the instrumentality of sport as enhancing the aerobic physiological system. Philip: "What I kind of figured out is that rollerblades are the socially acceptable skate tool … here's their big excuse, 'it's aerobic exercise.'" Doug also reflected this belief: "Rollerblading is such a mass appeal, it's an older person's sport, for a lot of people it's just cross training, it's an aerobic workout, that's what we (alternative sport shop) sell for."

Skaters also critiqued the instrumental use of skating. They were very critical of "posers," or people who dressed like skaters but did not skate. More generally, skaters are critical of people who buy the "alternative" style clothing, referred to as "beachwear," yet did not make the sacrifice or commitment to the values and the group.

The desire to maintain a process-oriented sport was passionately asserted by several skaters. Grace stated that she didn't want skateboarding to become a sport, she didn't want coaches, practices and specific tricks to learn. She felt that the creativity and freedom of skating "would be caged up and processed with everything else … [skateboarding] is a symbol of freedom, that can't be cut up and processed and sold, can't do that with freedom." Doug also made a claim for the expressive orientation of skateboarding:

> A lot of them [skaters] are really involved with artistic endeavors, are very artistic, you can see the parallel, it's kind of freedom of expression that skating is. How do you express yourself playing football?, playing basketball?, when you're skating it's, basically skating reflects your mood at the time and how you're skating, what you are doing, you know, it's definitely, you know, a way to express yourself.

A significant concern for skaters was the social relations they experienced in their physical activity. Francis and Eric discussed how friendships in organized sport are often instrumental, where they are not in skating. Eric said,

> In skating you're only responsible for you, if you mess up, you won't mess up the whole team, [you are] not going to lose friends over messing up in skating. ... If you're the worst one on the baseball team others give you shit, makes you feel bad, in skating if you are bad, no one makes you feel bad about that.

Exposing Contradictions in the American Dream

The American Dream is often exemplified through the stories of Horatio Alger, a young man who works hard, is honest, and with a few lucky breaks is financially successful. This American ideal of rugged individualism, freedom of expression, and that individual hard work and talent will be rewarded, are embraced by the skaters. Similar to most social practices, the subculture of skateboarding is laden with apparent contradictions and, in this case, contradictions which are indicative of mainstream American culture. In this situation, their subculture exposed the tension and contradiction that occurs between achieving success through individual effort and achieving success through the bureaucratic requirement of conforming to authorities' standards. My contention is that the skateboarders exposed this underlying and implicit tension of American culture making people uneasy which can lead to negative social sanctions.

Philip's description of the different social groups in his high school exemplifies this contradiction. Those who conformed or had the most money were ranked the highest, and the group to which he belonged, those who did not conform, were labeled "alternatives" or "individuals" which had the lowest ranking:

> After that comes the group I'm in, we're the alternatives and that basically we're, we're individuals. That's what they say we are, "you're an individual" [stated sarcastically]. We don't even have a skater class, there's not enough of us at our school to be our own class. I hang out with George, and he and I make up the alternative group.

A discussion Kathleen, Mark, and I had illustrated their concern with the emphasis on conformity as a means to achieve success. Kathleen described a pep rally at her high school where the football coach delivered an inspirational speech on taking control of one's life. While he spoke he held a corn stalk in one hand and a weed in the other. He stated that one could take control of his or her life by choosing to either be a weed or a plant. Mark noted that dandelions used to be considered plants. Kathleen commented that taking control of one's life is more than conforming to what the dominant group labels as valuable.

The skaters frequently pointed out that those who conformed to dominant standards are treated better than those who do not, including themselves. Alan, a fifth grade student, is part of a talented and gifted school program. He claimed that even though he is in the "advanced" group, the teachers don't like him and talk down to him. He felt that conformers such as "school girls" and "teachers' pets" could "get away with anything."

Doug, a substitute teacher and skater, talked about the prejudices he saw against skaters and claimed that it was prevalent:

> Oh, ya, because skaters they got an asymmetrical haircut, and wear their jeans rolled up and wear, you know, big airwalk shoes [skater brand name], you know, ya, and because they carry their skateboards with them to school, and that's bullshit, that angers me, maybe I'm biased to the other side, but I think they need some of those teachers.

I asked, "Is it just because they're not," and Doug interrupted, "conforming. Ya, I guess that's it."

Most of the skaters considered themselves to be more reflective than their peers. Philip: "We might look at everything twice whereas everybody else will just go "oh ya." The whole war thing (Persian Gulf war), I don't know it seems a little too, very convenient … We're not saying skating doesn't have any conformity, but it's more by your own choice." Jeff:

> It's not conformist conformity … I think skaters are more aware of conformity than jocks. I think jocks just seem to deal with it and say "OK, well that's just the way it is," but skaters go, "jeese, why do I have to do that, man."

Societal Response

Skaters recognized that their lack of conformity bestowed a label of deviance, and that label had the ramifications of being discredited and devalued. They explained discriminatory treatment as a reaction by mainstream people because skateboarding does not represent the dominant values associated with sport, especially a clean cut orientation. Francis and Eric stated that skating did not have a "healthy" or "family" image like bicycling or rollerblading, and that people understood the latter two because more people had participated in them. Mark and Kathleen described how they were stopped frequently by police because, as they related, "we don't like the way you look." Skateboarders tended to describe their stereotype in the manner that Jeff did: "and most people consider skaters, vandals and looters and pillagers and rapists and stuff…."

The following letter to the editor of a local newspaper exemplifies the strain the skaters felt between their desire for a unique subculture and the judgements of mainstream society, the tension between individuality and conformity:

> Skaters have a completely different culture from the norms of the world's society. We dress differently, we have our own language, use our own slang, and live by our own rules. People feel threatened by foreign attitudes. Everyone has his own views on different types of society and their own stereotypes. … Please stop viewing us as a totally negative race of people. The few people who have come up and watched us skate and spoken to us know that we are nice, educated, and intelligent. (Madea, 1991)

The inversion displayed by the subculture of skateboarders affected their relationship with mainstream society. Their daily exposure of some fundamental contradictions in the "American Dream" was not well received. The following describes a structural relationship between the subculture and dominant culture.

Relationship with the Dominant Culture

One specific example of this relationship was illustrated through the interaction of a group of skaters and the Jamestown city council. In February 1991, the council suggested that a task force should thoroughly investigate the possibility of a publicly financed skateboard park. Skaters, parents, and city recreation workers created a task force, and had two months to investigate the issue. I went to this March city council meeting with over 50 skaters and parents in a crowd of approximately 100 to 125 people. The city council unanimously supported the concept of a public skate park, but claimed they did not have the finances.

Four months later, July 1991, I talked to some of the skaters who were on that task force, and they said that the city is now building a model airplane runway on the south side of the city next to the country club. This group of skaters felt that this project was approved over theirs because it is an older wealthier peoples' hobby, and those people can vote.

In all the cities where I met skaters, skateboarding in public spaces was illegal. In addition, these cities provided no public and legal space for skaters. The rationale is that skateboarding is too physically risky which leads to frequent injuries and, therefore, not only is it unsafe, but the insurance is too high for the city to cover skateboarding. According to the Consumer Product Safety Commission, more injuries are reported in the non-professional activities of bicycling, basketball, football, baseball, and rollerskating than in skateboarding ("Watch your step," 1991). The other forms of physical activity are frequently positively sanctioned by the city either through their legal status or through subsidized public facilities.

It is my assertion that the public disregard for skateboarders is partially based in the subculture's inversion of dominant norms associated with mainstream sport and corporate bureaucratic relations. Their daily rituals of inversion promote discomfort with mainstream society because they challenge taken-for-granted norms and relations, and this discomfort can lead to antagonism and negative sanctions.

CONCLUSION

The social relations of mainstream sport in the United States have been linked with those of corporate bureaucracies. Especially noted is the emphasis on competition, extrinsic rewards, instrumental relations, and obedience to authority figures. The subculture of skateboarding inverts the norms associated with corporate bureaucracies by promoting the norms associated with play such as the participant as expert and intrinsic motivation. This inversion of corporate social relations has social consequences. Most apparently it challenges people by presenting a daily inversion to corporate bureaucratic relations. On a more implicit level, I contend that this daily inversion exposes a deeper contradiction regarding how one is to achieve the American Dream. The skaters exemplify many traditional American values such as individualism, hard work, and freedom of expression. On the other hand, they challenge other traditional forms of achieving success such as conformity with authority. The daily exposure of this contradiction disrupts people's perceptions of normalcy and, therefore, elicits negative social sanctions.

REFERENCES

Babcock, B. (Ed.). (1978). *The reversible world: Symbolic inversion in art and society.* Ithaca: Cornell University Press.

Foley, D. (1990). The great American football ritual: Reproducing race, class, and gender inequality. *Sociology of Sport Journal, 7,* 111–135.

King, N. (1982). Children's play as a form of resistance in the classroom. *Journal of Education, 164,* 320–329.

Lincoln, B. (1989). The dialectics of symbolic inversion. In *Discourse and the construction of society: Comparative studies of myth, ritual, and classification* (pp. 142–159). New York: Oxford University Press.

Madea, K. (1991, October). Rights for skateboarders [letter to the editor]. *Windsor Beacon,* p. 17.

McLaren, P. (1985). The ritual dimensions of resistance: Clowning and symbolic inversion. *Journal of Education, 167,* 84–97.

National Skateboard Association. (1990). Packet for new members.

O'Hanlon, T. (1980). Interscholastic athletics, 1900-1940: Shaping citizens for unequal roles in the modern industrial state. *Educational Theory, 30,* 89–103.

Scott, J. (1990). *Domination and the arts of resistance: Hidden transcripts.* New Haven: Yale University Press.

Sutton-Smith, B. (1983). Play theory and cruel play of the nineteenth century. In F. Manning (Ed.), *The world of play.* West Point: Leisure Press.

Szala-Meneok, K. (1994). Christmas janneying and Easter drinking: Symbolic inversion, contingency, and ritual time in coastal Labrador. *Arctic Anthropology, 31*(1) 103–116.

Watch your steps: Stairs No. 1 danger. (1991, May). *Denver Post,* p. 8a.

15

The Pleasures of Resistance: The Subversion of the Martial Arts

Margaret Carlisle Duncan

My purpose in this chapter is to offer a suggestive look at an area of research that I find compelling yet underexamined: the ways in which people subvert social systems in sport for their own pleasures. I will offer some examples of the different ways that people experience sport in the martial arts. Against the dominant discourses of the martial arts as they are practiced at one particular school or do jang, I will set the texts of practicing female martial artists to show how these are contesting voices that cannot and should not be reduced to a single text.

Here I invoke the ideas of Bakhtin, and in particular, the notion of *heteroglossia* (many voices), to argue that sport scholars must preserve a multiplicity of voices when studying sport culture. Bakhtin (1984) argued that every dominant perspective provokes oppositional perspectives, often irreverent and vulgar. Further, Bakhtin believed that scholars have both ethical and aesthetic obligations to preserve these discrepant readings alongside the mainstream readings (1984). Drawing on Bakhtin's ideas, I contend that sport scholars, too, have ethical and aesthetic obligations to recognize oppositional readings of sport. In this chapter I capture some widely discrepant sport texts and show that a number of female martial artists derive pleasure from subverting a specific martial system, Tae Kwon Do. I should add that this is a brief, exploratory effort, and by no means an attempt to pull off a full-dress treatment of my subject. I hope that this chapter will lay the foundation for a much more substantial research project in the future.

THE SUBVERSION OF FOOTBALL: AN ILLUSTRATION

I will start by describing the evolution of my own interest in the subversion of main-stream sport culture. Several years ago, a colleague and I set out to study the pleasures of televised sport spectating. We observed three groups of people watching televised professional football in the ordinary settings of their homes. One group was all male, one all female, and one mixed male and female. We had no idea what we would find, but we thought there might be some interesting gender differences. And indeed there were, although at first we were completely baffled in our attempts to understand those differences. At first we decided that women were simply less enthusiastic spectators, less involved, and less interested, since women were less physically and verbally exuberant and seemed to be less identified with the teams and players than were the men. Women also tended not to show off their football knowledge as extensively as the men who continually discussed the players' idiosyncrasies, eagerly displayed their intimate knowledge of the rules and strategies, and sprinkled their language with specialized game jargon.

Yet that didn't seem a very convincing explanation of the differences we witnessed, since the women *were* self-described *fans* and as knowledgeable as many men about football rules, strategies, jargon and about the teams and players' histories, even though they tended not to display that knowledge as frequently and argumentatively as the men in our groups. And the women clearly enjoyed their televised football watching, despite the fact that their expressive styles were quite different from the men's styles.

As we studied our transcripts of the conversations that took place in our viewing groups more carefully, we arrived at the following conclusion. Many of the women became televised football spectators largely for the purpose of subverting the activity itself. To do so, they relied on their own considerable technical knowledge of the game, but they used that knowledge ironically, against the institution of professional football itself. They tended to be more irreverent and less serious about the spectacle than men. For example, an obvious lapse by a quarterback prompted the following discussion:

Jane: All right, now *why* did he go through the middle? Why did he do that?
Molly: 'Cause that's where everybody else is ... That's where everybody else is. He doesn't want to be a loner. That's where everybody else is.
Jane: That frustrates me. That's totally dumb. What strategy is that? To run into a pile of people and fall down?

Another example: after eight or nine players zealously heaped themselves on the beleaguered quarterback with the ball, one woman exclaimed incredulously, "Do we need 85 people there? I'm surprised there aren't more dead football players." In short, in contrast to the male spectators whose discourse tended to be analytical and serious—and full of observations whose main purpose appeared to be to display their knowledge—our female spectators' comments tended toward the ironic, interspersed with rhetorical questions whose function seemed more to keep the social interaction going than to impress or enlighten.

We concluded that, at least in our small sample, women derived empowerment and pleasure from subverting the spectacle itself (Brummett & Duncan, 1992; Duncan & Brummett, 1993). The culture of professional football spectatorship in this country is one of male domination, and football is the ultimate physical expression of patriarchy (Messner, 1987; Real, 1982). The female spectators thus constructed subversive communities in opposition to the hegemonic community of fans that is encouraged by the patriarchal institution of professional football. Using their technical knowledge, they created the understanding necessary to read football ironically, and thus oppositionally. For these women, the pleasure and empowerment of football spectating derived from the joys of subversion.

TAE KWON DO

Now I switch to a discussion of a different set of texts, those centering on the martial arts. I offer a personal set of observations that comes from my own participation in the form of martial arts known as Tae Kwon Do. In particular, I show how female martial artists may subvert some of the dominant meanings of TKD culture as they are promoted in the school or do jang to which I belong. In this way I hope to demonstrate how these different texts represent a multiplicity of perspectives, a multiplicity of voices.

My two daughters and I began our TKD instruction in May 1991, about two and-a-half years ago for reasons having nothing to do with scholarship. Over the course of my instruction, however, I became interested in issues of subversion that came to my attention as I worked out with both women and men, girls and boys.

The Setting

The following is a sketch of the martial art culture as it is practiced and taught at my do jang. There, men, women, boys and girls are taught to master kicks, punches, various defensive moves, forms (continuous sequences of kicks and punches), sparring, and breaking boards. Students are put through a series of very physically demanding exercises and are expected to keep up and endure some pain and occasional injuries in order to progress. In our sparring matches, for example, students often receive minor injuries, jammed fingers, bruises, and sprains. These are considered an inevitable part of training, and one is expected to continue sparring—to persevere and show one's courage—unless the injury is debilitating. This is particularly true if one is male; female students are sometimes treated differently. For instance, the instructor will occasionally order the men not to make any physical contact with women during sparring (although women may connect with a punch or kick to their male partners), and light contact is more often the rule. Courage, and a certain imperviousness to pain, then, are expected, although more of these qualities are expected from males than from females.

Alongside these physical demands, students are also instructed in the philosophy of TKD. Classes begin and end with meditation, and are interspersed with lectures on concentration, confidence, and respect. Classes always end by the students' repeating the oaths of TKD—I shall observe the tenets of TKD, I shall never misuse TKD, I shall respect the instructors and seniors, I shall be a champion of freedom and justice, I shall build a more peaceful world—and the tenets—courtesy, integrity, perseverance, self-control, indomitable spirit. The final part of the ending ritual requires students to bow to the Master, the instructor, and then the highest ranking students, all of whom are supposed to exemplify the spiritual qualities promoted by TKD.

Like the military, Tae Kwon Do is profoundly hierarchical. In all schools students progress by attaining belts, each color representing a different level of competence. At my do jang, students line up in class according to their ranks, with the highest belts closest to the teacher and mirror at the front of the room, the lowest belts farthest away. Less advanced students must always bow and greet black belts (more advanced students). Lower belts are expected always to honor and obey the higher belts. The instructor, who is often a fourth degree black belt—or at least a high ranking belt—may levy punishments on students who are late (20 pushups) or who misbehave. At the top of the hierarchy is the master instructor, who at our do jang is a Grand Master, or 9th degree black belt. He has absolute authority over the other instructors and students. At testing time, he determines whether a student will be promoted to the next rank. He decides what moves students must be able to execute and what knowledge they must have in order to be promoted. He may also demote students for lack of discipline, respect, or self-control.

Instructors emphasize bringing honor to the school in general, and honoring the master, in particular, before each tournament. Students are encouraged to participate so as to win trophies that will bring acclaim to the do jang. Competing in area tournaments, even at the lowest ranks, is therefore highly encouraged.

The Subversive Voices of Female Martial Artists

Now it is time for me to set individual voices of female martial artists against the more general background of my do jang. These individuals include women and girls from ages 10 to 40, some students, some adults, some of whom work outside the home, others who do not, all who are all high colored belts and have been at the school for at least a year-and-a-half. Both their belt levels, which represent advanced skills, and their persistence suggest that they are in some ways quite committed to the discipline of TKD. Yet there are also clear indications that they enjoy subverting some aspects of it. I shall not argue that this is a representative sample in any sense, merely that their expressions of opposition to the martial arts culture, even as they embrace some of the discipline wholeheartedly, are noteworthy because it is clear that some of their empowerment and pleasure in the sport derive from these very expressions of opposition.

Here are some examples of subversive humor that took place in or around the do jang.

Ruth, a 30-year-old advertising executive, repeatedly entertained other students by doing her Bruce Lee imitation before class. This involved making high-pitched strangled cat sounds while punching and kicking the air in slow motion, and provoked much laughter among her other women friends. In Ruth's hands, this famous martial artist thus becomes a caricature of himself, and loses some of the awe and respect that otherwise might accrue to such a highly skilled black belt.

Sarah, a 12-year-old red-belt, liked to do an exaggerated version of a class exercise, favored by one of the more intense and serious male instructors, called the "groin stretch." This consisted of opening her legs and bending her knees, as though she was sitting astride a horse, then making a face like a constipated dog, and declaring, "I'm stretching my groin, oh, that feels so good." Part of her subversive enjoyment came from her identification of the word "groin" with male bodies. "Groin" is the term most often used in the do jang to indicate the below-the-belt region and is obviously male-centered. (No ob-gyn, for example, ever asks women how their groins are.) Sarah's way of subverting this male-oriented language was to make fun of it. She also seemed to delight in the absurdity of the posture, yet the seriousness with which the students assumed it.

Several students showed their enjoyment in oppositional pleasures shortly before testing time. For testing the Grand Master required students to memorize a poem titled "Just One Word" which is included here:

Just one uncaring word
   can spark a fight.
Just one cruel word
   can shatter a life
Just one harsh word
   can sow misunderstanding.
Just one disrespectful word
   can douse the fervor of love.

Just one kindly word
   can smooth a rocky path.
Just one joyful word
   can cheer a gloomy day.
Just the right word
   can lighten an uneasy heart.
Just one affectionate word
   can show the beauty of the world.

Although at testing, students respectfully intoned the lines of this poem, I heard two girls and one 40-year-old woman who showed neither respect nor courtesy when memorizing this poem beforehand. Jennie and Katie entertained each other on the way to the do jang by trying to guess what the one uncaring word might be: poophead? bozo? dorkface? and then mimed the poem with dramatic tragic gestures, voices quivering with pathos at appropriate moments.

Anne, the 40-year-old, came up with a creative variation on these verses by substituting "fuck" for "word" in the poem and primly reciting at various intervals:

> Just one uncaring fuck
>   can spark a fight.
> Just one cruel fuck
>   can shatter a life

and so on ending with

> Just one kindly fuck
>   can smooth a rocky path.

On another occasion, after a particularly hard class involving lots of high and difficult kicks, one of the teenage girls remarked, "I feel like my insides are splitting in two." Louise, a 30-year-old with a two-year young son, responded, "No, that doesn't happen until you have a baby." This is a very significant utterance, as Louise was offering an example from an exclusively female domain, childbirth, to counter the suggestion that the most strenuous, painful exercise one can undergo is at the do jang. The hardest workout, she suggested, was something men can never experience.

And the morning of testing, Patty, a 35-year-old homemaker with two children, declared, "There ought to be a 1-800 number you can call right before you test for your brown belt, so you could ask questions about how to do your forms." Patty's statement is interesting because it strips the ritualized TKD movements of their deep mystical significance and thus debunks one of the premises of hierarchy that underlies TKD. She treated the martial arts very matter-of-factly, as though learning about TKD is like studying for a CPA exam, merely a matter of knowledge, of acquiring the correct information.

These examples are illustrative of the kind of humor that subverts the seriousness of the martial arts endeavor and brings empowerment and pleasure to those women and girls who are, in other ways, quite committed to the discipline of TKD. In this respect, the females described here constitute a hegemonic community in opposition to at least some elements of the enterprise of TKD. I believe that one way to dismantle, or at least balance, the macho pretensions of the martial arts— the hierarchy, the potential for, if not the actual violence, the insistence on courage defined as being able to withstand the physical demands of working out and sparring—is through this kind of irreverent irony. As one of the previous examples shows, women sometimes define courage differently, as having a baby and withstanding labor pains, for example.

The Voices of Male Martial Artist

While it is possible that the men at our do jang also use oppositional humor, I have overheard or witnessed very little humor directed at the martial arts *as an enterprise* among the male members of our school.

On the contrary, I observed many instances of men and boys treating TKD with enormous seriousness. I have room to present only two examples to suggest the contrast in attitudes between men and women.

First, I have heard several of the male black belts, including the male instructors, speak admiringly of Jean-Claude Van Damme's moves in his latest films. (Van Damme, of course, is a superb martial artist who appears regularly in profoundly violent and bloody martial arts films such as "Bloodsport.") I have never heard women of any belt level praise Van Damme or mention any other martial artist in the near-worshipful tones that men employ.

Second, in the entryway of the school in a highly visible place, stands a towering trophy dedicated to the Grand Champion of one of the tournaments sponsored by our school. This trophy was won several years ago by one of the male stars of the do jang, Brian. Since then Brian joined ROTC at his university and became a member of an elite military unit. Brian's official military portrait, one in which he glares indomitably into the camera in his camouflage and beret, is framed and set against the trophy. And that particular spot in the room looks like nothing so much as a martial shrine to Brian. I have seen male students stop and speak to each other in awestruck, hushed tones about Brian's accomplishments and wonder themselves how long it would take to reach this pinnacle of TKD/macho perfection.

On the other hand, I have never witnessed women treat this display with anything approaching the reverence given to it by men.

CONCLUSION

To conclude, I argue that in order to talk about the experience of sport, researchers should reproduce the variety of voices, or texts, that constitute that sporting experience. In my research, the oppositional communities have interesting ways of subverting certain elements of the institution of sport that would otherwise oppress them, either literally or symbolically. Such subversion enables women to enjoy what is otherwise a profoundly masculinist undertaking. In line with Bakhtin's ideas, a completely irreverent poem like "Just One Fuck" is a way of disabling some elements of the androcentric culture of TKD. In a patriarchal world women may resist local, everyday examples of patriarchy as they occur, and TKD offers plenty of opportunities to do just that.

REFERENCES

Bakhtin, M. (1984). *Rabelais and his world.* Bloomington, IN: Indiana University Press.

Brummett, B., & Duncan, M. C. (1992). Toward a discursive ontology of media. *Critical Studies in Mass Communication, 9,* 229–249.

Duncan, M. C., & Brummett, B. (1993). Liberal and radical sources of female empowerment in sport media. *Sociology of Sport Journal, 10,* 57–72.

Messner, M. (1987). The life of a man's seasons: Male identity in the life course of a jock. In M.S. Kimmel (Ed.), *Changing men: New directions in research on men and masculinity* (pp. 53–67). Newbury Park, CA: Sage.

Real, M. R. (1982). The Super Bowl: Mythic spectacle. In H. Newcombe (Ed.), *Television: The critical view* (3rd ed., pp. 206–239). New York: Oxford University Press.

part VI
Intertextual Play

Part **VI**

Introduction

Alan Aycock

Much French structural and postmodern thinking about the world as text shares an emphasis on the trope of play or gaming (Bourdieu, Lyotard), while the playfulness of renowned French scholars such as Baudrillard, Barthes, and Derrida has often confounded American sociology, itself serious to the core. It is not surprising, perhaps, that the study of textual play and the antics of textual play remain less developed areas of analysis in North American play studies. In a spirit of experimentation the three articles in this section present diverse models for textual ludism.

Levin's deconstruction of Falstaff's significance in "The First Part of *Henry IV*" relies upon the character's refusal to be simply categorized according to Renaissance mores of masculinity and the succession of princes. Levin demonstrates that Falstaff occupies multiple sites of undecidable tension between court and battlefield, civility and decadence, restraint and libertinism. Falstaff's carnivalesque performances threaten to upend patriarchy with the excesses of commoners and feminine subversions. The structure of Shakespeare's "Henriad," in other words, is dissolved by the subtexts of Falstaff's mendacity, braggadocio, and scandal. Levin's remark that Shakespeare's attempt to "kill" Falstaff dramatically was thwarted by an intervention of Elizabeth herself seems most apposite in this context. For Levin, Derrida's playful aphorism that "nothing lies beyond the text" is an invitation to Shakespeare's textual play.

Aycock uses Bourdieu's apparatus of habitus and capital to interpret the commodification of chess as presented in the official catalog of books and equipment published by the United States Chess Federation (USCF). Aycock argues that chess books and equipment are textually imbued with advertising images such as officialdom, embodiment, mastership, and knowledge which produce hierarchy among USCF members. Even the aesthetic of chess, exemplified in the catalog's pictures and words that describe chess sets and chess-playing computers, mystifies the norms of chess and the roles of its players to sustain forms of dominance eventually acted out in casual games as well as in formal chess tournaments. For Aycock, Bourdieu's emphasis upon the game of cultural capital offers an opportunity to see how players may read capital as text.

Slowikowski and Kohn draw on Bergson, in many respects a forerunner of postmodern thought who stands somewhere between Nietzsche and Foucault in his insistence that bodies are figuratively inscribed as texts, cultural artifacts upon which social forces play out their interests. Kohn and Slowikowski treat their essay as a kind of performance art, a deliberate blurring of boundaries between experience and data. The essay develops both commentary and metacommentary as a textual device to express the joy of embodied movement in sport. Sport, for the authors, is an experience of physical and spiritual becoming forced into a rigid institutional milieu, much more goal- than process- oriented, that threatens to stifle it. The closing references to Trinh Min-ha remind us that physicality must be decolonized before we locate the Other in ourselves, ourselves in the Other. A process that itself resists closure is an appropriately playful way to close this book.

16

What's the Matter with Falstaff?: The Structure of Play in The First Part of King Henry IV

Kate Levin

INTRODUCTION: FALSTAFF IN THE HISTORY OF PLAY AND LITERATURE

In this chapter, I discuss Falstaff's significance in Shakespeare's history play *The First Part of King Henry IV* by considering him as play.[1] I am not the first critic to do so, nor am I by any means the first to engage in a theoretical discussion of play and literature. Indeed, we might say that literature *is* play; in the words of the editors of a recent volume of essays on play in literature, "it is not only playful authors who play, but that play characterizes all authors and all [literary] works" (Guinness & Hurley, 1986, p. 192). In this volume, which offers over 50 definitions of play in literature, Shakespeare is characterized as the play "master": his name is invoked and his plays cited more than any other author. In this volume, at least two critics refer to Falstaff as the exemplification of play (Lewis, p. 55, and Levin, p. 122, in Guinness & Hurley, 1986).

Unlike these critics, I do not use Falstaff to demonstrate what play means. Rather, I embrace all of play's multiple meanings (games, imitation, chance, competition, vertigo, wordplay, seduction, carnival, transgression, performance, etc., etc.) to attempt to say, not even what Falstaff *means*, but what he *does*. In my analysis, Falstaffian play

235

reconciles such seemingly incompatible literary-critical approaches as Derridean deconstruction (linguistic wordplay), Bakhtinian carnivalesque (material and sexual play), performance studies (theatre as play), psychoanalysis (the play of the unconscious that undoes a unified self), and gender studies (both "Woman" as play and playful feminism).[2] For example, Robert R. Wilson (1986) describes two supposedly disparate characterizations of play in literature, a materialist, carnivalesque, positive and purposeful play, and a Derridean, linguistic, random and intentionless play. However, these approaches are reconciled in theatrical play, the realm of carnivalesque performance *and* linguistic freeplay.[3] Wilson's distinction (like all other such critical distinctions) is thus collapsed by Falstaff. In the theatricality of Falstaff's grotesque materiality and linguistic free-for-all, he represents at once the purposeful, intentional creation of a once living author, and a fantasy that exceeds even Shakespeare's playfully masterful control.

THE MATTER WITH FALSTAFF

To attempt to define Falstaff is a dangerous undertaking: Falstaff has been dubbed "one of the nagging 'problems' of Shakespearean criticism" (Greenblatt, 1985, p. 41). Interpretations of Falstaff have a long and contradictory history. Some seventeenth- and eighteenth-century critics reviled him: "this view is best exemplified ... by John Dryden and Jeremy Collier, both of whom regarded Sir John as a 'coward' and a 'drunk' who hardly demanded the sympathy of a civilized society" (Harris, 1984, p. 283). Later critics have hailed him as a life spirit (Harris, 1984, p. 313). Who is this contradictory character? What should we make of these contradictions, what one critic calls Falstaff's "paradoxical opposites" (Humphreys, in Shakespeare, 1960, p. xliii)? What is the matter with Falstaff?

I suggest that Falstaff's meaning and matter exist in the very quandary that he creates for critics. Rather than finding a solution, we should embrace the problem. If the work of the critic is to resolve contradictions, Falstaff undoes that work through his inconsistencies, his paradoxical opposites. He is a nobleman ("Sir John") who prefers to be called "Jack." Bristol calls this "the most versatile and familiar name for every nameless hero of plebeian culture" (1985, p. 205). He is a drunken thief and the Prince's best friend. And most importantly, he is a fat *man* who is described both within the play and by critics as representing feminine matter rather than masculine mind.

Falstaff's character thus appears as an ambivalent construction. This ambivalence, rather than unsettling interpretations of the plays in which Falstaff is found, actually solicits interpretation. In the words of Montaigne, perhaps "'[w]e need to interpret interpretations more than to interpret things'" (quoted in Derrida, 1978, p. 278). Perhaps the meaning of *The First Part of King Henry IV* originates in the very ambivalence and indeterminacy that Falstaff represents.

THE STRUCTURE OF PATRIARCHAL HISTORY

Initially, the history plays in which Falstaff appears seem to resist this ambivalence. The project of patriarchal history upon which the plays are based, the chronicle of the deeds of fathers and sons, necessitates the construction of strict categories, sometimes characterized as binary oppositions.[4] Cixous and Clément give examples of such "dual, hierarchical oppositions" as activity/passivity, culture/nature, form/matter, mind/body, history/nature, and of course, man/woman (1986, pp. 64–65). In this construction, woman is always equated with the lower half of the hierarchical structure upon which patriarchy establishes its rule.

Woman as an abstract concept is thus absolutely necessary for the authority of patriarchy to remain viable: the "[s]ubordination of the feminine to the masculine order ... gives the appearance of being the condition for the machinery's functioning" (Cixous & Clément, 1986, p. 65). The bodies of actual women are also needed to produce the male heirs required for the structure's endurance. But herein lies the source of a potentially powerful contradiction. Patriarchy needs Woman/women to maintain its hierarchy. However, because of the invisibility of female sexuality, and the subsequent inability of women's procreative power to be controlled or even monitored, women are considered dangerous to patriarchy. As a result, patriarchal history has attempted to write out the mother, to do without her as much as possible:

> Because an adulterous woman at any point could make a mockery of the whole story of patriarchal succession, women were inevitably threatening to the patriarchal historiographic enterprise.... Patriarchal history is designed to construct a verbal substitute for the visible physical connection between a mother and her children, to authenticate the always dubious relationships between fathers and sons, and to suppress and supplant the role of the mother. (Rackin, 1990, pp. 160–161)

The "matter with Falstaff" is that he does not conform to the binary structure. Even worse, his presence, like the very existence of women in the history plays, actively works to undo such a structure. Falstaff destabilizes the strict gender categories upon which patriarchy establishes its authority. As Rackin notes, "Falstaff is ... the most fully developed embodiment of the disorderly conduct and subversive speech that express the threat both women and commoners represented in Shakespeare's historical world" (1990, p. 204). Because of the instability and interpretive ambivalence engendered by his presence, Falstaff reveals the categories as man-made structures. But Falstaff's paradoxical opposites do more than merely disrupt the patriarchal hierarchy (Rackin, 1990, p. 234); they expose the hierarchy itself as a fiction.

THE STRUCTURE OF PLAY/THE PLAY OF STRUCTURE

Several critics have characterized Falstaff as representing the absent feminine in *The First Part of King Henry IV*. Rackin describes Falstaff as repeat[ing] many of the features that Renaissance misogyny attributed to women. Not only his lack of military valor but also his lying, his inconstancy, and his outrageous incontinence locate him on the wrong side of the binary opposition that divided man from woman, spirit from matter, aristocrat from commoner. (1990, pp. 203–204)

From a psychoanalytic perspective, Traub also argues for Falstaff's femininity. She claims that the play's insistence on Falstaff's excessive materiality, his "grotesque body," positions him as a substitute for Prince Hal's absent mother. She thus reads Falstaff not only as the play's feminine presence, but as the actual replacement for the absent woman: "Prince Hal's subjectivity is constituted ... in his relation to Falstaff, whose somatic iconography metonymically positions him as the fantasized pre-oedipal maternal, against whom Hal must differentiate" (Traub, 1992, p. 53).

While Traub might accuse my analysis of "subsuming gender hierarchies under the aegis of the radical instability of all speaking subjects" (1992, p. 54), I maintain that her argument reinforces the structure that the play, through Falstaff, seeks to undermine. I posit that any analysis grounded in a psychoanalytic paradigm based on woman's "lack" reifies the binary opposition that the play, through Falstaff's presence, subverts and ultimately undoes. Cixous and Clément explain the dire consequences of Freud and Lacan's constructions of feminine sexuality for women:

> Starting from the relationship of the sexes to the Oedipus complex, the boy and the girl are steered toward a division of social roles such that women "inevitably" have a lesser productivity because they "sublimate" less than men, and that symbolic activity, hence the production of culture, is the work of men.... Freud starts from what he calls the *anatomical* difference between the sexes. And we know how that is represented in his eyes: by the difference between having/not having the phallus. By reference to those precious parts. Starting from what will take shape as the transcendental signifier with Lacan. (1986, p. 82)

Although Traub and I disagree on method and meaning, we concur on one crucial point: as "male dominated as it is, the *Henriad* contains within itself the means for its own meta-critique" (1992, p. 53). We both find the same hole at the center of *The First Part of King Henry IV*, the absence of the mother signified by Falstaff's presence. Traub reads this crucial absence *structurally*, as representing the Lacanian "lack" in reference to which the Phallus constructs its power.[5] In contrast, I read it *playfully*.

Derrida's essay "Structure, Sign and Play in the Discourse of the Human Sciences" helps to situate the difference in our interpretations of Falstaff. Derrida defines "structure" as that which refers to "a center ... a point of presence, a fixed origin" (1978, p. 278); "[i]ts matrix ... is the determination of Being as *presence*" (1978, p. 279). Structure, which demands stable definitions and fixed places, is both part of and equivalent to a history "oriented toward the appropriation of truth in presence" (1978, p. 291). Those who defend the sanctity of structure practice an interpretation that "dreams of deciphering a truth or an origin which escapes play" (1978, p. 292): they seek an absolute meaning and a history unthreatened by change. To those who desire such interpretation, "the notion of a structure lacking any center represents the unthinkable itself" (1978, p. 279).

"Play," which always occurs within this "structure," is that which the structure attempts to close down, but which always escapes its boundaries:

> there is something missing ... a center which arrests and grounds the play of substitutions ... this movement of play, permitted by the lack or absence of a center or origin, is the movement of *supplementarity* .... The movement of signification adds something which results in the fact that there is always more, but this addition is a floating one because it comes to perform a vicarious function, to supplement a lack on the part of the signified. (1978, p. 289)

By its very nature, play defies definition, mocking those who long for the stability of a hierarchical structure. Unlike those who dream of an impossibly "full presence beyond play" (1978, p. 279), I wish to practice interpretation "which is no longer turned toward the origin, [which] affirms play and tries to pass beyond man and humanism" (1978, p. 292). Because such interpretation welcomes indeterminacy and change, it embraces and exploits rather than fears and denies the seductive and subversive possibilities of play.

Thus, rather than reading Falstaff as representing the absent mother absolutely, I read him as that which the absent mother puts into *play*. I use "play" here in all its meanings, as for example "fun, jest, or trifling, as opposed to earnest," "the playing or conduct of a game," "to represent or imitate in jest or sport," "freedom of movement within a space" and especially, "a dramatic performance, as on the stage" (Urdang, 1973, p. 1018). Falstaff's excess and paradoxical opposites mark him as the representation of a "[p]lay [that] is the disruption of [historical] presence ... [the] play of absence and presence" (Derrida, 1978, p. 292). He becomes the play's Derridean "supplement," which by "suppl[ying] something which is missing ... [and] suppl[ying] something additional" (Translator's Note, Derrida, 1978, p. 339), "can take on any value required" (Derrida, 1978, p. 290). Falstaff is the playful supplement, the center that is inside and outside, present and absent, that can not be defined or banished and that has neither origin nor end. Falstaff thus represents the absent woman as she simultaneously bolsters and threatens the project of patriarchal history upon which the King attempts to ground his authority.[6]

But because the equation Falstaff = mother is not an exact match, Falstaff not only supplies something missing, but also something additional. He stands in for the absent mother, yet can not completely take her place. He thus supplements the absent mother by *pointing to* her absence, an absence that the patriarchal structure wishes but is unable to disguise and fill. The play cannot escape one important truth: *the mother is not there.* Without the bottom half of the binary opposition, the structure must ultimately collapse, leaving only Falstaff's playfully ambivalent presence.

THE MATTER WITH PRINCE HAL: ERECTING THE
STRUCTURE

From the very beginning of *The First Part of King Henry IV*, establishing the King's authority is a concern and a problem. King Henry is not a king by divine right but by usurpation: in *King Richard II*, he took the crown by force. Therefore, he needs to empower an invalid (sick/illegitimate) kingship. To justify his occupation of the King's/Father's position, Henry tries to police the myth of patriarchy. To succeed, he requires the symbolism of firm binary oppositions as the structure upon which to establish his rule.

Unfortunately, the greatest obstacle to Henry's tenuous grip on the kingship and kingdom is embodied by his own son, Prince Hal. If, as I quoted Rackin earlier, patriarchal history mandates the creation of an invisible bond between father and son, the bond between this King and Prince is made problematic from the beginning. Henry's invocation of Hal's name in his coronation scene associates Hal with the lower half of the binary structure:

> [Henry] BULLINGBROOK: Can no man tell me of my unthrifty son?
> 'Tis full three months since I did see him last.
> If any plague hang over us 'tis he.
> …Enquire at London 'mongst the taverns there,
> For there they say he daily doth frequent
> With unrestrained loose companions…
> While he, young, wanton and effeminate boy,
> Takes on the point of honour to support
> So dissolute a crew.
> …PERCY: …he would unto the stews
> And from the commonest creature pluck a glove
> And wear it as a favour. (Shakespeare, 1984, pp. 159–160)

Hal's absence from the court weakens his father's authority as legitimate king. Hal is also tainted and by affiliation, taints his father through his "loose" associations. Because Hal consorts with female prostitutes ("the commonest creature"), his own father labels him effeminate. In Renaissance England, the presence of women was considered dangerous to men. Unlike our own society's construction, which marks men effeminate who associate too closely with other men, this label was reserved for men who associated too closely with women (Traub, 1992, p. 51).

Because Hal's "loose" associations disrupt his status as legitimate heir, King Henry detaches himself from his son. At the beginning of *The First Part of King Henry IV*, Henry wishes for a different son:

> A son who is the theme of honour's tongue,
> Amongst a grove the very straightest plant,
> Who is sweet Fortune's minion and her pride;
> Whilst I by looking on the praise of him

See riot and dishonour stain the brow
Of my young Harry. O that it could be prov'd
That some night-tripping fairy had exchang'd
In cradle-clothes our children where they lay,
And call'd mine Percy, his Plantagenet!
Then would I have his Harry, and he mine. (Shakespeare, 1960, p. 8)

The substitute son for whom Henry wishes is Harry Percy. Percy, or Hotspur as he is called, seems to represent all that an heir to the throne should be: honorable, a warrior, and interested in that most masculine of domains, history. Even the name Hotspur associates him with masculinity. The Galenic branch of Renaissance medicine believed that only the proper amount of bodily heat kept men *men*: "[i]t could be assumed that men always had more of that precious heat than did women. But this heat, unless actively mobilized, might cool, leading even a man to approach the state of a woman" (Brown, 1988, p. 10). Hotspur thus seems created in direct opposition to Hal.[7] At least initially, Harry Percy (Hotspur) represents all that Harry Plantagenet (Hal) should be but is not.

Meanwhile, Hal is not at the court, the place of the masculine, but at the tavern. The tavern, run by the infamous Hostess, is the play's domain of dangerous feminine play. Naturally, it is also Falstaff's domain. Therefore, the Prince's first appearance, in spite of what we've heard, is bound to shock us. In the tavern scenes, Prince Hal breaks Shakespearean convention by speaking in prose. More scandalously, he and Falstaff are plotting a theft. Everything that we've heard about Hal thus seems true, and we don't wonder that the King needs to disown him.

What we must wonder, however, is the extraordinary weight that this play gives to Falstaff. Almost every other scene features him and his "dissolute crew." And the Prince is in the midst of these scenes, being dragged down by his association with these loose companions. Thus, a patriarchal hierarchy of high/low, court/tavern, present/absent, noble/common, honorable/loose, masculine/feminine *is* established. However, this hierarchy is already disturbing because of the Prince's place at the bottom.

But this hierarchy is no sooner erected than it is destabilized. The Prince not only seems aware of the hierarchy, but to *play* with it to his own advantage. Immediately after he plots the theft with Falstaff, at the same time planning to trick Falstaff, his speech switches from prose to verse:

I know you all, and will awhile uphold
The unyok'd humour of your idleness.
Yet herein will I imitate the sun,
Who doth permit the base contagious clouds
To smother up his beauty from the world,
...So when this loose behaviour I throw off,
...My reformation, glitt'ring o'er my fault,
Shall show more goodly, and attract more eyes
Than that which hath no foil to set it off.

I'll so offend, to make offence a skill,
Redeeming time when men think least I will. (Shakespeare, 1960, pp. 20–21)

Ironically, what steps in to put Prince Hal back in his proper place is the presence of play. However, the structure (in the voice of the Prince) claims that it can safely manipulate and contain this play. The Prince asserts that he is merely "playing holidays" (Shakespeare, 1960, p. 20), and that he knows his proper place in the hierarchy, on top. He transforms the tavern into a stage upon which he will play until it is no longer politic by characterizing his "loose behaviour" as a theatrical disguise that he can don and doff at will. He thus simultaneously participates in and directs a mock rehearsal of his future role as King, a rehearsal that prepares him to rule and the people of his kingdom to be ruled by him.

THE MATTER WITH HOTSPUR: COLLAPSING THE STRUCTURE

So the binary opposition, as exemplified by Hal and Hotspur, is disrupted by play almost from the beginning. However, even though Hal expresses his ability to play with its boundaries, the opposition still drives the plot. Hal continues to loiter in the tavern, while Hotspur talks of nothing but honor. At first, Hotspur appears to exist merely to uphold the fixed boundaries of the binary structure. For example, he refuses to surrender his prisoners to the King's emissary because the emissary is not manly enough: "[t]o see him shine so brisk, and smell so sweet,/And talk so like a waiting-gentlewoman/Of guns, and drums, and wounds, God save the mark!" (Shakespeare, 1960, p. 24). To give up his hard-won prisoners and thus, his honor, to one so effeminate, would taint him by association.

Because Hotspur helped Henry to usurp the "rightful king," he also worries about his family's place in history:

Shall it for shame be spoken in these days,
Or fill up chronicles in time to come,
That men of your nobility and power
Did gage them both in an unjust behalf
(As both of you, God pardon it, have done)
To put down Richard, that sweet lovely rose,
And plant this thorn, this canker Bolingbroke? (Shakespeare, 1960, p. 29)

Hotspur can only restore his place in history and cleanse his maligned honor by deposing King Henry. Only then will he restore his good name and by extension, his manhood.

Although Hotspur seems to represent the masculine half of the binary system, he also undermines the structure that he supposedly lives to uphold. His sport is described as the inversion of Hal's: his masculine desire for "fields, and blows, and groans" (Shakespeare, 1960, p. 36) contrasts with Hal's loose behavior. Hotspur also claims to speak roughly: "By God, I cannot flatter, I do defy/The tongues of soothers" (Shakespeare, 1960, p. 120). However, his own wordplay belies him. Like Falstaff, Hotspur multiplies discourse. Rather than using words as a means to an end, to bolster the structure, he allows words to run away with him and become a playful end unto themselves. Other characters blame him for this fault, calling his behavior "[d]efect of manners, want of government" (Shakespeare, 1960, p. 96) and even "this woman's mood" (p. 33). Parker describes how the Renaissance attempted to feminize the quality of verbosity:

> The opposition male/female often masks anxieties surrounding the figure of the feminized or effeminate male, just as in the misogynist diatribes against the female tongue the generative power inhabiting and generating the very discourse of misogyny often becomes the female loquacity which is its animating subject. (1987, p. 22)

In spite of Hotspur's best intentions, his verbal lapses into the feminine realm undermine his honor and threaten the structure's collapse. Ironically, honor, one of the central concepts upon which the gendered oppositions are established, often provokes Hotspur's verbal wanderings. Hotspur's obsession with the word honor actually reveals the structure's instability. In Act 1, Scene 3, Hotspur makes a long and excessively figurative speech about the necessity of redeeming "female" honor: "pluck up drowned honour by the locks,/So he that doth redeem her thence might wear/Without corrival all her dignities" (Shakespeare, 1960, p. 31). His uncle Worcester then criticizes Hotspur's use of language: "[h]e apprehends a world of figures here,/But not the form of what he should attend" (Shakespeare, 1960, p. 31). Worcester implies that Hotspur is obsessed with the (feminine) word rather than the (masculine) deed. This accusation not only undermines our view of Hotspur's masculinity, but also casts aspersions on the very honor that he wishes to redeem. This "feminine speech potentially out of control" (Parker, 1987, p. 27), linked as it is to female sexuality, threatens to undermine the historical project that maintains the patriarchal structure.

This scene is later doubled and in its doubling, parodied by Falstaff, the play's true master of wordplay. Derrida notes that wordplay is also play, "an infinite number of sign-substitutions" (1978, p. 280). Because Falstaff is a thief, he steals meaning from Hotspur, meaning that justifies Hotspur's very existence.[8] Falstaff illuminates what Worcester's earlier speech hinted, that honor is merely a *word*. Falstaff exposes honor as an empty signifier by contrasting this word with the materiality of the body and its wounds : "Can honour set to a leg? No. Or an arm? No. Or take away the grief of a wound? ... What is honour? A word ... Air" (Shakespeare, 1960, pp. 145–146).

In the end, honor metamorphoses from an abstract word into the absolutely material, as it is represented by Hotspur's dead body. Falstaff's philosophy prevails when Hotspur lies dead on the battlefield, when he who professed to live by deeds alone is undone by the word that sustained him. And the structure, upheld by a mere word, suddenly seems built upon a very flimsy foundation.

THE PLAYER-KING

Of course, both Falstaff and Hal are as guilty as Hotspur of multiplying discourse. The tavern scenes are a veritable cornucopia of wordplay, to which the heavily annotated editions of these scenes attest. Not only do words multiply their meanings, not only will two or more words serve where one would do, but stories become tall tales that wander far from the truth. The point of these tavern stories lies not in the truth, but in the playful telling.

In Act 2, Scene 4, Falstaff verbally misrepresents his participation in the theft. He transforms himself through words from a coward into a hero. In this scene, words not only grow and grow, but become embodied. As Falstaff's lies multiply, the truth of the story, a truth whose material reality has already been revealed, becomes distorted and unrecognizable. Words take on matter. The Prince comments on the fleshly quality of Falstaff's exaggerations: "O monstrous! Eleven buckram men grown out of two! … These lies are like their father that begets them, gross as a mountain, open, palpable. Why, thou clay-brained guts, thou knotty-pated fool, thou whoreson obscene greasy tallow-catch" (Shakespeare, 1960, p. 68).

Hal points here to Falstaff's multiplication of discourse. Falstaff's words are his children, which like their father, are fat and full of matter. Not surprisingly, this quality also infects Hal. The scene turns into a verbal competition between Hal and Falstaff, who compete to insult each other as copiously as possible. This part of the scene ends when the Prince reveals the truth of the story: "mark now how a plain tale shall put you down. Then did we two set on you four, and, with a word, out-faced you from your prize.… What trick, what device, what starting-hole canst thou now find out, to hide thee from this open and apparent shame?" (Shakespeare, 1960, pp. 70-71). Of course, Falstaff continues to find a verbal way out, and the scene continues on and on. It climaxes in a scene of play-acting in which Falstaff and Hal alternate playing the King and Prince.

This scene of play-acting serves as a synecdochic representation of the play: it dramatizes in miniature the undermining of the binaries and of the crown's authority. All of the disruptive play activated by Falstaff's presence culminates here. As Falstaff becomes the King and the Hostess, a known prostitute, the Queen, the world is turned upside-down.[9] As Hal orders Falstaff to "stand for my father and examine me upon the particulars of my life" (Shakespeare, 1960, p. 76), more than one serious subject is treated playfully. However, while speaking playfully, Falstaff often speaks the truth. The Player King tells Hal that as "pitch … does defile, so doth the company thou keepest" (Shakespeare, 1960, p. 79), a concern already voiced by the real King.

This scene of play-acting also contains the play's only allusions to the absent mother. Falstaff jokes "[t]hat thou art my son I have partly thy mother's word, partly my own opinion, but chiefly a villainous trick of thine eye" (Shakespeare, 1960, p. 78). This joke highlights the relationship between Falstaff's dangerous "feminine" use of language and the unreliability of female sexuality, those dual threats to the patriarchal structure. Play also "surrenders itself to *genetic* indetermination, to the *seminal* adventure of the trace" (Derrida, 1978, p. 292).

The relationship between these threats is fostered when Hal and Falstaff switch roles. The switch allows another serious subject to be treated playfully: *"Prince. Dost thou speak like a king? Do thou stand for me, and I'll play my father. Fal.: Depose me? If thou dost it half so gravely, so majestically, both in word and matter, hang me up by the heels"* (Shakespeare, 1960, p. 80). With these lines, the "word and matter" of the play, the threat to Henry's crown, is treated as a theatrical joke, as play. With these lines, Falstaff also traitorously implies that he is more effective at playing the King than either the King or Hal. The scene ends with Falstaff informing Hal that he can't be banished, the famous "banish plump Jack, and banish all the world" (Shakespeare, 1960, p. 82) and with Hal telling Falstaff that he *will* be banished: "I do, I will" (p. 82). Both of these claims ultimately prove true.

This scene is doubled by a later, far more serious scene between the King and his son. In this scene, Henry reiterates the concerns that were jokes in the playacting scene. He insists that Hal defiles himself by appearing in the "public eye": "let me wonder, Harry,/At thy affections, which do hold a wing/Quite from the flight of all thy ancestors" (Shakespeare, 1960, p. 102); "Not an eye/But is a-weary of thy common sight" (pp. 104-105). In his very long speech (over 60 lines), Henry tells Hal the right way to "play the King." *He* still possesses the crown because of his unwillingness to show himself. By contrast, Hal, "common-hackney'd in the eyes of men" (Shakespeare, 1960, p. 102), has become like one of the "harlotry players" (p. 77) admired by the Hostess in the playacting scene. By playing constantly to the public, Hal subverts the shaky structure upon which kingly authority is established.

In this scene, Henry replays the earlier tavern scene, but with a crucial difference that betrays his unspoken anxiety. While Falstaff as King claims to need the "mother's word" to confirm Hal's legitimacy, Henry professes to rely merely on his son's resemblance to his (male) ancestors. However, Hal's present lack of resemblance to those ancestors actually produces Henry's anxiety. In his anxiety, Henry reveals what he both needs to prove his son and heir's legitimacy and wishes he could circumvent, the mother's word.

Henry's attempt to write out the contribution of the mother in Hal's creation "articulates a patriarchal conception of the family in which children owe their existence to their fathers alone; the mother's role in procreation is eclipsed by the father's, which is used to affirm male prerogative and male power" (Kahn, 1986, pp. 35–36). Rackin defines Henry's problem somewhat differently: "[a]ll of Shakespeare's legitimate kings are equipped with wives. Lacking patriarchal authority, Shakespeare's usurping Henry IV ... also lacks a wife" (1990, p. 162). These interpretations complement each other. *Because* Henry's reign is illegitimate, he needs to insist on his self-sufficiency. He therefore must rely on the fiction that his authority, which he locates in an unbroken line of male ancestors, places him at the center of the realm.

This fiction attempts to erase the contribution of the always potentially subversive woman. Henry's need to erase the woman also explains why he views his own son's illegitimate behavior as a hindrance in establishing his own authority. Hal's behavior promotes his father's fear of Hal's actual illegitimacy, a fear verbalized by Falstaff.

However, Henry is more like Hal and Falstaff than we might realize. In his criticism of Hal's behavior, Henry obscures the theatricality that established his own kingship. Hotspur tells us that Henry did not achieve the crown in a manly way. This "king of smiles" gained the Percys' help, and thus the crown, by playacting. Hotspur blames Henry's deceit for tainting their honor: "what a candy deal of courtesy/This fawning greyhound then did proffer me!" (Shakespeare, 1960, p. 33). Henry's earlier playacting is literally made flesh in the battle scene where the King fights a war of false appearances: Hotspur announces that "[t]he King hath many marching in his coats" (Shakespeare, 1960, p. 152). Although Henry claims that his son is unlike him because of Hal's theatricality, they are actually most alike in this. Blanpied notes that "Henry ... commands the stage that *is* the realm" (1983, p. 14). The King and Prince's ability to manipulate this theatricality allows them to defeat Hotspur. At the same time, it necessitates the ultimate banishment of theatricality, and thus, of Falstaff and play, from the kingdom.

THE PLAY OF THE THEATRICAL/THE END OF STRUCTURE

Like play, the theatrical contains the potential to undo the binaries and collapse the patriarchal structure. In Shakespeare's theatre, gender and class confusion existed on the stage and in the audience: "men of low estate wear the clothes of noblemen and of women, and ... one's money, not one's blood or title, decide how high and how well one sat, or whether, indeed, one stood" (Howard, 1988, p. 440). The theatre thus represented a potential source of subversion. Rackin notes that because plays were *performed*, they provided opportunities for the potential evasion of censorial control (1990, pp. 236-237).

The subversive possibility of theatrical play is actually enacted within *The First Part of King Henry IV*. In the Wales scene (Act 3, Scene 1), a female character identified only as "the Welsh lady" has no actual lines. Instead, her speech is indicated by stage directions that say a variation of "the lady speaks in Welsh." Glendower, her father, must translate what she says to all other characters. This includes her husband Mortimer, the usurped heir to the throne.

The lacunae left by the lady's lack of lines provide a subversive space within the play in an actual historical sense. Mullaney remarks that Henry VIII outlawed Welsh in 1535, and compares the Wales scene to the tavern scenes: "[s]ome expressions [in the latter] remain as inaccessible to us as the Welsh we assume was spoken by Glendower and Lady Percy ... and may have been equally inaccessible to a large part of Shakespeare's audience" (1988, p. 84).

During Shakespeare's time, as in our own, very few people would have understood what the Welsh lady was actually saying. Therefore, the blank space represented by her discourse provided the possibility for subversive play, a space in which subversion of authority might have taken place.[10] This space plays the same role in miniature as Falstaff, theatricality and the feminine do at large. They all operate as playful disruptions of the enclosing structure that tries desperately but vainly to contain and control their power.

The power of such play also explains why, once King, Hal banishes Falstaff but is unable to vanquish him completely. Hal defeats Hotspur and acquires his honor precisely because Hal is a better *player* than Hotspur. Hal is thus better able to exploit the subversive possibilities offered by Falstaff's feminine presence.

But Falstaff is always there to remind Hal of play's dangers. It is true that Hal recovers his father's and his own authority. At the end of the play, Hotspur lies dead, having yielded his "budding honours" and "proud titles" to Hal (Shakespeare, 1960, p. 158). Even though the battle is not yet won, the authority of Henry's kingship and his son's succession seem guaranteed. However, Hal's final act provokes the same interpretive ambivalence generated all along by Falstaff's presence.

After Hal kills Hotspur, he leaves him next to Falstaff's (presumably dead) body. Falstaff rises from the dead to claim Hotspur's corpse as his own by stabbing him in the thigh. Falstaff then tells Hal that *he*, not Hal, has killed Hotspur. Rather than repudiating Falstaff, Hal acquiesces: "if a lie may do thee grace,/I'll gild it with the happiest terms I have" (Shakespeare, 1960, p. 162). Falstaff repeats himself by once again stealing honor from its true owner. Hal's acquiescence to Falstaff's lie thus seems a dangerous lapse into the realm of feminine play.

At this point, the audience might be tempted to protest, "but we *know* who killed Hotspur!" However, "who really killed Hotspur?" is left unanswered by the theatre's slippery, subversive nature. Blanpied remarks that "[s]ubtle differences in performance can crystallize major differences in perspective" (1983, p. 161). Therefore, whom should we believe?

We *think* that Falstaff lies because of what we have been led to expect from him. If so, the Prince makes an almost incomprehensible sacrifice. But this is only a play, and Falstaff a fictional character.[11] As a result, we will never know the "truth," a concept that, like the patriarchal structure of history, is sabotaged by theatrical play. Perhaps Falstaff really did kill Hotspur by stabbing him in the thigh, a most inglorious death for a noble warrior. Because we can't be sure, Falstaff wins. His presence predominates: he becomes what audiences remember and critics debate.

W. H. Auden remarks upon the unforgettability of Falstaff's scene-stealing playfulness: "[r]eading *Henry IV*, we can easily give our full attention to the historical-political scenes, but, when watching a performance, attention is distracted by our eagerness to see Falstaff reappear. Short of cutting him out of the play altogether, no producer can prevent him stealing the show" (1959/1992, p. 44). Because of the seductiveness of Falstaffian play, audiences even refuse to accept Falstaff's banishment and eventual death. Although Shakespeare tried to kill off Falstaff, rumor has it that Queen Elizabeth ordered him to resurrect Falstaff once more in *The Merry Wives of Windsor*: "[s]he was so well pleas'd with that admirable Character of *Falstaff*, in the two Parts of *Henry* the Fourth, that she commanded him to continue it for one Play more, and to shew him in Love" (Rowe, 1709/1992, p. 7). Because of Falstaff's banishment from the center of history, he is forever ensconced in the center of our minds. Thus, Falstaff's indeterminacy infects the play. Other characters who try to divorce themselves from all that he represents are like him or become like him. He also infects his critics, frustrating anyone who tries to make him mean *something* (as opposed to nothing or everything). Falstaff's excessive theatricality, both in his playacting within the play and the play engendered by his very character, releases possibilities that, once suggested, are not so easy to exclude. Once invaded and infected by theatrical play, the historical narrative's coherence appears more and more a nostalgic construction of a structure that never actually existed.

CONCLUSION: FURTHER POSSIBILITIES OF FALSTAFFIAN PLAY

Even those critics who describe Falstaff's playfulness seem to limit him in the end. For example, both Traub and Rackin characterize Falstaff as play without defining him as such (Traub in Falstaff's Bakhtinian "grotesque body," and Rackin in his "disorderly conduct and subversive speech"). I am indebted to their analyses, which have allowed me to see the gendered structures that Falstaff exceeds. But both Traub and Rackin reenclose Falstaff in psychoanalytic or historical structures that close down the infinite possibilities of his play.

I propose that Falstaffian play is not merely suggestive, but infinitely subversive of structure. I envision a utopian theatre that can never actually exist; after all, there is always *some* structure. But further possibilities of Falstaffian play might be discovered not only by analyzing Falstaff's reception history, but also his past and present performance history.

Such an analysis might reveal how individual performances of Falstaff have encouraged (or shut down) his playful possibilities. For example, Harold Bloom refers to a performance of Falstaff that continually plays in his mind: "I am suggesting that the disreputable Falstaff—glutton, boozer, womanizer—is a teacher of wisdom, a hilarious teacher. When I was fifteen, I saw Ralph Richardson play Falstaff … and I have carried the image of Richardson's exuberant and inventive Falstaff in my head for forty-five years now, and find the image informing the text every time I reread or teach the *Henry IV* plays" (1992, p. 2). Casting choices are also relevant; what of a production in which a woman plays Falstaff? Alan Aycock's discussion of the playful possibilities of chess resonates here: "there remains a 'je ne sais quoi' about a given game that overflows its authorial boundaries, but that lends to the play a pleasurable experience that is always somewhere else than merely in the recorded list of moves" (1993, no. 51). After all, a theatrical play is not merely the written record of characters created by an author, but is also informed (and exceeded) by the history of its interactions with actors, directors, critics and audience members. All of these players, whose personal histories affect their own performances and interpretations, also play with Falstaff's meaning. This points to the limits of my own theoretical discussion of Falstaffian play. After all, I too am constrained, not only by my personal history, but also by academic structures that force me to present a logically written argument, and that require me to "publish or perish" (the situation least designed to invite play). Without Falstaff's physical presence, can my readers be convinced? Wouldn't I best prove my point by standing in front of you and performing my own version of Falstaff rather than by offering a written substitute to supplement his absence? And of course, I can't control what you, my absent and only imagined readers, do with my version of Falstaff. Since I, like you and Falstaff, am also absent, we can only take each other's word for it. This too, of course, is play.

ACKNOWLEDGMENT

Thanks to Marian Eide for her thoughtful comments.

NOTES

[1] Falstaff appears throughout the *Henriad*, the trilogy about King Henry IV and his son. Although I focus on the first play, my argument extends to the entire trilogy.

[2] For a deconstructive approach to play in literature, see Zhang (1991). For *the* definition of carnivalesque play in literature, see Bakhtin (1984). For an example of performance studies and theatrical play, see Esslin (1986). Examples of psychoanalytic and feminist approaches to play in literature are too numerous to mention; some of them are cited in my chapter.

[3] Wilson himself locates such a possibility in Bakhtin's concept of carnival. Like Falstaff, Bakhtin's "carnival must always enhance the context in which it occurs.... Carnival's essential duality and metonymical on-goingness characterize the concept as much as do its spontaneous and free travesties" (1986, p. 87). For analyses of the carnivalesque in theatre, see Bristol (1985) and Levin (1986).

[4] I am indebted throughout this article to Rackin's excellent study of Shakespeare's "project of patriarchal history" (1990).

[5] In "The Purveyor of Truth," Derrida criticizes Lacan for the same reason that I disagree with Traub's reading of Falstaff: "[t]he truth is 'woman' as veiled/unveiled castration.... The link of Femininity and Truth is the ultimate signified of this deciphering" (1988, pp. 183–185).

[6] More than one feminist critic characterizes the space created by Derrida's "play" as a female or feminine space. See, for example, Irigaray (1985) and Jardine (1985).

[7] Rackin points out that "Hotspur, historically three years older than the king, is made the contemporary of Prince Hal so that he can serve as a foil to the heir apparent" (1990, p. 93).

[8] See Cixous & Clément (1986, p. 86) for the feminist implications of the word "to steal" ("voler") in its relationship to language and writing.

[9] For the cultural significance of the "world upside down," see Stallybrass and White (1986).

[10] I realize that if almost no one in the audience could understand the Welsh lady, the possibility for actual subversive acts issuing from her speech was highly unlikely. Thus, the possi-

bility of subversion is (mostly) metaphorical. Like the presence of Falstaff, this "space" stands for that which the dominant patriarchal discourse views as unrepresentable or incomprehensible and hence, potentially unmanageable. For another example of such a space, see Gubar (1985).

[11] Rackin relates Falstaff's fictionality to his theatricality: "he interrupts, retards, and parodies the historical action with his own theatrical plots and schemes" (1990, p. 235).

REFERENCES

Auden, W. H. (1992). The prince's dog. In H. Bloom (Ed.), *Falstaff* (pp. 43–44). New York: Chelsea House Publishers. Originally published in 1959. Reprinted in 1962 by Random House.

Aycock, A. (1993). Derri-da/fort-da: Deconstructing play. Unpublished version of article published in *Postmodern Culture, 3*(2).

Bakhtin, M. (1984). *Rabelais and his world.* H. Iswolsky (Trans.). Bloomington: Indiana University Press.

Blanpied, J. W. (1983). *Time and the artist in Shakespeare's English histories.* Newark: University of Delaware Press.

Bloom, H. (Ed.). (1992). *Falstaff.* New York: Chelsea House Publishers.

Bristol, M. (1985). *Carnival and theater: Plebeian culture and the structure of authority in Renaissance England.* New York: Methuen.

Brown, P. (1988). *The body and society: Men, women, and sexual renunciation in early Christianity.* New York: Columbia University Press.

Cixous, H., & Clément, C. (1986). *The newly born woman.* B. Wing (Trans.). Minneapolis: University of Minnesota Press.

Derrida, J. (1978). Structure, sign and play in the discourse of the human sciences. In A. Bass (Trans.), *Writing and difference* (pp. 278–293). Chicago: University of Chicago Press.

Derrida, J. (1988). The purveyor of truth. A. Bass (Trans.). In J. P. Muller & W. J. Richardson (Eds.), *The purloined Poe: Lacan, Derrida, and psychoanalytic reading* (pp. 173–212). Baltimore: Johns Hopkins University Press.

Esslin, M. (1986). Brecht and the scientific study of playfulness. In G. Guinness & A. Hurley (Eds.), *Auctor ludens: Essays on play in literature* (pp. 25–36). Philadelphia: John Benjamins Publishing Company.

Greenblatt, S. (1985). Invisible bullets: Renaissance authority and its subversion, *Henry IV* and *Henry V.* In J. Dollimore & A. Sinfield (Eds.), *Political Shakespeare: New essays in cultural materialism* (pp. 18–47). Ithaca, NY: Cornell University Press.

Gubar, S. (1985). The "blank page" and the issues of female creativity. In E. Showalter (Ed.), *The new feminist criticism: Essays on women, literature and theory* (pp. 292–313). New York: Pantheon Books.

Guinness, G., & Hurley, A. (1986). *Auctor ludens: Essays on play in literature.* Philadelphia: John Benjamins Publishing Company.

Harris, L. L. (Ed.). (1984). *Shakespearean criticism* (Vol. 1). Detroit: Gale Research Company.

Howard, J. E. (1988). Crossdressing, the theatre, and gender struggle in early modern England. *Shakespeare Quarterly, 39,* 418–440.

Irigaray, L. (1985). This sex which is not one. In C. Porter & C. Burke (Trans.), *This sex which is not one* (pp. 23–33). Ithaca, NY: Cornell University Press.

Jardine, A. (1985). *Gynesis: Configurations of women and modernity.* Ithaca, NY: Cornell University Press.

Kahn, C. (1986). The absent mother in *King Lear.* In M. W. Ferguson, M. Quilligan & N. Vickers (Eds.), *Rewriting the Renaissance: The discourse of sexual difference in early modern Europe* (pp. 33–49). Chicago: University of Chicago Press.

Levin, H. (1986). From play to plays: The folklore of comedy. In G. Guinness & A. Hurley (Eds.), *Auctor ludens: Essays on play in literature* (pp. 113–126). Philadelphia: John Benjamins Publishing Company.

Lewis, W. (1986). Playing with fire and brimstone: *Auctor ludens, diabolus ludicrus.* In G. Guinness & A. Hurley (Eds.), *Auctor ludens: Essays on play in literature* (pp. 47–61). Philadelphia: John Benjamins Publishing Company.

Mullaney, S. (1988). Strange things, gross terms, curious customs: The rehearsal of cultures in the late Renaissance. In S. Greenblatt (Ed.), *Representing the English Renaissance* (pp. 65–92). Berkeley: University of California Press.

Parker, P. (1987). *Literary fat ladies: rhetoric, gender, property.* London: Methuen.

Rackin, P. (1990). *Stages of history: Shakespeare's English chronicles.* Ithaca, NY: Cornell University Press.

Rowe, N. (1992). Some account of the life, &c. of Mr. William Shakespear. In H. Bloom (Ed.), *Falstaff* (p. 7). New York: Chelsea House Publishers. Originally published in 1709 by Jacob Tonson.

Shakespeare, W. (1960). *The first part of King Henry IV.* In A. R. Humphrey (Ed.), *The Arden Shakespeare.* London: Routledge.

Shakespeare, W. (1984). *King Richard II.* In A. Gurr (Ed.), *The new Cambridge Shakespeare.* Cambridge: Cambridge University Press.

Stallybrass, P., & White, A. (1986). *The politics and poetics of transgression.* Ithaca, NY: Cornell University Press.

Traub, V. (1992). *Desire and anxiety: Circulations of sexuality in Shakespearean drama.* London: Routledge.

Urdang, L. (1973). *The Random House college dictionary.* New York: Random House.

Wilson, R. R. (1986). Play, transgression and carnival: Bakhtin and Derrida on *scriptor ludens. Mosaic, 19*(1), 73–89.

Zhang, J. Z. (1991). Free play in Samuel Richardson's *Pamela. Papers on Language and Literature, 27*(3), 307–319.

17

Owning Up:
Bourdieu and Commodified
Play in the USCF Chess
Catalogue

Alan Aycock

We live inescapably in a world of commodities (Porter & Brewew, 1993; Carrier, 1995). It is nearly impossible to imagine an everyday encounter of any sort in which the meanings of the situation at hand are not at least partially sustained by manufactured devices intended to enhance the self-presentation of its participants, to facilitate their interactions, and to draw the occasion to a mutually satisfactory conclusion. Indeed, the pervasiveness of commodities is such that observations of the simple empiricism of co-presence must routinely be extended to include, as a component of its facticity, the market forces that construct its limits and possibilities.

Commodification in this sense is no less characteristic of play than of any other human domain. In some ways, perhaps, the commodifications of play are more significant than those in other realms of activity, since standard assumptions about play point to freedom and pretense as central features of its enjoyment (Huizinga, 1955, pp. 7–8), yet commodities, by their very nature, seem to fix experience in a rigid framework of objects and in a strict bourgeois economy of means and ends. Thus, if play is itself intrinsically paradoxical as Bateson (1972, pp. 182–183) has suggested, commodification renders it doubly so: not only must play stand at odds with the "real" world, as in Bateson's formulation, but commodified play must also, apparently, become self-contradictory as a result of its conflation of the regime of productive labor with the utopia of non-productive pleasures.

In order to explore this problem and to elaborate upon its nuances, I have selected as an example chess, the form of play with which I am most familiar from many years of participant observation. The instance of its commodification with which I shall be concerned is a catalog of books and equipment recently published by the United States Chess Federation (USCF), a large national organization which promotes and controls many aspects of formal play. The instrument of textual analysis which seems most useful to me for my purposes here is Pierre Bourdieu's method of generative structuralism as it has been set forward in numerous scholarly works and commentaries (e.g., Harker, Mahar, & Wilkes, 1990; Robbins, 1991; Jenkins, 1992; Calhoun, LiPuma, & Postone, 1993).

I shall begin by outlining the role of the USCF, and by sketching the USCF catalog and its contents in relation to it. I shall then briefly present those aspects of Bourdieu's method which seem most relevant. Next follows a detailed exegesis of my primary text along the lines that I have set out. After this, I shall offer a comprehensive discussion of the implications of the commodification of chess for its play, and for those who play it. I conclude by returning, perhaps more fully informed, to the initial remarks that I have made above, and by suggesting some directions for further research in this area.

THE USCF AND ITS CATALOG

The USCF is a corporation officially organized to promote chess in the United States. As such, it publishes a monthly journal, *Chess Life*, sells memberships (of which there are many tens of thousands) in the Federation, authorizes the organization of formal local, regional, and state tournaments under its aegis, sponsors national championships and teams for the chess olympics, maintains a sub-organization devoted to correspondence play, arbitrates disputes that arise from "serious" play, calculates ratings for tournament play and awards titles such as national master or senior master, provides programs for the development of junior and scholastic chess as well as women's chess, professional chess, and chess for the handicapped, liaises with the Federation Internationale des Échecs (FIDE), and lobbies in support of the interests of chess players in many venues, such as legislatures and government agencies. In addition to these multifarious activities, the USCF regularly publishes a catalog of books and equipment which may be purchased from the Federation (at a discount for its members).

Thus the USCF is a complex bureaucratic organization that combines among others the functions of a voluntary association, a political interest group, a hegemonic guarantor of "seriously" competitive play, a publisher, and a retailer of chess-related merchandise. Although to some extent its functions may compete with one another for resources and prominence (internecine struggles of one kind or another are often reported and intensely pursued in the pages of *Chess Life*), the stability of the USCF over many decades suggests its overall success in balancing the numerous claims that are placed upon it. Few, if any of those who go much beyond the level of casual games of chess at home can remain unaware of the USCF and its substantive influence on play in the United States.

"The Official USCF Chess Catalog" is mailed without delay to all who request it, whether or not they are currently members of the Federation. It is also available on electronic networks such as USA TODAY, and advertised on the Internet. The catalog is more than 20 pages long, replete with variable type to emphasize "sales" or "good buys," colored photographs of books and chess equipment, models who are portrayed as using chess sets, boards, or chess computers, and inset portraits and biographical sketches of the authors of books offered for the delectation and edification of potential customers. *Chess Life* annually includes the catalog in its pages (usually in the November issue to encourage Christmas buying), and publishes monthly updates as well.

The overwhelming impression that is given, and given off by the catalog, is that of commonsense. That is to say, readers of the catalog should assume without reservation or even conscious reflection that it is a privilege of their membership in the national association to gain special access to the latest and most profound chess knowledge, and to the skills that putatively follow from that knowledge. Even those who are not members will take from the USCF catalog a commonsense understanding that this is the sole means to improve their play to competitive standard, and thereby to participate fully in the elitist directions of the national, and international "metaculture" of chess (cf. Aycock, 1988b). A major share of the textual analysis that follows will be devoted to a demonstration of the manner in which this natural or commonsense perspective is accomplished through the devices of the "official" catalog.

BOURDIEU'S METHOD

Bourdieu has taken as his central project the elaboration of an approach which may loosely be termed constitutive, genetic, or generative structuralism (Bourdieu, 1990a, p. 14; Mahar, Harker, & Wilkes, 1990, p. 3). His approach attempts to supply a single framework for the interpretation of sociocultural data at many levels from the broadest operations of class and bureaucratic organization, to the fluctuations of taste in art and education, to the organization of personal experience and attitudes on a day to day basis. The full impact of Bourdieu's work is only now becoming manifest in the English-speaking world, with the recent translation of many of his major studies.

It is difficult to subsume Bourdieu's method to one particular school of thought simply because of the variety of thinkers whose specific influence he acknowledges (e.g., Marx, Weber, Durkheim, Bachelard, Sartre, Lévi-Strauss, Wittgenstein, and Goffman [Bourdieu, 1990a, ch. 1; Mahar, Harker, & Wilkes, 1990; Robbins, 1991: ch. 11]); however, Bourdieu's strong tendency to decenter individual consciousness and intention as an autonomous source of action (e.g., Bourdieu, 1990a, pp. 9, 91; 1991a, p. 18; Robbins, 1991, p. 113) seems to place him, if not as a true postmodernist (a term that he disparages [Bourdieu, 1988, pp. xii–xiii]), then certainly as a poststructuralist aligned with many postmodern directions. One further instance of this prospective alliance is Bourdieu's persistent use of space as a master trope of social forces (e.g., Bourdieu, 1977, p. 91; 1984, p. 114; 1990a, p. 14; 1991b, p. 229ff.; cf. Berman, 1988, p. 4). Another is his constant reference to games as a model of human relationships (e.g., Bourdieu, 1977, p. 56; 1984, p. 12; 1990a, ch. 3; 1991b, p. 58; Mahar, Harker, & Wilkes, 1990, p. 7; Robbins, 1991, pp. 85–89).

I cannot give full credit to the complexity and richness of Bourdieu's thought in a summary fashion. For my own purposes here, I shall focus upon two basic and related analytical units of Bourdieu's method: the first is habitus, and the second is capital. Together, habitus and capital create, and are themselves driven by forces of domination. I shall discuss each of these in turn.

Habitus, a concept borrowed from medieval scholasticism, designates the practical logic of a cultural game (Bourdieu, 1977, ch. 2). That is to say, if individual agents are to pursue the stakes of the game, whether the game lies in the domain of marital alliance or of conspicuous consumption, they must habituate themselves to its demands, and accustom themselves to follow out its strategies wherever they lead (Bourdieu, 1990a, p. 11; 1990c, p. 52). It is important to understand that players of the game need not be aware of its logic or self-conscious about its strategies (Bourdieu, 1977, p. 72; 1990a, pp. 11–12; 1990c, p. 53); instead, players are constituted as active agents by the immanent logic of the play, usually concealed as commonsense, mundane responses to its "obvious" necessities (Bourdieu, 1990a, p. 132; 1990c, p. 55). Habitus represents a practical mastery, a "feel for the game" (Bourdieu, 1990a, pp. 9, 62–63). Thus for Bourdieu the artifice of cultural games (equivalent to the homologous set of games that comprise a culture (Bourdieu, 1977, p. 86; 1984, p. 12; 1990a, p. 140) is disguised by the routine of daily life that comes to seem natural to those who function successfully within its strictures (Bourdieu, 1984, p. 86; 1988, p. 56; 1990a, pp. 109, 194). Subjectivity, from this perspective, is merely a by-product of the objective requisites of continued play.

Capital is roughly equivalent to the scarce and valuable resources that players may bring to bear upon their immediate situation (Bourdieu, 1977, p. 171ff.; 1990c, p. 112ff.). Although the many forms of capital are modelled upon the material substrata of given life styles (Bourdieu, 1977, p. 183; 1990c, p. 122), they do not often appear as such to those who accumulate and employ them. Indeed, when Bourdieu highlights the symbolic refractions of capital such as education or access to the legitimacy of office, he demonstrates that they are effective precisely because their contingent nature is misrecognized as such; thus, what is most arbitrary about the games at hand is taken to be, instead, natural or essential (Bourdieu, 1990a, p. 112; 1990c, p. 122). The uses of capital depend, then, upon an image of scarcity and desire transposed into habitus. As such, capital becomes readily available for distinctions of taste, the invidious aesthetic of consumption (Bourdieu, 1984, pp. 56, 173). When consumers purchase goods to pursue the cultural games in which they are immersed, they reproduce the material and symbolic conditions which render the games not only possible but also, in terms of their practical logic, necessary (Bourdieu, 1984, pp. 230ff., 466ff.; Codd, 1990).

Together, habitus and capital create fields of domination, in which agents struggle, according to their objective interests, to turn the moves of the game to advantage, and thereby to assert a practical mastery of its terms of play (Bourdieu, 1977, p. 183ff.; 1984, p. 244ff.; 1990a, pp. 111, 135; Mahar, Harker, & Wilkes, 1990, pp. 5, 13). For Bourdieu, strategies of domination are an effect of the historical conditions that produced capital and habitus as objective structures of accumulation and socialization (Bourdieu, 1977, pp. 78, 82; 1990a, pp. 62–63). The unfolding of these structures in time then reproduces history in their own image, generating a continuous cycle of production and reproduction that lends domination its authenticity, and renders its antagonists wholly oblivious to the objective circumstances of their own amor fati (Bourdieu, 1990a, pp. 14, 88, 91, 110; 1990c, p. 54). Freedom and determinism, from this viewpoint, are alike illusions of the games that people play, since the warp of habitus and the weft of capital weave textures of domination in which an implacable logic both arises from and interpenetrates the "free" choices that agents devise to further their own objective interests (Bourdieu, 1990a, p. 15; 1990c, p. 54; Robbins, 1991, p. 75).

In summary, Bourdieu's approach carries forward a philosophical tradition of will and representation (Bourdieu, 1990a, p. 53; 1991b, p. 133) that may readily be discovered also in the thought of Schopenhauer, Nietzsche, and Wittgenstein (Snook, 1990). However, Bourdieu's signal contribution to this tradition is that he has formulated a macro-sociology of force that takes its impetus from Marx, Durkheim, and Weber, linked with a micro-sociology of practice that owes much to Erving Goffman (cf. Harker, Mahar, & Wilkes, 1990, p. 206ff; Robbins, 1991, p. 179). The alliance of these diverse directions permits Bourdieu to offer a comprehensive method, analogous perhaps in some ways to the work of Derrida, Foucault, or the earlier Baudrillard, though far superior to them for my present needs, to analyse specific bodies of data simultaneously from numerous points of view and at many levels of empiricism. It is to this analytic challenge that I now turn.

THE USCF CATALOG: CONTENT ANALYSIS

As a preliminary means to organize my presentation, I have selected five pervasive images of the USCF catalog that appear, on an intuitive basis, to be significant: (1) officialdom, (2) embodiment, (3) authorial presence, (4) knowledge, and (5) aesthetics. I shall elaborate each in its turn, and refer to appropriate aspects of Bourdieu's methodology to support my discussion.

Officialdom

The official status of the commodities offered is proclaimed initially by placement on the front cover of the logo of the USCF (evocatively, a stylized representation of the central chess piece, the king), and by an accompanying inset photograph of "your USCF Sales Specialist." Inside the catalog, the USCF's "money-back guarantee" of "confidence and satisfaction" is repeated no fewer than seven times, each time with a telephone number whose final four digits spell "king." Further, the emblems of social honor in the domain of commodities (cf. Bourdieu, 1977, p. 10ff., on honor as a game), major credit cards, are iterated in association with the guarantee. Finally, at the centre of the catalog, order pages summarize all of these themes—the logo, the guarantee, and the availability of approved credit—and emphasize them by a lengthy statement from the USCF's Executive Director: "U.S. Chess chooses only the very best ... Our staff has checked and approved each item ... Rely on U.S. Chess." The capacity of an official discourse to control words such as "king," "guarantee," and "approval" produces the things which are named, and thereby generates a powerful social recognition of authorized relations of dominance (Bourdieu, 1990a, pp. 54, 82, 136; 1991b, pp. 45, 109). Such legitimized modes of expression produce and reproduce the game and its stakes (Bourdieu, 1991b, p. 58).

Thus there is an intense effort to create an inextricable relationship among the U.S.C.F as the "ruler" of American chess, official approval of their merchandise, and the bourgeois super-solvency of their subjects/customers. Bourdieu points to the decoding of the messages of consumption as a primary mechanism by which agents' interests are constituted, and as a consequence, by which they are drawn into conflict over control of the goods essential to the specific arena of their play (Bourdieu, 1984, pp. 2, 66, 280). This protracted struggle to monopolize access to the symbolic capital of play, or to dispense it only under strict surveillance, is likewise apparent in the descriptions of chess equipment, and even in the manner of its use.

For example, in serious chess tournaments and even in casual play (skittles), chess clocks are used to discipline the thought and movements of the players (Aycock, 1992a). Although a variety of clocks are sold in the catalog, only one is singled out on several occasions: the "USCF's Master Quartz Clock." The ambiguity of mastership is perhaps significant here: who is master of the play, the organization, the clock, or the player?

Again, while numerous chess sets are depicted, two are featured in particular: one set which is "used by the *Chess Life* crew," and another which is designated a "tournament-approved set." That all sets sold conform to the Staunton design which is universally required for formal play is a further indication of the hegemonic status of this kind of chess equipment: Harry Staunton, an English master of the previous century, produced a design of chess pieces that was adopted throughout the world in large measure because of the historical prominence of English chess at the precise juncture when national chess organizations, championship tournaments and titles, and widely subscribed rules of play were introduced (Aycock, 1988a; cf. Bourdieu, 1990, p. 66ff. on the disciplinary significance of official codifications of practice).

Somewhat lesser forms of equipment such as rule books, score sheets, materials for the use of tournament directors, and devices used to record games in correspondence play are also proclaimed to be "U.S. Chess Official Equipment," "Official Rules of Chess," and "Official Tournament Kit." Thus the complex hierarchy of chess organization replicates itself fully in the bureaucracy of formal play, and in the dominant circumstance of literacy that pervades chess by contrast with many other games and sports (Parry & Aycock, 1991; cf. Bourdieu, 1977, p. 187 on the role of literacy as symbolic capital).

By the same token, "Official USCF Videos" and the "USCF Chess Academy," the latter a program of interactive computerized learning, transform the mere novice into sacred novitiate, a role conferred by the "official instruction" to which the catalog frequently alludes. As Bourdieu has remarked, such "rites of institution" separate those who have undergone them from those to which they do not pertain (Bourdieu, 1991b, p. 117): pedagogic authority reproduces the power relations, the "system of cultural arbitraries," that establish dominance (Bourdieu, 1990b, p. 10). In effect, therefore, even the knowledge of play is made an element of the capital essential to participate in the game of chess officialdom, an access parcelled out according to the acolyte's ability to pay.

Finally, chess-playing computers, the supreme icons of technological modernity and the simulacra of disembodied rationality (Aycock, 1990), are officially ranked by the "U.S.C.F. Computer Rating Agency" as "certified" Experts or Masters. The fact that 90 percent of all USCF members fail to attain this exalted level of skill only points up another facet of the operation of commodities, their barely concealed, but safely "misrecognized" authority to consume and possess those who, notionally, consume and possess them.

In summary, the commodity fetishism of officialdom, Bourdieu's "mystery of the ministry" (Bourdieu, 1991b, p. 206), is functionally multidirectional: (1) it constitutes the organization itself "by endowing itself with the set of things which create groups" (Bourdieu, 1991b, p. 205); (2) it "ensures the reproduction of the structure of the distribution of capital which ... reproduces the structure of the relations of domination and dependence" that characterize it (Bourdieu, 1977, p. 184); (3) it objectifies consumers by generating a "tight control" between them and the objects of their consumption (Bourdieu, 1990a, p. 94); and (4) it inscribes action with "rituals of social magic," the purchases that are contingent upon the capital they require to achieve a practical mastery of the game (Bourdieu, 1991b, p. 111). The rhetoric of officialdom involves a thorough-going relationship between "authorization, persons authorized to speak, and the state of affairs authorized" (Snook, 1990, p. 175). Cultural producers, in this context, have the "symbolic power to show things and make people believe in them" (Bourdieu, 1990a, p. 144).

Embodiment

Since chess has a reputation as a competition of minds, not of bodies, it is all the more interesting to examine the role that embodiment plays in the sale of chess commodities. To the extent that the body may be said to be rigorously "unthought" in chess (Aycock, n.d.[d]), the presence of bodies as images in the USCF catalog betrays, perhaps, unconscious Others of play.

Bourdieu emphasizes the importance of the body as a tool which objectifies social space by making visible relationships of dominance while constructing such relationships as "natural" and therefore lending itself ideologically to their misrecognition (Bourdieu, 1990a, pp. 81, 115). The habitus of embodiment allows agents to construe their experience as consistent and centred, thus domesticating subjectivities through their bodily discipline (Bourdieu, 1977, p. 15; 1990a, p. 167; 1990c, p. 72; 1991b, p. 87). Further, symbolic capital reproduces itself by inscribing upon the body an overdetermination of every sort of social distinction (Bourdieu, 1977, p. 87; 1990c, p. 71).

Generally speaking, the portrayal of bodies in the USCF catalog falls into three categories: hands, heads, and torsos, in decreasing order of frequency. There is only one shot that could reasonably be called a full body, and in this picture the person is seated behind a chess table that conceals much of his figure.

This absence of "whole" bodies and their replacement by body fragments may suggest, if not the disembodiment of chess, at least a degree of its passivity. For Bourdieu, the dignity of the body in a class society is closely linked to the manner of its activity in sport: lower-class sport produces and is then reproduced by strong, violent bodies acting in concert with one another, while upper-class sport involves slim, fit bodies acting alone and at relative ease in their surroundings (Bourdieu, 1984, pp. 215–218; Wilkes, 1990, p. 118). Thus games such as chess bear the aesthetic and ethical markers of class distinction, a conflation of "is" and "ought" (Bourdieu, 1984, p. 339). In this context, all of the persons depicted in the catalog are white and well groomed; some are shot in shirt and tie, while others wear leisure clothing (slacks and sweater) appropriate to the winter season in which the catalog was originally produced. None seems to be burdened by necessity, sweat, or a concern with physical violence. Each of the categories that I have identified appears to carry analogous implications.

Photographs of hands in the USCF catalog are overwhelmingly those of women, with children's hands a distant second, and only one shot of male hands. This precisely reverses the demographics of actual membership in the USCF, which is predominantly male and adult. Since the catalog was originally published just before Christmas, it seems possible that this theme of engenderment represents an expectation that women as primary caregivers will be presenting the commodities portrayed as gifts, and that men (or occasionally children) will be the usual beneficiaries. Another interpretation might be that the goods themselves have been engendered to meet normative standards of American culture, in which most advertising is imbued with images of heterosexual desire; this latter interpretation is strengthened somewhat by the fact that the women's hands, with few exceptions, hold items in such a manner as to display extremely long, lacquered, "sexy" fingernails. In either case, the photographs reproduce the image of the sexual (and, secondarily, age) divisions of labor in an ideal American family. By doing so, the photographs map bodies into cosmic and social spaces associated with dominant class, gender, and ethnic relationships in America (cf. Bourdieu, 1977, p. 91; 1990c, p. 77).

The head shots in the catalog are exclusively inset photos of authors of the books presented for sale; all of these are adult males, and all are named as chess masters. The sense of authorial presence that these insets convey is reinforced by the fact that all of the head shots look directly into the camera, inviting the reader to assume the position of the encountered Other, the consumer of authorial wisdom, and the flattered object of non-threatening, if not actually friendly, attention by a stereotype of the ideal person in American culture, the white adult male. As Bourdieu has observed, embodiment offers many "opportunities to experience or assert one's position in social space, as a rank to be upheld or a distance to be kept" (Bourdieu, 1984, p. 57). In this instance, the "rank" or "distance" has to do with American notions of authorial dominance (of which I shall speak further below).

Finally, the torso photographs are more varied than either hands or face shots. They are divided roughly equally between male and female. Most of the male torso shots display identifiable chess masters carrying or using equipment such as a chess table or wall board, while the remaining male torso photograph is of a man (designated as both a "national master" and as an official "sales specialist") holding a phone. The female torso photographs are nearly all of a young, attractive woman smiling at a piece of chess equipment, and in one instance of the slim, shapely lower body of a woman in high heels carrying chess equipment. This sharp division between the male torsos, who are all accomplished chess players, and the female torsos, who appear to be mere appurtances of the items they purvey, is very striking: in the former case, mastership is the strongest impression of the photograph; in the latter, sexuality.

Where faces may be discerned, both male and female torso models are smiling to indicate their satisfaction with the item in question (although very few women in actual practice use the items that the models are enjoying, and the women who do employ them generally, in my experience, are not at the moment of use wearing artificial fingernails, elaborate makeup, and high heels, nor are they smiling fatuously). These dispositions of the body, termed "bodily hexis" by Bourdieu, reveal primordial social facts about distinctions which are to be ideologically misrecognized, and therefore to be recognized, by agents (Bourdieu, 1984, p. 173). Here the ethic of fun or pleasure is joined to an aesthetic of self-presentation to contain politically the features of class, gender, ethnicity, and age that constitute American society (cf. Bourdieu, 1984, p. 367).

To summarize, the practices of culture are not a state of mind, but of the body transformed as "mythology," a "durable way of standing, speaking, walking, and thereby of feeling and thinking" (Bourdieu, 1990c, pp. 68–70). The USCF catalog, through embodiment, reproduces the symbolic capital which controls access to diverse social distinctions or spaces at a most fundamental level: "the body believes what it plays at" (Bourdieu, 1990c, p. 73).

Authorial Presence

Chess is a strongly authorial game from two perspectives: first, it is a seldom-challenged assumption that its players are the "authors" of their games (cf. Aycock, 1992b); second, it is widely understood that chess skill is inherently hierarchical, a quality measured by its system of formal ratings and titles (Elo, 1978). Both beliefs, true or not, are invidiously reflected in the USCF catalog and in the organization that produces it.

I will consider three aspects of the portrayal of authorial presence in the USCF catalog: the first, biographical insets, speaks to the issue of the authorship of games; the second, references to ratings, titles, and champions, addresses the matter of hierarchy; the third, chess-playing computers, is a curious amalgam of the first two.

There are eight biographical insets in the 24 pages of the catalog. Each inset includes a photograph of the author (which I have dealt with above), date and place of birth and titles awarded, a short "chess biography," and two lists of books written, and books recommended by the author in question.

I have developed more fully the notion of the chess biography elsewhere (Aycock, n.d.[a]); suffice it to say that such extensions in time, retroactively configured, of a coherent moral career strengthen the sense of authorial presence by arranging personal anecdotes of play in a vividly causal sequence, leading "inexorably" to success at play and even mastership. For Bourdieu, it is crucial to perceive how individual subjectivities become constructed and attached to agencies, lending them their sense of full authenticity, their intuition of their "place" in social arenas (Bourdieu, 1988, pp. 2–3; 1990a, pp. 91, 128; Robbins, 1991, pp. 113). In Bourdieu's thought the subjective struggle over strategies of self-presentation collapses into an objective contest of collective interests of which the singular is merely a trace (Mahar, Harker, & Wilkes, 1990, pp. 5–6).

The insets of the catalog establish autobiographical sequences (1) by tracing the author's initial encounter with the game (e.g., "When he was 14 ... walked into the New York Public Library and confronted a life-changing revelation"; "learned chess at age five by watching his father and brother play"; "had known chess for only 10 months when ... played and drew GM [Grandmaster]..."); then (2) by supplying a reinforcing anecdote (four of the insets refer to Bobby Fischer, an American legend of cold-war heroism against the Soviets, and one to escape from the Soviet Union); and finally (3) by adducing a motive for writing (e.g., "to increase chess knowledge and proficiency"; "to solve realistic tactical problems"; "to make sure [essays in a chess column] survive in a more permanent form").

These chess biographies, then, demonstrate a common pattern of socialization, and absorption into the mythos of play, including prominence in nationalistic endeavors (i.e., those supported by the USCF), and an ascription of "correct" motives for authorship. In effect, they reproduce the cycle of mastership and play that is subserved to nationally-oriented goals, inviting readers to subsume their own moral careers to these parameters. The initial connection with the hegemony of the USCF as an institution is fairly explicit, and it is emphasized by the lists of books written and recommended: by coincidence, all the volumes on these lists are sold in the present catalog! Thus, the USCF catalog attempts to present its legitimacy, and that of the USCF, by tying the purchase of goods inextricably to the habitus of the self embedded in the autobiographical situation of authorial play (Bourdieu, 1990a, p. 112); as it does so, consumers fall quite imperceptibly into the logic immanent in the game, not only of chess, but of subjectivity and of the mastership whose desire has been systematically induced (Bourdieu, 1990a, p. 90).

Similarly, the hierarchies of ratings, titles, and champions pervades the catalog. Authors of books are invariably identified by their titles ("NM," "IM," "GM"), and the contents of the books focus on the activities of titled players and champions (e.g., "used today by top GM's"; "complete GM games"; "the World Champ's real ideas"; "Best games and career highlights"). These book descriptions iterate ceaselessly a "commonsense" claim that ordinary players should wish to imitate professional masters and champions in their own games. This claim constitutes the sacred credentials that form the symbolic capital of a chess theocracy "behind the impeccable appearance of equity and meritocracy" (Bourdieu, 1990a, p. 151; 1990b, p. xi).

Because this claim is unexamined (for instance, rating statistics strongly suggest that very few players will indeed enter such an elite), it becomes entirely unexceptionable, and thereby itself partakes of an important mythology, the ability of commodities purchased from the USCF to ensure successful play (cf. Bourdieu, 1990a, p. 132ff, on the symbolic struggle to produce commonsense as an arbitrary reality misrecognized as such). Further, this claim disguises a contingent circumstance of play, the achievement of titles and championships, as an essential standard, in the process making it necessary for those who have a stake in the game to enter the realm of domination by professional players and the national organization that symbolically represents their interests (Bourdieu, 1990a, pp. 31, 80). The social space of commodification may then "present itself in the form of agents provided with different properties that are systematically linked" (Bourdieu, 1990a, p. 132).

Finally, the role of chess-playing computers combines the authorship of play with its hierarchy. Computers are, as I have noted above, awarded official ratings by the USCF, and referred to by titles ("Travel Master," "own the World Champion," "watch this certified expert think," "Kasparov portable advanced trainer," "USCF 2325 rating in a custom attaché case," "Chessmaster 3000"). Alternatively, computers are endowed with authorial designations of demonic intensity ("Scorpio," "Diablo," "Knightstalker," "Phantom"), and in one instance, programmed to simulate a human personality ("Chesster, the talking chess expert").

Thus chess-playing computers offer both the promise of hierarchical achievement through high technology and the threat of the displacement of authorial presence through an eclipse of human capacities, an irresistible challenge to many because it evokes strong emotions associated with both themes of authorship and hierarchy (Aycock, 1990). By giving the chess-playing computer a form that is legitimized by the iconography of esoteric machinery, it becomes possible to express openly a "wish or practice that might otherwise be unacceptable" (Bourdieu, 1990a, p. 85); that is to say, a desire to excel in a social field where the emblems of excellence are disproportionately restricted to a tiny elite.

In summary, authorial presence in institutionalized and commodified chess is an "ideological discourse" both individually and collectively misrecognized, "history turned into nature and denied as such" (Bourdieu, 1977, p. 78; 1991b, p. 153). Competence in play is acquired by buying the authors (organic or silicon), the organization, and even the autobiographies that guarantee success, necessitating an expensive pursuit of the symbolic capital to realize what is, symbolically, at stake in this social space (Bourdieu, 1984, p. 65; 1990a, p. 128). Precisely because authorial presence legitimizes the "objective structures of the social world" of competitive chess as self-evident, the purchase of books and computers permits consumers to forget the limits of their situation, generating "investments of time, money, work, etc." to overcome them (Bourdieu, 1984, p. 471; 1990a, pp. 87–88, 135).

Knowledge

Chess is reputed to be a game of the mind, and chess players themselves are often said to possess supreme qualities of reason (Aycock, 1991, p. 33; Aycock, 1992a). One immediate consequence is that chess reproduces a cultural division between working-class sport, perceived as typically focussed on the body, and middle- or upper-class leisure, more often associated with the intellect (cf. Bourdieu, 1984, pp. 215–217; he uses chess as an example). Another implication is discovered in the substantial industry of academic psychology, which takes skill in chess as a centrepiece of theory and experimentation on cognition (e.g., Holding, 1985), thus responding to and reinforcing cultural beliefs about thinking and about the game of chess itself. In this sense, the habitus of chess play carries a semblance of rationality which need not be based on reason to render it effective (Bourdieu, 1990a, p. 11).

Consonant with such broadly construed cultural themes, chess privileges literacy as a mode of learning, and chess literature numbers in the tens of thousands of volumes (cf. Bourdieu, 1977, p. 187, on literacy as a means to monopolize cultural capital; and Bourdieu, 1990a, p. 103, on the "game of references referring mutually to one another" that are "at the same time differences and reverences, contradictions and congratulations"). It is not surprising, therefore, that the USCF catalog takes advantage of this situation to promote the purchase of chess books as the primary symbolic capital of the game.

There are several fundamental motifs of the chess books offered for sale in the USCF catalog: aggression, progressive learning, esoterica, and systematic knowledge. I shall deal with each in turn.

The idea of aggression represents a symbolic violence deeply embedded in the game itself (Bourdieu, 1977, p. 191), and closely tied to the notions of hierarchy, mastership, and championship that I have addressed above. Some examples: "hones killer instinct"; "early knockouts"; "sharpest system"; "maximize your chances"; "deadly use"; "counterpunching"; "forcing"; "fight on your turf"; "score sudden points"; "classic attacking techniques"; "the winning edge." The imagery of winning through sudden, implacable violence represents chess as an enterprise which is inherently zero-sum, intensely expropriative, and formidably masculine (cf. Bourdieu, 1990a: 183; 1990b: 4, on the close relationship between knowledge and symbolic violence). That chess seems to share these characteristics with bourgeois culture in general argues strongly for the resonance of such attitudes in homologous cultural games: "the homology between ideological production and class struggle produces euphemized forms of economic and political struggle" (Bourdieu, 1991b, p. 169).

Progressive learning as an ideal of play is likewise consistent with the powerful mythos of eternally upward progress in a culture based on class and upon the accumulation of capital: "'Become who you are': that is the principle behind the performative magic of all acts of institution" (Bourdieu, 1991b, p. 122), here the institution of knowledge as an objective structure of capital. Some key descriptors that are repeated throughout the catalog: "improvement"; "updating"; "progress"; "get better"; the "latest"; the "newest"; "new levels of understanding"; "vast new library of chess knowledge"; "rushed to you"; latest technology." Thus the educational capital that constitutes players' interests is assumed to be cumulative: the new always surpasses the old, and access to the most recent knowledge involves a frantic effort to purchase that knowledge before others, providing oneself with the paraphernalia of expertise. That this educational capital is symbolic permits its material aspects to be misrecognized, and thus recognized in the habitus of purchase (Bourdieu, 1991b, pp. 111, 122).

Esoterica is a common motif in book descriptions that becomes an important device to express the fetishistic power of knowledge, and thereby to dominate the game of consumption (Bourdieu, 1991b, p. 184). For instance: "secret Soviet methods"; "confidential adjournment analyses from Karpov's inner circle"; "secret stock of sound but little-known surprises"; "secret Soviet training methods"; "GM analysis"; "analysis by the World Champion"; "Yugoslav and Russian sources"; "unlock Russian chess literature." The predominance of references to Eastern European, Russian, or Soviet play is, of course, consonant with cold-war demonologies (cf. Bourdieu, 1977, p. 82, on the practical coherence of symbolic systems), while the use of analysis by grandmasters or champions authenticates the books as I have suggested in the section above. As Bourdieu has suggested (following Veblen in his image of the costume of servitude), the "livery of the word" structures the perception of symbolic capital as scarce and desirable, the "primordial illusio without which there would be no stakes to play for, nor even any game" (Bourdieu, 1988, p. 56; 1990b, p. 125; 1991b, p. 105).

Finally, there is a strong emphasis placed on systematic knowledge, a symbolic ordering of play guaranteed by the masterly elite (Bourdieu, 1990a, p. 80). In a cosmological sense, the consumers of chess books are forcefully invited to enter and control a self-contained universe: "complete and systematic"; "wisdom"; "the chessplayer's bible"; "the right opening moves"; "a complete system"; "covers all the main variations"; "really complete"; "comprehensive." The act of purchase has both "technical and symbolic dimensions, the latter a practical metadiscourse by which the person acting shows off certain remarkable properties of his action" (Bourdieu, 1990a, p. 30). Such acts sharpen and consecrate boundaries between the uninitiated and the illuminati, producing an apparent consensus on their effects which situates books on chess within a field of social forces (Bourdieu, 1990a, p. 82; 1991b, p. 118; Codd, 1990, p. 154). In this fashion symbolic and economic structures determine one another (Bourdieu, 1990a, p. 18).

Thus chess knowledge as it has been commodified in the USCF catalog draws its customers in two directions at once: on the one hand, knowledge is purchased in fragments, a ritual act which must be endlessly renewed and progressive to be efficacious; on the other hand, players are invited to perceive themselves as gaining access to symbolic capital that is "secret," "complete," and "comprehensive" in itself. The power of this contradiction ("the refusal to know and the illusion of knowing" [Bourdieu, 1990a, p. 183]) elicits the most compelling desire to maintain an elaborate and expensive library of chess books, constantly adding and discarding its elements. The logic immanent in the act of purchase, then, plays itself out in the objective structures of domination that comprise a "serious" relationship to the game. From this perspective, the habitus of the commodification of chess constitutes its agents' feelings as well as their thought, overdetermining their actions by strengthening the illusio that drives investment in the stakes of play (Bourdieu, 1977, pp. 82, 110; 1990a, p. 195).

Aesthetics

The aesthetic dimensions of pleasure in commodities are essential components of their capacity to serve as symbolic capital, and thereby to reproduce relationships of domination in the habitus of play (Codd, 1990, p. 142). Chess books, sets, clocks, computers, and boards are meticulously designed to appeal to the taste of their consumers, who produce the objects they consume by "a labour of identification and coding" (Bourdieu, 1984, p. 100; Codd, 1990, p. 154). For Bourdieu, discriminations of taste are fundamental markers of difference and commonality, and thus represent wider social affiliations: "(t)aste classifies, and it classifies the classifier. Social subjects ... distinguish themselves by the distinctions they make" (Bourdieu, 1984, p. 6).

I discern three broad categories of distinction in the USCF chess catalog: accessibility, mobility, and solidity. I shall explain and instantiate each of these.

The accessibility of chess goods is both financial and pragmatic. On the financial side, many items in the catalog are highlighted in red letters with exclamation points as "discounted," on "sale," a "best" value, a "real bargain." From a pragmatic viewpoint, other items are described as "clear, easy to see," "convenient," "handy," "accessible," "easy to understand," "easy to read," "easy to use," "ideal for players with limited time to study," "a good road map," "thoroughly explained," "clear and concise, "easy to follow," "entertaining," "fascinating," "fast," and "quick."

At first glance these two kinds of accessibility may seem to function quite differently in the sale of chess goods, and indeed it may be difficult to understand why financial accessibility "counts" as aesthetic. However, it is one of the virtues of Bourdieu's approach that it becomes possible to relate these apparently disparate qualities. In Bourdieu's terms, "taste" operates as "social orientation, a sense of one's place" (Bourdieu, 1984, p. 466):

> Nothing more rigorously distinguishes the different classes than the disposition objectively demanded by the legitimate consumption of legitimate works, the aptitude for taking a specifically aesthetic point of view on objects already constituted aesthetically—and therefore put forward for the admiration of those who have learned to recognize the signs of the admirable—and the even rarer capacity to constitute aesthetically objects that are ordinary or even "common" ... or to apply the principles of a "pure" aesthetic to the most everyday choices of everyday life ... (Bourdieu, 1984: 40)

Here the "pure" aesthetic is one quite basic to bourgeois culture, an item that may be purchased at a low cost and used with significant ease (cf. Fiske, 1989b, ch. 2, on bargain-hunting as a resistant tactic of everyday life). This aesthetic of easy access is derived in its original form from an upper-class stance of freedom from necessity, and symbolically mimics it (Bourdieu, 1984, p. 55). In addition, accessibility, both of cost and use, provides a symbolic entrée to the elite of formal chess by an acquisition of the cultural capital that is believed to be essential to play the game successfully. Thus the desire for accessibility among consumers of chess goods is an aspect of consumers' "disposition to establish and mark differences by a process of distinction" (Bourdieu, 1984, p. 466).

The mobility of books and equipment is equally to be prized: "portable," "lightweight," "travelmaster," "take your chess anywhere," "your constant companion," "chess on the go," practically indestructible," "handy, inexpensive traveler," "spacesaving." In part, of course, the desire for mobility is a feature of the practical logic of play, since most tournaments require travel from one city to another: "the most efficacious strategies of distinction are those which find their principle in the practical, pre-reflexive, quasi-instinctual choices of habitus" (Bourdieu, 1990a, p. 115). To put the same matter in another way, "each social space [here the space of the chess tournament] functions as one of the sites where competence is produced and as one of the sites where it is given its price" (Bourdieu, 1984, p. 88). Thus movement from one place to another requires the purchase of a technology which makes mobility possible.

In a deeper sense, as well, mobility is an aesthetic tied to the practices of middle- or upper-class lifestyles, such as travel on the job, radical changes of work site in pursuit of career advancement, and fashionable tourism. Bourdieu:

Taste, the propensity and capacity to appropriate (materially or symbolically) a given class of classified, classifying objects or practices, is the generative formula of life-style, a unitary set of distinctive preferences which express the same expressive intention in the specific logic of each of the symbolic sub-spaces... (1984, p. 173)

Thus the mobility of chess commodities is linked more broadly to mobility in chess itself, and analogously to mobility in the practices of social class.

Finally, the solidity of books and equipment is replete with images of endurance and craftsmanship: "rugged," "durable," "heavy," "solid," "firm," "your position stays put," "deluxe," "quality," "the look of wood," "accuracy," "precision," "long-lasting use," "heavy-duty," "extra heavy," "endure for years to come," "solid hardwoods," "sturdy," "tough," "protect your investment for many years to come," "luxury is yours!"

The solidity of chess equipment—its size, weight, and durability—is an embodiment of the solidity of chess itself as a social enterprise (Aycock, 1988a). Chess boards, pieces, sets, clocks, and computers slide easily in this fashion from a "model of reality to the reality of the model" (Bourdieu, 1990c, p. 39). In two meanings of the term, the feel for the game is "sensible" (Bourdieu, 1990c, p. 66): equipment pleasurable to the senses, culture grounded in nature and thereby misrecognized as legitimate (Bourdieu, 1990a, p. 112); and commonsensical in the habitus of formal chess competition, the "practical affirmation of an inevitable difference" (Bourdieu, 1984, p. 56).

Once more, there is also a class distinction implied in the taste for well-crafted chess equipment. In the prevalent circumstances of mass production, those who can afford commodities produced one at a time of "natural" materials such as wood have converted "differences in the mode of acquisition of culture into differences of nature" (Bourdieu, 1984, p. 68); thus, the purchase of "deluxe" equipment by a presumptive elite satisfies Bourdieu's proposition that "taste is a class culture turned into nature through embodiment" (1984, p. 190).

In summary, therefore, the language of aesthetics in the USCF catalog is an "instrument of action and power" (Bourdieu, 1991b, p. 37). It draws a "veil of enchanted relationships" (Bourdieu, 1977, p. 191) across commodities, disguising the social conditions of taste (Bourdieu, 1984, p. 11) as a "feel for the game" (Bourdieu, 1990a, p. 9). By so doing, aesthetic judgements as they are materialized in the descriptive words of the catalog produce the conditions by which Self and Other are classified in social positions, both within the game of chess and without, the fateful games of class (Bourdieu, 1990a, p. 131).

DISCUSSION

The five dimensions of the USCF catalog that I have analyzed—officialdom, embodiment, authorial presence, knowledge, and aesthetics—by no means exhaust the range of comments that might be made of its content, but they do suggest something of its subtleties. I will now draw together these five elements to show some relationships among them.

Officialdom is especially a property of the USCF catalog as an institutional production, and as a reproduction of the institution itself. However, officialdom is also an intimation of authorial presence, and reverberates strongly in the official knowledge of chess that books provide, and in the official jargon of aesthetics that the catalog employs. The embodiment of chess as a legitimate arena of struggle is apparent in the catalog's designation of particular items as officially guaranteed, and the monopoly that the USCF exercises over the award of many ratings, titles, and championships.

Embodiment is an instrument of domination which grounds cultural values such as knowledge and aesthetics objectively in books and chess equipment. The presence of play is a subjective quality that is perceptibly enhanced as an objective structure by photos of authors, and by the hegemony of the USCF. Even such broad social traits as gender, age, and race are called into service as bodies which simultaneously sell desire and successful play.

Authorial presence is conveyed in the first instance by the official status of the USCF catalog, and in the second, by the bodies of authors presented to consumers both pictorially and autobiographically. Authorial presence transforms knowledge into desire, constituting it as a symbolic capital essential to the game of chess. Aesthetics, likewise, is a kind of authorial presence, because it lends to apparently inanimate objects the authority of play within the domain of chess—its solidity, accessibility, and its mobility—and within the wider domain of social class, a game which is "intended" by the immanent logic of chess and the life style to which players become habituated.

Knowledge is never neutral, though it exerts a more powerful force because it is misrecognized as such. Its efficacy is legitimated by the USCF logo, by the USCF agency that rates computers, by money-back guarantees, by the recommendations of authors, and by the sexually alluring women who are depicted in the pages of the catalog. Knowledge is also aesthetic, because its symbolic violence is utterly masculine, its progressive nature is thoroughly capitalistic, its esoterica is comprehensively elitist, and its systematization is wholly reassuring.

Finally, the USCF catalog is aesthetic through and through, in the diverse political and economic guises of which Bourdieu speaks so forcefully. In a modern state and class culture, officials define the categories of recognition and classification to which ordinary folk must subscribe. Bodies, as Foucault has often reminded us, are imbued with a "micro-physics" of discipline and action that is both beautiful and ethically prominent. Authorial presence offers the essential illusion of subjectivity as a self committed to creative goals, a charisma that is objectively constructed in aesthetic language. Knowledge itself is all of these: official, embodied, and authorial, offering the aesthetics of distinction in the special sense in which Bourdieu relates taste to the situating of selves in social space.

In short, the USCF catalog is a nexus of images that depend upon one another for their sustenance. Together, the five dimensions that I have selected here constitute the commodities that may be purchased as a symbolic capital that produces and reproduces the relationships of domination in chess. There are at least two habitus of play that arise: first, the habitus of the game of chess itself, whose logic necessitates access to symbolic capital to enter the elite of mastership; second, the habitus of buying and owning, whose logic is essential to various games such as those of gender, race, national pride, class distinction, credit and bargain-hunting, self-improvement, victory, and yes, even the simple pleasures of formal or casual competition.

CONCLUSION

I began this essay with a paradox: play signifies freedom, while commodifications of play seem to be far more deterministic; how shall I reconcile this apparent contradiction which arises so frequently in the circumstances of modern, bourgeois culture? Part of the answer lies in Bourdieu's "illusio" (Bourdieu, 1984, p. 86; 1988, p. 56) which is not really very dissimilar to Huizinga's characterization of play as "pretense" (1955, p. 8) or to Bateson's use of "metacommunication" (1972, p. 178) to deal with the nature of playful actions as both meant and unintended in their consequences. The "illusio" of play, for Bourdieu, is not simply a definitional quality as Huizinga (and perhaps Bateson) believed; it must be produced, and must in turn reproduce the relationships of the game. The production of the illusio requires a misrecognition, and therefore a recognition, of what is at stake and the manner in which agents' interests are constituted (Bourdieu, 1984, p. 250). Thus when play is considered as fantasy, it is insufficient to argue that this seemingly ethereal feature of play is a universal, free-floating essence. Bourdieu has demonstrated quite convincingly that fantasy is always contingent upon the social arrangements which situate it as such in particular moments of history and culture (Bourdieu, 1990a, pp. 11–12, 70), and I have taken his demonstration seriously with respect to bourgeoisified play.

Another part of the answer devolves from Bourdieu's concept of the habitus, the objective structure of dispositions that governs play at every level (Bourdieu, 1977, p. 77). Again, Huizinga only thought of "rules" that defined each cultural game, to which players must consciously subsume their actions (1955, p. 11). Bateson lodged play in framings which presupposed, perhaps, a formal and explicit intention of the parties to conform to the discourse of their games (1972, pp. 186–189). Bourdieu's habitus, however, is neither conscious nor intentional: the production of the game as such implicates its agents in a specific range of strategies which must be entered upon to meet the needs of their continued participation, and in its turn, players' habitus generate and reproduce the game and its stakes (Bourdieu, 1977, pp. 82–83; Robbins, 1991, p. 102). This departure from subjectivity decentres the issue of freedom and constraint by representing it as an objective factor of play, empirically visible to the analyst and therefore capable of analysis in a way that conscious intentions are not: "why is there action rather than nothing?" (Bourdieu, 1990a, p. 194). My discussions of commodification thus interact with the habitus of chess as I have argued above, dissolving my initial paradox in the flux of structured relationships with the game.

Yet a third aspect of the answer requires a careful examination of Bourdieu's notion of symbolic capital. For Huizinga (Bateson is rather oblique on this point [1972, pp. 191–193]), the games of culture propose resources inherent in the rules of play (Huizinga, 1955, ch. III). Bourdieu's symbolic capital is more dynamic than this: such resources are embodied social forces that are themselves subject to strategies of access and accumulation (Bourdieu, 1977, p. 184). At once the agents of play are limited in their freedom to construct the situation of the game, because they must acquire and sustain the capital that constitutes its arena as a field of struggle; yet they are also free to achieve alternative combinations of capital to meet their needs as agents, and to outdo others in the process. Symbolic capital, further, is never merely given, for it must be produced and reproduced as a condition of the game's continuance in history (Bourdieu, 1984, p. 244ff.; 1990a, pp. 18, 137). In accord with this position, I have presented the commodifications of the USCF catalog as symbolic capital that seems to liberate consumers from their ignorance and amateurish play, yet simultaneously enmeshes them in the exigencies of scarce and desirable goods which make this elevation possible.

The title of this chapter, "Owning Up," catches up all three parts of my resolution of the Huizinga/Bateson paradox as I have originally stated it, by emphasizing the play on words that is implicit there. "Owning" is the appropriation of the symbolic capital that comprises the games of chess, consumption, and life in bourgeois culture. "Up" signifies the relationships of domination that suffuse the fields of play in all of these cultural domains. Yet "Owning Up" has a colloquial meaning as well, that of taking responsibility in a strict regime of cause and effect: it is the responsibility of the habitus to which I now refer, implacable and onerous because it carries with it the illusio of freedom (cf. Bourdieu, 1991b, p. 94). Thus my title, and my content analysis of the USCF catalog, flow directly from my interpretations of Bourdieu's work, and seem to substantiate its directions as I have represented them.

There are of course numerous problems yet to be considered, which suggest further opportunities for research. Some of these have to do with critiques of Bourdieu's own thought, which are profound and potentially disabling; the circularity of his conceptual schema is one such difficulty that is not easily overcome (Harker, Mahar, & Wilkes, 1990, p. 210ff.). Others arise from my own limitations; for instance, I have not dealt satisfactorily with the historical context of commodification, nor with the grosser empirical issues such as the social origins of players or their class alignments, matters that Bourdieu thoroughly addresses in his massive studies on art and education. Finally, I have not mentioned one of Bourdieu's basic concerns, the reflexivity of sociological understanding (e.g., Bourdieu, 1988; 1990a; 1990b; 1991a; Barnard, 1990).

I have worked out the premise of this essay as a first approximation to a later, more mature comprehension of the central device of modernity, its commodification of lived experience. Perhaps Bourdieu says it best:

In order to escape the realism of the structure ... it is necessary to pass from the opus operatum to the modus operandi ... and to construct the theory of practice, which is the precondition for establishing an experimental science of the dialectic of the internalization of externality and the externalization of internality, or more simply, of incorporation and objectification (Bourdieu, 1977, p. 72).

REFERENCES

Aycock, A. (1988a). The anthropology of play equipment. *Newsletter of The Association for the Study of Play, 14*(1).

Aycock, A. (1988b). "Gens una sumus": Play as metaculture. *Play and Culture, 1*(2): 124–137.

Aycock, A. (1990). Play without players, players without play: The world computer chess championship. *Play and Culture, 3*(2): 133–145.

Aycock, A. (1991). The desire of kings and the silence of their subjects: Play as intertextuality. *Play and Culture, 4*(1): 31–42.

Aycock, A. (1992a). Finite reason: A construction of desperate play. *Play and Culture, 5*(2).

Aycock, A. (1992b). Three assumptions in search of an author: Some textual problems in the study of play. *Play and Culture, 5*(3).

Aycock, A. (n.d.[a]). *Body matters: An exploration of the senses at play.* Unpublished manuscript.

Aycock, A. (n.d.[b]). *The postmodern 'situation': Erving Goffman's selves at play.* Unpublished manuscript.

Barnard, H. (1990). Bourdieu and ethnography: Reflexivity, politics, and praxis. In R. Harker, C. Mahar, & C. Wilkes, (Eds.), *An introduction to the work of Pierre Bourdieu: The practice of theory,* (pp. 58–85).

Bateson, G. (1972). A theory of play and fantasy. In G. Bateson, *Steps to an ecology of mind,* pp. 177–193. New York: Ballantine Books.

Berman, A. (1988). *From the new criticism to deconstruction: The reception of structuralism and post-structuralism.* Chicago, IL: University of Illinois Press.

Bourdieu, P. (1977). *Outline of a theory of practice.* Cambridge: Cambridge University Press.

Bourdieu, P. (1984). *Distinction: A social critique of the judgement of taste.* Cambridge, MA: Harvard University Press.

Bourdieu, P. (1988). *Homo academicus.* Stanford, CA: Stanford University Press.

Bourdieu, P. (1990a). *In other words: Essays towards a reflexive sociology.* Stanford, CA: Stanford University Press.

Bourdieu, P. & Passeron, J.-C. (cited as Bourdieu, 1990b). *Reproduction in education, society, and culture* (2nd ed.). London: Sage.

Bourdieu, P. (1990c). *The logic of practice.* Stanford, CA: Stanford University Press.

Bourdieu, P., Chamboredon, J-C, & Passeron, J-C. (cited as Bourdieu, 1991a). *The craft of sociology: Epistemological preliminaries.* Mouton: de Gruyter.

Bourdieu, P. (1991b). *Language and symbolic power.* Cambridge, MA: Harvard University Press.

Brewer, J., & Porter, R. (Eds.). (1993). *Consumption and the world of goods.* New York: Routledge.

Calhoun, C., LiPuma, E., & Postone, M. (Eds.). (1993). *Bourdieu: Critical perspectives.* Chicago: University of Chicago Press.

Carrier, J. (1995). *Gifts and commodities: Exchange and western capitalism since 1700*. New York: Routledge

Codd, J. (1990). Making distinctions: The eye of the beholder. In R. Harker, C. Mahar, & C. Wilkes (Eds.). *An introduction to the work of Pierre Bourdieu: The practice of theory*, (pp. 132–159).

Elo, A. (1978). *The rating of chessplayers, past and present*. New York: Arco Press.

Fiske, J. (1989). *Reading the popular*. Boston, MA: Unwin Hyman.

Harker, R., Mahar, C., & Wilkes, C. (Eds.) (1990). *An introduction to the work of Pierre Bourdieu: The practice of theory*. London: MacMillan.

Holding, D. (1985). *The psychology of chess skill*. Hillsdale, NJ: Lawrence Erlbaum Associates.

Huizinga, J. (1955). *Homo ludens: A study of the play element in culture*. Boston, MA: Beacon Press.

Jenkins, R. (1992). *Pierre Bourdieu*. New York: Routledge.

Mahar, C., Harker, R., & Wilkes, C. (1990). The basic theoretical position. In R. Harker, C. Mahar, and C. Wilkes (Eds.). *An introduction to the work of Pierre Bourdieu: The practice of theory*, (pp. 1–25).

Parry, K. & Aycock, A. (1991). *When Minnesota Fats meets Bobby Fischer: Rules and style in billiards and chess*. Paper presented at the Annual Conference of The Association for the Study of Play, Charleston, SC.

Robbins, D. (1991). *The Work of Pierre Bourdieu: Recognizing Society*. Buckingham: Open University Press.

Snook, I. (1990). Language, Truth, and Power: Bourdieu's Ministerium. In R. Harker, C. Mahar, & C. Wilkes (Eds.). *An introduction to the work of Pierre Bourdieu: The practice of theory*, (pp. 160–179).

Wilkes, C. (1990). Bourdieu's Class. In R. Harker, C. Mahar, & C. Wilkes (Eds.). *An introduction to the work of Pierre Bourdieu: The practice of theory*, (pp. 109–131).

18

(Un)toward Joy: Movement, Sport, and (the Meaning of) Life

Synthia Slowikowski
Nate Kohn*

In the creation scene of a recent remake of the Frankenstein story, the camera fore-grounds the monster's hand. Punctuated by a musical spike, the fingers twitch and we know it is alive. The miracle of life, even man-made life badly done on a television screen, is defined by a simple movement. I watch my new born daughter sleep. She is still as death. For a long time, she does not move. A fear rises within me, a churning, pulsating, crescendoing fear, as I search her motionless form for a sign. Suddenly, her hand twitches and with a sharp and shameless laugh disguised as a simple sigh, the fear escapes my body and, for a little while, disappears.

Giorgio Agamben says that "the root of all pure joy and sadness is that the world is as it is. Joy or sadness that arises because the world is not what it seems or what we want it to be is impure or provisional. ... In the highest degree of their purity ... sad-ness and joy refer not to negative or positive qualities, but to a pure *being-thus* with-out any attributes" (Agamben, 1994, Appendix 90.1). Agamben's tenet can be used to think about movement, particularly the joyful movements that are fixed within the cultural bounds of sport performances.[1] We are specifically interested in the pure *being-thus* that Agamben addresses in *The Coming Community* and that Henri

---

* This chapter was equally coauthored.

275

Bergson touched on in his work a century ago, and how this *being-thus* may be understood in a sport context. We focus in our dialogue on describing, interpreting, and deconstructing[2] the look and feel of the actions and the movements involved in sport performances, how joy might be generated at those sites for both athlete and audience, how *being-thus* might be glimpsed in the spectacle of such joy, unbridled and unattributed.

Cornel West's glancing reference to cultures as "...in part, what human beings create (out of antecedent fragments of other cultures) in order to convince themselves not to commit suicide" (West, 1992, p. 40) brings to mind Sansone's definition of sport as "the ritual sacrifice of energy" (Sansone, 1988, p. 142) wherein the athlete becomes the ultimate sacrificial victim, spreading joy as he naively proceeds to ritualize his own prolonged suicide through ever more challenging physical acts/movements. Such a life-long dedication to self-sacrifice is indeed a joyful act, though not necessarily a pleasurable one—particularly if we invoke Cornel West's distinction:

> pleasure ... tends to be inward. You take it with you, and it's a highly individuated unit. ... But joy cuts across all that. Joy tries to get at those non-market values—love, care, kindness, service, solidarity, the struggle for justice—values that provide the possibility of bringing people together. (Dent, 1992, p. 1)

So we have the possibility of the athlete as a Christ-like figure, one who foregoes personal pleasure to spread joy through the act of dying, if not for our sins then at least for our pleasure, forging through extraordinary movement what passes for a cultural bond in this postmodern age.

With Agamben and with other philosophers who have sought to dissect movement (such as Bergson or Patsy Neal,[3] a physical educator) and also with our work, an important question about movement must be asked at this point. Is the movement that is philosophized that of the watcher or the mover?[4] We know that we want to focus on theorizing the joy of movement that we have felt in the past as we watched others move, and as we ourselves moved in athletics, dance, sex, ritual, and everyday life. But whose movement counts in our text? Do we understand movement in this present narrative as authors, voyeurs, athletes, choreographers? Or, towards even a loftier question, as we move in bodies that have been constructed (as Foucault and others tell us) by our cultures (Mauss, 1934), is there a coming body that speaks in movements common to all of us on this planet? We do not clearly answer these questions in this text, nor do we ever choose one standpoint of interpretation (mover, watcher, etc.). We simply: (1) lay out some of the general theoretical parameters for wondering about the above questions; (2) introduce Agamben's idea of the coming community and how it may be a provocative and redeeming way to comprehend the joy of sport movement. (3) alight briefly betwixt and between the standpoints that theorists of movement occupy in their own analyses.

Agamben's idea of "coming community" is illuminated most clearly in a review of his work, *The Coming Community,* by Heesok Chang in the online *Postmodern Culture*:

> The basis of the coming community, the singular being, is *whatever being*—not in the sense of "I don't care who you are," but rather, "I care for you *such as you are.* As such you are freed from belonging either to the emptiness of the universal or to the ineffability of the individual ... human identity is not mediated by its belonging to some set or class (being old, being American, being gay). Nor does it consist in the simple negation of the negative community. ... Such a singularly exposed being wants to belong— which is to say, it belongs to want, or for lack of a less semantically burdened and empty word, to love: The singularity exposed as such is whatever you *want* that is lovable ... In [this] work, philosophy becomes once again, perhaps, a kind of homesickness, a longing to belong. To a permanent disorientation. To oscillation. To whatever. (Chang, 1993)

As we move in different bodies (like these above listed in our text), we ask whether the singular *whatever being,* the pure *being-thus,* is manifested in the movement that comprises sport. We focus on such a question because we wonder if the actual act of sport/movement/performance is a working cultural strategy of the coming community. We forward this idea not as romanticists, Olympists, or idealists of sport; rather, we see sport performances as one of the strategies of resistance[5] in postmodernity. We want to map out the theoretical issues that are evoked when such movement is abstracted into scholarly narratives such as ours.

To the dismay of my Alexander Technique teacher who believes there is much to be unlearned if we are to return our bodies to a tensionless, efficient way of being, I find I am constantly leaning into things these days—into the computer monitor, the car windshield, the television screen. Chin jutted out, shoulders rotated forward, neck muscles chronically tensed, I find myself reaching out, forcing myself into the images in front of me, mostly trying to become what I see before me, particularly if it is Michael Jordan defying gravity or Martina volleying at the net with dazzling speed and grace. That I am laying the foundation for later back and neck pain goes unnoticed—it is not that I don't care but that I am completely unaware— as I join the image before me, actually catch a fleeting glimpse of my visage dancing on Michael Jordan's shoulders. And for me there is a wonder in that, how suddenly I am more than me, able to be an unquestioning part of one of life's grander leaps, completely guiltless and guileless in such a virtual union. "Vicariousness," as Olalquiaga notes, "is a fundamental trait of postmodern culture" (Olalquiaga, 1992, p. 39). "The postmodern broadening of the notion of reality," she continues,

> *whereby vicariousness is no longer felt as false or secondhand but rather as an autonomous ... dimension of the real, facilitates the current circulation and revaloration of this aesthetics ... the logic of organization is anything but homogeneous, visual satu-*

ration is obligatory, and the personal is lived as a pastiche of fragmented images from popular culture. (Olalquiaga, 1992, p. 42)

Yup, I think, that's me and I thank God for small pleasures; one of the few joys life allows me these days, I say, grateful for the readily available cliches that so perfectly express my every feeling.

Agamben says that "there is a good that humanity must learn to wrest from commodities in their decline." This good involves linking "together image and body in a space where they can no longer be separated, [thus forging] the whatever body whose *physis* is resemblance" (Agamben, 1994, p. 50). *Whatever bodies. Being-thus.* The space and time of sport may be seen as terrains where these constructs have been historically realized, both by audience and performers. Moreover, joy may be a phenomenon that articulates to audience and movers these universal becomings[6] that are staged in sport movement.

As we watch and participate in sport, we marvel at the joy of movement that we see and feel. At the same time, in our academic community and in our communities-at-large, we witness sport dissected and criticized,[7] as it should be, as it is our job as sport scholars to do. Yet we wonder if we have forgotten something in our contemporary cynicism; we wonder whether scholarly commentary on joy and movement can be rediscovered within the ontological and epistemological stand-points of sport sociology/anthropology. What are the foundations of a sociology of movement that would link abstractions of joy to emerging concepts of community and identity?

I am on my bicycle now, peddling into the wind, feeling the strain on my leg muscles, that leaden sign of weakness or fatigue that so distresses me, but I persevere, standing up to get more leverage, seeing the crest before me and within reach, ascending, finally reaching the top, my lungs breathing hard, my body drenched in sweat. As I glide along the moraine, I find a new strength in my thighs, the peddling suddenly effortless, painless, as natural as the sky is blue. I feel the breeze cooling my skin, my whole body relaxed and loose, now beyond restraint and inertia-free, and I know that I could go on forever. I ride high on my bike, a proud smile on my face, and I see people in their gardens look up and wave at me as I glide by, and I see in their faces a joy at my exhilaration, and they share the moment with me, sensing my aliveness and wanting to join me in it. Or at least so I think then, in that boundless becoming space that movement made for me.

It may seem that we are taking some of the same theoretical detours that sport philosophy has already taken. Indeed, we are revisiting some of this work because we believe that these narratives offer forgotten examples of theoretical discourse concerning the fascination, seduction and joy of sport. Such discourse shows how such literature and theory are not (only) postmodern places of nihilism or complicity, but are also redemptive sites.[8] The moves in sport and narratives (visual, virtual, written, oral, etc.) about these moves are sites where it is possible, we think, to get outside the construction of difference, to move (un)toward Agambens coming community where it is possible to always be in the act of becoming. For example, when Patsy Neal says:

Often I have asked myself what is it that has touched my life in such a personal way … that draws countless millions to participate in and to watch sports and athletics? Has every athlete felt what I have felt? Has every individual that has thrown a ball and hit a spike felt that intimate involvement … that inward laughter … *aware* of the lifeline that one can come into contact with … that gives one the chance for *open* and boundless joy. … It is joy in the purest sense … the fluidity of movement, the instant reactions under stress, the sense of control over body and mind, the creativeness of *being*. One is joyful because one is alive in the fullest sense. Why? Why there … in the sports world? (Neal, 1972, p. 3)

Indeed, in such narratives it is not only the writer but also the reader who is transported to the liminality of sport, to that threshold where the body is free to fly, soar, speed, to always be in the act of becoming.

We are thinking too, of sites like MTV Sports where video artists create fragmented, blurred, gorgeously colored and musically choreographed rushes of sport scenes that provide opportunities for aesthetic experiences for watchers in living rooms, bars, prisons, malls.[9] And it's not only TV sport that provides such out-of-museum works of art.[10] Seen from the bleachers, the wondrous save of a goal by a five-year-old goalie of a local kindergarten soccer league, his body flying parallel to the ground, perfectly stretched as he tips a ball away, offers a joyful exhilaration. The giant Nike Town statue of Michael Jordan that freezes his unique movement reifies joy as it promotes consumerism through its proximate associations.

Copy from a Nike print ad, looking as if it were written on an old Remington manual typewriter, words on a wrinkled brown sheet with Jackie Joyner-Kersee's running body coming out of the page, a blurred personification of movement:

THERE WERE TIMES WHEN YOU WERE GROWING UP IN EAST ST. LOUIS WHEN YOU THOUGHT YOU WOULD NEVER FIT IN. AND YOU THOUGHT YOU WOULD ALWAYS STAND OUT. AND YOU'D TALK TO YOUR MOTHER SAY TO YOUR MOTHER AND COMPLAIN TO YOUR MOTHER because that's what mothers are there for THAT YOU WISH THAT YOUR LIFE COULD BE NORMAL AS OTHER PEOPLE'S NORMAL LIVES SEEMED TO BE. AND THEN ONE DAY YOUR MOTHER'S NOT THERE ANYMORE. AND THERE WAS NOTHING NORMAL ANYWHERE ANYMORE.

BUT SHE TAUGHT YOU THAT YOU HAD A BODY AND YOU KNEW IT COULD MOVE. AND YOU HAD A BODY AND YOU KNEW IT WAS FAST. AND NOW WHEN YOU RUN IT'S HER FACE YOU SEE. AND WHEN YOU HEAR THE WIND IT'S HER WORDS YOU HEAR. AND YOU FIND SHE IS IN YOUR LEGS IN YOUR ARMS IN YOUR FEET IN YOUR BODY JUST AS YOU WERE ONCE IN HERS. AND YOU ARE

*GLAD THAT YOU GREW UP FAST. YOU ARE GLAD THAT YOU GREW UP SO
FAST.[11]*

*The words tug at me, the manipulative sentimentality notwithstanding. The link-
ages: movement with body with speed with mother with generational continuity with
transcendent humanity with fastness with shoes—Oops, I mentioned the product.
Sorry about that. I didn't mean to do it; it just slipped out. And that's what linkages
are about in the postmodern world of advertising. Taking something that might be
essential to life—movement, in this case—and maneuvering it with cunning affect
through communal touchstones until it becomes one with the product, indistinguishable from it. A necessary relationship or articulation is created. Of course, as
Lawrence Grossberg (1992, p. 16) points out, there are no necessary relationships in
the normal world, the world, say, of Jackie Joyner's childhood. But perhaps things are
different in the space of the coming community, on the track and on the field, dream
spaces where natural laws seem not apply.*
  "THIS IS THE BODY," the ad ends

*YOU WILL RACE WITH AND LIFT WEIGHTS WITH AND HAVE FUN WITH
AND PRACTICE UNTIL YOU ARE PERFECT WITH AND PLAY AND PLAY AND
PLAY WITH UNTIL YOU ARE JUST TOO darn TIRED TO PLAY ANYMORE.*

Or, we might add, until the shoes fall apart and you are obliged to buy a new ones.
  *The advertisement captures me, though, makes me remember Jackie Joyner on the
Olympic fields, her legs, the muscles, the tendons, the stride, each step reaching ever further, defying both the limits of the body and the laws of gravity. The memory makes me
forget the ache in my legs from too much bicycling, takes me into that imaginary world
where anything is possible and pain is just a grimace without a referent, inconsequen-
tial and unfelt. I rub the top of my thighs and think about buying a new pair of shoes.*

Many would use our ideas here to point out how, sadly, sport is an opiate of the
masses, that "noble sport" is now tainted with the frantic consumerism of capitalism;
they would point out how tragic, that in these technological, televisual times, we are
a world of sickly watchers instead of healthy doers, that it is wrong to make athletes
our heroes, instead of poets, statesmen, or scientists. It could be said that culture is
oppressive and limits movement.[12] Critics could say that what we are describing is
Baudrillard's orgy, "a state of repletion and abundance where we are gorged with
meaning and it is killing us" (Baudrillard, 1988, p. 63).
  We do agree that sport is an opiate; we agree that sport is the site of frenzied col-
lecting; we realize that oppression may limit movement; (Deleuze, 1992, p. 282),
we concur that the joy of movement may be orgiastic. We disagree that these activities and emotions are immoral. As scholars whose calling has been to anthropolo-
gize sport, we have decided to self-reflexively celebrate the exotic, erotic, sensual
quality of sport.

Now, what paradigms, issues, philosophies, does such a reflexive anthropology/ sociology of sport/movement center on? As we said above, we forward the poetics of joy as one of the tactics that can be used to navigate this anthropology.[13] Such joyfulness may have something to do with elemental passions—perhaps the universality of such passions—that are enabled by sport/movement. Such joyfulness may come from the potential of the androgyny of movement in sport today. The mover is not sexed or raced, abled or disabled; the mover is a blur, thin, neuter, one of the coming community. Humans[14] continue to be fascinated by movement, continue to create movement, continue to enjoy watching movement, because, we think, the performing, moving body displays for us what we are, shows us ourselves as we wish we were, as we know we could be if only we tried a little harder.[15]

From Bergson:

> Our body, with the sensations which it receives on the one hand and the movements which it is capable of executing on the other hand, is then, that which fixes our mind, and gives it ballast and poise. (Bergson, 1896, p. 173)

In sport, then, we see what the mind is, we witness in sport movement a tableau, a concretization, of all that humanity may be capable of becoming.

Bergson goes on to speak of dreams, of how dreams are one state of mind in which the human is not concretized, is not "fixed by the sensori-motor equilibrium of the body" (Bergson, 1896, p. 174). With our anthropology, we suggest that in postmodernity sport is a cultural dream of the body that is made flesh, "acted" (Bergson, 1896, p. 174), instead of merely dreamed; in sport, the dream *is* fixed by the sensori-motor equilibrium of the body. The dream, once an ephemeral psychic form, is in sport played out in real-time, performed for whole communities.[16]

You know that feeling, walking into a sports stadium, coming out of a dark tunnel into brilliant autumnal sunlight just as 70,000 people spring to their feet loudly cheering some fullback muscling his way 15 yards down the field. You know that feeling, the sense of a flower opening in fast-motion, the embrace of a sea of humanity moving in concert, the live all-around fullness of the sound of human voices in joyful cheer, the lightness of it, the pure sensuality of it, the tickle of it. It is a place like no other, a magical place, where identity loses its link to individual concerns, where the edges of people blend into each other and you suddenly become a part of a great and wondrous happening, a union, a melding, a solidarity—at least until the hard concrete seat and chilling wind pluck you from the dream and urge you toward the safety and comfort of your Strato-lounger.

Yet in those few initial minutes, when the rush hits you like a breath of fresh air from a sensual god, you are captured and you wonder, given what it is for you, how much more it must be for the athletes, those down on the field, running out of their tunnel, bounding suddenly and miraculously into the gaze of tens of thousands, millions if you count television. Think of the joy they must feel, these boys from the ghet-

tos of Chicago and the farms of Moultrie County, as they live the impossible dream, feel it coming true now and here, bask in it as the sound of their pounding feet becomes one with the martial music and the rhythmic chanting of the crowds. No matter how plastic, how contrived, how overdetermined, how man-made, how sexist, how racist, how untoward, it becomes a dominion of joy. Give pause and think about that. Wonder why it works every time. And then thank God that it is only football players (not gladiators or storm troopers) down on that field.

In our scheme, we also problematize the liminality of sport movement, the in-betweeness of moving in sport, the idea of "becoming" within the rhythms of sport performativity. Sport may be a unique (but not the only) site where this act of becoming is realized. This may be due to the "unrolling" character of sport:

> an unfolding of states wherein our interest prompts us to look at that which is unrolling, and not at that which is entirely unrolled. (Bergson, 1896, p. 150)

In sport/movement's unrolling, we need to understand how rest and death, with their absence of movement, play a part in the creation of joyful sport movement. Rest is part of our anthropology of movement, as joy may also arise from the juxtaposition of the nanoseconds of rest against the exuberance of moving: the micro-rests involved in trampolining; the stillness before the bungee jump or before the ski descent of a mountain.

Danger, speed, vertigo can be inserted into our anthropology of movement as well. We are aware that it has been frequently hypothesized (Elias & Dunning, 1986) that modern humans have it easy, that they have no thrill, excitement, danger in their lives and thus sport becomes the (post)modern substitute for such experiences. We would suggest that discourse that has to do with playing with death, with danger and sexual rituals, is important to an anthropology of sport movement. Sport movement is closely tied to eros. We need to theoretize how sexual and sport cultural performances seep into, terrorize, play off and into, one another.

There are criticisms, too, about constructs like speed: Abbas, for example, cautions that "after a certain critical point is reached, speed becomes a form of inertia, the accelerator another kind of brake, and the experience of speed an experience not of liberation but of carceration" (1990, p. 70). Speed for Abbas brings about disappearance; when something does not exist, there is no joy. But in our scheme, this disappearance is yet another construct that is layered around or juxtaposed with joy.

That is, to disappear through joyful movement may be the closest that we come to being free.

Bergson:

> Whether we consider it in time or space, freedom always seems to have its roots deep in necessity and to be intimately organized with it. Spirit borrows from matter the perception on which it feeds and restores them to matter in the form of movements which it has stamped with its own freedom. (Bergson, 1896, p. 249)

Gunner Breivik says, "It is more 'natural' or 'normal' for humans to move than to be at rest" (Breivik, 1993, p. 1). He wonders if we think better when we move, wonders if we should run and think instead of sit and think. He also wonders, if philosophy is a form of adult play, could philosophy also include physical play? What, he wonders, is the epistemology of the movement? These are not idle concerns. As I sit and watch that new born baby girl, the one whose stillness so concerned me earlier, I marvel at how she moves, at her obvious need to move, to stretch, at how flexible and agile she is, even in her awkwardness, even with her lack of control, how moving is her most natural and pleasurable act, how her moving spreads joy among all who watch her with captivated eyes.

Then I look at myself in my 50th year and agonize over chronically contracted major muscle groups in my trunk and legs, how inhibited and self-conscious my limited range of movement has become. I think about how I have problematized movement and about how lack of movement has problematized me. I worry that I now seek movement vicariously, outside my body through watching and projection and dreams. I fear that my attempt to regenerate movement in myself comes too late and is too meager, that I have allowed myself to atrophy beyond repair. I don't believe the therapists and the exercise gurus who tell me otherwise, that there is still hope, even for me. I try to massage my gnarled and knotted hamstrings and know the experts are wrong. I understand the need to move and I yearn for the joy that is so evident in movement. I search and find the memory of it; I hunger for the freedom and the possibilities inherent in uninhibited, unrestricted movement. I wish it for myself now, as I feel myself groping along the time-line of life, as I find myself becoming more concerned with the realities of salvation than with the abstractions of theory, yet still hoping that the latter will somehow illuminate a path toward the former.

I seek reassurance in the words of Trinh Minh-ha, wondering if middle age might be viewed as a moment of quiescence:

> Quiescence [is] necessary to the dawning of a new awareness ... Nothingness produces snow; quiescence produces yellow sprouts (Chang Po-tuan). When stillness culminates, there is movement. The living potential returns afresh, the cycles of the moon go on regularly, again and again the light will wane. In the process of infinite beginnings, even immortality is mortal. (Minh-ha, 1991, p.1)

The words, inscrutable as they are, move me. Yet the knowledge that I and my abilities to move/not-move are part of a larger cycle of life cannot penetrate my own irreversible occidental obsession with me.

I return, as if against my will, knowing full well the hopelessness of it, to the unanswerable "if-only," looking to it as a mantra, still hoping that by repeating it endlessly I will someday find in it a revelation:

If only I could figure out how to truly think with my body, if only I could unlearn everything that has brought me to this state of chronic, movement-stifling tension, if only I could start my life over again with the knowledge I now possess, then, perhaps, I say, I might rediscover the free sensuality of movement and the joy it liberates.

We might stop here, after having laid out some of the problems involved with studying movement/sport as a segment of coming communities. But what of the place of sport, the spaces of sport? Bergson reminds us that "space, by definition, is outside us;" yet "the separation between a thing and its environment cannot be absolutely definite and clear-cut; there is a passage by insensible gradations from the one to the other" (Bergson, 1896, pp. 202, 209). In his introduction to "Mediators," even Gilles Deleuze wonders about the spaces of sport:

> Running, throwing a javelin and so on: effort, resistance, with a starting point, a lever. But nowadays we see movement defined less and less in relation to a point of leverage. Many of the new sports—surfing, windsurfing, hang-gliding—take the form of entry into an existing wave. There's no longer an origin as starting point, but a sort of putting-into-orbit. The basic thing is how to get taken up in the movement of a big wave, a column of rising air, to "come between" rather than to be the origin of an effort. (p. 281)

Our approach to understanding joy, movement and sport would consider the spatiality of coming communities: their potential chaos, order, beauty; such an approach would recognize and move (un)toward the modern sensibilities that created time and space.

In conclusion, we are seeking, at the least, to expose and wonder about the whatevernesses that have been designed by philosophers like Bergson and re-theorized in recent works by Agamben, Trinh and Abbas. We are trying to see what happens when we ruminate on *being-thus*, the whatevernesses of joy, movement and sport as this sport/movement/joy may hint at (the meaning of) life in coming communities.

NOTES

[1] We use the term "sport" loosely here, not wanting to restrict our discussion only to mainstream sport, like basketball or skiing. Leaving the sport label open allows discussion of activities like virtual-computer generated sport performance, skateboarding, hang-gliding, frisbee, football, and those sports that are created everyday that sometimes comprise outlandish equipment, rules, and/or participants such as land luge or sumo diving. In our work, sport can be anything the reader/author wants it to be—for example, prostitution, dance, or working on an assembly line may be sport. With this tactic, we make an effort towards de-colonailizing the grammar of sport.

[2] This is not intended as a formal reference to deconstruction. We use the term here in the familiar sense, in that we are attempting to "unwrap," "consider," "call attention to," "interpret," some of the meanings and issues linked to sport and movement as they are informed by the ideas of the authors mentioned in the text (i.e., Agamben, Bergson). Although we have been influenced by the work of Derrida and others, we have not allied ourselves to any one school of deconstruction here.

3 Listing Neal alongside Bergson is our ploy to acknowledge the mostly unrecognized, but in our opinion, valuable work of some physical education philosophers of the past century (see Neal, 1972).

4 For instance, Jean-Paul Sartre (in Gerber & Morgan, 1956), makes a distinction between body as "being-for-itself" and body as "being-for-others" (p. 164). We try to explore whether being-for-others and being-for-itself may perhaps meld together in the realm of sport movement.

5 For example Abbas (1990, p. 68) speaks of strategies of resistance. He does not discuss sport/movement, but does contemplate speed. See also Virilio (1991).

6 See Bergson (1896): "But this special image which persists in the midst of the others, and which I call my body, constitutes at every moment, as we have said, a section of the *universal becoming* (emphasis added).

7 For example, sexism, racism, consumerism, colonialism, and so forth—are all written into sport by journalists, researchers.

8 See for example, work such as Kroker, Kroker, and Cook (1989, p. 172): "No longer sports as about athletic competition, but postmodern sports now fascinating because the athlete's body is a blank screen for playing out the darker passions of triumph and scapegoatism.

9 Foster (1992, p. 494) describes an MTV body as a "hired body," and "video dancing body." She criticizes such bodies and would not agree with us that these bodies produce joy. She sees these bodies as only producing a "permanent" record to be used in historicizing dance in the choreographic process:

The video dancing body is often constructed from the edited tapes of dance movement filmed from different angles and distances. Its motion can be slowed, smeared or replicated so that it performs breathtaking feats, and yet projects none of the tensive qualities of movement, the body's situation in space or the charisma of a live performance.

10 For instance, in the film, *The Autumn Ritual,* Alan Ginsburg called sport: "display of the human form divine ... some of the things Swan (professional football player) did with his body I hope art historians will do something with."

11 Seen in *US Magazine* (August 1994), pp. 12–13.

12 For example, in certain cultural and historical contexts, female bodies cannot move freely in male sports (like boxing); the economically poor land-bound cannot surf an ocean wave, etc., etc. See the passage often quoted by Foucault (1978, p. 25): "[such practices] invest, mark, train and torture the body: they force it to carry out tasks, to perform ceremonies and to emit signs."

13 Novak (1976) approaches some of the themes that we are trying to develop, but he does this within the confines of what he calls the "holy trinity"—baseball, football, basketball. Novak hints at being-thus:

to live at such instantaneous intensity forever, all gathered up like the sweetness of a plum at peak of ripeness, would be joy indeed (p. 131).

Novak is interested not so much in movement (he does speak of grace and speed), as on the contest\agon of sport:

The heart that refuses to give in, refuses to panic, seizes opportunity, slips through defenses, exerts itself far beyond capacity, forges momentarily of its bodily habitat an instrument of almost perfect will...I love it when a last set of calculated, reckless, free and impassioned efforts is crowned with success (pp. 150–151).

Above also, is a sample of the 1970s philosophy of physical education that (although the same language was not used) began to contemplate the third spaces, coming communities, that are currently being theorized by Agamben, Bhabha, and Trinh.

[14] Mauss says the body is

Man's first and most natural technical object, and at the same time his first technical means is his body (Sansone, 1988, p. 461).

[15] "Despite the incredible number of creatures out there...there aren't that many ways to move" (Wheeler. 1994, p. A6).

[16] Seen this way, sport may be conceptualized as a communal ritual (as many have argued). But when we suggest that sport is a communal dream, we expand the boundaries of sport beyond that of ritual or myth. We say that sport is life itself.

REFERENCES

Abbas, A. (1990). Disappearance and fascination: The Baudrillardian Obscenario. In A. Abbas (Ed.), *The provocation of Jean Baudrillard.* Hong Kong: Twilight.

Agamben, G. (1994). *The coming community.* M. Hardt, (Trans.). Minneapolis: University of Minnesota Press.

Baudrillard, J. (1988). *The ecstasy of communication* (B. Schultze & C. Schultze, Trans.) New York: Semiotext(e).

Bergson, H. (1896). *Matter and memory* (N.M. Paul, Trans.). New York: Zone Books (reprinted 1991).

Breivik, G. (1993). *On the move: Some comments on the epistemology of movement.* Unpublished manuscript.

Chang, H. (1993, September). *Postmodern Culture,* 4, n. 1Is. 48–50, 60 (pmc@unity.ncsu.edu).

Crary, J., & Kwinter, S. (Eds.) (1992). *Incorporations.* New York: Urzone, Inc.

Deleuze, G. (1992). Mediators. In J. Crary & S. Kwinter (Eds.), *Incorporations.* New York: Urzone Inc.

Elias, N., & Dunning, E. (1986). *The quest for excitement: Sport and leisure in the civilizing process.* New York and Oxford: Blackwell.

Foster, S.L. (1992). Dancing bodies. In J. Crary & S. Kwinter (Eds.), *Incorporations.* New York: Urzone, Inc.

Foucault, M. (1978). *Discipline and punish: The birth of the prison* (A. Sheridan, Trans.) New York: Pantheon.

Gerber, E.W., & Morgan, W.J. (Eds.). (1956). *Sport and the body: A philosophical symposium.* Philadelphia: Lea & Febiger.

Grossberg, L. (1992). *We gotta get out of this place.* New York: Routledge

Kroker, A., Kroker, M., & Cook, D. (1989). *Panic encyclopedia: The definitive guide to the postmodern scene.* New York: St. Martins Press.

Neal, P. (1972). *Sport and identity.* Philadelphia: Dorrance and Company.

Novak, M. (1976). *The joy of sports: End zones, bases, baskets, balls and the consecration of the American spirit.* New York: Basic Books.

Olalquiaga, C. (1992). *Magalopolis.* Minneapolis: University of Minnesota Press.

Trinh, T. M-ha. (1991). *When the moon waxes red.* New York: Routledge.

Virilio, P. (1991). *The aesthetics of disappearance* (P. Beitchman, Trans.). New York: Semiotext(e).

West, C. (1992). Nihilism in black America. In G. Dent (Ed.), *Black popular culture.* Seattle: Bay Press.

Wheeler, D.A. (1994, May 25). The secrets of Motion. *The Chronicle of Higher Education,* p. A6.

Author Index

Subject Index